*Routledge Re*

# The Lonely Tower

First published in 1965, this reissue of the second edition of T. R. Henn's seminal study offers an impressive breadth and depth of meditations on the poetry of W. B. Yeats. His life and influences are discussed at length, from the impact of the Irish Rebellion upon his youth, to his training as a painter, to the influence of folklore, occultism and Indian philosophy on his work. Henn seeks out the many elements of Yeats' famously complex personality, as well as analysing the dominant symbols of his work, and their ramifications.

# The Lonely Tower

## Studies in the Poetry of W. B. Yeats

### T. R. Henn

Routledge
Taylor & Francis Group

First published in 1950
Second Edition published in 1965
by Methuen & Co. Ltd

This edition first published in 2011 by Routledge
2 Park Square, Milton Park, Abingdon, Oxon, OX14 4RN

Simultaneously published in the USA and Canada
by Routledge
711 Third Avenue, New York, NY 10017

*Routledge is an imprint of the Taylor & Francis Group, an informa business*

© 1965 T. R. Henn

**Publisher's Note**
The publisher has gone to great lengths to ensure the quality of this reprint but
points out that some imperfections in the original copies may be apparent.

**Disclaimer**
The publisher has made every effort to trace copyright holders and welcomes
correspondence from those they have been unable to contact.

A Library of Congress record exists under LC Control Number: 65006945

ISBN 13: 978-0-415-50060-9 (hbk)
ISBN 13: 978-0-203-12913-5 (ebk)
ISBN 13: 978-0-415-50358-7 (pbk)

# THE LONELY TOWER

This famous study of the poetry of W. B. Yeats has been unobtainable for some years, but in this new edition, published to coincide with the centenary of Yeats' birth, has been revised and largely rewritten. A new chapter has been added, and the author has taken the opportunity to modify some of his earlier views in the light of new researches of his own and of other scholars. New illustrations have also been added as a result of the author's travels in America, France and Italy.

UNIVERSITY PAPERBACKS

U.P. 126

*by the same author*

\*

THE PLAYS AND POEMS OF J. M. SYNGE

THE HARVESTS OF TRAGEDY

THE APPLE AND THE SPECTROSCOPE

Samuel Palmer: The Lonely Tower
*'An image of mysterious wisdom won by toil'*

# The Lonely Tower

## Studies in the Poetry of W. B. Yeats

T. R. HENN c.b.e., m.a.

*Hon. D. Litt. (Dublin). Fellow of St Catharine's*
*College, Cambridge, University Lecturer in English*

UNIVERSITY PAPERBACKS

METHUEN : LONDON

*First published 1950*
*First published in this series 1965*
*Copyright © T. R. HENN*
*Printed in Great Britain by*
*Cox & Wyman Ltd., Fakenham*
*Catalogue No 02/6846/49*

*University Paperbacks are published by*
METHUEN AND CO LTD
11 NEW FETTER LANE, LONDON, E.C.4

*Thou look'st through spectacles; small things seeme great*
*Below; But up unto the watch-towre get,*
*And see all things despoyl'd of fallacies.*

DONNE

*His soul had wedded Wisdom, and her dower*
*Is love and justice, clothed in which he sate*
*Apart from men, as in a lonely tower . . .*

SHELLEY

*I declare this tower is my symbol . . .*

With Gratitude
for
M. E. H.

# Acknowledgements

I wish to tender grateful acknowledgements to the following for their permission to quote or reproduce: Mrs Yeats and Messrs Macmillan for the quotations from Yeats' Prose and Verse; the Director of the National Gallery, Dublin, for Poussin's 'The Marriage of Peleus and Thetis',[1] Bordone's 'St George and the Dragon', and the picture of the Virgin at Her Sewing (by an unknown artist); the Director of the Courtauld Institute for the drawing of the mosaic of the Dolphin and for the photograph of Ricketts' *Don Juan and the Statue*; the Director of the Louvre for Ingres' 'Oedipus and the Sphinx'; the Director of the Whitworth Art Gallery, Manchester, for Blake's 'The Ancient of Days'; the Director of the Victoria and Albert Museum, London, for Palmer's 'Lonely Tower'; and to the Director of The Denver Art Museum for 'The Triumph of Death' (School of Mantegna) which was formerly at Washington.

[1] Now re-ascribed.

# Contents

# Illustrations

# Introduction to the First Edition

I

A year or two before his death I spoke with Yeats, and he asked
me what quality in his work I valued most. I replied 'Wisdom';
though it was, indeed, an imprecise word. I meant that his writing
had given me pleasure through its revelation of stable values in
thought and in mood; that its assertions of gaiety, courage, bitterness, sorrow, seemed to me of the great tradition; and that much
of its symbolism carried in itself that quality of expansion and
resonance in the mind which he sought to give it. At the time, I
think, I saw his work against a background which we shared,
and particularly in relation to the Ireland of the period between
1916 and the Treaty. Of that period I have written in the opening
chapter.

Although the events of his life are available from many sources,
I have found it convenient to recapitulate them in outline under
the title of 'Choice and Chance' in so far as they bear on the arguments I have sought to develop. To those events I have related his
own theories of the mask, as justifying his complex and apparently
contradictory personality. I have shown some of the factors which
determined his early style, and then gone on to consider the development of his maturer poetry. But before this stage could be reached
it seemed important to survey the whole series of poetic
springs represented by his exploration of magic, astrology, and
mystical mathematics in general; to consider at some length his
dominant symbols and their ramifications; and to trace in outline
the dramatic work, which, together with much of the prose, must
be considered side by side with the poetry before the latter can be
understood.

## II

I have argued that Yeats' use of symbols shows a consistency that is unusual in poetic practice; that the choice of symbols is less capricious than certain critics have thought; and that his development is related to the steady discarding of the inessential and to the concentration and expansion of those symbols which he thought could ultimately be related to the stream of *Anima Mundi,* that strange company of spirits or witnesses that take shape in human minds, revealed to him in the mythologies of the world and confirmed by the evidence of controlled vision and dream. To this process the theory of the 'ancestral memory' is the key. Because of this development it is important to consider the relationship between the poetry of different periods. Yeats does not lend himself readily to anthologies; even the simplest poems may demand cross-reference to a passage in an essay or a play, or a parallel usage in another poem, before its full significance becomes apparent. I have therefore found it necessary to quote more fully than is customary in such essays.

## III

It seems to me likely that Yeats' early training as a painter, and his use of pictorial symbols to stimulate his imagination, established a habit of peculiar sensibility to visual art. If this is so – and there is ample evidence of the importance of this poetic practice in the work of Spenser, Shakespeare and Keats – then some clue as to the origins and perhaps the significance of the symbols can be found by a study of the allusions to pictures, statues and mosaics. I have considered a number of these in the chapter 'Poet and Painter'. I think that other clues may well emerge at some later stage when the results of Yeats' visits to galleries and museums, together with his reading-matter at certain critical periods of stimulation, have been more thoroughly assessed.

## IV

I am concerned to show what I consider to have been the impact of the Irish Rebellion and the subsequent 'Troubles' upon Yeats' development. I have given more weight to these events than is usual; but I believe that the evidence will be found ultimately to support this view. The poet who writes of modern war is aware of it as single or fragmentary experiences: the scale of it is too vast, the actions too complex, to be perceived as a whole; and the poet may well fall back from the imitation of an action of this magnitude to the intricate turnings of his own sensibility. But for Yeats, the Rebellion gave, for perhaps the last time in literature, an experience which was small enough to be perspicuous, and of which the causes were linked at every stage to his own artistic and political views; an experience which had its roots in Ireland's long history of bloodshed and defeat, but which was also in some sense an image of the larger disintegrations of the world. It could be typified by his own hero Cuchulain, who is the only one of the mythological figures to be retained to the end, and who stands for loneliness, and exaltation, and defeat, but who draws his strength from many heroic ages:

> When Pearce summoned Cuchulain to his side,
> What stalked through the Post Office? . . .

From that experience he gathered, after an initial period of bewilderment, a clearer and more bitter picture of his own self and anti-self. At the outset, a 'terrible beauty' was born; later, with warring Sinn Fein and Free State soldiers about the Tower, he was aware of his own inadequacy and confusion of thought. For Yeats is perhaps the only poet who believed, or half believed, that he was responsible for starting a war:

> Did that play of mine send out
> Certain men the English shot? . . .
> Could my spoken words have checked
> That whereby a house lay wrecked?

The discrepancy between the active life he dreamed of, and the poet who was terrified of the London Zeppelin raids, and yet would deliberately go out into the firing in the Dublin streets, had to be reconciled by the making and wearing of many masks. I have tried to indicate how these masks were made; and, more important, their complex effect upon his thought.

V

Yeats' poetry reflects at every turn his esoteric studies, his gatherings of folk-lore, his occultism; the background of his Sligo boyhood; the patronage and protection of Lady Gregory; his concern with Indian philosophy and myth; his readings of Plotinus, Henry More, Cudworth, Swedenborg; the mosaics which he saw in Sicily and at Ravenna; his studies of Blake and Calvert; his obsession, at a certain stage, with Greek and Roman sculpture; his readings of Castiglione, Boehme and Spengler; his many friendships, and that passionate hatred through which, as I believe, he grew.

I am well aware of my ignorance in many fields. It will be necessary for the future editor of Yeats[1] to have mastered in detail much esoteric literature, including the *Kabbala* and Boehme; Spenser, Swift, Berkeley, Burke; Balzac, Lionel Johnson, Dowson, Sturge Moore, Gogarty, Dorothy Wellesley; Plato, Plotinus, Julian, Vico, Gentile, McTaggart, Croce, von Hügel, Spengler, Whitehead; a fair amount of nineteenth-century French poetry; Japanese and Chinese translations; portions of the *Upanishads*; some theosophy and Rosicrucian literature; the Irish patriot poets of the nineteenth century; the poems of Michelangelo and Mallarmé. He will need a working knowledge of statuary and of mosaics, of Egyptian, Greek, and Byzantine art, of painting from Michelangelo to Edmund Dulac, of

Calvert and Wilson, Blake and Claude.

He will have to be a musician, although Yeats was not; for it seems that the influence of Irish folk-song upon the rhythms is subtle and far reaching. He should have a knowledge of Gaelic, not only for Irish mythology, but to help to explain those difficult overtones which Irish idiom and construction appear to carry when they are wholly or partly transposed into English. He should be a Shakespearean and Elizabethan scholar; for Yeats, under his father's stimulus, read the plays widely and continuously, and there are many traces of Ben Jonson, of Beaumont and Fletcher, and especially of Chapman, in his verse; and part of the final self-dramatization was the phase of *Timon* and of *Lear*. I am not suggesting that

[1] The definitive and fully annotated edition will be a life-time's work.

Yeats was in any sense a scholar, and indeed he denies, though inconsistently, that imputation. He read widely, voraciously, and probably unsystematically; ransacking artists, philosophers, poets, to reject or confirm his theories, or to supply him with images. He had a powerful, imprecise and ingenious memory, and there was much laid aside in

> the foul rag-and-bone shop of the heart.

All that he saw and read and thought must one day be examined. It will be objected by some that such consideration is a laborious and uncertain undertaking, unlikely to repay the reader. To this we must reply that there is still a residue of complexity and uncertainty, of interpretation, and only through such study will the full significance of the poetry become apparent. It seems possible that in another age Yeats might have been a writer of epic, and given us, as an essential part of the body of his poetic work, much of the commentary that is now isolated in essays, prefaces, and the mystical writings. In spite of their predominantly lyrical structure, the poems have seldom the isolation and self-sufficiency proper to the lyric.

## VI

I have not attempted to deny to Yeats what he himself listed under the heading of 'Detractions' in his noble essay on Synge. There is vanity, misjudgement at times of poems, and of people, and of poems for the sake of their authors; intolerance, and the handling of lust and rage; though I believe that this last was of set purpose, justified (as he thought) in the history of past poets. There is a perpetual self-dramatization, an oscillation between opposing aspects of personality, real or imaged; and this, a stumbling block to many readers as evidence of Yeats' 'insincerity', I have attempted to explain and to justify. But the lives of the poets teach us how easy it is to 'mock at the great', how speculation and scandal may be joined (as some have joined them recently), to turn our eyes from a living poetry to 'an imagined image' of the life. Other detractions of recent critics I have attempted to refute, believing that much criticism errs by blaming a poet for failure to achieve what was never his intention, or for not writing in a manner that would have been wholly impossible to his traditions and temperament. But perhaps one of the difficulties of Yeats' poetry is that his work demands continuously some knowledge of, and sympathy with, the Christian tradition; though he was incapable of accepting Christianity.

## VII

This poetry does demand, perhaps more than most, a personal response, with all the dangers and exaltations that a strictly impersonal criticism might wish to avoid. Therefore the reader of Yeats should have some knowledge of the background of the poet's race and time, presented with whatever shortcomings are inevitable in a picture coloured by personal experience. He should be, at the least, not unsympathetic towards a practice of vision that, whatever its ultimate explanations in the neuro-physiology of the future, has sufficient precedent in Blake and Rilke to deserve some measure of acceptance. It seems inconsistent to accept without comment the voices of the *Duino Elegies*, and to reject the vision of a man shooting an arrow at a star. Many today are afraid of rhetoric, and there is much of it in Yeats. They are suspicious of 'traditional' attitudes, of a poet who thinks of himself as among 'the last Romantics', of political beliefs that appear to run counter to the catch-phrases of the moment, of poetry which appears to be independent of the crisis-waves of thought. They demand, from verse that relies upon symbol, a greater clarity and precision than is or can be proper to such technique. These preconceptions must be rejected. We must realize that the 'reality' expressed by the symbol is, in terms of an algebraic analysis, infinitely complex; and though the variation of meaning is decreased by the selective impact of one symbol upon another, the total effect must always be that of a richly cumulative but indeterminate complexity.

## VIII

It is well to remind ourselves of the peculiarities of this poetry. It grows out of experience, but does not, and cannot, summarize experience. It is moulded at many stages by the unconscious activities of the mind, and its connection with physical experience is complex, remote, and often speculative. I am aware that some, perhaps much, of what I have to say may deserve this last adjective; but I suggest that such interpretation is an intermediate stage; useful if for the moment it provides a framework in which the poetry can be seen, as I believe it must be, in a coherent pattern. For the poet himself cannot always trace the links in the chain of poetical responsibility, and those who make the attempt must, in the last resort, suggest what is no more than a personal interpretation or response.

I am indebted to many for their help, encouragement and advice; to Joseph Hone for his friendship and criticism, as well as to his *Life* of the poet and his Selections from J. B. Yeats' Letters, and for the loan of certain manuscripts; to Peter Allt, for much help in many ways, for the loan of the manuscripts of his Variorum Edition, and for his reading of the proofs; to A. Norman Jeffares for his published and unpublished material, and for his advice; to Patric Dickinson; to many friends in Dublin, Sligo and Clare, and to the Directors of the Dublin National and Municipal Galleries. I owe certain ideas to Dr C. M. Bowra's essay on Yeats in *The Heritage of Symbolism* (I take this to be the most illuminating study of the subject that has yet been made); to Louis MacNeice's *The Poetry of W. B. Yeats*, though I disagree with certain of his conclusions; to the essay in Edmund Wilson's *Axel's Castle*; and to Miss Ellis-Fermor's *The Irish Dramatic Movement*, with the admirable chapter on Yeats' Plays. To Dr Tillyard, Miss Lloyd Thomas, Oliver Edwards, Theodore Redpath, and J. E. M. White I am also grateful for much assistance and criticism.

While these essays have been in the press four important works have been published which deal wholly or in part with Yeats. Dr Norman Jeffares' *W. B. Yeats: Man and Poet* is the most fully documented study that has yet been made, and contains much source-material not available elsewhere. Together with Hone's *Life* it seems likely to become a standard work. Richard Ellmann's *W. B. Yeats: The Man and The Masks* is also based on the examination of much unpublished material, and approaches the problem of the 'divided consciousness' in the poetry through Yeats' relationship to his father. Graham Hough's *The Last Romantics* is specially notable for the chapter on Yeats, which I would set beside Dr Bowra's essay for its sympathy and insight. Donald A. Stauffer's *The Golden Nightingale* is mainly concerned with a study of the lyrics. Where the work of these authors has corrected or amplified my own I have endeavoured to give, within the limits now possible, appropriate reference or acknowledgement.

Above all others I am indebted to Mrs Yeats; for much unpublished information, for her help in correcting errors in others' writing, and in my own; for the gift of her husband's slides of Blake, Calvert and Palmer; for her unfailing courtesy and encouragement; and finally for her most generous permission to quote from the published and unpublished works.

Cambridge, 1949

# Introduction to the Second Edition

I

For some years this book has been out of print, and there have been many requests for its re-issue. Yet I have approached the problem of a new edition with some reservation. I began to write the book in 1947, after my return from war service, and in the midst of many other tasks. I had owed much to the encouragement of my friend and sometime teacher, E. M. W. Tillyard; but another incitement was the anger I had felt when confronted with Yeats' image in 'the mirror of malicious eyes' in post-war Dublin. In its first form *The Lonely Tower* owed much to my friend and pupil G. P. D. Allt, who fell so tragically to his death, and whose posthumous monument is the great Variorum Edition which he shares with Russell Alspach. And this might have been succeeded by the book which Peter Allt and I had planned, the Prolegomena to Anglo-Irish Literature, which would have begun with Spenser, or beyond.

Then H. R. Bachchan of Delhi came to work with me on Yeats and his Eastern sources. He was succeeded by F. A. C. Wilson, whose books *W. B. Yeats and Tradition* (in substance the thesis for his doctorate) and the later *Yeats' Iconography*, are as important as the controversies they have aroused. His work confirmed much that I had suspected regarding the traditional nature of Yeats' imagery, and a debt to complex esoteric sources which had been outside my knowledge. At the same time I had the privilege of directing some work on the Nōh plays by the Japanese poetess and scholar, Hiroko Ishibashi; and of reading in manuscript or for press a number of other works. Of these I remember with gratitude William Becker's Oxford thesis on the Plays and Professor A. G. Stock's *W. B. Yeats, his Poetry and Thought*; and Edward Engelberg's *The Vast Design* which has drawn together so much of Yeats' artistic beliefs. I am also grateful to Professor Johannes Kleinstück, to his pupil, Rolf Lass of Hamburg, who has worked with me on the Anglo-Irish background of the Big House and its 'mythology'; as well as to the Lecturers of the past four years at the Yeats International Summer School at Sligo –especially to Marion Witt, Myles Dillon and Frank O'Connor – and to the members of the Advanced Seminar Group at those meetings. I owe a particular debt to Francis Warner, for reading this edition both in script and in proof. It is possible that I have inadvertently taken ideas from others which I have not acknowledged; if so, I ask their pardon.

Over the past fifteen years critical works have emerged in a steady stream. Among those that seem to me most important (since 1950) are Ellmann's *The Identity of Yeats*, Kermode's *Romantic Image*, Virginia Moore's *The Unicorn*, Melchiori's *The Whole Mystery of Art*, Ure's *The Plays of W. B. Yeats*. George Brandon Saul, perhaps the most learned of all the American critics, has produced his *Prolegomena* both to the Poems and to the Plays. Unterecker's *Reader's Guide* also gives assistance.

Much work has been done on the lines of one of my first concerns, Yeats' interest in the pictures in Dublin and elsewhere. Our understanding has been notably enlarged by Professors Melchiori[1] and Kermode,[2] and particularly to Kermode's Reading Exhibition catalogued as *Images of a Poet*. Wind[3] has illustrated dramatically and cogently the projection into the Renaissance of pagan esoteric imagery. Fr. Hugo Rahner's *Greek Myths and Christian Mystery*[4] is also relevant. Hatzfeldt's *Literature Through Art* and Kenneth Clark's *Landscape into Art* have contributed much, from wholly different approaches. Charles Madge appears to have solved, once and for all, the iconographic origin of *Leda and the Swan*.[5] Stallworthy's *Between The Lines*, and his unpublished lectures, have added greatly to our knowledge of the manner in which the drafts of the poems were forged and filed. I owe much to Raymond Lister and his book on Calvert.

During the same period Alan Wade's great *Letters* has made redundant or misleading many of my earlier references, including

[1] *The Whole Mystery of Art* 1960.
[2] *Romantic Image* 1957.
[3] *Pagan Mysteries in the Renaissance* London 1958.
[4] English Translation, London 1963.
[5] *T.L.S.* Sept. 1962.

those to certain letters in my own possession. I have used Wade's text throughout. Macmillans have brought out, in addition to the *Collected Poems* (1950) and the *Collected Plays* (1954), *Mythologies*, *Explorations*, and *Essays and Introductions*, *Autobiographies*, and *A Vision;* these have made much material more readily available, and the references in the first edition have been, in general, revised to correspond with them. But there have been instances where I have kept to the earlier editions, usually because the newer ones are, at times, only selections from these.

## II

This second edition has been brought up to date so far as the scale and plan of the original allowed. I have tried to correct my earlier mistakes of fact or judgement. I am much indebted to my critics, including the reviewers (particularly the late Edwin Muir) and to George Brandon Saul, Marion Witt, Frank Wilson, and the late L. A. G. Strong. A new chapter has been added. That called 'Poet and Painter' has been largely re-written in the light of my visits to the galleries and works which Yeats saw on his travels in America, Italy and France. But I have made no attempt to consider the innumerable exegetical essays and commentaries which have grown or twined themselves about the poems. To accept, modify, or reject would have swollen the book out of all reason; much of this writing and explanation is fruitful, more is sheer ingenuity. I do not think that more than a dozen of the poems demand or admit, because of their complexity, widely different interpretations. At the same time I believe that we should be chary of imputing to Yeats consistently elaborate or weighted meanings. Poets are often less exact than we should like to imagine; a study of the re-draftings shows that there are many reasons, not all of them obedient to the logic of thought or ear, for the apparently final version. He was not averse to mysti-fication; nor was he less guilty than other poets have been of sacri-ficing semantic precision to the rhetoric of a phrase.

Theses for doctorates and other degrees have now multiplied beyond counting. For the English Post-Graduate Faculties, par-ticularly in the U.S.A., Pound, Yeats and Joyce remain the most popular of quarries. I find the results a little depressing. The attractiveness of the subject for 'research' is easily explained. Yeats and Eliot remain the most considerable poets of the century, though the reputation of both wavers in certain balances. Both have made dark words upon the harp. Eliot's bones – we may be thankful – cannot yet be beaten; Yeats' are being ground in the mills of many minds. Much remains to be done; it is, for example, probable that a new text of Cornelius Agrippa, about to be produced by F. le P. Warner, will throw a good deal of light on some dark places. 'The seventeenth century English Translation of . . . *De Occulta Philosophia* was once so famous that it found its way into the hands of Irish farmers and wandering Irish tinkers. . . .'[1]

### III

The main quarrel (if it be a quarrel) in Yeatsian criticism appears to be that of the relevance of much of our present-day 'scholarship'. I should be the first to condemn *Quellenforschung* for its own sake, whether of pictorial or esoteric sources. A key problem is that of the relevance of *A Vision*. But I believe that it is misleading to regard every poem as a self-sufficient whole needing no ancillary comment:[2] with the corollary that we should disregard the notes that Yeats himself supplied. This kind of poetry is forged out of the substance of Yeats' own life and experience. It is often, deliberately, oblique and obscure; the meaning in depth depends, as he himself said, on a rich poetical memory. To decide what is or is not relevant to the *understanding* of any great poet, the process that precedes evaluation, is an age-old problem. But even the new critics are, it seems to me, compelled to rely on knowledge that is, strictly speaking, alien to the overt form of the statement. I do not think we have yet understood fully the esoteric basis of Yeats' thought, and I do not agree with those who seek to minimize its significance. On this Wind has spoken wisely:

> In recent years, esoteric studies of Donne, Herbert, Blake, and Yeats have raised the question of their poetic utility. While it is certain that readers repelled by recondite meanings are likely to miss some magnificent poetic metaphors,[3] on the other hand those addicted

[1] *Four and Twenty*, p. 59. But I am a little sceptical.
[2] *v.* (e.g.) Kleinstück's recent book.
[3] And, I would add, of meaning-in-depth.

to esoteric studies may lose sight of the poetry altogether. But the danger of these studies does not lessen this importance. In each instance the relevance is a question of poetic tact; that is, it cannot be settled in the abstract, but depends on that altogether indefinite but unmistakable sense of pitch which distinguishes a pertinent from a rambling disquisition.'[1]

I still believe that for Yeats, as for Shakespeare, it is necessary to consider the work as parts of a whole which approaches an epic totality. With that in mind, the experience of the individual work emerges in its completeness, and then (and only then) it affords the opportunity to assess its total impact. And at this stage of progressive integration I believe that many considerations are relevant: Yeats' reading (that brings us sometimes to a greater certainty as to what he had in mind); many of the textual redraftings (for the same reason); the realization that Yeats was to some extent a writer in an esoteric tradition, and that the symbolism demands wherever possible a knowledge of what he appears to have accepted, consciously or unconsciously, from those sources. But at the last (and this is always the great danger of those who 'cough in ink') the poems are to be read aloud for only then there is released the full subtlety of sound and accent and rhythm. Many recordings have been made, but not more than three or four professional readers seem to me capable of producing satisfactory interpretations, of releasing the full subtleties of sound and accent and rhythm; fewer still are capable of giving weight to the subtleties of the Anglo-Irish intonation, of the occasional regional idiom, and the Spenserian brightness of brave and glorious words.

It is difficult to predict the winding paths which future scholarship will follow. Alspach's Variorum Edition of the Plays will provide as much fresh fuel for the bonfires of research as that of the Poems has done. We still know little about 'the bundle of German plays' which Yeats mentions. A great mass of new material will become available if and when certain papers and notebooks are released; for example the unpublished *Bridegroom* is not generally available, and I do not know anything of the mysterious 'Black Jester', which is perhaps related to the Tarot Pack.

It seems possible that, by the time this edition is published, the

[1] Edgar Wind, *op. cit.* (p. 22 *n.*).

pendulum will have swung farther to the left in the disestimation of Yeats. There is much that will be contrary to the predominant temper of the nineteen-sixties. His beliefs cannot be 'distanced' as readily as those of Donne or Blake. These include 'belief' in the supernatural (whether proven, modified or refracted); in ceremony and sainthood, in autocracy and aristocracy; in war; and in 'the wasteful heroic virtues'. His rhetoric is of a special kind, not readily accepted now. The whole Anglo-Irish background lacks the interest, perhaps the microcosmic significance that it appeared to have gained thirty years ago; when *The Tower* and *The Winding Stair* seemed the major poetic achievement for a hundred years. But however critical opinion may drift about

As fashion or more fantasy decrees

the perfection and permanence of the work does not seem to be in doubt.

Cambridge, 1964

# Texts and Abbreviations

Many new editions of Yeats' works have become available since the first edition of this book was published. In order to simplify reference and quotation, I have altered the previous references, as far as possible, to conform to these. Among these the 'composite' volumes *Mythologies* (1959), *Essays and Introductions* (1961) and *Explorations* (1962) are especially valuable. But there are instances where, for example, the newer edition has omitted footnotes, or modified the text, and I have then retained the reference to the works which I had used. For example, the two texts of *A Vision* differ in many ways; I have kept the original references to the 1925 version as (A) and to the 1937 as (B). Wade's Bibliography has made superfluous the previous lists of dates of publication. The references to Hone's Life are to the First Edition.

Abbreviations etc. used for convenience in the footnotes, are:

| | |
|---|---|
| *E. & I.* | *Essays and Introductions*, 1961. |
| *Autobiographies* | 1955 Edition. |
| *C.P.* | *Collected Poems*, 1950. |
| *C. Plays* | *Collected Plays*, 1953. |
| *Wade* | *The Letters of W. B. Yeats*, Edited by Alan Wade, 1954. |
| *Bibliog.* | *A Bibliography of the Writings of W. B. Yeats*, Edited by Alan Wade, 1951. |
| *Variorum* | *The Variorum Edition of the Poems of W. B. Yeats*, Edited by Peter Allt and Russell K. Alspach, 1957. |
| *P.A.S.L.* | *Per Amica Silentia Lunae*, 1918. |
| *W. & B.* | *Wheels and Butterflies*, 1934. |
| *P. & C.* | *Plays and Controversies*, 1923. |
| *1930 Diary* | *Pages for a Diary Written in Nineteen Hundred and Thirty* (Cuala Press), 1934. |
| *Four and Twenty* | *If I were Four and Twenty* (Cuala Press) 1940. |

| | |
|---|---|
| *T.S.M. Letters* | *W. B. Yeats and T. Sturge Moore, Their Correspondence* 1901–1937, Edited by Ursula Bridges, 1953. |
| *D.W. Letters* | *Letters on Poetry from W. B. Yeats to Dorothy Wellesley*; Oxford, 1940. |
| *J.B.Y. Letters* | *Letters to his son, W. B. Yeats, and others,* Ed. Joseph Hone. London, 1944. |
| Vision (A) | *A Vision* (1925) |
| Vision (B) | *A Vision* (1937) |

CHAPTER ONE

# The Background

'You have come again,
And surely after twenty years it was time to come.'
I am thinking of a child's vow sworn in vain
Never to leave that valley his fathers called their home.[1]

Sligo town lies in a cup of the hills, where a short but broad river
takes the waters of Lough Gill into the Atlantic. As you stand facing
the sea, there are two mountains: Knocknarea on the left hand, with
a tumulus on the summit, said to be Queen Maeve's grave, and called
in the Irish *Árd-na-riagadh*, the Hill of the Scaffolds.[2] On the
right, far beyond the town and river, a great shoulder of mountain
drops to the plain that stretches towards Lissadell and the sea; this
is Ben Bulben, where Diarmuid and Grainne were pursued by Finn,
and where Diarmuid, Adonis-like, was wounded by the enchanted
boar. The river flows through a long twisting estuary, guarded
towards the mouth by a beacon, The Metal Man, which is to be seen
in Jack Yeats' foreshortened drawing of Rosses Point; the little
village that lies among the sand-dunes, with the sea to the west of
it. The two mountains are full of legend. An old servant of Yeats'
uncle, George Pollexfen, described Maeve and her women on
Knocknarea:

> ... They are fine and dashing looking, like the men one sees riding
> their horses in twos and threes on the slopes of the mountains with
> their swords swinging.[3]

[1] 'Under Saturn,' *C.P.*, p. 202.
[2] 'Old bones upon the mountain shake'? But there are many ancient graves
on the north and east slopes, as well as prehistoric monuments. Some
authorities give *Árd-na-Ríagh*, 'the height of the Kings'.
[3] *Autobiographies*, (1955) p. 266.

Both mountains and plains are ancient battlegrounds. After the Battle of Sligo in A.D. 537 Eoghan Bel 'was buried standing, his red javelin in his hand, as if bidding defiance to his enemies'.

> There in the tomb stand the dead upright . . .

Beside Glencar there is a precipice where a troop of horsemen were led to their death; and one of my friends had heard on Ben Bulben the beat of miniature horse-hoofs on the plateau at the mountain-top, and seen the grass beaten down and springing up again as if a troop of horse had passed that way:

> *What marches through the mountain pass?*
> *No, no, my son, not yet;*
> *That is an airy spot,*
> *And no man knows what treads the grass.*[1]

The whole neighbourhood is 'airy':[2] perhaps because of the battle-fields that the conformation of the ground has determined through the centuries, perhaps because the fresh and the salt waters from the mountains and the estuary meet so violently and quickly there.[3]

At the head of the lake, which is studded with wooded islets (Innisfree among them), there is the village of Dromahair, where a man stood among a crowd and dreamed of faery-land.[4] Near the coast, north-west of Sligo town, is the village of Drumcliff ('An ancestor was rector there'); the church among its rook-delighting trees beside the river that flows out of Glencar. It is full of ancient history; near it there is a monastery said to have been founded by St Columba, and this part too of the Sligo Plain was an ancient battlefield. On the wooded sides of the lake stood the great houses, Hazelwood of the Wynnes, Cleaveragh of the Wood-Martins, Markree of the Coopers, and many more up and down the country-side; Lissadell of the Gore-Booths was the most important in Yeats' boyhood and manhood. In and about Sligo there were relatives of the Yeats family; and farther south, in Mayo and Galway, the

---

[1] 'Three Marching Songs,' *C.P.*, p. 377.
[2] Yeats' note: '"Airy" may be an old pronunciation of "eerie", often heard in Galway and Sligo.'
[3] Jack B. Yeats spoke to me of this, but something of the kind was a belief in the seventeenth century.
[4] *C.P.*, p. 49.

'half-legendary men', the ancestors whom he drew into his own legend of great place.

To the south-west, beyond Ballisodare (the scene of a spirited battle with the French who landed at Killala Bay in 1798), are the Ox Mountains. At Collooney the Sligo Plain ends and the mountains begin. Near by is Tullaghan Well, said to have burst forth as a spring at the prayer of St Patrick, and whose waters ebb and flow mysteriously, perhaps in relation to the far-away tides. Such wells are often sacred, in past myth and as places of Christian pilgrimage; they may be linked to poetic inspiration. Of this last kind, 'each is surrounded, it is said, by nine imperishable hazel trees, from which the showers of ruddy nuts were dropped periodically into the spring. These nuts were eagerly watched by the salmon at the bottom of the spring who, when they saw them drop upon the surface, dashed up and ate them as fast as they could, after which they glided into the neighbouring rivers.'[1] Beside are two rocks, The Hungry Rock and the Hawk's Rock: and this is perhaps the setting of '*At the Hawk's Well*'.

The society and life of the early part of the century was in many ways peculiar. It is a very different world from that of Synge or of O'Casey. Everywhere the Big House, with its estates surrounding it, was a centre of hospitality, of country life and society, apt to breed a passionate attachment, so that the attempt to save it from burning or bankruptcy became an obsession (in the nineteen-twenties and onwards) when that civilization was passing. The gradual sale of the outlying properties, as death duties and taxation rose higher, is recorded in Lady Gregory's struggle to save Coole Park, and was the fate of many estates.[2] The great families were familiar with each other and with each other's history; often, perhaps commonly, connected by blood or marriage. They had definite and narrow traditions of life and service. The sons went to English Public Schools, and thence to Cambridge, or Oxford, or Trinity College, Dublin: the eldest would return to the estate and its management, the younger went to the Services, the Bar, the Church. There were

[1] Wood-Martin, *History of Sligo*. Vol. III. Ch. XXVI.
[2] See Lady Gregory, *Journals*; in particular the chapters called 'The Terror' and 'The Civil War'.

> . . . Great rooms where travelled men and children found
> Content or joy; a last inheritor
> Where none has reigned that lacked a name and fame
> Or out of folly into folly came.[1]

The great age of that society had, I suppose, been the eighteenth and early nineteenth centuries; from the eighteen-fifties onwards it seems to have turned its eyes too much towards England, too conscious of its lost influence in its hereditary role of The Ascendancy. By 1912 it was growing a little tired, a little purposeless, but the world still seemed secure:

> We too had many pretty toys when young:
> A law indifferent to blame or praise,
> To bribe or threat; habit that made old wrong
> Melt down, as it were wax in the sun's rays;
> Public opinion ripening for so long
> We thought it would outlive all future days.[2]

The image of the house and its fall lingered with Yeats to the end, as in the play *Purgatory*:

> Great people lived and died in this house;
> Magistrates, colonels, members of Parliament,
> Captains and Governors, and long ago
> Men that had fought at Aughrim and the Boyne . . .
> . . . to kill a house
> Where great men grew up, married, died,
> I here declare a capital offence.[3]

In the furnishings of a great house, or in its library, one became aware that most of the work had been done between, say, 1750 and 1850, over the bones of a rebellion and two famines. The original building might date from Cromwell's time, or before; modernized, perhaps, by adding a frontage from a Loire chateau, or a portico from Italy. Some of these were of great beauty:

> Many ingenious lovely things are gone
> That seemed sheer miracle to the multitude,

1 'Coole Park and Ballylee, 1931', *C.P.*, p. 275.
2 'Nineteen Hundred and Nineteen,' ibid., p. 232.
3 *Purgatory*, *C. Plays*, p. 681.

> Protected from the circle of the moon
> That pitches common things about.[1]

But the whole Anglo-Irish myth, the search for beauty and stability in the midst of poverty and defeat, the dreams that oscillated between fantasy and realism, has yet to be described.

It is against this background, I believe, we must see the Recognition and Reversal in Yeats' poetry that came out of the Rebellion and its aftermath. Before the First World War that aristocratic culture seemed to have given so much: pride of race, independence of thought, and a certain integrity of political values. It could be perceived (even then) in relation to the great eighteenth-century tradition, which, foreshortened and perhaps not wholly understood, held so much fascination for Yeats. It could be seen as representing the Anti-Self or Mask to which he was striving: whether in the image of the hero, or soldier, or horseman, or that symbolic Fisherman who occurs repeatedly:

> . . . I choose upstanding men
> That climb the streams until
> The fountain leap, and at dawn
> Drop their cast at the side
> Of dripping stone; I declare
> They shall inherit my pride,
> The pride of people that were
> Bound neither to Cause nor to State,
> Neither to slaves that were spat on,
> Nor to the tyrants that spat,
> The people of Burke and of Grattan
> That gave, though free to refuse –
> Pride, like that of the morn. . . .[2]

Lady Gregory and the Gore-Booths had shown him the security that came from the wealth of the great estates, and the life, leisured and cultured, that it seemed to make possible:

> Surely among a rich man's flowering lawns,
> Amid the rustle of his planted hills,
> Life overflows without ambitious pains;
> And rains down life until the basin spills,
> And mounts more dizzy high the more it rains

[1] 'Nineteen Hundred and Nineteen,' C.P., p. 232.
[2] 'The Tower,' iii, ibid., p. 223.

As though to choose whatever shape it wills
And never stoop to a mechanical
Or servile shape, at others' beck and call.[1]

To this society, in the main Protestant, Unionist, and of the
'Ascendancy' in character, the peasantry was linked. The great
demesnes had their tenantry, proud, idle, careless, kindly, with a
richness of speech and folk-lore that Lady Gregory had been the
first to record.[2] The days of *Castle Rackrent* and the absentee landlord were, in the main, over; the relationship between landlord and
tenant varied, but was on the whole a kindly one, and carried a
good deal of respect on either side. The bitterness of the Famine,
the evictions and burnings described by Maud Gonne in *A Servant
of the Queen*, belonged to an earlier period. The members of the
family would be known either by the titles of their professions: the
Counsellor, the Bishop, the Commander, and so on: or by the
Christian names of their boyhood. They mixed with the peasantry
more freely and with a greater intimacy (especially in childhood)
than would have been possible in England.[3] Yeats' memories of
conversations with servants, and particularly with Mary Battle,
gave him much material. Sport of every kind was a constant bond:
the ability to shoot, or fish, or ride a horse was of central importance.
At its best there was something not unlike a survival of the Renaissance qualities:

. . . Soldier, scholar, horseman, he,
And all he did done perfectly
As though he had but that one trade alone.[4]

But even at its best the tradition had outlived its usefulness, as
Yeats knew:

O what if gardens where the peacock strays
With delicate feet upon old terraces,
Or else all Juno from an urn displays

[1] 'Meditations in Time of Civil War,' *C.P.*, p. 225.
[2] As in *Visions and Beliefs*. She had popularized it, though Standish O'Grady
and Douglas Hyde were the pioneers.
[3] See *Autobiographies*, pp. 258, 261. George Moore gives a good account
of this in his boyhood: adding the interesting opinion that the best and purest
English was spoken by gamekeepers.
[4] 'In Memory of Major Robert Gregory,' *C.P.*, p. 148.

Before the indifferent garden deities;
O what if levelled lawns and gravelled ways
Where slippered Contemplation finds his ease
And Childhood a delight for every sense,
But take our greatness with our violence?[1]

There were other aspects of that life. Land or local troubles flared out from time to time. There were times, even in my own boyhood, when one did not sit in the evening between a lamp and the open; though Lady Gregory, in reply to threats on her life during the Civil War, replied proudly that she was to be found each evening, between six and seven, writing before an unshuttered window.[2] Violence had its curious paradoxes: there is a perfect description in Lord Dunsany's *The Curse of the Wise Woman*. A father and his schoolboy son of fifteen or so, on holiday from Eton, are living alone. The house is raided: a band of men have come to shoot the father, who slips out of the study by a secret passage, bidding his son to wait and delay the men. They question him: he denies that his father is in the house. On the table there is a fragment of the True Cross, embedded in crystal (the family are Catholics). They make the boy swear on the relic that he is telling the truth. He perjures himself, and then hears in the distance the beat of horse-hoofs that means his father has got away. At last the men decide to go: their leader calls the boy and tells him that the wild geese are coming to a bog near his house and that he should come up one night for a shot. Finally, he grows confidential and gives the boy the most valued piece of advice he knows:

And if it ever comes to it, and God knows the world's full of trouble, *aim a foot in front of a man walking, at a hundred yards!*

In this society there was (outside the big cities) no middle class, and this was in itself a fundamental weakness. A barrister was honoured for his profession: a solicitor was in a very different category. The doctor and the clergyman had positions in the social scale not wholly unlike those in the world of Swift. The relations

[1] 'Meditations in Time of Civil War,' i, *C.P.*., p. 225.
[2] 'Beautiful Lofty Things,' *C.P.*, p. 348.

between Protestants and Catholics might be bitter, and memories of the Penal Laws were long; but in the years before the First World War I remember little trouble in the West. Indeed, my grandfather had given land for the local chapel, so that the front pew was reserved for members of the family in case they should one day be converted. And for many years, in accordance with some old tradition, a light was kept burning on our behalf in the ruined abbey on one of the islands in the Shannon – a ritual that hardly belonged to Protestantism, but was accepted as natural and proper. In every district there were many superstitions, with a curiously ambivalent attitude to them on the part of country-folk and gentry alike. The early Christian missionaries had taken over many of the features of the Elder Faiths of the locality. Holy wells are numerous and display the offerings of the pious. In my own youth pieces of gorse were placed on the lintels of the cottages on May Day to discourage the Good People from alighting there. A relic of the Baal Fire ritual was rehearsed in the lane below our house on St John's Eve when young men leaped through the flames of bonfires.[1] The sacred pilgrimage to Croagh Patrick fired Yeats' mind with a vision of a new synthesis of paganism and Christianity. The 'cleft that's christened Alt'[2] is near Sligo, and has magical associations; it was no violence of Yeats to think of it in terms of the chasm at Delphi, just as the Sphinx might be transplanted to the Rock of Cashel.[3] A good Catholic might well half-believe in the older magic and yet go to Mass with a clear conscience; a Protestant, while in theory superior to all superstitious practices, might yet catch something of a fearful half-belief from speech with servants, grooms and fishermen, and innate romanticism could readily build upon their stories.

I believe that it is important to realize something of this background of Yeats' work. It has many bearings. The world of the great houses offered security, a sense of peace, beautiful things to

[1] See the account of this ceremony in Honor Tracy's *The Straight and Narrow Path*.

[2] 'The Man and the Echo,' *C.P.*, p. 393.

[3] 'The Double Vision of Michael Robartes,' ibid., p. 192. See p. 250, *infra*.

look on and handle:

> Great works constructed there in nature's spite
> For scholars and for poets after us,
> Thoughts long knitted into a single thought,
> A dance-like glory that those walls begot.[1]

The truth about the great houses of the South and West lies, perhaps, somewhere between Yeats' pictures of Coole Park, the romantic descriptions of some recent novelists, and MacNeice's 'snob idyllicism'. For every family that produced 'travelled men and children' there was another that produced little but 'hard-riding country gentlemen', who had scarcely opened a book. An eighteenth-century house might be half-filled with Sheraton and Adam work, and half with Victorian rubbish. Families nursed the thought of past greatness, fed their vanity with old achievement or lineage or imagined descent from the ancient kings; and in the warm damp air, with its perpetual sense of melancholy, of unhappy things either far off or present, many of them decayed. Standish O'Grady could write bitterly of *The Great Enchantment*, that web of apathy in a country with an alien government and an alien religion, subject at every turn to patronage and the servility it brings, into which Ireland had fallen. That, too, is a narrow view of the whole. The aristocracy had, at its best, possessed many of the qualities that Yeats ascribed to it: the world of Somerville and Ross, the Dublin of Joyce or of Sean O'Casey differ merely in accordance with the position of the onlooker.

Of the paradox of Ireland, and its challenge, Yeats was aware almost from the beginning. He wrote to 'A.E.': 'But remember always that now you are face to face with Ireland, its tragedy and its poverty, and if you would express Ireland you must know her to the heart and in all her moods. You will be a far more powerful mystic and poet and teacher because of this knowledge. . . . You are face to face with the heterogeneous, and the test of one's harmony is our power to absorb it and make it harmonious. . . . Absorb

---

[1] 'Coole Park, 1929,' *C.P.*, p. 273. The idea of the dance and story are linked elsewhere: perhaps a memory of Nietzsche's remark as to the connection between the dance and tragedy. Compare the fourth stanza of 'Byzantium'.

Ireland and her tragedy and you will be the poet of a people, perhaps the poet of a new insurrection.'[1]

One effect of this society, organized into sharply divided classes, living a life that was perpetually seeking reassurance from the past, was to accentuate a certain rhetorical habit of thought and speech. The attitude to 'brave and glorious words' had something Elizabethan about it; just as the richness of idiom, of a certain happy valiancy of phrase that is so easily parodied or misunderstood, goes back to that tradition of speech. This instinct lies deep, but does lead to what is normally described as 'insincerity'. It is deliberate, cultivated, but still an essential part of the Irish character: remembering always that it is false to speak of any constant feature in that heterogeneous race. The reply of Nora in Synge's *In the Shadow of the Glen* to the Tramp's outburst of poetry is a fair comment:

> 'I'm thinking it's myself will be wheezing that time with lying down under the Heavens when the night is cold: but you've a fine bit of talk, stranger, and it's with yourself I'll go.'

Yeats found in these surroundings security, companionship, encouragement, and some honour as a poet. The passing of that world, as it passed between 1916 and 1923, was a magnificent theme. There was a war within a war; Hugh Lane's drowning on the *Lusitania*, Robert Gregory's death in Italy in 1918, were symbols of the outer conflict that was imaged in the larger movement of the gyres, the cyclic movements of history. It was a kind of phoenix-ending of Ireland's great past; the burning of the eighteenth-century houses was half a terror, half the price of resurrection. The poet's ancestors were in the great tradition of political or literary achievement, men who had protested against tyranny or social decay:

THE FIRST.     My great-grandfather spoke to Edmund Burke
                       In Grattan's house.
THE SECOND.                    My great-grandfather shared
                       A pot-house bench with Oliver Goldsmith once.[2]

---

[1] Wade, *Letters*, p. 294. Compare the quotation from Standish O'Grady's speech: 'We have now a literary movement, it is not very important; it will be followed by a political movement, that will not be very important; then must come a military movement, that will be important indeed.' (*Autobiographies*, p. 424.)

[2] 'The Seven Sages,' *C.P.*, p. 271. It is worth noting, as Peter Allt has pointed out, that the three men were sprung from the professional middle class, not from the great land-owning families.

In contrast with the great past, the fall was greater:

> Even from that delight memory treasures so,
> Death, despair, division of families, all entanglements of mankind grow,
> As that old wandering beggar and these God-hated children know.[1]

In that setting he would be the last Romantic, or Lear, or Timon, or the prophetic Blake; the roles were infinite. From the present he could go back through ancestral memories and see the folk-lore of the Sligo and Galway mountains behind those men and women who were fighting for the Irish Republic: so that the mythologies seem to meet and blend, the great eddies of history repeating themselves in rhetorical patterns. Cuchulain, bound by the belt to a pillar in his last fight, as in that great statue in the Post Office in Dublin, stood for the great paradox of heroic defeat:

> Some had no thought of victory
> But had gone out to die
> That Ireland's mind be greater,
> Her heart mount up on high. . . .[2]

The irony was apparent, too; that life with which he identified himself was to be broken by the very forces which he believed he had launched. So, of the burning of the houses:

> But is there any comfort to be found?
> Man is in love and loves what vanishes,
> What more is there to say? That country round
> None dared admit, if such a thought were his,
> Incendiary or bigot could be found
> To burn that stump on the Acropolis,
> Or break in bits the famous ivories
> Or traffic in the grasshoppers or bees.[3]

In all this there was, of course, a certain vanity. Yeats was a great actor; but his pose, while it was of the skin of his poetry, was never of its bone. (I shall suggest that this is in part true of his psychical investigations.) For though he knew his ancestry far back, among the farmers and traders of the West, his world was, initially, outside

---

[1] 'From Oedipus at Colonus,' *C.P.*, p. 255.
[2] 'Three Songs to the One Burden,' ibid., p. 371
[3] 'Nineteen Hundred and Nineteen,' i, ibid., p. 232.

that with which he tried to identify himself.[1] Nor did he attempt to falsify his pedigree, as many romantic writers have done. Dublin's gossip might tell malicious stories of his preoccupation with his ancestry, but it does not matter greatly. It was an easy and harmless game to magnify his lineage in verse, to claim entry into that pathetically pedigreed world that linked itself to Ormondes or Butlers or the High Kings.[2] But, in point of fact, it is the other side of his genealogy, his descent from the smaller professional families, that he seeks to stress. Ancestral virtues came from seafaring men, from horsemen, from an integrity of the blood that had passed through no huxter's loin:

> He that in Sligo at Drumcliff
> Set up the old stone Cross,
> That red-headed rector in County Down,
> A good man on a horse,
> Sandymount Corbets, that notable man
> Old William Pollexfen,
> The smuggler Middleton, Butlers far back,
> Half-legendary men.[3]

The West, like the Roman Campagna, is a country of ruins. There is a perpetual reminder, in dún and rath and the hill-forts of Tara or Emain, in ruined Norman castle and round tower, in the mysterious forts of Aran, of the heroic age, of past power that conjures up the emotions that Dryden, or Dyer in *The Ruins of Rome*, or Richard Wilson, found in the Roman scene. There is endless melancholy, sprouting easily in the soft rain, in the setting of a shiftless and idle countryside, beneath the drums and tramplings of four conquests. A ruined castle, with a couple of cottages beside, could be bought for thirty pounds and become a dominant symbol with memories of Spenser, Herbert,[4] Thomson,[5] Shelley:

---

[1] Mr Day Lewis is, I think, wrong when he suggests that Yeats belonged as of right to this aristocracy, or was accepted by it until he was 'taken up' by Lady Gregory. There was a vast gap between the 'squirearchy' to which he refers and the great houses. (*v. Yeats and the Aristocratic Tradition: Scattering Branches*, ed. Stephen Gwynn, pp. 162, 163, 166.)

[2] George Moore is particularly lucid on this subject; *v. Vale*, p. 101.

[3] 'Are You Content?' *C.P.*, p. 370.

[4] 'Is all true doctrine in a winding stair?'

[5]                          'The lonely tower
Is also shunned, whose mournful chambers hold,
So night-struck fancy dreams, the yelling ghost.'

There, on blood-saturated ground, have stood
Soldier, assassin, executioner,
Whether for daily pittance or in blind fear
Or out of abstract hatred, and shed blood. . . .[1]

It is something that is easy to stigmatize as fantasy, escapism, self-dramatization, snobbery, nostalgia, and so forth: but all such dismissals are too simple. Unless the duality of mood is realized and accepted for what it is, unless we cease to laugh at Yeats as not conforming to Arnold's 'criticism of life', or to deride the plays on the grounds that Aristotle would not have considered them as plays at all, we are condemned to a supercilious critical attitude that will vitiate all understanding.

The rebuilding of the Tower, Thoor Ballylee, near Lady Gregory's place at Coole, was a gesture, too: half-believed in, half-mocked at, but serving as a symbol, by turns cosmic and absurd; viewed with that peculiar irony that was necessary to preserve a sense of mystery, an incantation of power and benediction:

Blessed be this place,
More blessed still this tower;
A bloody, arrogant power
Rose out of the race
Uttering, mastering it,
Rose like these walls from these
Storm-beaten cottages —
In mockery I have set
A powerful emblem up,
And sing it rhyme upon rhyme
In mockery of a time
Half dead at the top.[2]

For the Tower was never finished; and a great empty room remained at the top. This empty room would be connected with the traditional symbol of the Seventh Room in alchemy[3] and the ultimate room in St Teresa's *The Interior Castle*, which Yeats had read. The last, topmost, empty room would be that in which spiritual revelation is given; compare the last 'house' of the 'Phases of the Moon'. I suggest that 'half dead at the top' refers not to the flat cement roof as Hone[4] thought, but to the impossibility of religious or

[1] 'Blood and the Moon,' iii, *C.P.*, p. 269.
[2] 'Blood and the Moon,' i, ibid., p. 267.
[3] *v. The Chymical Marriage of Christian Rosencrux.*
[4] *Life*, p. 331.

spiritual enlightenment in this era. Yeats used to say that *A Vision* would be finished when the room was finally restored; neither was ever completed. But, in mockery or not, it could foreshorten history for him:

> I declare this tower is my symbol; I declare
> This winding, gyring, spiring treadmill of a stair is my
> ancestral stair;
> That Goldsmith and the Dean, Berkeley and Burke have
> travelled there.[1]

He could pace upon the battlements, where the crumbling stone or a jackdaw's nest at a loop-home, gave other images —

> ... And send imagination forth
> Under the day's declining beam, and call
> Images and memories
> From ruin or from ancient trees,
> For I would ask a question of them all.[2]

As first used in 'The Phases of the Moon', the Tower is closely linked to necromancy, to '*Il Penseroso*'s Platonist', as well as to *Axël's* Castle. Through meditation on it Yeats found new significance in its many aspects. Among them are its qualities, real or imagined, in the Anglo-Norman occupation, which was itself related to the Easter Rising through the story of Dermot and Devorgilla in *The Dreaming of the Bones*. In the unpublished play *The Bridegroom* it has sexual connotations. Hero's tower has its winding stair by which man ascends to the topmost room, to find spiritual peace. In *Ideas of Good and Evil* Yeats describes the tower as the symbol of the mind looking outward upon men and things, as well as the symbol of the mind turned inward upon itself. At night bats fly round it, butterflies beat their wings against it. Both are traditionally souls or disembodied spirits. They seek to gain entry, to communicate the wisdom of the dead, but are too fragile to do so.

By 1928 the Tower had served its purpose as a symbol. It was no longer the dwelling of '*Il Penseroso*'s Platonist' or 'Shelley's visionary prince,'[3] and sickness was approaching. By 1927 there

---

[1] 'Blood and the Moon,' ii, *C.P.*, p. 267.
[2] Ibid., p. 219. cf. the ending of George Moore's *Vale*
[3] Taken, I think, from 'Prince Athanase':
> His soul had wedded Wisdom and her dower
> Is love and justice clothed in which he sate
> Apart from men as in a lonely tower ...

were the first serious warnings of tuberculosis. Time was running on; and the next transformation of the symbol is The Great Clock Tower and its mysterious King, in *A Full Moon in March*; with

> A slow low note and an iron bell.

If, as I shall suggest later, his philosophy from 1928 to 1934 was much concerned with his own theory of the Phases of the Moon, he was passing into the phase of the Saint, who might be perceived as Ribh, 'the critic of St. Patrick'.

> Now his wars on God begin;
> At stroke of midnight God shall win.[1]

Much of Yeats' work seems to have that curious clarity of vision which is not a clarity of detail, but rather of imaginative focus; a sense of the processional element in life and in history. Perhaps that clarity arises in part from the elimination or stylization of the immediate foreground detail, as by a short-sighted man; but I think it is rather because he had this intense awareness of the significant things in his surroundings which could be used for the structure of his thought. His lineage, the birth of his child, the building of the Tower, the breaking of a civilization – these things are the scaffolding of the arch. The material might be thought of (at first) as belonging to the conventional Romantic pattern; the nostalgia for the past, the dilettantism of history and ruins, the self-aggrandizement and posturing of the Poet. But a certain bitterness of insight, a continuous wrenching back of all that might become sentimental, a consciousness of depth in the whole picture, disperse continually any such impression.

In one mood —

> We were the last romantics – chose for theme
> Traditional sanctity and loveliness;
> Whatever's written in what poets name
> The book of the people; whatever most can bless
> The mind of man or elevate a rhyme. . . .[2]

---

[1] 'The Four Ages of Man,' *C.P.*, p. 332. The explanation is a letter to Olivia Shakespear 'These are the four ages of individual man, but they are also the four ages of civilization. The first is earth (vegetable): the second, water (blood and sex): the third, air (brain, intellect): the fourth, fire, which is soul.'

[2] 'Coole Park and Ballylee, 1931' *C.P.*, p. 275.

In the next, the bitter gaiety comes out. The strong violent rhythms, and an almost impish reining back of language to normality, break all suggestion of sentimentality; if need be by the coarseness or even vulgarity of rhythm or word, which are used thus more frequently as he grows older.

There is, I think, much truth in Chesterton's description of the Irish chief who came to fight at Ethandune:

> And all were moved a little,
>     But Colan stood apart,
> Having first pity, and after
> Hearing, like rat in rafter,
> That little worm of laughter
> That eats the Irish heart.

The laughter can be arrogant, bitter, self-dramatizing, and sometimes all three at once:

> Those that I fight I do not hate,
> Those that I guard I do not love;[1]

The Rebellion of 1916, and the Troubles that followed it, were other acts of the tragedy. It was then uncertain for what issue men like Robert Gregory had died; or how the 'drunken soldiery' of 'Byzantium' or of 'Nineteen Hundred and Nineteen', in Clare or Galway, justified that bloodshed. Cowley's epigram is familiar enough: 'A warlike, various and tragical age is the best to write of, but the worst to write in.' Its validity is doubtful today. Perhaps the difficulty lies in the fact that the pattern of modern war is seldom clearly seen; nor is the part of the individual poet ever sufficiently defined, as actor or spectator. Hardy could see *The Dynasts* as a single great action, but only after a long interval and by an effort of the will to raise it above the level of immediate experience. Of the Six Years War the poets have written only of small and fragmented experiences, and no symbol or myth can ever be built great enough to include it all.

The Irish 'war' was of a different type. It was tiny in scale and it was therefore perspicuous: a series of actions of which the ramifications could be clearly seen, and whose origins might be perceived

---

[1] 'An Irish Airman Foresees His Death,' *C.P.*, p. 152.

by a poet, as capable of being traced back to him.[1] In a sense, too, it was (as Allt has suggested) the last of the wars on the Renaissance model; that is, it was deliberately planned and executed by men who had a definite object before them, and whose poetry, literature, religion, had been co-ordinated to that end. It was war conceived as a definite political act, rational, directed by bold and resolute men:

> Because I helped to wind the clock
> I come to hear it strike.[2]

It had many aspects. For the Nationalists, it was defeat, the shooting of the Sixteen Men, the hanging of Roger Casement, the dispersal or imprisonment of the leaders. That phase was seen later by Yeats as what I have called the New Mythology; the Republican leaders become, in *Last Poems*, the successors of the long historic line of rebels and the inheritors of some of the virtues of the Celtic heroes. But the fight dragged on into the aimless brutal warfare of the Black and Tans, and that in turn into the fight between the Free-Staters and the Republicans; at the end, political ideologies seemed to count for very little. In 1919 the whole was vivid. In my own county, three known murderers lived within a short distance of my home; atrocities were frequent, and on both sides. The night raid, the digging of a grave on the lawn, whether for use or as a warning to leave the country, were normal preludes to the burning of the 'big houses', and the destruction of the 'famous ivories'. When the Auxiliaries and the Black and Tans appeared, they were ill-disciplined, badly officered and without clear orders as to what their duties might be; bands of them in Crossley tenders drove through the countryside, firing and burning indiscriminately:

> Now days are dragon-ridden, the nightmare
> Rides upon sleep: a drunken soldiery
> Can leave the mother, murdered at her door,

---

[1] 'I count the links in the chain of responsibility, run them across my fingers, and wonder if any link there is from my workshop.' Though this was written of a mob riot in Dublin, there is some evidence that Yeats felt, then and later, a personal responsibility for the Rebellion; compare Hone's statement that he was annoyed because the Rebellion had started without consulting him.

[2] 'The O'Rahilly,' *C.P.*, p. 354.

To crawl in her own blood, and go scot-free;
The night can sweat with terror as before
We pieced our thoughts into philosophy,
And planned to bring the world under a rule,
Who are but weasels fighting in a hole.[1]

Yeats and his friends did not fight. It was part of the general irony of things that the race of Protestant leaders who had left great names in history – Lord Edward Fitzgerald, Wolfe Tone, Emmet, Smith O'Brien, Parnell – were almost wholly absent from this, the only successful rising in Irish history. Armed rebellion, resistance for conscience' sake, had been to a great extent a Protestant achievement and invention. Now, in 1916, many of The Ascendancy were growing old, or were bewildered by conflicting loyalties in that critical year. Many were still concerned with the larger war in Europe; and in the guerilla warfare of the Black and Tans both Catholic and Protestant gentry were in the main neutral. The best of the younger generation, who might have been leaders, on either side, in the critical period after 1921, had been killed with the Irish regiments in France or at Gallipoli. For those who remained, it was not in their tradition to lead a rebellion, nor could they crush it who had themselves, in fact or in fancy, commended its objects; and this neutrality was, perhaps, the last act in their fatal severance, throughout Irish history, from any true identification with their people:

We are closed in, and the key is turned
On our uncertainty; somewhere
A man is killed, or a house burned,
Yet no clear fact to be discerned:
Come build in the empty house of the stare.[2]

This is of the second phase, the phase of the Civil War. In its senseless cruelties and destruction this seemed to image the post-war disintegration throughout Europe. To Yeats it was a confirmation

---

[1] 'Nineteen Hundred and Nineteen,' *C.P.*, p. 232. The weasel image is a favourite one; it occurs in *The Countess Cathleen*:

'. . . though the whole land
Squeal like a rabbit under a weasel's tooth.'

An admirable personal account is in Ernie O'Malley's book, *On Another Man's Wounds*.

[2] 'The Stare's Nest by My Window,' *C.P.*, p. 230.

of the cyclic theory of history, and a source of perplexity, and a basis for a fantasy of himself; for there is in every poet the image of himself as a man of action.[1] In the simplification of *Last Poems*, the soldier is seen as this Anti-Self; Yeats' own physical fear sublimated in the brave ranting words:

> You that Mitchel's prayer have heard,
> 'Send war in our time, O Lord!'
> Know that when all words are said
> And a man is fighting mad,
> Something drops from eyes long blind,
> He completes his partial mind,
> For an instant stands at ease,
> Laughs aloud, his heart at peace.
> Even the wisest man grows tense
> With some sort of violence
> Before he can accomplish fate,
> Know his work or choose his mate.[2]

In action there might have been some respite from the complexities of mire and blood; but there was nothing to be done, except to be envious and to dream:

> An affable Irregular,
> A heavily-built Falstaffian man,
> Comes cracking jokes of civil war
> As though to die by gunshot were
> The finest play under the sun.

> A brown Lieutenant and his men,
> Half dressed in national uniform,
> Stand at my door, and I complain
> Of the foul weather, hail and rain,
> A pear-tree broken by the storm.

> I count those feathered balls of soot
> The moor-hen guides upon the stream,
> To silence the envy in my thought;
> And turn towards my chamber, caught
> In the cold snows of a dream.[3]

---

[1] Consider de Vigny's: 'If any man despair of becoming a poet, let him take his knapsack and march with the troops.'

[2] 'Under Ben Bulben,' *C.P.*, p. 397. *vide* Mitchel, *Jail Journal*, p. 358: 'Czar, I bless thee, I kiss the hem of thy garment. I drink to thy health and longevity. Give us war in our time, O Lord!'

[3] 'The Road at My Door,' *C.P.*, p. 229. Note the third line of the last verse.

To attribute the change in Yeats' poetry to the Rebellion and the Civil War would be to simplify unduly. The tightening and hardening of style is foreshadowed in the writings between 1909 and 1914, when he seems first to have experienced the astringency of a great and enduring anger, well calculated to modify the earlier naïve romantic view of Ireland. But the stresses set up in his mind by the Rebellion helped, I think, to produce a peculiar quality of balance. The word he uses again and again is 'coldness', a quality that George Russell had noted as characteristic of medieval Irish poetry. War was immediate, outside his door; the larger war in Europe had passed him by. But in Ireland there was the microcosm of an epoch that was disintegrating: his fear for the safety of the Tower is imaged in the ending of a great cycle of history. It was clear that a civilization was passing.[1]

> Turning and turning in the widening gyre
> The falcon cannot hear the falconer;
> Things fall apart; the centre cannot hold;
> Mere anarchy is loosed upon the world,
> The blood-dimmed tide is loosed, and everywhere
> The ceremony of innocence is drowned;
> The best lack all conviction, while the worst
> Are full of passionate intensity.[2]

Other springs brought water to the pool that was to clear his eyes. In 1912 Grierson's edition of Donne gave him a new understanding of metaphysical poetry, and from 1913–14 onwards he appears to grow much more aware of the historical patterns of English literature, and the tradition of the great classical stylists. Long before his marriage began to consolidate the raw material of *A Vision*, he was reading More, Glanvil, Cudworth, and some of the minor Neo-Platonists; together with Arthur Avalon's books on the Tantra. Between 1917 and 1924 he was reading more carefully, and with a different range: Berkeley, Swift, Locke; Landor and Donne; Plato and Plotinus. And this reading was to be supple-

[1] 'The Anglo-Irish were the best Irish but I can see very little future for them as the present belongs to that half-crazy Gaeldom which is growing dominant about us.' (*Letters*, 'A.E.' to W. B. Y., p. 63.)

[2] 'The Second Coming,' *C.P.*, p. 210. For a consideration of the symbolism, see Chapter 6.

mented later, as he sought to justify both the mystical mathematics of *A Vision* and the darker sayings of his verse by investigations of Spengler, Frobenius, Whitehead and G. E. Moore. He was reconsidering Blake and Calvert, and their engravings lay on his table in the Bodleian Library. He was learning something of Greek and Roman sculpture and of Byzantine art: this last to be further stimulated by his visit to Italy and Sicily in 1924–25. The long and chivalric love affair with Maud Gonne had died down, lit at the last by a half-paternal, half-platonic relationship with her daughter Iseult; a relationship which indeed culminated in a curious proposal of marriage. And all these fell into place in the procession of images that support this 'distinguished and lonely' poetry.[1] His marriage in 1917, and the discovery of his wife's automatic writing, produced that strange imprecise pseudo-mathematical structure of *A Vision*: incoherent in its mysticism, exasperating in its fragmentation or distortion of history.

And behind it all there was the problem of growing old. By 1920 the 'tattered man' was fifty-five.

> Now shall I make my soul,
> Compelling it to study
> In a learned school
> Till the wreck of body,
> Slow decay of blood,
> Testy delirium
> Or dull decrepitude,
> Or what worse evil come –
> The death of friends, or death
> Of every brilliant eye
> That made a catch in the breath –
> Seem but the clouds of the sky
> When the horizon fades;
> Or a bird's sleepy cry
> Among the deepening shades.[2]

In that new synthesis it was necessary to take stock of many things; of women, of death, of ancestry, of the great cycles of history and

---

[1] 'Ireland cannot put from her the habits learned from her old military civilization and from a church that prays in Latin. Those popular poets have not touched her heart, her poetry when it comes will be distinguished and lonely.' (*Autobiographies*, p. 101.)

[2] 'The Tower,' iii, *C.P.*, p. 218.

of the latest cycle which seemed to be disintegrating them; of Ireland passing from romantic Fenianism to murder, and from murder to politics; of the poets of the Rhymers' Club, whose art had once seemed so perfect, and of the great song that would return no more.

# CHAPTER TWO

# Choice and Chance

'Oh no, Kusta ben Luka has taught us to divide all things into Chance and Choice; one can think about the world and about man, or anything else until all has vanished but these two things, for they are indeed the first cause of the animate and inanimate world.' – Note to *Calvary*.

> For though love has a spider's eye
> To find out some appropriate pain —
> Aye, though all passion's in the glance —
> For every nerve, and tests a lover
> With cruelties of Choice and Chance. . . .
> 'Solomon and the Witch.'

The purpose of this chapter is to establish, as it were, a series of reference points in Yeats' life, sufficient only to form a framework to which the subsequent arguments can be tied. Readers to whom the chronology of Yeats' life is familiar will not require it. I am, of course, indebted continually to Hone's *Life*, to Jeffares' admirably documented study, and to Wade's Bibliography.

The background is that of a middle-class family – 'The Yeats's were always very respectable'[1] – with relatives who were comparatively wealthy by the standards of that day: but Yeats' father depended largely on the diminishing rents of a small estate, and was continually in straitened circumstances. 'I remember little of childhood but its pain' is an often-quoted statement, and twice he alluded to the 'ignominy' of boyhood; but it seems clear from *Autobiographies* that this period was, in part at least, pleasurable and vigorous. 'The boy I knew was darkly beautiful to look on, fiery yet playful and full of lovely and elfin fancies.'[2] Much of his youth

---

[1] *Autobiographies*, p. 19.

[2] 'A.E.,' *Imaginations and Reveries*, p. 39. It is perhaps fair to counter-quote Yeats' description of 'A.E.': 'A wild young man who would come to school of a morning with a daisy-chain hung round his neck' (*Autobiographies*, p. 80).

was spent with relations in Sligo, then a sleepy, half-commercial, half-market town, with a constant traffic of small vessels, which entered the harbour by the winding estuary from Rosses Point. The crowded quays, full of excitement for a boy, remained in his imagination, and provided the setting of *On the Boiler*. He frequently took passage by long-sea from Liverpool to Sligo for his holidays. To the admiration of his grandfather, William Pollexfen, and perhaps to his fear of him, we can trace his delight in 'passionate' men, and his quest for that quality as he himself grew old. He believed that the Pollexfen race had given him his sense of adventure and love of the sea. "Yet it was a Yeats who spoke the only eulogy that turns my head: 'We have ideas and no passions, but by marriage with a Pollexfen we have given a tongue to the sea-cliffs.'"[1] His subsequent concern with ancestry and with eugenics is rooted both in this conviction and in the desire to re-establish himself, by recalling Butlers and Corbets, in a social position which he believed that he had lost.

He was subjected to childish disillusionment on the subject of sex; and the disgust arising from this reinforced the tendency towards fantasy. He sailed model yachts; this remained a passion with him, and with his painter brother. He acquired, through family and local legend, a dramatic sense of the supernatural. A seabird was the omen that announced death or danger to a Pollexfen.[2] But his education was unhappy, calculated to produce instability and fear. 'The only lessons I had ever learned were those my father taught me, for he terrified me by descriptions of my moral degradation and he humiliated me by my likeness to disagreeable people.'[3] And this uncertainty was reinforced by schooldays at a second-rate establishment in Hammersmith, 'an obscene bullying place', where he became acutely aware of the loss of social position which an Irish schoolboy might experience in an English school. In 1881, when the family returned to Ireland, he was at school in Dublin, where his father had a studio; and in 1884 he entered the Metropolitan School of Art, where he met George Russell and the two sculptors, John

---

[1] *Autobiographies*, p. 23.
[2] Ibid., p. 10.
[3] Ibid., p. 32. This deliberate suppression by depreciation seems to have been a precept for Victorian parents. Yeats was, perhaps, happiest with his grandparents.

Hughes and Oliver Sheppard, as well as a number of the younger Irish writers. His first poems, which included 'The Island of Statues', were published in the *Dublin University Review* of 1885. The same year saw the foundation of the Hermetic Society, and Yeats' interest in esoteric practices – strongly disapproved by his father – was confirmed. He met 'the Brahmin', Mohini Chatterji, who came to Dublin as the representative of the Theosophical Society, and whose visit bore fruit long afterwards in the poem named after him.[1] The Indian romantic setting had traditional attractions for a young poet, and precedents in Shelley; it is used in the idylls of *Crossways*.

In 1887 the family again moved to London, and 'King Goll' was published. 1889 saw the publication of 'The Wanderings of Oisin'; a considerable work, which the critics compared favourably with Tennyson's *Maeldune*. It was the first of the 'old themes':

> What can I but enumerate old themes?
> First that sea-rider Oisin led by the nose
> Through three enchanted islands, allegorical dreams,
> Vain gaiety, vain battle, vain repose,
> Themes of the embittered heart, or so it seems,
> That might adorn old songs or courtly shows;
> But what cared I that set him on to ride,
> I, starved for the bosom of his faery bride?[2]

That year also marked the beginning of a great and enduring love, when Maud Gonne, fired with enthusiasm and admiration for the poem, came to visit for the first time. Together they planned to take the Abbey Stone, the Stone of Destiny, back to Ireland, and talked of Danaan symbols, the stone, the cauldron, the spear and the sword. Later, they met in Yeats' rooms in Woburn Buildings, and talked with William Sharp, and Sarojini Naidu, 'the little Indian Princess', with Lionel Johnson and Florence Farr. He started *The Countess Cathleen*, important both as embodying the first projection of his own love and despair, and as the first effective step to drama. Both the play and *Oisin* underwent extensive and minute revisions.

He met Madame Blavatsky, in whose circle his innate love of ritual and secret societies (perhaps fostered by his own awkwardness

---

[1] *C.P.*, p. 279.
[2] 'The Circus Animals' Desertion,' ibid., p. 391.

and loneliness) found full scope. In 1890 he had joined the Order of the Golden Dawn, under the leadership of MacGregor Mathers,[1] who taught Yeats the technique of 'controlled vision' stimulated by pictorial symbols. He began to study Blake's prophetic books; and therefrom Boehme, Swedenborg, and Thomas Taylor on Plotinus. A friendship grew from his meeting with Florence Farr, for she was a great actress, and, of all speakers of verse, had seemed to come nearest to his ideal in that art; though he subsequently repudiated his hope: 'she was a chalk egg he had been sitting on for years'.[2] The withering of her beauty, and her consequent self-exile, affected him most powerfully.

In 1891 the two tales of *John Sherman* and *Dhoya* were published under the pen-name of 'Ganconagh'. *John Sherman* is important as depicting the early stages of the Self and Anti-Self developing their Hegelian conflict in Yeats' mind. His fellowship with the Rhymers' Club, 'the companions of the Cheshire Cheese' and members of 'The Tragic Generation', began. He met George Moore and Edward Martyn, later to be his colleagues, and, at the finish, his enemies. *Dorian Gray* was published that year. Yeats was deeply interested in Wilde's work, and I shall suggest later that *Salome*, and Ricketts' illustrations for it, underlie the obsession with the image of the severed head and of the 'virgin cruelty' of woman towards her lover. Parnell died, and Yeats met Maud Gonne on her way to the funeral, though he refrained from going to the graveside. The star which, according to many present, fell as the coffin was lowered,[3] seemed later to be yet another of the archetypal and cosmic signs:

> . . . a brighter star shoots down;
> What shudders run through all that animal blood?
> What is this sacrifice? Can someone there
> Recall the Cretan barb that pierced a star?[4]

In 1892 *The Countess Cathleen* was published with 'Various

[1] Who had written *The Kabbalah Unveiled*.
[2] T. Sturge Moore, *English*, Vol. II, 1939.
[3] See Maud Gonne, *A Servant of the Queen*, p. 175. In *John Sherman* a shooting star falls at the moment when the hero is making up his mind to propose to Margaret. This dominant image is discussed in Chapter 9.
[4] 'Parnell's Funeral,' *C.P.*, p. 319. The original title was 'A Parnellite at Parnell's Funeral'.

Legends and Lyrics', and also *The Rose*, which was dedicated to Lionel Johnson. The edition of Blake, in collaboration with E. J. Ellis, was in progress, and was published the following year; in it we can trace this intense interest in symbolism, and the study of Blake's illustrations to Dante that were to supply images at a later stage. Certain of the essays in *Ideas of Good and Evil* were written. The National Literary Society was founded in Dublin in 1892, and Yeats' association with Irish literary politics (for the two converged rapidly), began. In 1893 he published *The Celtic Twilight*.

In 1894 *The Land of Heart's Desire* was performed in London; Yeats went to Paris and saw *Axël* there; he met Bergson and Olivia Shakespear. The same year he returned and visited Lissadell, then one of the great country houses of Sligo. There he met Eva Gore-Booth, a poetess who subsequently achieved a considerable reputation, writing somewhat in the manner of 'A.E.,' and Constance Gore-Booth, afterwards Madame Markiewicz and a leading figure in the political agitations that preceded the Rebellion. I think this visit was Yeats' first contact with such surroundings, and was o great importance. He celebrated the two girls in the opening to 'The Winding Stair'.[1]

> ... The older is condemned to death,
> Pardoned, drags out lonely years
> Conspiring among the ignorant.
> I know not what the younger dreams —
> Some vague Utopia – and she seems,
> When withered-old and skeleton-gaunt,
> An image of such politics.[2]

In 1895, *Poems* was published by Fisher Unwin; this contained, in separate sections, *Crossways* and *The Rose*. This last included 'Innisfree', and ended with the poem 'To Ireland in the Coming Times'.[3] In it he asserted his kinship with the Irish poetic tradition:

> Nor may I less be counted one
> With Davis, Mangan, Ferguson,
> Because, to him who ponders well,
> My rhymes more than their rhyming tell

[1] *C.P.*, p. 263.
[2] Compare 'On a Political Prisoner,' ibid., p. 206.
[3] Ibid., p. 56.

Of things discovered in the deep,
When only body's laid asleep.

In this year he took rooms in Woburn Buildings, which remained his London quarters for many years.

1896 was perhaps the most fateful of all years, for Yeats met Lady Gregory, and began the long association with Coole, where he spent many summers. Lady Gregory even asked Maud Gonne, bluntly, whether she would 'marry Willie Yeats'. The conflict of women for the poet had begun. The same year he met Synge; I have suggested some results of that friendship in a subsequent chapter. With Arthur Symons he visited Aran, then untouched and unexploited. In 1897 he published *The Tables of the Law* and *The Adoration of the Magi*, written in that resonant and ornate prose, well suited to mirror his mystical thinking, which he had taken from Pater, and Pater had taken from Sir Thomas Browne. He spent some time at Coole, collecting folk-lore with Lady Gregory; involved at the time, he himself says, 'in a miserable love affair'. This was, perhaps, the second reaction from Maud Gonne's obduracy; the first had been an affair with 'Diana Vernon', to whom two of the poems of *The Wind Among the Reeds* are addressed.

In 1898 Yeats became President of the Wolfe Tone Memorial Association. In all his concern with Irish nationalism, whether literary or political, there is a curious ambivalence; which can be explained, I think, partly in terms of his background, partly in terms of a temperament that saw, passionately, a vision of what might be, and recoiled in disgust from the slow poisoned world of conflicting personalities and intrigues. As a nominal Protestant, a member of the Ascendancy (at least by reason of the circle to which he was now becoming attached), his status as a Nationalist was liable at that time to suspicion – a suspicion that was only partly lulled by the crowd's half-reverent, half-contemptuous view of the poet, which is admirably summed up in a conversation at his burial at Drumcliff:

'Did you ever read anything he wrote?'
'Well, I did, mind you. 'Tis high-class stuff, of course, but in my private opinion the most of it is great rambling.'[1]

The sensitive plant, with visions of an Ireland regenerated by a

[1] Kate O'Brien, *The Spectator*, 24 September 1948.

new *Prometheus*, was ill-fitted for Irish politics at the turn of the century and the popular demonstrations over the Boer War. Maud Gonne's flaming example led him on; but the conflict between the world of Coole Park and that of the Dublin cabals was calculated to emphasize the oscillation in his mind; typified, perhaps, by the romantic enthusiasm of *Cathleen-ni-Houlihan*, and the bitter tone of the Essays in *Estrangement*. I have written later of the same conflict over the Easter Rising itself; and events were not forced into a pattern in his mind till the last wave of studied hatred and exaltation in the patriotic ballads of *Last Poems and Plays*.

In 1899, *The Wind Among the Reeds* was published, and *The Countess Cathleen* was produced; he visited Maud Gonne in Paris, and again proposed to her. Plans were drawn up for the Irish Literary Theatre that was to bring to Yeats long years of drudgery and frustration. In 1900 the first version of *The Shadowy Waters* was finished, and the first poems of *In the Seven Woods* were written. These were prefaced with an important introduction, since suppressed:

> I made some of these poems walking about the Seven Woods, before the big wind of nineteen hundred and three blew down so many trees, and troubled the wild creatures, and changed the look of things; and I thought out there a good part of the play that follows [i.e. *On Baile's Strand*]. The first shape of it came to me in a dream, but it changed much in the making, foreshadowing, it may be, a change that may bring a less dream-burdened will into my verses. . . .

It is a curious phrase, this 'dream-burdened will'; perhaps suggesting that the result of MacGregor Mathers' training in controlled visions was now wearing thin, and that something at once more personal and more prophetic was taking its place. From about this time he dated the appearance of 'the brazen wingéd beast that signified laughing ecstatic destruction'; and it is of great psychological interest that this, which I believe to be connected with Ricketts' illustrations to Wilde's *Sphinx*, should appear at the same time as the projection of himself into the Cuchulain story.

In 1901 Yeats collaborated with Lady Gregory over *Where there is Nothing* and *The Pot of Broth*; and the next year saw the production of Synge's *In the Shadow of the Glen*, and of his own *Cathleen-ni-Houlihan*, with Maud Gonne in the title part.

Again 1903 is a critical year. Maud Gonne married MacBride; and Yeats' bitterness is apparent in many poems after the event, though his rejection in 1899 had left its mark on 'the mirror of perfection'. 'The Folly of Being Comforted'[1] and 'Adam's Curse'[2] were both published in 1902. The anger against MacBride flared up again in *Responsibilities*; the tenderness for the image of Maud Gonne, the 'sweetheart from another life', remained. Yeats went on his first lecture tour in the United States.

The following year saw the opening of the Abbey Theatre, the production of Synge's *Riders to the Sea*, and *On Baile's Strand*. In 1905 Maud Gonne separated from her husband. In 1906 *Poems 1899–1905* was published, a reprint of *In the Seven Woods* together with three plays. In 1907 *Deirdre* was written, and Yeats began to revise his collected works. The same year he visited Italy with Lady Gregory, and saw for the first time the pictures and mosaics which affected him so powerfully, and to which he was to return in the great period.

> I have prepared my peace
> With learned Italian things
> And the proud stones of Greece,
> Poet's imaginings
> And memories of love. . . .[3]

The proud stones of Greece were to become important in his theories of statuary, together with the 'drilled eyes' and their historical significance, which appear prominently in *A Vision*.

In 1907 Synge's *Playboy* was produced and reviled. It is difficult to realize now the virulence which the controversy raised. Yeats was denounced by Arthur Griffith, the representative of the Sinn Fein movement. In the year preceding he had quarrelled with George Moore and with 'A.E.'. The temperature was rising in preparation for the period of 'Estrangement'.

The year 1908 saw the production of the prose version of *The Green Helmet*. The next year was one of triumph and bitterness. The eight volumes of his collected works were produced. Lady Gregory fell ill – from overwork, and the long violence of controversy that

[1] *C.P.*, p. 86.
[2] Ibid., p. 88.
[3] 'The Tower,' iii, ibid., p. 223.

had started with the production of *The Playboy of the Western World* in 1907, and the slanders levelled against their joint work in the Abbey. It seemed as though she might die; and in 'A Friend's Illness'[1] and 'These are the Clouds',[2] his emotion is crystallized out:

> ... And therefore, friend, if your great race were run
> And these things came, so much the more thereby
> Have you made greatness your companion. ...

The next year Synge died. I have written of this in the chapter called 'Yeats and Synge'.

The year 1909 is thus of central importance. Yeats severed his connection with the Abbey; and for the next five years the emotions that I have suggested in the chapter 'The Study of Hatred' were generated. These, seen in conjunction with Maud Gonne's marriage and separation, and the period of the 'entanglement' with other loves, determine the increasing astringency of his verse, to be later reinforced by his understanding of metaphysical poetry. In 1910 he was again at Coole, and in 1911 visited the United States with the Abbey Theatre Company. 1912 saw the fourth version of *The Countess Cathleen*,[3] and it is not fantastic to trace, in certain of the revisions, the changes which he desired to portray in the projections of Maud Gonne and of himself in Cathleen and Aleel, and so to release the 'imposthume in his brain'. That same year, while staying with the Gonnes in Normandy, he met Miss Hyde-Lees, whom he afterwards married. The great and bitter controversy over the Lane Pictures, which was an important pretext for the study of hatred, began. In 1911 *The Hour Glass* was published; Yeats fell ill, and for a time shared a house in Sussex with Ezra Pound. In 1914 *Responsibilities* was published and he started work on the Nōh plays, perhaps drawing from Pound the stimulus that he had previously found in Synge. He went on the second lecture tour in the United States.

Lane was drowned on the *Lusitania*, and his death enabled the fires of his picture controversy to smoulder on in Dublin opinion and in Yeats' mind. In 1916 he refused a knighthood, and the Easter Rising flared up and failed; the Sixteen Men, including

---

[1] *C.P.*, p. 109.
[2] Ibid., p. 107.
[3] The texts in *Poems*, 1919, and in *Plays and Controversies*, 1923, are the fifth version.

MacBride, were executed. From now onwards the critical events came quickly upon Yeats. *At the Hawk's Well* was published in 1917. That summer he was again with Maud Gonne in Normandy, proposed to her daughter, Iseult, and was refused. He had watched her childhood:

> O you will take whatever's offered
> And dream that all the world's a friend,
> Suffer as your mother suffered,
> Be as broken in the end. . . .[1]

On 21 October he married Miss Hyde-Lees. Shortly after the wedding he discovered that she produced 'automatic writing': and this, together with a mass of memories of earlier occult investigations and continuous and excited reading in history and its byways, became the raw material of *A Vision* (1925). In 1918 Major Robert Gregory, the Irish airman, was killed in Italy. Maud Gonne, a political prisoner in England, escaped to Dublin, and sought temporary refuge, without success, in her house which she had let to Yeats and his wife.

The year 1919 saw the publication of *The Wild Swans at Coole* in its new form, with an elegy on Robert Gregory, and the pastoral poem, 'Shepherd and Goatherd', to his mother. The poem on the birth of his daughter brings out the tone of this collection, far gentler than that of *Responsibilities*. In 'A Prayer for my Daughter' –

> My mind, because the minds that I have loved,
> The sort of beauty that I have approved,
> Prosper but little, has dried up of late,
> Yet knows that to be choked with hate
> May well be of all evil chances chief.[2]

In 1920 *Calvary* was published: and Yeats spent much time in the Bodleian at Oxford, among pictures and Arabic manuscripts. The Tower had been in danger of burning through the Troubles, and the opening lines of 'The Second Coming'[3] refer to its possible destruction. He went on the third lecture tour in the United States, and spoke against British policy there, and at the Oxford Union.

*Michael Robartes and The Dancer* is dated 1920, and in it appeared the first poetic effects of the Easter Rising, the heroic action whose

[1] 'Two Years Later,' *C.P.*, p. 137.
[2] Ibid., p. 211.
[3] Ibid., p. 210. Written January 1919 (Mrs. Yeats).

significance he was trying to assess. It includes 'Easter 1916', 'Sixteen Dead Men' and 'The Rose Tree'; as if the poet were dazed by those events and striving to relate them to 'The Second Coming'. The draft of *A Vision* was in progress, and the attempt to co-ordinate the enormous body of notes that the automatic writing had provided took much of his energy. But, as I shall suggest subsequently, it is the first effort to see the Rising as a whole, as part of a pattern of world history. Leda and the Swan had produced the eggs of Love and War from that fierce union:

> A shudder in the loins engenders there
> The broken wall, the burning roof and tower
> And Agamemnon dead.[1]

1922 is the first year of the Irish Free State.

Part of *A Vision* was finished at Thoor Ballylee in 1922; and the poem 'The Gift of Harun Al-Rashid'[2] deals with the automatic writing of his bride. Early in 1922 he was elected a Senator, largely through Gogarty's influence. In 1924 he was awarded the Nobel Prize, celebrated in the essay 'The Bounty of Sweden'. In 1925 he was again travelling in Sicily and Italy, and writing *The Trembling of the Veil*. The whole focusing of childhood and adolescence into a clear outline is, I think, to be perceived as part of his theories of history and personality in *A Vision*, and *Autobiographies* should be read beside that work. In 1925, too, the first or 'A' version of *A Vision* was published, with its elaborate 'spoof' introduction. He travelled again in North Italy, and began a correspondence on philosophy with T. Sturge Moore.

In 1926 *The Resurrection* was written; and this, too, is to be linked to *Calvary* and to portions of *A Vision*, as aspects of his attempt to perceive Christianity in its relationship to world history. *Oedipus at Colonus* was performed, and that tale of destiny and fortitude was suited to fire his imagination at such a stage as this. The year 1927 saw the first signs of illness, perhaps brought on by the damp of Ballylee. In 1928 *The Tower* was published; his term as Senator came to an end; and from then till 1934 the great creative period was at its height.

[1] *C.P.*, p. 241.
[2] Ibid., p. 513.

The next six years show an astonishing activity. *A Vision* was being redrafted, to be published again, greatly altered, in 1937. In 1929 *Fighting the Waves* was published, and the Cuchulain myth, that had been working in his mind for more than a quarter of a century, was nearing its final form. In 1930 he was at Rapallo; Swift had been haunting him, with thoughts of strong ghosts, and a new Ireland that had cast off England, as Byzantium had cast off Rome; and *The Words Upon the Window-pane*, with its important Preface, was published, and produced at the Abbey. In 1932 *Words for Music Perhaps* was published, with Crazy Jane and Old Tom as mouthpieces. In 1932 de Valera's government came into power; an event which Yeats seems to have construed as a further sign of the disintegration of the traditional Irish values, and which accounts for much of the violence of his denunciation of the new rulers; though he was impressed by the personality and sincerity of de Valera himself. Yeats went on his last lecture tour in the United States; and Lady Gregory died. 1933 saw the publication of *The Winding Stair*, and in it 'Byzantium', and the beginning of his momentary interest in the Blue-shirts of General O'Duffy. 1935 is the date of *A Full Moon in March*, and the little-known but important 'Supernatural Songs' in it. The friendship with Dorothy Wellesley, the progress of which is outlined in her *Letters*, starts from this year. *The Oxford Book of Modern Verse* was published in 1936, *On the Boiler* was written in 1938, and the second version of *A Vision* produced in 1937. *Last Poems and Plays* (1936–9) contains poems dated as late as 21 January of the latter year, and the two plays *Purgatory* and *The Death of Cuchulain*. The mysterious play *The Herne's Egg* was published in 1938.

Against such a bare list of dates there emerges, as it were through the screen of netting that Mancini used when painting, a pattern for the life. There are, perhaps, six major phases which overlap and blend; Sligo, childhood and the supernatural; his pre-Raphaelite background, and the London of the Nineties, with its spiritualism and the many secret societies to satisfy his taste for mystery and ritual; the Irish Nationalist, poet, politician, theatrical manager, with Lady Gregory's comfort and protection behind him; the period of estrangement, sensual bitterness and hatred, culminating in *Responsibilities* in 1914; the Easter Rebellion and the Troubles, from

1916 to 1923, in which experience of war about him, and a philosophy of history, are so blended that they can ferment in passion and clarify into the poetry of 1928–33; the remaining six years of political excitement, ill-health, and an attempt, as I have tried to show in the chapter on *Last Poems*, to read the book of life (whether holy or daimonic) by a new light.

# CHAPTER THREE

# The Masks — Self and Anti-Self[1]

If we cannot imagine ourselves as different from what we are, and try to assume that second self, we cannot impose a discipline upon ourselves though we may accept one from others. Active virtue, as distinguished from the passive acceptance of a code, is therefore theatrical, consciously dramatic, the wearing of a mask. . . . – *Per Amica Silentia Lunae.*

The other self, the anti-self or the antithetical self, as one may choose to name it, comes but to those who are no longer deceived, whose passion is reality. – *Ibid.*

If you are separated from your opposite, you consume yourself away.
*A Vision.*

I

Any understanding of Yeats' poetry depends upon a realization of his theory of the Mask, and, I believe, some sympathy with that theory. His imagination was by nature intensely active, quick moving, and perpetually excited by the dramatic qualities of men's lives, and it was therefore natural that he should try to draw into himself those aspects of their personalities which he admired. They served to supply psychological compensations, to reinforce his success or justify his failure, to excuse the evil or folly that he might have done; and it is probable that he had lingering memories of his father's comparison of him to 'disagreeable people', and was therefore sensitive on the matter. His personality thus oscillated, as it were, between the poles of opposing aspects of personality; one the seeming, the present, the other the wished for, which could, at moments, appear to be justified in action. He could be a romantic lover in the great medieval tradition of Dante, and, like Dante, present the paradox of high constancy and sin. He could exploit the

[1] Ellmann's *The Man and the Masks* was published after this was written. It is, of course, a standard work.

image of the swordsman, and take fencing lessons, and justify the opposition, in himself, of the swordsman and the saint. He could be the man of action, whose word had sent out an army, or the scholar-saint in the lonely tower that Palmer had drawn in his illustration for *Il Penseroso*; something of a pastoral recluse in the manner of Calvert or Morris; a politician, the 'sixty-year-old smiling public man'; the prophetic poet who could answer the riddle of the Sphinx, now transplanted to the ancient Rock of Cashel, the symbol of ancient and holy Ireland, and who would one day reconcile the warring religions.

Somewhere between these poles of assumed personalities there was reality, but here again the term is misleading. Yeats speaks continually of 'the last knowledge': as if the end would be, not the certainty of self-knowledge, but a kind of mystic receptiveness in the phase of the Fool, to whom all knowledge comes from God. It is therefore wrong to search for a previous stability of mind or consistency of beliefs. The lyric poet is, by his nature, subject to the ebb and flow of moods. An epic poet, by balancing incident with pattern, can achieve consistency. But that which links Yeats' poems into a unity is the prose and dramatic work, which is complementary at every turn to the verse; and the latter can only be understood when both have been examined. The complexity appears to be of a triple character. I find, firstly, the deliberate exploitation, the encouragement, of conflict; distinguishing between the internal conflict in himself of which the poetry is made, and the external conflict with circumstance, the 'Body of Fate'; for only through these conflicts can man progress towards perfection of knowledge. Secondly, there is the assumption of the Mask from a desire to preserve the poetic personality intact; and this is most important for any poet whose poise and consequent sense of reality must be kept at all times delicately adjusted. Speech through mouthpieces, the creation of puppet characters, is an easy way to preserve this aloofness and prophetic role, and to generate, in addition, a sense of mystery. Thirdly, there is an extraction, from the personalities of others, of those characteristics which appealed to him; either as justifying his theory of the Daimon (since their attributes were called down from *Anima Mundi*), or as offering psychological compensations for his own deficiencies, or as providing a kind of magical reassurance as to his own position in the historical cycles.

Of the literary figures on whom he modelled himself, the first are those of the two men whose work he edited. Spenser is approved as the first great representative of the Anglo-Irish tradition, the poet who drew from 'the book of the people', the practical and ferocious author of *A View of the Present State of Ireland*, a title which might indeed be applied (with some allowance for the irony of the content) to the pamphlet *On the Boiler*. The editing of Blake with E. J. Ellis, was one of his earliest attempts at scholarship. The edition was a failure, and is now forgotten, but the results of the impact of Blake's philosophy and poetic practice are permanent and complex. From him comes, through Boehme, the idea of progression through contraries that justifies the doctrine of the Anti-Self. Blake had found it necessary to build his mythology out of Ossian and Swedenborg and his own dreams, and had failed in his purpose because that mythology was too personal; Yeats' own mythology was, he believed, merely dormant in the thought and knowledge of the people, and ready to be brought to life. Blake was 'the first writer of modern times to prove the indissoluble marriage of all great art with symbol'.[1] Yeats approved Blake's belief in the figures seen upon the mind's eye – a doctrine that must have seemed curiously akin to the theory of the images suggested by images, and all the mirror figures. And, finally, Blake's doctrine of fidelity to outline, to the 'hard and wiry line', is a guiding principle in Yeats:

> And as I look backward upon my own writing, I take pleasure alone in those verses where it seems to me I have found something hard and cold, some articulation of the Image, which is the opposite of all that I am in my daily life. . . .[2]

There was satire to be found in Ben Jonson, Swift, Blake, models for the little bitter epigrams, precedents for the contemptuous dismissal of the stupidities of politicians and academic critics of painting, who failed to appoint Hugh Lane to the Directorship of the National Gallery.[3] Above all things there was passion, and the

[1] *E. & I.*, p. 116.
[2] *Autobiographies*, p. 274.
[3] 'An Appointment,' *C.P.*, p. 141. For details of this, see Lady Gregory's *Hugh Lane*, pp. 83 et seq.

belief that 'Passions, because most living, are most holy . . . and man shall enter eternity borne upon their wings'.[1] So, in 'An Acre of Grass',[2]

> Grant me an old man's frenzy,
> Myself must I remake
> Till I am Timon and Lear
> Or that William Blake
> Who beat upon the wall
> Till Truth obeyed his call. . . .

The effect upon Yeats of Blake's illustrations to Dante are considered in a later chapter, but there is a curious little poem in *Last Poems* that picks up the Blake rhythms, and may well suggest a debt to *The Marriage of Heaven and Hell*, perhaps from the illustrations on the first page of 'A Memorable Fancy', and remembering that these 'images' had occurred on the 'device' of Madame Blavatsky:

> Seek those images
> That constitute the wild,
> The lion and the virgin,
> The harlot and the child.
>
> Find in middle air
> An eagle on the wing,
> Recognise the five
> That make the Muses sing.[3]

It seems as though the end of his life brought a return to Blake; he quotes, with approval, as 'the most beautiful of all the letters', Blake's:

> I have been very near the gates of death, and have returned very weak, and an old man feeble and tottering, but not in spirits and life, not in the real man, the imagination which liveth forever. In that I am stronger and stronger as this foolish body decays. . . .[4]

This is the theme of 'Sailing to Byzantium' and of 'The Tower'.

Among the other Romantics, Wordsworth had in some sort failed: 'great poet though he be, [he] is so often flat and heavy partly because his moral sense, being a discipline he had not created, a

[1] *E. & I.*, p. 113.
[2] *C.P.*, p. 346.
[3] 'Those Images,' ibid., p. 367.
[4] *Letters to the New Island*, p. 94.

mere obedience, has no theatrical element'. Yeats speaks continually of creating his discipline, both of technique and of thought, and we are constantly reminded of the 'theatrical element'.[1] Landor, on the other hand, was a model of greatness: 'while Savage Landor topped us all in calm nobility when the pen was in his hand, as in the daily violence of his passion when he had laid it down'.[2] Landor was the aristocrat, the master of calm and ordered prose, of the same phase as Talma the revolutionary actor, and Napoleon, and Irving; a kind of paradox, the many-sided man, faintly ridiculous in the impro-visations of his life —

> What made the ceiling waterproof?
> Landor's tarpaulin on the roof.[3]

Violence of heroes and of lovers, of poets who were also men of action, was to be desired in poetry, and should be justified by precedents in the lives of poets. 'The last knowledge has often come most quickly to turbulent men, and for a season brought new turbulence. When life puts away her conjuring tricks one by one, those that deceive us longest may well be the wine-cup and the sensual kiss.'[4] That might serve for a text on which to rationalize one's own desires, and the intense sensual excitement that continued into old age. The other figure to set beside Landor is Donne:

> And I may dine at journey's end
> With Landor and with Donne.

From Donne he learnt much in technique from 1912 onwards, but it seems probable that he found other precedents in that life; the fusion of intense religious experience with sensuality; the obsession of the tomb-haunter, the concern with apparitions and strong ghosts; poetry which set, for the first time in English poetry, the full theme of *Odi et Amo*.

Two eighteenth-century figures, Swift and Berkeley, were to become central to his thought. Yeats seems to have possessed the faculty of thinking himself into such tragic and rhetorical parts:

---

[1] *Mythologies*, p. 334.
[2] Ibid., p. 328.
[3] 'A Nativity,' *C.P.*, p. 387. *Tarpaulin* was originally *hammer*. I do not understand the allusions.
[4] *Mythologies*, p. 332.

> Who thought Cuchulain till it seemed
> He stood where they had stood?[1]

They are of the great age of Protestant-Anglo-Ireland, men who are simultaneously political writers, philosophers, perhaps mystics. 'But now I read Swift for months together, Burke and Berkeley less often but always with excitement, and Goldsmith lures and waits. . . . Swift haunts me; he is always just round the next corner.'[2] This was in 1931, when the thought of the political nationality of Ireland was much in Yeats' mind. As for the Mask-aspect, Swift symbolized action, passion, and a vision of a world that would soon decay under democracy and revolution. He proved that 'Rome and Greece were destroyed by the war of the Many upon the Few'. And Swift was in himself the prototype, the prophet of the passing of the civilization that Yeats himself had seen, for the gyres run on:

> Swift . . . saw civilization pass from comparative happiness and youthful vigour to an old age of violence and self-contempt. . . .[3]

Besides the translation of the great epitaph of Swift, and the reference in 'The Seven Sages', there are less obvious echoes:

> Civilization is hooped together, brought
> Under a rule, under the semblance of peace
> By manifold illusion . . .[4]

To Swift's philosophy of aristocracy the aristocracy of Yeats owes much; as in the conflict between the One, the Few and the Many which underlies his interpretation of history. There is some debt to Swift in the bitter epigrams that deal with history in terms of the gyres, never of the straight line:

> Parnell came down the road, he said to a cheering man:
> 'Ireland shall get her freedom and you still break stone.'[5]

or (concerning the hatred of the abstract):

[1] *The Death of Cuchulain*, C. Plays, p. 693
[2] *Explorations*, p. 345
[3] Ibid., p. 354.
[4] 'Meru,' *C.P.*, p. 333. For the explanation of the title, see the Preface to *The Holy Mountain*.
[5] 'Parnell,' *C.P.*, p. 359. Compare Grattan, *Speeches* (1822), Vol. I, p. 53: 'I never will be satisfied so long as the meanest cottager in Ireland has a link of the British chain clanking to his rags; he may be naked, he shall not be in iron. . . .'

c

> 'Those Platonists are a curse', he said,
> 'God's fire upon the wane,
> A diagram hung there instead,
> More women born than men.'[1]

But perhaps there is Swift's thought in the reduction of man to the bundle of rags, and love to the sexual act; that made Crazy Jane (as Swift had made Vanessa) to see that unaccommodated men or women must be stripped in just this way before wisdom can replace illusion. At the last

> 'Fair and foul are near of kin,
> And fair needs foul' I cried.
> 'My friends are gone, but that's a truth
> Nor grave nor bed denied,
> Learned in bodily lowliness
> And in the heart's pride.'[2]

Political resemblances were to be found and developed. Swift's challenge to English stupidity, greed and exploitation, was worth imitating and, when necessary, those same vices in Ireland could justly be attacked. Defiance might go to the lengths of incitement to violence: 'And I will shoot Mr. *Wood* and his Deputies through the Head, like *High-Way Men* or *House-breakers*, if they dare to force one Farthing of their Coin on me in the Payment of an Hundred Pounds',[3] is not far different in tone from the patriotic ballads of *Last Poems*, or the fulminations of *On the Boiler*. Swift and Berkeley are in the procession of ancestors:

THE THIRD.    My great-grandfather's father talked of music,
              Drank tar-water with the Bishop of Cloyne.
THE FOURTH.   But mine saw Stella once.[4]

There were elements in Berkeley's life that must have seemed strangely like his own: the American tours, the journeys in Italy and Sicily; the long stay at Oxford (where Berkeley died); the return (in *Siris*) to occult learning, and the alchemical essences of things; a belief that the philosophers had not dared to take the final

---

[1] 'Statistics,' *C.P.*, p. 271. 'He' is Spengler, of *The Decline of the West*.
[2] 'Crazy Jane talks with the Bishop', *C.P.*, p. 294.
[3] *Drapier's Letters II*. Consider, too, the image: 'Only when I am in danger of bursting I will go out and whisper among the Reeds . . . "Beware of Wood's Half-pence."'
[4] 'The Seven Sages,' *C.P.*, p. 271.

steps in thought that the poets could take; even the strange injunc-
tion in Berkeley's will to let his body lie for five days undisturbed
before burial – was it so that the 'confusion of the death-bed' might
pass? And Yeats finds, deliberately, aspects of Berkeley's many-
sidedness to correspond with his own image, finding that Berkeley,
too, had his Mask.

As I enumerate these thoughts I forget that gregarious episcopal
mask and remember a Berkeley that asked the Red Indian for his
drugs, an angry unscrupulous solitary that I can test by my favourite
quotations and find neither temporal nor trivial – 'An old hunter
talking with gods, of a high-crested chief, sailing with troops of friends
to Tenedos', and the last great oracle of Delphi commemorating the
dead Plotinus, 'That wave-washed shore . . . the golden race of mighty
Zeus . . . the just Æacus, Plato, stately Pythagoras, and all the choir
of immortal love.'[1]

'Angry', 'solitary' are keywords in the later poetry. The value of the
solitary man, Goldsmith or Synge, not in his contemplation, but in
his responsibility as a link between the hierarchical levels of society.
He is the interpreter of the people. So in 'The Municipal Gallery
Revisited':

> John Synge, I and Augusta Gregory, thought
> All that we did, all that we saw or sang
> Must come from contact with the soil, from that
> Contact everything Antaeus-like grew strong.
> We three alone in modern times had brought
> Everything down to that sole test again,
> Dream of the noble and the beggar-man.[2]

These values are permanent, opposed to the materialistic and
mechanistic philosophies that Swift and Berkeley had attacked:

> Born in such community Berkeley, with his belief in perception,
> that abstract ideas are mere words, Swift with his love of perfect
> nature, of the Houyhnhnms, his disbelief in Newton's system and
> every sort of machine, Goldsmith and his delight in the particulars
> of common life that shocked his contemporaries, Burke with his
> conviction that all states not grown slowly like a forest tree are

---

[1] Introduction to Hone and Rossi's *Berkeley*, p. xxvii. 'The Old Hunter'
is from Browning's *Pauline*.
[2] *C.P.*, p. 368

tyrannies, found in England the opposite that made their thought lucid or stung it into expression.[1]

The pattern is now growing clearer. Both Swift and Berkeley are Anglo-Irish, Protestants, and in a sense 'expatriates'; but they are also the champions of Ireland:

> As a boy of eighteen or nineteen he [Berkeley] called the Irish people 'natives' as though he were in some foreign land, but two or three years later . . . defined the English materialism of his day in three profound sentences, and wrote after each that 'We Irishmen' think otherwise – 'I publish . . . to know whether other men have the same ideas as we Irishmen' – and before he was twenty-five had fought the Salamis of the Irish intellect.[2]

There was in both men a sense of responsibility that Yeats found to justify and reinforce his own:

> I cannot look thereon,
> Responsibility so weighs me down.[3]

> Furthermore I understood now, what I once but vaguely guessed, that these two images, standing and sounding together, Swift and Berkeley, concern all those who feel a responsibility for the thought of modern Ireland that can take away their sleep.[4]

This is the theme of 'The Man and the Echo'.[5]

> I lie awake night after night
> And never get the answers right.

In Berkeley's writings he found much to justify his own theories of vision. How much he had read of the philosopher himself is not clear; certainly he knew the *Dialogues between Hylas and Philonous*, the *Notebooks*, and *Siris*. There are whole passages in this last curious disquisition that slides so easily between tar-water, Neo-platonism, chemistry and metaphysics, that may well have served Yeats as sources. The long discourse, § 153, on 'The Aether or pure invisible Fire' is full of traditional fire and light images; allusions to Pythagoras, Empedocles, the derivation of Greek philosophy from Eastern or Egyptian sources (§ 177); the comments of Ficino on Plotinus

---

[1] Introduction to Hone and Rossi, op. cit., p. xx.
[2] *Explorations*, p. 348.
[3] 'Vacillation,' v, *C.P.*, p. 282.
[4] Introduction to Hone and Rossi, op. cit., p. xvi.
[5] *C.P.*, p. 393.

(§§ 206, 283); the doctrine of *Anima Mundi* in relation to souls 'derived from celestial luminaries' (§ 282): all these are possible sources for some of the speculations in *A Vision* and of certain images in the verse. Some aspects of Berkeley's Neo-platonic thinking in the last phase marched very closely with the world of *A Vision* and with Yeats' own doctrine of the immortality of thought. Compare, for example, the following from *Per Amica Silentia Lunae*:

> The soul has a plastic power, and can after death, or during life, should the vehicle leave the body for a while, mould it to any shape it will by an act of imagination, though the more unlike to the habitual that shape is, the greater the effort. To living and dead alike, the purity and abundance of the animal spirits are a chief power.[1]

He believed, too, that Coleridge, when writing his best poetry, was under Berkeley's influence.[2] There are repeated allusions in the poems and elsewhere:

> About our tradition I said, 'Berkeley was the first to say the world is a vision; Burke was the first to say a nation is a tree. And those two sayings are a foundation of modern thought.'[3]

This becomes:

> And haughtier-headed Burke that proved the State a tree,
> That this unconquerable labyrinth of the birds, century after century,
> Cast but dead leaves to mathematical equality;

> And God-appointed Berkeley that proved all things a dream,
> That this pragmatical, preposterous pig of a world, its farrow that so
> solid seem,
> Must vanish on the instant if the mind but change its theme. . . .[4]

Berkeley taught that there is no substance of matter, but only a substance of mind which he terms 'spirit'; that there were two kinds of spiritual substance, the one eternal, and uncreated, the substance of the Deity, the other created, and, once created, eternal; that the universe as known to created spirit has no being in itself, but is the result of the action of the substance of the Deity on the substance of those spirits. Such a doctrine, if the Deity be replaced by *Anima*

[1] *Mythologies*, p. 349.
[2] *Explorations*, p. 298.
[3] Lady Gregory, *Journals*, p. 265.
[4] 'Blood and The Moon,' ii, *C.P.*, p. 267.

*Mundi,* appeared to Yeats to give a philosophical justification for many of his beliefs – for the immortality of the spirit world, the ancestral memories, the complexities of all the phenomena of sensation, the early experiments in magic; and – though this sounds strange enough – to the description of 'Nature or reality as known to poets or tramps' (here are Goldsmith and Synge) 'which has no moment, no impression, no perception like another, everything is unique and nothing unique is measurable'. Like Swift and Blake he attacked the abstraction of thought and the mechanization of man. 'No educated man today accepts the objective matter and space of popular science, and yet deductions made by those who believed in both dominate the world. . . .'[1] Berkeley had justified Plotinus; Yeats would no longer 'baulk at this limitlessness of the intellectual'.

## II

It seems clear, then, that Yeats, a deliberate and self-conscious artist, moulded his personality on aspects of previous poets, politicians and philosophers. The doctrine of evolution by the fusion of opposites was very much part of the intellectual current of the early nineties. Dowden was an exponent of it. There were many aspects. The poet could mould himself consciously to conform with some admired action, or rationalize his deficiencies by finding that great men suffered them. By a recognition of intellectual kinship he could reassure himself as to his political and regenerative mission; and at the same time find precedent for invective against his country:

> Come, fix upon me that accusing eye.
> I thirst for accusation. All that was sung,
> All that was said in Ireland is a lie
> Bred out of the contagion of the throng,
> Saving the rhyme rats hear before they die.[2]

Much of his own personality, sanctioned by 'Ah, that is I', was justified as being in the great tradition. But Dante, Donne, Swift, Berkeley, Goldsmith – with whom he might claim kinship by

[1] *Explorations,* pp. 435–6.
[2] 'Parnell's Funeral,' *C.P.,* p. 319; cf. Rosalind's Irish rats in *As You Like It.*

having walked with Lady Gregory among the tenantry at Coole — Blake, Landor, and Morris (also a violent and heroic man) were insufficient. More subtle projections of personality were needed, puppet figures that might in their initial lives deceive the reader into thinking of them as real beings, and to whom he could give a licence of expression that would make them important quasi-dramatic mouthpieces. The three most important figures are Michael Robartes, Owen Aherne, and Kusta-ben-Luka. The first projection, Owen Aherne, is part ascetic, part the demoniacal principle: something like Blake's 'angel who is now become a devil' in *The Marriage of Heaven and Hell*. He possesses a secret book of Joachim of Flora called *Liber Inducens in Evangelium Æternum*. The first book is called *Fractura Tabularum*. 'It has swept the commandments of the Father away, . . . and displaced the commandments of the Son by the commandments of the Holy Spirit.'[1] He teaches a dangerous doctrine; Aherne comes to misery, Faust-like: 'I have lost my soul because I have looked out of the eyes of the angels.' He is the 'I' in the dialogue between 'I' and Heart in 'Owen Aherne and his Dancers',[2] which describes the incident of the proposal to Iseult Gonne. The dancers are the delighted senses, the principle of desire.[3]

In the same way, Michael Robartes is the scholar, the visionary, the recluse; holding converse with the same principle in the Dance. He is the writer in the tower, from whom another aspect of Yeats' personality has taken over:

> On the grey sand beside the shallow stream
> Under your old wind-beaten tower, where still
> A lamp burns on beside the open book
> That Michael Robartes left, you walk in the moon
> And though you have passed the best of life, still trace,
> Enthralled by that unconquerable delusion,
> Magical shapes.[4]

The two men meet in 'The Phases of the Moon'. The poem is

[1] *Mythologies*, p. 298.
[2] *C.P.*, p. 247.
[3] The depth and richness of the dance-imagery has been admirably dealt with by Kermode in *The Romantic Image* (q.v.).
[4] *C.P.*, p. 180. The image source in Calvert's illustration to 'Il Penseroso' is discussed later.

considered more fully in the chapter of that title. In the person of Robartes, Yeats develops his philosophy of the Wheel. In the dialogue form, the quick subtle play of thought fixes the position and characteristics of the third character outside them: Aherne says little; but his role becomes significant by his interjections:

'All dreams of the soul
End in a beautiful man's or woman's body.'

Aherne is the older of the two; he foreshadows, I think, the last projection of personality, Ribh of 'Supernatural Songs'.

The two men, Aherne and Robartes, meet in the Introduction to *A Vision*. They have both quarrelled with Mr Yeats. The whole elaborate make-believe of the Arabic manuscripts is abandoned in the later version and it is not clear that the two serve any useful purpose. But the earlier divisions of the book – *What the Caliph partly learned* and *What the Caliph refused to learn* – become clear in the light of the poem 'The Gift of Harun Al-Rashid' written in 1923, and published in *The Cat and the Moon*, 1924. This is 'part of an unfinished set of poems, dialogues and stories about John Aherne, Michael Robartes, Kusta-ben-Luka, a philosopher of Bagdad, and his Bedouin followers'. It owes much, in structure and rhythm, to Browning's 'Karshish'. The story is given in a suppressed note.[1]

This poem is founded upon the following passage in a letter of Owen Aherne, which I am publishing in *A Vision*.

After the murder, for an unknown reason, of Jaffar, head of the family of the Barmecides, Harun-al-Rashid seemed as though a great weight had fallen from him, and in the rejoicing of the moment, a rejoicing that seemed to Jaffar's friends a disguise for his remorse, he brought a new bride into the house. Wishing to confer an equal happiness upon his friend, he chose a young bride for Kusta-ben-Luka. According to one tradition of the desert she had, to the great surprise of her friends, fallen in love with the elderly philosopher, but according to another, Harun bought her from a passing merchant. Kusta, a Christian like the Caliph's own physician, had planned, one version of the story says, to end his days in a Monastery at Nisibis, while another story has it that he was deep in a violent love-affair that he had arranged for himself. The only thing upon which there is general agreement is that he was warned by a dream to accept the gift of the

[1] I am indebted for this footnote, and for the next, to Peter Allt.

Caliph, and that his wife a few days after her marriage began to talk in her sleep, and that she told him all those things which he had searched for vainly all his life in the great library of the Caliph and in the conversation of wise men.

This latter part is, of course, autobiographical, of the automatic writings of Mrs Yeats:

> Upon a moonless night
> I sat where I could watch her sleeping form,
> And wrote by candlelight; but her form moved,
> And fearing that my light disturbed her sleep
> I rose that I might screen it with a cloth.
> I heard her voice, 'Turn that I may expound
> What has bowed your shoulder and made pale your cheek',
> And saw her sitting upright on the bed;
> Or was it she that spoke or some great Djinn?
> I say that a Djinn spoke.[1]

So the diagrams of *A Vision* are produced:

> 'The signs and shapes,
> All those abstractions that you fancied were
> From the great Treatise of Parmenides;
> All, all those gyres and cubes and midnight things
> Are but a new expression of her body
> Drunk with the bitter sweetness of her youth.'[2]

Yeats has a footnote, subsequently suppressed:

'All those gyres and cubes and midnight things' refers to the geometrical forms which Robartes describes the Judwali Arabs as marking upon sand for the instruction of young people, and which, according to tradition, were drawn or described in sleep by the wife of Kusta-ben-Luka.'

We can now group together some of the aspects of the Anti-Self. The lives of past poets and writers served to reassure him as to his place in Irish history; and at times to excuse aspects of conduct which belonged to the Dionysiac self. Irish mythology had provided Cuchulain, whose heroism, love affairs, and fight with 'the ungovernable sea', appealed perpetually and most powerfully to his need for self-dramatization. Robartes and Aherne were puppet figures, to suggest both the scholar-saint and the violent Faust-like

[1] *C.P.*, p. 513.
[2] Ibid., p. 519.

figure whose cabbalistic device in the Order of the Golden Dawn was *Demon Est Deus Inversus*. And Robartes had discovered the mystical writings of Kusta-ben-Luka, to serve at once as a mask and framework for *A Vision*. The puppet figures do not appear in *The Tower* or *The Winding Stair*, but there is a curious passage in 'The Gift of Harun Al-Rashid' that links Kusta-ben-Luka with Byzantium:

>               – but I
> Who have accepted the Byzantine faith,
> That seems unnatural to Arabian minds
> Think when I choose a bride I choose for ever. . . .

In 'Supernatural Songs' Yeats creates a further image, Ribh, the Saint and critic of early Christianity; and, as I suggest later, this character is the mouthpiece for Yeats' final answer to the conflict of lover and ascetic. For the moment, the mouthpieces of Aherne and Robartes serve their turn. They help to give precision and subtlety to dialogue; to achieve a delicate balance, and to prepare for the form in which the interlocutors are merely 'Hic' and 'Ille'[1] or more simply, 'Soul and Self.'[2] It seems that his own interpretation of his character, as well as those of others, was further modified by that part of *A Vision* that deals with the Phases of the Moon. For the present it is necessary to consider Michael Robartes and his bride, and the more general characteristics of Yeats' women, and their psychology.

[1] 'Ego Dominus Tuus,' *C.P.*, p. 180.
[2] 'A Dialogue of Self and Soul,' ibid., p. 265.

CHAPTER FOUR

# Women Old and Young

'You must first be married,' some god told them, 'because a man's good
or evil luck comes to him through a woman.'

*Per Amica Silentia Lunae.*

Does the imagination dwell the most
Upon a woman won or woman lost?

'The Tower', ii.

My dear, my dear – when you crossed the room with that boyish movement, it was no man who looked at you, it was the woman in me. It seems
that I can make a woman express herself as never before. I have looked out
of her eyes. I have shared her desire. – *Letters to Dorothy Wellesley*, p. 118.

I

The friendship and love of women were essential to Yeats. His
experience and knowledge followed the pattern of development
that appears normal in the life of a Romantic poet; adoration, the
taking fire of the mind at women's beauty; the recoil from disappointment and frustration into affairs that were unsatisfactory in
varying degrees; a return to his idealized portrait, and a desperate
attempt to rediscover it in the next generation; his marriage, and its
overwhelming consequences in his philosophy; parenthood, and a
certain stability; then (after the pattern of the lives of poets), a
growing excitement and intensity as the imagination seized new
significance in the elements which it could now combine. For as the
physical realities receded, the images took on a continually sharpen-
ing edge: the gap between the extremes of sensuality and the
spiritual, 'the intercourse of angels', widened as both became
emphasized in the 'passionate coldness' that marks the later thought.

The early women are thin, fragile, delicately passive; wavering like the rhythms derived from Moore and Ferguson; sentimental, charged with a nostalgia built on Sligo memories, themselves based on dreams. (The incident of the night expedition to Sleuth Wood, and the old servant's Rabelaisian deductions from it, are good comment.) His disgust at the first revelations of sex, also recorded in *Autobiographies*, served no doubt to intensity the fantasy-making of this period. And the pre-Raphaelites were perpetually at hand, in their pictures, in their verse, and in the prose stories of Morris, to intensify that decorated kindly solitude where life was to become ceremonious and simple:

> Here we will moor our lonely ship
> And wander ever with woven hands,
> Murmuring softly lip to lip,
> Along the grass, along the sands,
> Murmuring how far away are the unquiet lands:[1]

Sometimes the manner is nearer to Moore than to Morris, even to the clichés:

> The hour of the waning of love has beset us,
> And weary and worn are our sad souls now;
> Let us part, ere the season of passion forget us,
> With a kiss and a tear on thy drooping brow.[2]

The women themselves are phantoms, brain-spun, languid, and decorated:

> You need but lift a pearl-pale hand,
> And bind up your long hair and sigh;
> And all men's hearts must burn and beat . . .[3]

Images and language are vague and timid:

> O cloud-pale eyelids, dream-dimmed eyes,
> The poets labouring all their days
> To build a perfect beauty in rhyme
> Are overthrown by a woman's gaze
> And by the unlabouring brood of the skies . . .[4]

But there is another side to this conventional world. If Yeats were to align himself with the great traditional lovers, there was

---

[1] 'The Indian to his Love,' *C.P.*, p. 15.
[2] 'The Falling of the Leaves,' ibid., p. 16.
[3] 'He gives his Beloved certain Rhymes,' ibid., p. 71.
[4] 'He Tells of the Perfect Beauty,' ibid., p. 74.

precedent in that tradition for a compensating sensuality. There is evidence that the story of Dante and Beatrice appealed powerfully to Yeats, both in terms of Self and Anti-Self. For

> . . . I am always persuaded that he celebrated the most pure lady poet ever sung and the Divine Justice, not merely because death took that lady and Florence banished her singer, but because he had to struggle in his own heart with his own unjust anger and his lust; while unlike those of the great poets, who are at peace with the world and at war fought themselves, he fought a double war. 'Always', says Boccaccio, 'both in youth and maturity he found room among his virtues for lechery.'[1]

A passage from Landor's *Petrarca and Boccaccio* is relevant to this and to the antinomies; and the form of Landor's dialogue is borrowed in *Red Hanrahan's Vision*:

> The features of Ugolino are reflected full in Dante. The two characters are similar in themselves, hard, cruel, inflexible, indignant, but, wherever moved, moved powerfully. In Francesca, with the faculty of divine spirits, he leaves his own nature (not indeed the exact representative of theirs) and converts all his strength into tenderness. The great poet, like the original man of the Platonists, is double, possessing the further advantage of being able to drop one half at his option and to resume it. Some of the tenderest on paper have no sympathies beyond; and some of the austerest in this intercourse with their fellow-creatures have deluged the world with tears. It is not from the rose that the bee gathers her honey, but often from the most acrid and the most bitter leaves and petals.

So he might be Dante, or Petrarch; and both Beatrice and Laura, as well as Helen, find a reincarnation in the great and long friendship with Maud Gonne, who married MacBride and later separated from him. That admiration runs like a glittering thread, vanishing and reappearing, through nearly the whole course of his work. He met her first, in London, in 1889; he first proposed to her, at Howth, in 1891: she married MacBride in 1903.

Mother and daughter were with Yeats in Normandy in the spring of 1916 and of 1917; and Iseult Gonne seems to have become a kind of reincarnation to call up and intensify the past. In that year, following the Easter Rising, many things were being reconsidered

[1] *P.A.S.L.*, p. 18. cf. 'Ego Dominus Tuus': 'Being mocked by Guido for his lecherous life.'

in Yeats' mind. Love, war, the problem of growing old, and the reshaping of a philosophy under the stress of disillusionment and hatred – all these were working together in a ferment. The meeting in Normandy must have seemed intensely dramatic to him: as if Prospero had met Perdita, and seen, for the moment, a new vision, which might resolve all the bitter moments of the conflict with Iseult's mother. In one mood:

> Maud Gonne at Howth station waiting a train,
> Pallas Athene in that straight back and arrogant head . . .[1]

In another she could be the symbol of hatred and fanaticism:

> I thought my dear must her own soul destroy,
> So did fanaticism and hate enslave it,
> And this brought forth a dream and soon enough
> This dream itself had all my thought and love.[2]

'This dream itself' was the play *The Countess Cathleen*; and that shadow-sweet woman was perhaps an early projection of what Yeats desired. The bitterness and arrogance which Irish nationalism appeared to have bred in the women, Constance Markiewicz among them, had hurt him. So in 'A Prayer for my Daughter' he remembers Maud Gonne, the 'sweetheart from another life':

> An intellectual hatred is the worst,
> So let her think opinions are accursed.
> Have I not seen the loveliest woman born
> Out of the mouth of Plenty's horn,
> Because of her opinionated mind
> Barter that horn and every good
> By quiet natures understood
> For an old bellows full of angry wind?[3]

From 1903 onwards this shadowy romanticism is blowing aside. There are sign of this even before Maud Gonne's marriage:

> We sat grown quiet at the name of love;
> We saw the last embers of daylight die,
> And in the trembling blue-green of the sky
> A moon, worn as if it had been a shell

---

[1] 'Beautiful Lofty Things,' *C.P.*, p. 348.
[2] 'The Circus Animals' Desertion,' ibid., p. 391.
[3] Ibid., p. 211.

Washed by time's waters as they rose and fell
About the stars and broke in days and years.

I had a thought for no one's but your ears:
That you were beautiful, and that I strove
To love you in the old high way of love;
That it had all seemed happy, and yet we'd grown
As weary-hearted as that hollow moon.[1]

The texture is closer, and the verse is starting to grow from within; though the shadow of Morris is still there, and a certain syntactical vagueness. But it is an image out of the common thought, and, most important of all, there is the cardinal realization of the emptiness of words.

There follows a silence of three or four years. The earliest poem in *The Green Helmet* of 1910 appears to have been first published in July 1908: the latest in *In the Seven Woods* in October 1905 ('O do not love too long'). In *The Green Helmet* the tone has changed completely. He is finding words to match the bitterness and complexity of love:

Why should I blame her that she filled my days
With misery, or that she would of late
Have taught to ignorant men most violent ways,
Or hurled the little streets upon the great,
Had they but courage equal to desire?[2]

Madame MacBride's performance as a political agitator was a source of bewilderment and anxiety to Yeats; and his conflict found expression in a growing complexity of imagery when he wrote of her. She might be embodied in the Countess Cathleen, idealized in Cathleen-ni-Houlihan, or find a shadow (as I think) in the pale fierce queen of *On Baile's Strand*. She had beauty, wit, high birth and vigour of bone; a royal bearing and eccentricities of behaviour which marked her out wherever she went; at once the object of scandal to Dublin and of worship to the peasantry of the West. It was still the Edwardian era, and here was a woman whose beauty and conduct alike were the reverse of the early pre-Raphaelite dreams:

[1] 'Adam's Curse,' *C.P.*, p. 88.
[2] 'No Second Troy,' ibid., p. 101.

What could have made her peaceful with a mind
That nobleness made simple as a fire,
With beauty like a tightened bow, a kind
That is not natural in an age like this,
Being high and solitary and most stern?[1]

There is a short poem which foreshadows something of the attitudes
in *A Woman Young and Old*:

'Put off that mask of burning gold
With emerald eyes.'
'Oh no, my dear, you make so bold
To find if hearts be wild and wise,
And yet not cold.'
'I would but find what's there to find,
Love or deceit.'
'It was the mask engaged your mind,
And after set your heart to beat,
Not what's behind.'

'But lest you are my enemy,
I must enquire.'
'O no, my dear, let all that be;
What matter, so there is but fire
In you, in me?'[2]

We may quote from Reynolds:
'She [Maud Gonne] is Yeats' *Laura*, and he who would understand much of Yeats' very allusive poetry must learn of her. . . .
Maud Gonne, filled with a destroying energy, as Florence Farr was
with a destroying curiosity, grew daily more shrill in argument,
more violent in action, while Yeats looked on, furious that Demeter,
banner in hand, should lead the Dublin lines that picketed the first
performances of *The Plough and the Stars*.'[3]

In *Responsibilities* (1914) the change is more marked. It is as if
Yeats had picked up, examined, and tightly twisted the strands of
his experience into a new complexity. At the centre there is still the
red marking strand of the great love affair, but there is a new hardness in the fibre as of violence and lust. There is a gaiety akin to
hatred that leads to Crazy Jane and The Wild Old Wicked Man, and

---

[1] *C.P.*, The MS. is dated Sept. 1908 (Mrs Yeats).
[2] 'The Mask,' ibid., p. 106. Beatrice in the *Purgatorio* has emerald eyes
(xxxi).
[3] *Letters to the New Island*, Introduction, p. 59.

a knowledge of the clay and worms like that of Synge. At first it comes slowly, with refrains that are becoming integrated with the meaning:

> 'Time to put off the world and go somewhere
> And find my health again in the sea air',
> *Beggar to beggar cried, being frenzy-struck,*
> 'And make my soul before my pate is bare'.

> 'And get a comfortable wife and house
> To rid me of the devil in my shoes',
> *Beggar to beggar cried, being frenzy-struck,*
> 'And the worse devil that is between my thighs.'[1]

The poet must take stock of it all; and especially of the sordid love affairs in which he had tried to find relief from the treatment of his love 'ennobled and poetic'. Like Dante, he had 'found room among his virtues for lechery'. That is the explanation of the last line in this stanza; and of the first draft of 'The Witch', where the third line originally read 'like some stale bitch'.[2] Old age is approaching: it is blended with the new political hatreds and violence, and the memory of the woman lost. The verse becomes hard-cored:

> And from the fortieth winter by that thought
> Test every work of intellect or faith . . .[3]

The lover must be tested, for love has a spider's eye; the thought perhaps from Donne.

The image seems to me to be a complicated one. We have of course the familiar aspect of the spider, the female destroying the mate after copulation. There is Donne's 'spider love, that *transubstantiates* all' in 'Twickenham garden', with the Jacobean trade in dried spiders for poison distillation, or the steeping of the spider of jealousy in a man's drink.[4] Yeats would have known the memorable Arachne in Doré's *Illustrations to Dante*, as well as Blake's 'Black and White Spiders'. But I suggest that the image is also from natural history. The spider's eye is large, containing a great

---

[1] 'Beggar to Beggar Cried', *C.P.*, p. 128. For the autobiographical background to this poem, see Ellmann, *The Man and The Masks*, pp. 211–12 and Jeffares, *W. B. Y.: Man and Poet*, pp. 175–6.
[2] I owe this variant to Jeffares.
[3] 'Vacillation,' iii, *C.P.*, p. 282.
[4] See *A Winter's Tale*, II, 1, 38.

number of refracting and magnifying lenses, covering many angles. And this gives superbly the capacity of lovers to discover, reflect, enlarge each other's shortcomings. It is well to quote the whole passage for its rhythmic energy and certainty of control:

> For though love has a spider's eye
> To find out some appropriate pain –
> Aye, though all passion's in the glance –
> For every nerve, and tests a lover
> With cruelties of Choice and Chance;
> And when at last that murder's over
> Maybe the bride-bed brings despair,
> For each an imagined image brings
> And finds a real image there;
> Yet the world ends when these two things,
> Though several, are a single light,
> When oil and wick are burned in one;
> Therefore a blessed moon last night
> Gave Sheba to her Solomon.[1]

In this important poem there are many seeds of Yeats' subsequent thought: the passion of love, its disillusionment, the hope for 'the intercourse of angels' that he finds at the end in 'Ribh at the Tomb of Baile and Aillinn' – all these recur in different shapes. 'That Arab lady', of the poem's opening links it to 'The Gift of Harun Al-Rashid' as part of this epithalamic group.

Women are being tested with the rest:

> We sat as silent as a stone,
> We knew, though she'd not said a word,
> That even the best of love must die,
> And had been savagely undone
> Were it not that Love upon the cry
> Of a most ridiculous little bird
> Tore from the clouds his marvellous moon.[2]

The 'most ridiculous little bird' seems to recur as a symbolic commentary on the act of love or, 'the disarming isolation of suddenly realized love', as in *A Woman Young and Old*:

> And now we stare astonished at the sea,
> And a miraculous strange bird shrieks at us.[3]

[1] 'Solomon and the Witch,' *C.P.*, p. 199.
[2] 'A Memory of Youth', ibid., p. 137.
[3] 'Her Triumph', ibid., p. 310.

It comes to disturb the lovers in 'Parting', and again in 'A Last Confession':

> There's not a bird of day that dare
> Extinguish that delight.[1]

The bird seems to have among its values a kind of eternalizing function: it is not merely the link with day, and the dissipation of the lovers' ecstasy, but also a half-malicious, half-mystical symbol that suggests a supernatural and eternal commentary on the act. It is 'ridiculous', 'miraculous', 'betraying'. Perhaps it is linked to the golden bird of 'Byzantium'; something permanent and spiritual, and mocking, beside love's ecstasy.

## II

There is little great love poetry in English, perhaps no more than a dozen poems that are objectively developed and single in their desires. It seems as if the greater writing comes from a more delicately perceived balance between lover and mistress, 'between the emotion and the act', between violence and receptivity: the whole shot through with an ironical detachment that can lose itself for a moment in emotion, and then recover its poise. Yeats had been reading Donne, and perhaps Meredith, and certainly Landor, after 1912; his debt to the metaphysical tradition, its hard quick thinking, grows steadily. The old nostalgia has been sharpened, felt more poignantly; but the subjective elements of his own experience are forced into the background, to be perceived as part of some processional unity. Maud Gonne may be Helen, or Beatrice, or 'the girl in *The Revolt of Islam*'. Yeats may dramatize himself as Dante, and there were several parallels to be found. Brutality and coarseness are the correlatives of a growing abstraction: the personal experiences of the past are being adjusted to the new integration. There is still an ideal woman, not obsessed with politics, not arrogant:

> May God be praised for woman
> That gives up all her mind,
> A man may find in no man
> A friendship of her kind

[1] 'A Last Confession', *C.P.*, p. 313. See *Romeo and Juliet*, III, v, 2.

> That covers all he has brought
> As with her flesh and bone,
> Nor quarrels with a thought
> Because it is not her own.[1]

This was the woman lost: but there was her daughter who might perhaps make up for it all:

> My imagination goes some years backward, and I remember a beautiful young girl singing at the edge of the sea in Normandy words and music of her own composition. She thought herself alone, stood barefooted between sea and sand; sang with lifted hand of the civilizations that there had come and gone, ending each verse with the cry: 'O Lord, let something remain.'[2]

The experience is central. It is handled repeatedly in different keys, with a new tenderness:

> My dear, my dear, I know
> More than another
> What makes your heart beat so;
> Not even your own mother
> Can know it as I know,
> Who broke my heart for her
> When the wild thought,
> That she denies
> And has forgot,
> Set all her blood astir
> And glittered in her eyes.[3]

Iseult's song becomes the refrain of a poem in *The Winding Stair*:

> From man's blood-sodden heart are sprung
> Those branches of the night and day
> Where the gaudy moon is hung.
> What's the meaning of all song?
> 'Let all things pass away'.[4]

It is repeated in 'Long-legged Fly', where the girl has joined in retrospect the processional symbols of Helen and Cleopatra:

---

[1] 'On Woman,' *C.P.*, p. 164. Compare, 'Women, because the main event of their lives has been a giving themselves and giving birth, give all to an opinion as if it were some terrible stone doll.' *Autobiographies*, p. 504.
[2] *A Vision* (B), p. 220.
[3] 'To a Young Girl,' *C.P.*, p. 157.
[4] 'Vacillation,' vi, ibid., p. 282.

That the topless towers be burnt
And men recall that face,
Move most gently if move you must
In this lonely place.
She thinks, part woman, three parts a child,
That nobody looks; her feet
Practise a tinker shuffle
Picked up on a street.
*Like a long-legged fly upon the stream*
*Her mind moves upon silence.*[1]

Iseult Gonne rejected the 'ageing' man; he was fifty-two. That
summer the 'Presences' haunted him:

This night has been so strange that it seemed
As if the hair stood up on my head.
From going down of the sun I have dreamed
That women laughing, or timid or wild,
In rustle of lace or silken stuff,
Climbed up my creaking stair. They had read
All I had rhymed of that monstrous thing
Returned and yet unrequited love.
They stood in the door and stood between
My great wood lectern and the fire
Till I could hear their hearts beating;
One is a harlot, and one a child
That never looked upon man with desire,
And one, it may be, a queen.[2]

After his marriage the emphasis has changed, though the ghosts of
the past still walk:

A sweetheart from another life floats there
As though she had been forced to linger
From vague distress
Or arrogant loveliness,
Merely to loosen out a tress
Among the starry eddies of her hair
Upon the paleness of a finger.[3]

(These are relics of the idioms of the nineties with a new rhythmic
pointing; contrast the passages quoted on page 52.) But Maud
Gonne had been imprisoned, and escaped. She had crossed from

[1] *C.P.*, p. 381.
[2] Ibid., p. 174.
[3] 'An Image from a Past Life,' ibid., p. 200.

England to Dublin, and had come to her own house that she had
let to Yeats and his bride at 73 St Stephen's Green. Newly married,
and with illness in the house, Yeats refused her admittance.[1] The
incident gave rise to much scandal 'in this blind bitter town'. They
quarrelled, but were reconciled again.

Her leadership of the crowd, her fierce and uncompromising
Republicanism, represented some denial of the aristocratic ideal.
So had Countess Markiewicz betrayed her sex and tradition:

> Did she in touching that lone wing
> Recall the years before her mind
> Became a bitter, an abstract thing,
> Her thought some popular enmity:
> Blind and leader of the blind
> Drinking the foul ditch where they lie?[2]

In contrast he had written, memorably, of the dignity and malicious
gaiety of the dying Mabel Beardsley:

> She has not grown uncivil
> As narrow natures would
> And called the pleasures evil
> Happier days thought good;
> She knows herself a woman,
> No red and white of a face,
> Or rank, raised from a common
> Unreckonable race;
> And how should her heart fail her
> Or sickness break her will
> With her dead brother's valour
> For an example still?[3]

In *Last Poems* Maud Gonne is both a memory and an enigma: the
subject of speculation upon the ultimate nature of women, and yet
another addition to the symbols afforded by sculptures, or by the
memory of Spenser, or by neo-Platonic speculation:

> . . . her form all full
> As though with magnanimity of light,
> Yet a most gentle woman; who can tell
> Which of her forms has shown her substance right?

---

[1] Hone, *Life*, p. 314.
[2] 'On a Political Prisoner,' *C.P.*, p. 206.
[3] 'Upon a Dying Lady,' ibid., p. 177.

Or maybe substance can be composite,
Profound McTaggart thought so, and in a breath,
A mouthful held the extreme of life and death.[1]

## III

Marriage and the coming of old age unite to focus more sharply
the experiences of the past; and from the women old and young a
kind of essence is expressed. That essence is hard to define: there
is, first, the perception of sensuality in its most naked elements, as
Swift perceived it, but fused by laughter that is ironical, and can turn
suddenly to tenderness. There is, too, the divided and balanced
mind of the poet: the realization that two disparate values may be
apprehended simultaneously, though they be opposites, and that
the poem so formed explains, adequately and perhaps finally, the
dualism of love:

> O but there is wisdom
> In what the sages said;
> But stretch that body for a while
> And lay down that head
> Till I have told the sages
> Where man is comforted.
>
> How could passion run so deep
> Had I never thought
> That the crime of being born
> Blackens all our lot?
> But where the crime's committed
> The crime can be forgot.[2]

For women who are old passion remains in the memory: and old
men and women are endued with this violence of the imagination
which flings their sensuality into relief against myth or symbol.
So in 'Her Vision in the Wood'[3] the Adonis image comes to the hag:

[1] 'A Bronze Head,' *C.P.*, p. 382. See the illustration of the plaster bust by
Laurence Campbell and the portrait by Sarah Purser, reproduced by Hone.
[2] 'A Woman Young and Old,' v. ibid., p. 308. The echo from Sophocles
is plain; v. 'From "Oedipus at Colonus"' ibid., p. 255. It is profitable to compare the last two lines with the ending of Donne's 'A Valediction: Forbidding
Mourning'.
[3] Ibid., viii.

> Dry timber under that rich foliage,
> At wine-dark midnight in the sacred wood,
> Too old for a man's love I stood in rage
> Imagining men. . . .

Against the myth, imaged in painting, the perfection of art stands timeless. It is still the theme of 'Byzantium' and the 'Grecian Urn': with Yeats' processional world giving depth to the experience:

> All stately women moving to a song
> With loosened hair or foreheads grief-distraught,
> It seemed a Quattrocento painter's throng,
> A thoughtless image of Mantegna's thought —
> Why should they think that are for ever young?[1]

This 'lust and' rage take both men and women when they are old; but to the old is given a clarity of insight into the nature of both:

> Hidden by old age awhile
> In masker's cloak and hood,
> Each hating what the other loved,
> Face to face we stood:
> 'That I have met with such,' said he,
> 'Bodes me little good.'

> 'Let others boast their fill,' said I,
> 'But never dare to boast
> That such as I had such a man
> For lover in the past;
> Say that of living men I hate
> Such a man the most.'[2]

But behind the hatred of the 'maskers' – for human loves carry their illusions and self-delusions to the end – there is a merging into tenderness:

> 'A loony'd boast of such a love,'
> He in his rage declared:
> But such as he for such as me —
> Could we both discard
> This beggarly habiliment —
> Had found a sweeter word.

[1] *C.P.*, p. 312.
[2] Ibid., p. 314.

IV

'It seems that I can make a woman express herself as never before. I have looked out of her eyes, I have shared her desire.' That is a bold claim for any man to make, and Yeats had not the psychological insight of a dramatist. But there is some substance in the claim provided we understand what Yeats was trying to do. As an example of failure to realize Yeats' intentions, James Stephens' indictment is of interest:

> He worried about love, conceiving it as a passion, as a drama, and not the simplest, the most abundant thing in our otherwise bedevilled world, for love is complete trust, unremitting attention. . . . He thought he could pin it down and rhyme it into reason. . . . Love and pity and hate were not absolutely real to him. . . .[1]

Against these statements, which invite destructive comment at every turn, we can set Yeats' own intention:

> Love is created and preserved by intellectual analysis, for we love only that which is unique, and it belongs to contemplation not to action, for we would not change that which we love.[2]

Such intellectual analysis gives rise to the traditional questions of any poet who writes of love. Is it ecstasy of soul or of body? And if the answer is (as it must be) 'of both', then at what times in the lives of men and women does one or other predominate? Does it endure, outlive the body, in reality or only in the mind? What place does ecstasy take, either in itself or as emblem of union with God? All these questions are set and answered in terms of contemplation and analysis. It must be seen to be variable (as all things are) under the Phases of the Moon: it must lie behind the processional image of history and the ravings of Crazy Jane. It is, as Meredith knew, 'a thing of moods'.

> Eternity is passion, girl or boy
> Cry at the onset of their sexual joy
> 'For ever and for ever'; then awake
> Ignorant what Dramatis Personae spake. . . .[3]

---

[1] Broadcast, January 1948. Beside this we may set Frank O'Connor's view that Yeats is a great poet of friendship, not of love.
[2] *A Vision* (A), p. 187.
[3] 'Whence had they come?' *C.P.*, p. 332.

It can be realized in a little-known poem with a dramatic and authentic rhythm:

> And now my utmost mystery is out.
> A woman's beauty is a storm-tossed banner;
> Under it wisdom stands, and I alone —
> Of all Arabia's lovers I alone —
> Nor dazzled by the embroidery, nor lost
> In the confusion of its night-dark folds,
> Can hear the armed man speak.[1]

He portrays through the women of these lyrics that duality of mood, that perception of a balance which appears to represent stable and satisfactory values, in this quintessence of womanhood. It is, I think, something quite unconnected with the psychological insight of the novelist or dramatist; the women become mere mouthpieces for the truth they have seen and for the strange and terrifying impersonality of their desires. There is no Romantic colouring:

> What lively lad most pleasured me
> Of all that with me lay?
> I answer that I gave my soul
> And loved in misery,
> But had great pleasure with a lad
> That I loved bodily.[2]

It is a very far cry from the mystical eroticism of Rossetti or Patmore: but it is perhaps nearer the image of a woman's desire. The bitterness is wholesome, not destructive or hysterical:

> I gave what other women gave
> That stepped out of their clothes —

This stripping down to the common impulse of the body is necessary lest there should be confusion of shadow with substance. The thought occurs again:

> ... And maybe we are all the same
> Where no candles are,
> And maybe we are all the same
> That strip the body bare.
> *O my dear, O my dear.*[3]

---

[1] 'The Gift of Harun Al-Rashid,' *C.P.*, p. 513.

[2] 'A Last Confession,' ibid., p. 313. Cf. 'The tragedy of sexual intercourse lies in the perpetual virginity of the soul.' (Yeats to John Sparrow.)

[3] 'The Three Bushes,' ibid., p. 341.

and again:

> What sort of man is coming
> To lie between your feet?
> What matter, we are but women.
> Wash; make your body sweet . . .[1]

But the union of soul with soul is the cleaner and more transcendent for the knowledge.

> But when this soul, its body off,
> Naked to naked goes,
> He it has found shall find therein
> What none other knows,
>
> And give his own and take his own
> And rule in his own right;
> And though it loved in misery
> Close and cling so tight,
> There's not a bird of day that dare
> Extinguish that delight.[2]

The 'Crazy Jane' poems set forth that stage of womanhood in which, the body failing, the memory of its pleasures carries the soul forward into a synthesis founded upon a denial of sentimentality and a fierce exultation in the wild dance rhythms: which are based, many of them, on concertina music, strident and violent. (The ballad of 'Colonel Martin' was intended for whistle and concertina.) Outside and beyond lust and rage – rage against the Bishop, or a king, or circumstance – are the remains of the processional and historical world; against which these Synge-like peasants move in a peculiar solitude of their own. Sometimes the fusion is not complete:

> I care not what the sailors say:
> All those dreadful thunder-stones,
> All that storm that blots the day
> Can but show that Heaven yawns;
> Great Europa played the fool
> That changed a lover for a bull.
> *Fol de rol, fol de rol.*
>
> To round that shell's elaborate whorl,
> Adorning every secret track
> With the delicate mother-of-pearl,
> Made the joints of Heaven crack:

[1] 'The Lady's Second Song,' *C.P.* p. 344.
[2] 'A Last Confession,' ibid., p. 313. v., also p. 58.

> So never hang your heart upon
> A roaring, ranting journeyman.
> *Fol de rol, fol de rol.*[1]

Suddenly the last three lines change rhythm, and one hears the
fiddle and concertina bringing out the kick-step of the couplet
upon that arrogant rhyme; just as the words 'made the joints of
Heaven crack' wrenches us back – the thought-sequence is plain –
to the Creation in the Sistine Chapel.[2]

Old Tom and Crazy Jane confront the girl and the young man
with their songs; each facing the problem of love in old age. They
stand for the images of many women: for 'Florence Farr coming
to her fiftieth year, dreading old age and fading beauty', she who
had helped him with his first experiments in speaking verse to
music 'in an effort to release poetry from its slavery to music in
song'. It is all part of the high tradition: for 'it has always seemed
to me that all great literature at its greatest intensity displays the
sage, the lover, or some image of despair' ('Maybe the bride-bed
brings despair') 'and that there are traditional attitudes. When I
say the lover I mean all that heroic casuistry, all that assertion of the
eternity of what Nature declares ephemeral. . . .'[3]

The young have their answer, bravely, in the heart, in a neo-
Platonic vision:

> 'She will change,' I cried,
> 'Into a withered crone.'
> The heart in my side,
> That so still had lain,
> In noble rage replied
> And beat upon the bone:
>
> 'Uplift those eyes and throw
> Those glances unafraid:
> She would as bravely show
> Did all the fabric fade;
> No withered crone I saw
> Before the world was made.'[4]

---

[1] 'Crazy Jane Reproved,' *C.P.*, p. 291.
[2] Cf. 'Under Ben Bulben,' iv, ibid., p. 397.
[3] *Explorations*, p. 295. Compare:
> 'Eternity is passion girl or boy
> Cry at the onset of their sexual joy' . . .
[4] 'Young Man's Song,' *C.P.*, p. 296.

To the woman, the physical love of man is seen as oscillating between two poles; it can be completed and satisfying, a giving and a receiving, the exercise of a mystery and a power.

> 'Three dear things that women know,'
> *Sang a bone upon the shore;*
> 'A man if I but held him so
> When my body was alive
> Found all the pleasure that life gave':
> *A bone wave-whitened and dried in the wind*[1]

She is well aware of the man's romantic attitude; her own woman's knowledge goes beyond it:

> Flinging from his arms I laughed
> To think his passion such
> He fancied that I gave a soul
> Did but our bodies touch,
> And laughed upon his breast to think
> Beast gave beast as much.[2]

Woman is at once the victim and the torturer and the mystic partner in the union: with that curious arrogant acceptance of passion, and her dispassionate contemplation of it. And she is part of the historical procession, for there was warrant for it in Spengler:

> Here in man and in woman, *the two kinds* of History are fighting for power. Woman is strong and wholly what she is, and she experiences the Man and the Sons only in relation to herself and her ordained role. In the masculine being, on the contrary, there is a certain contradiction; he is this man, and he is something else besides, which woman neither understands nor admits, which is robbery and violence upon that which to her is holiest. This secret and fundamental war of the sexes has gone on ever since there were sexes, and will continue – silent, bitter, unforgiving, pitiless – while they continue.[3]

So the end is Blake's wife or harlot, and 'the lineaments of gratified desire':

> 'The third thing that I think of yet,'
> *Sang a bone upon the shore,*
> 'Is that morning when I met
> Face to face my rightful man

---

[1] 'Three Things,' *C.P.*, p. 300.
[2] 'A Last Confession,' ibid., p. 313.
[3] *The Decline of the West*, vol. II, p. 328.

And did after stretch and yawn':
*A bone wave-whitened and dried in the wind.*[1]

Yeats' women are stripped and not dishonoured; their art of love is brought into a sharp clear focus, while their tenderness and mystery remain. The body passes with old age; but Crazy Jane is only one puppet in the dialogue that debates the endless problem of growing old. In that process the images of desire still haunt the poet: images which are of the brain and not of the loins, memories that have become part of a pattern. It is indeed as if, at the last, his women had become like the stylized women Blake drew to illustrate the *Purgatorio*; with passion, and knowledge, yet with a curious translucent uniformity of coldness:

> For maybe we are all the same
> Where no candles are . . .[2]

In that uniformity they join the procession of symbols: till at the last the idea of aristocracy and beauty return in that stately poem to Dorothy Wellesley:

> 'What climbs the stair?
> Nothing that common women ponder on
> If you are worth my hope! Neither Content
> Nor satisfied Conscience, but that great family
> Some ancient famous authors misrepresent,
> The Proud Furies each with her torch on high.[3]

But this is not the last word. As I have suggested elsewhere, the last and greatest Mask of Yeats is Ribh, 'the critic of St Patrick' in *A Full Moon in March*. Love is purified by tragedy; and a great light shines from the last intercourse of angels. He had followed Donne's advice:

> Thou look'st through spectacles; small things seeme great
> Below; But up unto the watch-towre get,
> And see all things despoyl'd of fallacies.[4]

These processes of analysis and disintegration as a prior condition of synthesis is the dominant method of Yeats' work in the last

[1] *C.P.*, p. 300.
[2] 'The Three Bushes' ibid., p. 341.
[3] Ibid., p. 349.
[4] 'The Second Anniversarie.'

period. We can see its application to many aspects; to Celtic mythology, the rejection of 'Irish' pastoralism, the attack on the new
political and social patterns of the post-treaty world, and an increasingly violent association of the antinomies between the physical and
the spiritual side of love. Once so despoiled, love must become
mystical again. What reality there is on earth lies between extremities, and the final answer is to show yet another mystery:

> What matter that you understood no word!
> Doubtless I spake or sang what I had heard
> In broken sentences. My soul had found
> All happiness in its own cause or ground.
> Godhead on Godhead in sexual spasm begot
> Godhead. Some shadow fell. My soul forgot
> Those amorous cries that out of quiet come
> And must the common round of day resume.[1]

[1] 'Ribh in Ecstasy,' *C.P.*, p. 329.

# CHAPTER FIVE

# Yeats and Synge

And here's John Synge himself, that rooted man,
'Forgetting human words', a grave deep face.
'The Municipal Gallery Revisited.'

Yeats and Synge first met in 1896, in Paris, where Yeats had gone
to make a ritual for an Order of Celtic Mysteries by which Young
Ireland was to be initiated 'into a mystical philosophy which would
combine the doctrines of Christianity with the faiths of a more
ancient world, unite the perceptions of the spirit with those of
natural beauty'.[1] A contemplative order was to be founded at Rock
Castle, on Lough Key: to be a shrine of Irish tradition, an emblem
of holy Ireland. There were magical preparations to be made:
'Maud Gonne & myself are going for a week or two perhaps to get
as you do the forms of Gods & Spirits and to get sacred earth for
our invocation.'[2] The verses 'Into the Twilight' are typical enough:

> Out-worn heart, in a time out-worn,
> Come clear of the nets of wrong and right;
> Laugh, heart, again in the grey twilight,
> Sigh, heart, again in the dew of the morn.
>
> Your mother Eire is always young,
> Dew ever shining and twilight grey;

[1] Hone, *Life*, p. 133.

[2] Letters to 'A.E.,' Wade, p. 295 When the Senatorships were offered to
Yeats and George Russell, the latter replied that he must first consult the
gods.
  But the account given by Maud Gonne differs a good deal from this. The
institute was to be a practical one – in part a hospital for those who had been
wounded fighting for Ireland against England, in part a house of refuge for
writers, scholars, and the old. (I owe this to Peter Allt.)

Though hope fall from you and love decay,
Burning in fires of a slanderous tongue.

Come, heart, where hill is heaped upon hill:
For there the mystical brotherhood
Of sun and moon and hollow and wood
And river and stream work out their will;

And God stands winding His lonely horn,
And time and the world are ever in flight;
And love is less kind than the grey twilight,
And hope is less dear than the dew of the morn.[1]

The accounts of that momentous meeting read ironically now: and
the irony is reinforced if we remember that an ancestor of Synge
had gone to the West as a missionary to convert the people to
Protestantism. Yeats, true to his own faith in Ireland as the new
source of European culture, gave Synge the best of advice. 'Give
up Paris, you will never create anything by reading Racine, and
Arthur Symons will always be a better critic of French literature.
Go to the Aran Islands. Live there as if you were one of the people
themselves; express a life that has never found expression.'

Synge had many qualities to offset those of Yeats. Like him he
was under the influence of the Nineties; but unlike him he had a first-
hand knowledge, through his Wanderjahre, of the continental
tradition. (Perhaps this Goldsmith-aspect had attracted Yeats.) He
had read Villon,[2] Petrarch, Rabelais, Ronsard, Nashe, Cervantes,
Herrick, Burns. A full and generous alignment with the continental
tradition was, in a sense, a deficiency of the whole movement, and is,
I believe, the explanation of its subsequent provincialism. And the
growth of this was accelerated when compulsory Irish sealed off
any European language from Irish normal education. On this point
Stephen MacKenna had stood firm:

> His ideal was an Ireland Irish in speech, in culture, in institutions,
> but not an Ireland cut off from the fertilizing waters of the great
> European tradition.[3]

[1] *C.P.*, p. 65. This might easily be taken for some of 'A.E.''s work.
[2] Villon seems to have appealed in a special manner to the poets of the last
two decades of the century; there are numerous translations of his poems.
Perhaps it was an aspect of the contemporary cult of *Les Fauves*.
[3] *Memoir*, p. 38.

D

His profound and meditative temperament combined with his
Anglo-Irish heritage and his continental travels to give him a
clear disillusioned outlook; yet this melancholy, his perception of
present sorrow in birth and death, was counterpointed with a strong
Elizabethan *bravura*, a rhetoric which could be savage, or splendid,
or ironic. He was something of a Wordsworthian too:

> I knew the stars, the flowers and the birds,
> The grey and wintry sides of many glens,
> And did but half-remember human words,
> In converse with the mountains, moors, and fens.

Yeats celebrates him as the 'solitary man', the 'enquiring man';
perhaps that powerful, taciturn and receptive genius supplied some
need in himself, some knowledge of 'the book of the people' that
he envied.

In a curious passage of *A Vision* he groups him with Rembrandt;
both are typical figures belonging to No. 23 of the Phases of the
Moon. 'Both will work in toil and pain, finding what they do not
seek . . . but that which they reveal is joyous.'[1] Both are full of pity,
the 'pity for man's darkening thought' that is inseparable from
wisdom. But Synge changed after his contact with the true life of
the peasantry. 'In Synge's early unpublished work, written before
he found the dialects of Aran and of Wicklow, there is brooding
melancholy and morbid self-pity. He had to undergo an aesthetic
transformation, analogous to religious conversion, before he
became the audacious joyous ironical man we know.'[2] These qualities
are seen perhaps at their most vivid in Yeats' *Last Poems*.

Like Yeats himself Synge found compensation for ill-health in
imagined brutality and violence. He was thus in some measure
Yeats' Anti-Self, human enough to understand the peasant mind,
ready to share its brutalities, patient, self-effacing, curious; enough
of a scholar to have a little Gaelic, some German, and a good deal
of French to broaden his point of view. He was a keen fisherman
and a great rambler in the Wicklow glens, and in that curious and
important poem 'The Fisherman' there may be some memory of
Synge, 'The dead man that I loved':

[1] 'A', p. 99. Also: 'Synge must find rhythm and syntax in the Aran Islands'
(Ibid.).
[2] Ibid., p. 100. But 'joyous' is used in a Yeatsian sense.

> Imagining a man,
> And his sun-freckled face,
> And grey Connemara cloth,
> Climbing up to a place
> Where stone is dark under froth,
> And the down-turn of his wrist
> When the flies drop in the stream;
> A man who does not exist
> A man who is but a dream. . . .[1]

But this image of an Anti-Self occurs frequently. Compare:

> Some have known a likely lad
> That had a sound fly-fisher's wrist
> Turn to a drunken journalist . . .[2]

His father speaks with pride of the family's prowess as fishermen,[3] and Yeats valued the approval that a critic had given (rightly) to the accuracy of the phrase, 'the down-turn of his wrist'. But he himself had little practical skill, and the fisherman was but another mask or compensation; to give a sense of wisdom, simplicity, the integrity of the lonely man, and maybe a certain aristocratic skill of hand and eye that could be related to the Renaissance tradition. Hence his own imagined pride in it, as in the horsemanship of his ancestors or in the lessons which he took in fencing.

In retrospect Yeats saw Synge's career as an image of his own journeying. The Aran Islanders had become vested with a mystical significance:

> But that, long travelling, he had come
> Towards nightfall upon certain set apart
> In a most desolate stony place,
> Towards nightfall upon a race
> Passionate and simple like his heart.[4]

Yeats set at the head of his Introduction to the posthumous edition

[1] 'The Fisherman,' *C.P.*, p. 166. Babette Deutsch gives an admirable account of this much-misunderstood poem in *This Modern Poetry*, p. 215.
[2] 'Why should not Old Men be Mad?' *C.P.*, p. 388.
[3] *J. B. Y. Letters*, p. 246.
[4] 'In Memory of Major Robert Gregory,' *C.P.*, p. 148. The ambiguity of 'stony' for the Aran Islands, where the fields are mere pockets of earth in the rock, is worth notice. Stone and coldness, rock and thorn, are also associated with the Burren in North Clare.

of Synge's poems the quotation from Proclus: 'The Lonely returns to the Lonely, the Divine to the Divinity.'

Synge was much concerned with death and with the horror of old age; but both were treated with an objectivity and grim humour which he learnt, perhaps, from Villon. Yeats had seen the Irish peasantry in a pale and holy light; Synge saw them with a kind of dispassionate mocking sympathy. On the stage there was to be reality and joy, the 'rich joy found only in what is superb and wild in reality'. 'In a good play every speech should be as fully flavoured as a nut or apple' (he had learnt much from Elizabethan drama) 'and such speeches cannot be written by anyone who works among people who have shut their lips on poetry.'[1]

His drama was to give 'the nourishment, not very easy to define, on which our imaginations live. . . . Of the things which nourish the imagination, humour is one of the most needful, and it is dangerous to limit or destroy it.' This is in contrast to Yeats' practice, which was more in Arnold's tradition, the selective use of the great subject; he was incapable of that flexibility of intelligence, of the acute observation of significant detail, that is the gift of Synge; in whom he saw that 'hunger for harsh facts, for ugly surprising things, for all that defies our hope'.[2]

Synge's theory of poetry was much like his theory of drama. Men were losing or had lost their poetic feeling for ordinary life. Hence exalted poetry was likely to lose its strength of creation. In the age of Coleridge and Shelley it went with verse that was not always human. Then follows the famous passage:

> In these days poetry is usually a flower of evil or good, but it is the timber of poetry that wears most surely, and there is no timber that has not strong roots among the clay & worms. Even if we grant that exalted poetry can be kept successful by itself, the strong things of life are needed in poetry also, to show that what is exalted, or tender, is not made by feeble blood. It may almost be said that before verse can be human again it must learn to be brutal.

Such a doctrine was a healthy corrective to the 'pure poetry' of the Nineties, to the 'hard, gem-like flame', to the exalted poetry of *The Wanderings of Oisin*. It had much to do with Yeats' rejection

[1] Preface to *The Playboy of the Western World*.
[2] Preface to Synge's *Poems and Translations. E. & I.*, p. 308.

of his dreams of a mythology dedicated to high nationalistic ideals. '... I did not see, until Synge began to write, that we must renounce the deliberate creation of a kind of Holy City in the imagination, and express the individual. The Irish people were not educated enough to accept images more profound, more true to human nature, than the schoolboy thoughts of Young Ireland.'[1] His collaboration with Lady Gregory, particularly over *Poets and Dreamers*, had shown him something of the resources of the peasant vocabulary, translated though this might be in Lady Gregory's 'Kiltartanese'. Synge had found himself and a new source of experience in the Aran Islands and in Kerry: he had succeeded, as Yeats never did, in catching, through rhythm and idiom, the gaiety and tragedy and profound monotony of the Irish peasant lives, of the loneliness of the farmsteads in the West, of the lonely Wicklow glens where a woman may sit

> hearing nothing but the wind crying out in the bits of broken trees were left from the great storm, and the streams roaring with the rain.

The life of tinkers, parish priests, the talk in a Mayo public-house, the love-making of women, the cringing of beggars; these were Synge's reading in 'the book of the people', a knowledge that Yeats had praised so highly in the blind poet, Raftery. There was a new store of imagery to be handled in this strange idiom, phrases 'with a skin on them', the product of an imaginative people who read little and talk and listen much. So Raftery, of a woman —

> Her breast is the colour of white sugar, or like bleached bone on the card-table.

There is a healthy brutality, itself rhetorical in tone, bred of the knowledge of the clay and the worms:

> ... when it's sooner on a bullock's liver you'd put a poor girl thinking than on the lily or the rose?

or

> At your age you should know there are nights when a King like Conchubor would spit upon his arm ring, and queens will stick their tongues out at the rising moon.

[1] *Autobiographies*, p. 493.

It is of interest that Yeats alluded to Synge's very slight verse in the Preface to the *Oxford Book*, and found room for no less than eleven pieces in it: an instance of the many and perverse misjudgements of that anthology. There was perhaps something in Synge that accorded not only with Yeats' desire for brutality and violence, but also with his ironic laughter at heroic legend. Of the Catalogue of Queens in the Villon manner:

> Queens who wasted the East by proxy,
> Or drove the ass-cart, a tinker's doxy,
> Yet these are rotten – I ask their pardon —
> And we've the sun on rock and garden,
> These are rotten, so you're the Queen
> Of all are living, or have been.

It is of a piece with the two-pole treatment of the Deirdre legend, the exaltation and the brutality – 'for death should be a poor untidy thing, though it's a queen that dies'. We may remember Yeats' favourite quotation from Nashe:

> Brightness falls from the air.
> Queens have died young and fair.
> Dust hath closed Helen's eye.

And Synge's Island woman on Aran:

> You've plucked a curlew, drawn a hen,
> Washed the shirts of seven men . . .

There were Synge's ballad-rhythms too, a little sophisticated but new to Yeats: there was even a renunciation, like that in *Responsibilities*, of the Celtic Twilight, and of 'A.E.''s 'spirit' pictures. (Yeats did not refer to them by title.)

> Adieu, sweet Angus, Maeve and Fand,
> Ye plumed yet skinny Shee,
> That poets played with hand in hand
> To learn their ecstasy.

> We'll stretch in Red Dan Sally's ditch,
> And drink in Tubber fair,
> Or poach with Red Dan Philly's bitch
> The badger and the hare.[1]

[1] It is significant that the sub-title of the poem is: 'After looking at one of "A.E." 's pictures'; but I do not know which

All Synge's better verse – there is not much of it – is in the *Playboy* tradition, which Yeats had called 'this strange, violent, laughing thing'. It is picaresque, quick-moving, grotesque in rhymes; we are reminded of parts of the Crazy Jane poems (Villon is surely a common factor), and of 'Colonel Martin'. The production of the *Playboy* occasioned a long and bitter attack; greater than that which Yeats had known at the performance of his own *Countess Cathleen*, when the suggestion that an Irishwoman would sell her soul to the devil had been held to be a libel on that nation of saints. It was the same disapproval that he was to meet again over the publication of 'Leda and the Swan'. The *Playboy* was blasphemous, suggesting that parricide and murder were approved by public opinion, as represented by a small public-house in Mayo. Irishwomen were depicted in an unflattering manner: both as pursuing the Playboy, and in immodest images. The line 'a drift of chosen females, standing in their shifts itself' caused a riot, as did the first run-on line of Hugo's *Hernani*, at every performance. The numerous appeals to the Saints, so common in the normal peasant speech, were irreligious on the stage. And finally, Synge, a Protestant and the son of a barrister, was suspected of lack of patriotism, lack of reverence for women, and actual blasphemy:

> 'Is it killed your father?'
> 'With the help of God I did surely, and that the Holy Immaculate Mother may intercede for his soul.'

To all this Synge replied with dignity:

> The *Playboy* . . . is not a play with a purpose in the modern sense of the word, but, although parts of it are, or are meant to be, extravagant comedy, still a great deal that is in it and a great deal more that is behind is perfectly serious when looked at in a certain light. This is often the case, I think, with comedy, and no one is quite sure today whether Shylock or Alcestis should be played seriously or not. There are, it may be hinted, several sides to the *Playboy*.

To Yeats the controversy drove home the realization of the force of irrational ignorant opinion in arms against him, though he had seen something of it before in the response to his political speeches. It was a realization that was to be strengthened by the events of 1928 and afterwards. Now in his comments, as well as in the bitter epigrams that appeared in *Responsibilities*, there is a more realistic approach to the problems of a national literature and national politics:

> Ireland is passing through a crisis in the life of the mind greater than any she has known since the rise of the Young Ireland party. ... Many are beginning to recognize the right of the individual mind to see the world in its own way, to cherish the thoughts which separate men from one another, and that are the creators of distinguished life: instead of those thoughts that had made one man like another if they could, and have but succeeded in setting hysteria and insincerity in place of confidence and self-possession.[1]

And again:

> Indeed, I have Ireland especially in mind, for I want to make, or to help some man some day to make, a feeling of exclusiveness, a bond among chosen spirits, a mystery almost for leisured and lettered people. Ireland has suffered more than England from democracy, for since the Wild Geese fled who might have grown to be leaders in manners and in taste, she has had but political leaders.[2]

Synge's knowledge of the Irish peasant, shopkeeper, priest, tinker, fisherman, is intimate, cool, dispassionate. He is aware of their melancholy, violence, drunkenness, exaltation, poverty, cruelty. Yeats is concerned with a somewhat idealized peasantry, sometimes refracted in the timelessness of Celtic myth, sometimes discerned (a little shyly) through his expeditions with Lady Gregory to collect folk-lore. Of this, the magical or supernatural aspects appealed powerfully to Yeats, certifying as they did a world-wide body of visions and beliefs. His hint to Synge to investigate such matters on Aran was very properly disregarded, though Synge was well aware of the immanence of the supernatural, there and elsewhere, and was (I believe) frightened by what he found. Yeats' knowledge is most vivid when it is related to his boyhood knowledge, and, at the end, to an imagination fired by the rhythms of the street-ballads. The middle of Irish humanity he never really knew. For

---

[1] *Plays and Controversies*, p. 198. I find no evidence for the recent suggestion that Yeats' interest in the *Playboy* controversy was conditioned by his own Oedipus complex.

[2] Ibid., p. 215. Compare also, 'Civilization dies of all those things that eed the soul, and both die if the Remnant refuse the Wilderness,' *Auto-biographies*, p. 467.

that we must go to the early works of J. B. Yeats and his illustrations to Synge's *The Aran Islands*; when the little spirited sketches give the very smell of porter and wet frieze, the muddy streets and characterless pubs and shops, the ragged swashbuckling tinkers, showmen, cattle drovers; the delighted movement of horses in 'the races on the strand'.

Yeats learnt little of dramatic technique from Synge. He had none of the true dramatist's incessant curiosity for character, nor the gift of its detailed creation or development. Of this he was fully aware. 'I have sometimes asked her [Lady Gregory's] help because I could not write dialect and sometimes because my construction had fallen into confusion.'[1] This is not surprising, since Yeats' own theory of drama ran counter to all that Synge demanded. In the first place, he was influenced by the static drama of Maeterlinck, with its conception of action as a distracting and unnecessary framework, and its concentration on atmosphere and the phases of the soul. He works towards a 'pure' drama by the exclusion of the extraneous and irrelevant. From this follows his unduly high valuation of the Japanese Nōh plays as a model. That limited, stylized, aristocratic and remote drama, giving full play to mask, song and music, allowed him to express both his gifts for lyric and the mystical doctrines of the Self and Anti-Self. (These aspects are treated more fully in the chapter 'The Poetry of the Plays'.) There was an inherent element of ritual to which he attached increasing importance from 1920 onwards; and it looks as if he rationalized that ritualistic element (with memories of his early Mysteries and Orders) as part of his philosophy:

> The Japanese labour leader and Christian saint Kagawa, perhaps influenced by Vico though his millennium-haunted mind, breaks Vico's circle, speaks of that early phase of every civilization where a man must follow his father's occupation, where everything is prescribed, as buried under dream and myth.[2]

So the drama is to be deliberately remote. 'The theatre began in ritual, and it cannot come to its greatness again without recalling words to their ancient sovereignty.' His revolt against the 'modern

---

[1] Preface to *Plays*, p. vii. But I think that the general debt was in the other direction.

[2] Introduction to *The Cat and the Moon*, *W. & B.*, p. 135.

intellectual drama' is never in the direction of the 'book of the people'. There was, moreover, safety in the stylized ritual of the Nōh drama as a model for the brief one-act plays, based on Irish mythology, designed as curtain-raisers for an intimate theatre and an audience of his friends. The conflict of the market-place was over; the less strenuous conflict of the Senate was yet to come.

Nor did Yeats ever catch Synge's rhythms, with the subtle over-stressing of idiom, the mannerisms which are, perhaps, at their worst in *Deirdre*, which produced St John Ervine's indictment of him as a 'faker of peasant speech'; although that criticism (which set Barrie's speech above Synge's) appears to have considered neither the heightening and compression that dramatic speech involves, nor the basic soundness of Synge's memory of idiom and construction. It is of interest to compare the three stages in *Deirdre*: the prose material in Lady Gregory, a little stilted and Ossianic; and then the two poets working upon it.

First:

> Sorrowful was my journey with Fergus, betraying me to the Red Branch; we were deceived all together with his sweet, flowery words. I left the delights of Ulster for the three heroes that were bravest; my life will not be long, I myself am alone after them.
>
> I am Deirdre without gladness, and I at the end of my life; since it is grief to be without them, I myself will not be long after them.
>
> After that complaint Deirdre loosed out her hair, and threw herself on the body of Naoise before it was put in the grave and gave three kisses to him, and when her mouth touched his blood the colour of burning sods came into her cheeks, and she rose up like one that had lost her wits, and she went on through the night till she came to where the waves were breaking on the strand.[1]

The ending of Synge's play shows the momentum of the rhythms and the restraint behind the speech:

> I have put away sorrow like a shoe that is worn out and muddy, for it is I have had a life that will be envied by great companies. It was not by a low birth I made kings uneasy, and they sitting in the halls of Emain. It was not a low thing to be chosen by Conchubor, who was wise, and Naisi had no match for bravery. It is not a small

---

[1] *Cuchulain of Muirthemne*, pp. 136–7. Compare Morris's description of the death of Gudrun at the end of *Sigurd the Volsung*.

thing to be rid of grey hairs, and the loosening of the teeth. [*With a sort of triumph.*] It was the choice of lives we had in the clear woods, and in the grave we're safe, surely. . . .

CONCHUBOR. She will do herself harm.

DEIRDRE [*showing Naisi's knife*]. I have a little way to unlock the prison of Naisi you'd shut upon his youth for ever. Keep back, Conchubor; for the High King who is your master has put his hands between us. [*She half turns to the grave.*] It was sorrows were foretold, but great joys were my share always; yet it is a cold place I must go to be with you, Naisi; and it's cold your arms will be this night that were warm about my neck so often. . . . It's a pitiful thing to be talking out when your ears are shut to me. It's a pitiful thing, Conchubor, you have done this night in Emain; yet a thing will be a joy and triumph to the end of life and time.

In comparison with this the stiff pseudo-Elizabethan verse of Yeats, the shadowy chorus, are lifeless:

CONCHUBOR.    How do I know that you have not some knife,
                      And go to die upon his body?

DEIRDRE.                       Have me searched,
                      If you would make so little of your queen.
                      It may be that I have a knife hid here
                      Under my dress. Bid one of these dark slaves
                      To search me for it. [*Pause.*]

CONCHUBOR.    Go to your farewells, queen.

DEIRDRE.        Now strike the wire, and sing to it a while,
                      Knowing that all is happy, and that you know
                      Within what bride-bed I shall lie this night,
                      And by what man, and lie close up to him
                      For the bed's narrow, and there outsleep the cock-
                      crow.          [*She goes behind the curtain.*]

FIRST MUSICIAN.  They are gone, they are gone.
                      The proud may lie by the proud.

SEC. MUSICIAN.  Though we were bidden to sing, cry nothing loud.

FIRST MUSICIAN.  They are gone, they are gone.

SEC. MUSICIAN.  Whispering were enough.

FIRST MUSICIAN.  Into the secret wilderness of their love.

SEC. MUSICIAN.  A high, grey cairn. What more is to be said?

FIRST MUSICIAN.  Eagles have gone into their cloudy bed.

The recognition and expression of 'ugly surprising things' was an element of poetry that Yeats did not master till later in life. It is apparent most clearly in the 'Crazy Jane' and 'Old Tom' poems. The derivation is through Synge from Villon; here is Synge's translation of 'An Old Woman's Lamentations':

The man I had a love for – a great rascal would kick me in the gutter – is dead thirty years and over it, and it is I am left behind, grey and aged. When I do be minding the good days I had, minding what I was one time, and what it is I'm come to, and when I do look on my own self, poor and dry, it wouldn't be much would set me raging in the streets. . . .

It's the way I am this day – my forehead is gone away into furrows, the hair of my head is grey and whitish, my eyebrows are tumbled from me, and my two eyes have died out within my head – those eyes that would be laughing to the men – my nose has a hook on it, my ears are hanging down, and my lips are sharp and skinny. That's what's left over from the beauty of a right woman – a bag of bones, and legs the like of two shrivelled sausages going beneath it.

Beside this we can set:

> Come, let me sing into your ear;
> Those dancing days are gone,
> All that silk and satin gear;
> Crouch upon a stone,
> Wrapping that foul body up
> In as foul a rag:
> *I carry the sun in a golden cup,*
> *The moon in a silver bag.*[1]

or 'Crazy Jane talks with the Bishop', or 'Crazy Jane on the Mountain' – and Yeats' characteristic refusal to change the adjective of 'great-bladdered Emer' at a publisher's request.[2] An old phrase remembered from a notable line: 'they say in the Aran Islands that if you speak overmuch of things of Faery your tongue becomes like a stone', is recast in a 'Dialogue of Self and Soul':

> Only the dead can be forgiven;
> But when I think of that my tongue's a stone.[3]

But Synge's characters with their wildness and sorrows seem to return in the later poetry. The Fools and Blind Men of Yeats' early plays are puppets; Crazy Jane and Red Mannion have vitality though not roundness; they are mouthpieces, crying aloud their disillusionment. Yeats uses his peasant characters as Wordsworth

[1] 'Those Dancing Days are Gone,' *C.P.*, p. 302.
[2] The account of the contest between the women in the snow has many sources: e.g. *Die Irische Helden* . . . by Rudolf Thurneysen, p. 428. The capacity of the bladder was thought to be related to sexual potency.
[3] *C.P.*, p. 265

used his, for a specific end, as symbols taking their place in the historical procession, foreshortening time. They are violent, brutal: reflected in rhythms that owe much to the Irish street-ballad, yet swerving from its clichés and its sentimentality with the deliberateness of high technique. It is a roaring drunken copulating world, foreshortened at the last with the vision of a hierarchical society:

> Sing the peasantry, and then
> Hard-riding country gentlemen,
> The holiness of monks, and after
> Porter-drinkers' randy laughter;
> Sing the lords and ladies gay
> That were beaten into the clay
> Through seven heroic centuries. . . .[1]

Indeed, in *Last Poems* there is much of Synge's brutality:

> Go your ways, O go your ways,
> I choose another mask,
> Girls down on the sea-shore
> Who understand the dark;
> Bawdy talk for the fishermen;
> A dance for the fisher-lads;
> When dark hangs upon the water
> They turn down their beds.
> *Daybreak and a candle-end.*[2]

Perhaps it was an aspect of the Anti-Self, or a simplification of civilization that was about to disintegrate. Perhaps it was a vision of what was heroic in the 1916 Rebellion, and old quarrels could be pardoned. But more likely it was the image of Goldsmith, joining hands with Swift, models on which he would remake himself in the knowledge of what Goldsmith, a wanderer like Synge, had gained:

> They walked the roads
> Mimicking what they heard, as children mimic;
> They understood that wisdom comes of beggary.[3]

Yeats seems to have been drawn to the beggar and the related imagery during the period of disillusionment, 1909–14. We may recognize a deliberate polarity between king and beggar, queen

---

[1] 'Under Ben Bulben,' *C.P.*, 397.
[2] 'The Wild Old Wicked Man,' ibid., p. 356.
[3] 'The Seven Sages,' ibid., p. 271.

and doxy, both now and in the period from 1930 onwards. The
dancing girl of 'Long-legged Fly' is also a queen and carries, like
Cleopatra, the doom of empires as well as her unselfconscious
childhood:

> . . . her feet
> Practise a tinker shuffle
> Picked up on the street.

Synge's demands for 'reality and joy', for the imagination that is
'fiery and magnificent and tender', seem to me emphasized in this
period.

To Yeats the long collaboration with Synge and Lady Gregory
became a kind of epic memory with the same thought:

> We three alone in modern times had brought
> Everything down to that sole test again,
> Dream of the noble and the beggar-man.[1]

But the death of one, and the rejection of the other, were part of
his tragedy. 'While Lady Gregory has brought herself to death's
door with overwork, to give us, while neglecting no other duty,
enough plays, translated or original, to keep the Theatre alive, our
base half-men of letters, or rather half-journalists, that coterie of
patriots who have never been bought because no one ever thought
them worth a price, have been whispering everywhere that she takes
advantage of her position as director to put her own plays upon the
stage. When I think, too, of Synge dying at this moment of their
bitterness and ignorance, as I believe, I wonder if I have been right
to shape my style to sweetness and serenity. . . .'[2]

It was, perhaps, fortunate that such shaping should have been
incomplete.

How Yeats might have developed, if Synge had lived, is a large
problem. I think myself that Synge's particular vein of ore had been
worked out, and that the mannered rhythms were, at the end,
growing monotonous and self-conscious. Yeats required support
and stimulus. He found his next dramatic models in the Nōh plays,
his next companionship with Ezra Pound: whose wild 'deliberate

[1] 'The Municipal Gallery Revisited,' *C.P.*, p. 368.
[2] *Autobiographies*, p. 482. See also Lady Gregory's *Hugh Lane*, Chapter XI,
and Joyce's *The Day of the Rabblement*.

nobility' gave Yeats at once an example and a warning. For the moment, the 'sweetness and serenity' of the 1910 publications is the last that can deserve those epithets for nearly eight years. There were plenty of events between 1910 and 1914 to enable him to study hatred.

# CHAPTER SIX

# The Study of Hatred

... I dreamed of enlarging Irish hate till we had come to hate with a passion of patriotism what Morris and Ruskin hated ...

*Poetry and Tradition.*

I study hatred with great diligence,
For that's a passion in my own control ...

'Ribh Considers Christian Love Insufficient.'

A poet, when he is growing old, will ask himself if he cannot keep his mask and his vision without new bitterness, new disappointment.

*Per Amica Silentia Lunae,* p. 41.

You say that we must not hate. You are right, but we may, & sometimes must be indignant and speak it. Hate is a kind of 'passive suffering' but indignation is a kind of joy. – *Letters to Dorothy Wellesley,* p. 126.

*Saeva Indignatio* and the labourer's hire. ...

'Blood and the Moon', ii.

The turning-point, or watershed, as a recent critic has called it, of Yeats' poetry is usually considered to be the period that produced the poems in *Responsibilities.* There were, it seems, two important experiences. The first was the affair of the Lane Pictures. Hugh Lane had collected a number of French paintings of great importance; they were part of a modern art exhibition in Dublin in 1905. The group consists of thirty-nine pictures, including works by Pissarro, Mancini, Renoir, Manet, Puvis de Chavannes, Corot, Courbet, Philippe Rousseau, Ingres, Daumier, Forain, Fantin-Latour, Vuillard, Boudin, Bonvin, Maris, J. L. Brown and Alfred Stevens. Of these, Puvis de Chavannes, Corot and Ingres are mentioned by Yeats, as of special significance to him. Lane thought that his pictures should be suitably housed by the Corporation of Dublin. Lutyens had designed a bridge building for the new collection: the choice of both architect and site met with furious and abusive opposition from the Nationalist Press. Private subscriptions were called for to obviate an increase of the rates. Tempers ran high; Lane took away the pictures and lent them to the National Gallery in London. In 1915, before sailing to America, he drafted a codicil to his will, revoking his intended gift of the pictures to the National Gallery, and bequeathing them to Dublin, on condition that a suitable gallery to house them was provided within five years of his death. Lady Gregory was appointed sole trustee, an act which seems clear evidence of Lane's intention to give the pictures to Ireland.

But the codicil was not witnessed, and Lane was drowned on the *Lusitania*. In the welter of war-time politics, continually importuning all who might have political, or financial, or aesthetic interest, to see that the spirit of the codicil was fulfilled, Lady Gregory laboured till 1928 without result. For many years the Dublin Municipal Gallery, with a fine dramatic instinct, kept ready for them a large empty room, tenanted only by a bust of Hugh Lane. They have now been returned.

The whole incident, the revelation of sectarian and political animosity as well as the philistinism of the mob, affected Yeats profoundly. The second poem in *Responsibilities* (the first is in the earlier manner), is addressed 'To a Wealthy Man who promised a Second Subscription to the Dublin Municipal Gallery if it were proved the People wanted Pictures'.[1]

> You gave, but will not give again
> Until enough of Paudeen's pence
> By Biddy's halfpennies have lain
> To be some 'sort of evidence',
> Before you'll put your guineas down,
> That things it were a pride to give
> Are what the blind and ignorant town
> Imagines best to make it thrive.

Yeats had taken a great interest in Lane's collection for a considerable time before the incident, but his indignation against the mob had been simmering for some years in prose. Even in 1909 he was writing of the new 'ill-breeding in Ireland' in relation to the *Playboy* controversy, and that too, bred a six-line epigram in

[1] *C.P.*, p. 119.

*Responsibilities.* 'Those who accuse Synge of some base motive are the great-grandchildren of those Dublin men who accused Smith O'Brien of being paid by the Government to fail. It is of such as these Goethe thought when he said "The Irish always seem to me like a pack of hounds dragging down some noble stag."'[1] And again: 'When *The Countess Cathleen* was produced, the very girls in the shops complained to us that to describe an Irishwoman as selling her soul to the devil was to slander the country.'[2] As Charles Ricketts had commented, 'Yeats is obviously discouraged by Ireland and things Irish. . . . The Irish are odious with their barn-door politics and hen-run ethics.'[3] But throughout this controversy Yeats had tried, at least, to shape his style to 'sweetness and sincerity'. Now he let himself go. The refrain takes on a fiercer cleaner note in what is perhaps the most powerful of the political ballads:[4]

> What need you, being come to sense,
> But fumble in a greasy till
> And add the halfpence to the pence
> And prayer to shivering prayer, until
> You have dried the marrow from the bone;
> For men were born to pray and save:
> Romantic Ireland's dead and gone,
> It's with O'Leary in the grave.

O'Leary, who died in 1907, had become for Yeats a kind of symbol of national integrity. He stood high in the councils of the Fenian Brotherhood, and for a time Yeats shared lodgings with him.[5] 'There are things a man must not do to save a nation,' he had once told me, and when I asked what things, had said 'To cry in public'.

In the verses that follow there is an account of the 'patriot' party that, in cold print, runs on the edge of sentimentality. But Yeats twists and lightens it with the ambivalent 'delirium' in the sixth line, lending an edge to the theme of 'heroic defeat' that is developed so fully in *Last Poems*:

[1] *Autobiographies*, p. 483. Yeats returns frequently to this image; e.g. 'Pull down established honour . . .'
[2] 'The Irish Dramatic Movement,' *P. & C.*, p. 63.
[3] *Self Portrait*, p. 121. This is in 1905.
[4] 'September 1913,' *C.P.*, p. 120. I think it probable that the poem owes something, in rhythm and general character, to Villon's *Ballade des Pendus*, which he had read in Swinburne's translation as well as in Synge's prose.
[5] *Autobiographies*, pp. 209 et seq.

> Was it for this the wild geese spread
> The grey wing upon every tide;
> For this that all that blood was shed,
> For this Edward Fitzgerald died,
> And Robert Emmet and Wolfe Tone,
> All that delirium of the brave?
> Romantic Ireland 's dead and gone,
> It 's with O'Leary in the grave.

Now it is at least arguable that the Lane affair was seized on by Yeats as the pretext for the expression of an anger that had been simmering since the death of Synge. The Lane pictures, though of undisputed excellence, have acquired a notoriety that owes more to the debate over their ownership than to their merits as pictures. If tempers had not flared so high, on either side, a reasonable settlement could have been negotiated.[1] But there was much emotion waiting to be transposed from prose to verse:

> The root of it all is that the political class in Ireland – the lower-middle class from whom the patriotic associations have drawn their journalists and their leaders for the last ten years – have suffered through the cultivation of hatred as the one energy of their movement, a deprivation which is the intellectual equivalent to a certain surgical operation. Hence the shrillness of their voices. They contemplate all creative power as the eunuchs contemplate Don Juan as he passes through Hell on the white horse.[2]

This becomes, with memories (I believe) of the Ricketts painting, 'On those that hated "The Playboy of the Western World", 1907:'

> Once, when midnight smote the air,
> Eunuchs ran through Hell and met
> On every crowded street to stare
> Upon great Juan riding by:
> Even like these to rail and sweat
> Staring upon his sinewy thigh.[3]

Living and dead converge processionally in the flame of anger. Lady Gregory and Hugh Lane had suffered equally from the journalists who had attacked them:

[1] I am indebted to Jack B. Yeats, and to Mr. Kelly of the Municipal Gallery, for these opinions.

[2] *Autobiographies*, p. 486.

[3] *C.P.*, p. 124.

> Now all the truth is out,
> Be secret and take defeat
> From any brazen throat,
> For how can you compete,
> Being honour bred, with one
> Who, were it proved he lies,
> Were neither shamed in his own
> Nor in his neighbours' eyes?[1]

He thinks himself into the stream of history: 'To a Shade'[2] is addressed to Lady Gregory, who is compared with Lane:

> A man
> Of your own passionate serving kind . . .
> . . . has been driven from the place,
> And insult heaped upon him for his pains. . . .

The bitter fable of 'The Three Beggars'[3] shows Yeats himself as the lonely heron, another version of The Fisherman, which became the dominant image of *The Resurrection*:

> *I've stood as I were made of stone*
> *And seen the rubbish run about,*
> *It's certain there are trout somewhere*
> *And maybe I shall take a trout*
> *If but I do not seem to care.*

Four of the poems in *Responsibilities* deal with beggars. Naked man is the theme; the sequence of the poems is a gesture of renunciation in the face of defeat as well as a katharsis of anger. We know the great Platonic image of man as the spiritual beggar; this archetype occurs in the Irish poems of Raftery, and in the Nōh plays. But behind them all there is the image of Lear, and 'unaccommodated man'. The past is thrown away: the famous 'A Coat', the rejection of the 'embroideries', is well known, but rings a little false. I do not know what special comments in the Irish Press evoked it: but there is evidence throughout the minor verse of the period for Bowra's

---

[1] 'To a Friend Whose Work has Come to Nothing,' *C.P.*, p. 122. (This is, according to Lady Gregory, of Lane. But Yeats points out (ibid., pp. 444–5) that he meant Lady Gregory.
[2] Ibid., p. 123. Compare 'An Appointment' (*C.P.*, p. 141); and Lady Gregory, *Hugh Lane*, Chapter VIII.
[3] *C.P.*, p. 124. The mysterious 'lebeen-lone' of the opening stanza is a phonetic rendering of *libín leamhan*, small fish or minnows.

suggestion that Yeats' Celtic mythology was then being widely exploited by others. Perhaps it is an echo of the controversy with 'A.E.' and his circle. It was not a complete renunciation, for he returned to the embroideries again. More vivid and direct is the ending of 'The Dolls', with its touch of pity.

But the most impressive poem in the volume is 'The Cold Heaven', the first in which the debt to the metaphysical poets appears to be clearly defined. In 1912 Sir Herbert Grierson had sent him the new edition of Donne; to which Yeats had replied: 'I . . . find that at last I can understand Donne. Your notes tell me exactly what I want to know. Poems that I could not understand or could but vaguely understand are now clear and I notice that the more precise and learned the thought the greater the beauty, the passion; the intricacy and subtleties of his imagination are the length and depths of the furrow made by his passion. His pedantry and his obscenity – the rock and loam of his Eden – but make us the more certain that one who is but a man like us all has seen God.'[1]

It is necessary to give 'The Cold Heaven'[2] in full. It was occasioned by the marriage of Maud Gonne to MacBride.

> Suddenly I saw the cold and rook-delighting heaven
> That seemed as though ice burned and was but the more ice,
> And thereupon imagination and heart were driven
> So wild that every casual thought of that and this
> Vanished, and left but memories, that should be out of season
> With the hot blood of youth, of love crossed long ago;
> And I took all the blame out of all sense and reason,
> Until I cried and trembled and rocked to and fro,
> Riddled with light. Ah! when the ghost begins to quicken,
> Confusion of the death-bed over, is it sent
> Out naked on the roads, as the books say, and stricken
> By the injustice of the skies for punishment?

Here is a new metre and a new rhythmical treatment, sinewy and economical and direct. Perhaps it marks the return of vision – which he had misdoubted was still alive, through such long pre-occupation with affairs[3] – with an intensity which begins to purify

[1] Grierson, Preface to Menon, *The Development of William Butler Yeats*, p. xiii; Wade, p. 570.
[2] *C.P.*, p. 140.
[3] See p. 110.

the verse. Intellect and emotion are 'wild', and the word has overtones in Irish idiom of fierceness, gaiety and abnormality of conduct,
along with energy and sexual power.[1] The rooks, in that aerial tumult
of wildness one sees sometimes in winter, form an image which has
enough of the ominous, the overtones of the 'rooky wood', to
balance the metaphysical fire and ice. But the image is even more
complex than it appears. Yeats may have had in mind Empedocles'
statement that there are two suns, one of fire,[2] and one a reflection
in the concave mirror of ice we call the sky. He alludes to Empedocles several times, as in 'The Gyres':

> Empedocles has thrown all things about.[3]

But the ice-fire image may be a memory of his much-read Pater —

> In Michelangelo's poems frost and fire are almost the only images –
> the refining fire of the goldsmith.[4]

In the early manner, Yeats would have lingered on the images,
drawn them out; now they are touched and tossed aside in the
slip-stream of the rhythm. In this moment all evil and error are
accepted, with their pain; 'out of all sense' is again an Irish idiom
which may be unfamiliar – 'to an extent far beyond what common
sense could justify' – combined with the ambiguity 'beyond the
reach of sensation'. The experience embodies, mystically, old age
and death. All that remains are the great moments of his love, the
faint potential nostalgia redeemed from sentimentality by the setting,
and he will nurse that memory to the end. Now for a mystical instant
it is all apparent, and he himself, dying that death for love – perhaps
a Donne-memory? – is a ghost; that is not set free from the body
until some days after apparent death.[5] In the prevision of the
ghost's destiny he is thinking of this 'living backward' which is the
fate of spirits. 'They examine their past if undisturbed by our

---

[1] Cf. 'The Wild Old Wicked Man,' *C.P.*, p. 356.
[2] Eisler, *The Royal Art of Astrology*, p. 234.
[3] *C.P.*, p. 337.
[4] *The Renaissance*, 'The Poetry of Michelangelo'. But perhaps we tend to
search for over-complicated sources. Yeats uses throughout much elemental
and commonplace symbolism.
[5] This is Berkeley's belief also. Compare, too, *A Vision* (A), p. 223: 'Now
in its turn the *Spirit* gradually awakens, and it is said that the awakening may
begin with the sight of a flower upon the grave. . . .'

importunity, tracing events to their sources, and as they take the form their thought suggests, seem to live backward through time.'[1] This is again the thought of 'A Dialogue':

> I am content to follow to its source,
> Every event in action or in thought;
> Measure the lot, forgive myself the lot![2]

Again the thought appears in the later poems: a moment of vision, in which a particular setting clarifies past and present, precipitating what is irrelevant. So in 'Stream and Sun at Glendalough':

> Repentance keeps my heart impure;
> But what am I that dare
> Fancy that I can
> Better conduct myself or have more
> Sense than a common man?

> What motion of the sun or stream
> Or eyelid shot the gleam
> That pierced my body through?
> What made me live like these that seem
> Self-born, born anew?[3]

It is significant that Yeats is now aware of events forming a time pattern: Maud Gonne's daughter is the centre of the two songs 'To a Child dancing in the Wind.' He is building his legend about that love, dramatizing it; there are precedents in Dante and Petrarch:

> And what of her that took
> All till my youth was gone
> With scarce a pitying look?
> How could I praise that one?
> When day begins to break
> I count my good and bad,
> Being wakeful for her sake,
> Remembering what she had,
> What eagle look still shows. . . .[4]

---

[1] *Wheels and Butterflies*, p. 34.
[2] 'A Dialogue of Self and Soul,' *C.P.*, p. 265. But this was not the original reading.
[3] Ibid., p. 288. 'Shot the gleam' is the Annunciation-image; see Chapter 10.
[4] 'Friends,' ibid., p. 139.

Besides 'The Cold Heaven', the important poem in *Responsibilites* is 'The Magi'.[1] It is of interest because it seems to be the first mention of the birth of Christ regarded as a world-breaking event, the end of a gyre, the beginning of a new one. It is complicated because the centre is a personal vision, but we can see, like the rock strata in a quarry, the historical pattern of Yeats' technique:

> Now as at all times I can see in the mind's eye,
> In their stiff, painted clothes, the pale unsatisfied ones
> Appear and disappear in the blue depth of the sky
> With all their ancient faces like rain-beaten stones,
> And all their helms of silver hovering side by side,
> And all their eyes still fixed, hoping to find once more,
> Being by Calvary's turbulence unsatisfied,
> The uncontrollable mystery on the bestial floor.

The vision may have its origin in some remembered Italian or pre-Raphaelite Nativity, perhaps Mantegna's, and there is a possible clue in Yeats' Preface to W. T. Horton's *A Book of Images*:

> I closed my eyes a moment ago, and a company of people in blue robes swept by me in a blinding light, and had gone before I had done more than see little roses embroidered on the hems of their robes,[2] and confused, blossoming apple boughs somewhere beyond them, and recognized one of the company by his square, black, curling beard. I have often seen him; and one night a year ago, I asked him questions which he answered by showing me flowers and precious stones, of whose meaning I had no knowledge, and seemed too perfected a soul for any knowledge that cannot be spoken in symbol or metaphor.[3]

It is clear that this is something different from Horton's own picture of the Magi, which is a bad piece of drawing that owes much to William Morris; and indeed the description of the decoration suggests that painter. The Magi are, however, a part of Yeats' 'capricious and variable world'. As in Ben Jonson, they tell of a prodigious and monstrous birth, a threat to their land.

The period of *Responsibilities* coincides with that in which he found further cause for hatred. The Dublin mob that had rejected

---

[1] *C.P.*, p. 141.
[2] This appears to be associated with the 'red-rose-bordered hem' of 'To Ireland in the Coming Times,' ibid., p. 56.
[3] P. 13.

Lane's pictures, set upon Parnell, and vilified *The Playboy*, had led
women like Constance Markiewicz astray:

> Blind and leader of the blind
> Drinking the foul ditch where they lie.[1]

So, too, with the 'loveliest woman born', though she, indeed, was
taking little part in politics by then. This political scene seems to
have provided Yeats with just that pretext he wanted for cultivating
his self-frustration, so that it might be released. In this he had the
approval of Ezra Pound, who reviewed *Responsibilities*:

> There is a new robustness; there is the tooth of satire which is
> in Mr Yeats' case, too good a tooth to keep hidden. . . . There are
> a lot of fools to be killed and Mr Yeats is an exultant slaughtermaster
> when he will but turn from ladies with excessive chevelure appearing
> in pearl-pale nuances.[2]

Synge, from whom he might have drawn a more dispassionate
stability, was no longer there to help. Pound's mind and talk
offered many things; pity for the under-dog, a studied violence
of language, an attempt to combine a classical impatience with the
Nineties and all they stood for in pattern and form with the intensity
of the last Romantics. And perhaps, as Häusermann has suggested
in his study of Yeats as a figure of Phase 23,[3] he learnt from Pound's
defects of formlessness, over-emphasis on technical devices, and
occasional unintelligibility.

At the end of *Responsibilities* he is again at Coole Park under
Lady Gregory's roof. There is some quietening of the anger, but
Yeats seems to be doing no more than argue himself into a temporary
calm of mind:

> *I can forgive even that wrong of wrongs,*
> *Those undreamt accidents that have made me*
> *– Seeing that Fame has perished this long while,*
> *Being but a part of ancient ceremony –*

---

[1] 'On a Political Prisoner,' *C.P.*, p. 206. Compare *Upanishads*, p. 51:

> Fools brag of their knowledge, proud, ignorant, dissolving;
> staggering to and fro, blind and led by the blind.

The image is used in the second movement of 'A Dialogue of Self and Soul'.

[2] Quoted by H. W. Häusermann, *W. B. Yeats' Criticism of Ezra Pound.*
v. p. 52.

[3] H. W. Haüsermann, *op. cit.*

> *Notorious, till all my priceless things*
> *Are but a post the passing dogs defile.*[1]

But he could never forgive them. The image of hatred and bitterness was too valuable a mask to set aside. I do not understand James Stephens' contention[2] that Yeats was incapable of hatred, but could only achieve scorn; since his every instinct was to control the expression of hatred into a traditional form with the restraints proper to it, and this was in turn proper to the aristocratic poise and pose. I do not suggest that Yeats' attitude was disinterested, for always the experience is related to himself. It was a method of cultivating a specific antithetic personality:

> To oppose the new ill-breeding of Ireland, which may in a few years destroy all that has given Ireland a distinguished name in the world. . . . I can only set up a secondary or interior personality created out of the tradition of myself, and the personality (alas, only possible to me in my writings) must be always gracious and simple. It must have that slight separation from interests which makes charm possible, while remaining near enough for passion.[3]

Now this was written in 1909. It shows another side of Yeats, and a less pleasant one; a possibility (which the Body of Fate was to spare him) of a studied literary pose deriving from Pater. But fortunately he was not consistent in this, and the allegiance to Pater was fading. 'Surely the ideal of culture expressed by Pater can only create feminine souls. The soul becomes a mirror not a brazier.'[4]

The final self-justification is seen in *A Full Moon in March*, in the poem 'Ribh Considers Christian Love Insufficient'. Hatred is 'a passion in my own control'. His soul, freed by it from terror and impurities, can find its true nature, the truth belonging to its past life, and to its future. As such, it breaks down into mysticism, the union of opposites:

---

[1] 'Closing Rhyme,' *C.P.*, p. 143. In 1916 he said to Ricketts: 'Ireland is like a man diseased who can only think of his disease' (Ricketts, op. cit., p. 268). The reference in the last line is to a passage in George Moore's early version of *Hail and Farewell*, which had been serialized in some magazine. The metaphor is taken from Erasmus (*1930 Diary*, p. 46).

[2] Broadcast, January 1948.

[3] *Autobiographies*, p. 463.

[4] Ibid., p. 477.

> Thought is a garment and the soul's a bride
> That cannot in that trash and tinsel hide:
> Hatred of God may bring the soul to God.[1]

But that is the last stage. From *Responsibilities* onward the mask of hatred will serve so many imagined aspects of the Anti-Self; Swift, Blake, Landor, Lane, Timon, all could be dramatized.

> Out of Ireland have we come.
> Great hatred, little room,
> Maimed us at the start.
> I carry from my mother's womb
> A fanatic heart.[2]

The ten years that followed were to complicate that fanaticism in many ways.

[1] 'Supernatural Songs,' *C.P.*, p. 330. The image seems to come from Porphyry: 'The body is a garment with which the soul is invested.' See also Shelley's *Epipsychidion*.
[2] 'Remorse for Intemperate Speech,' *C.P.*, p. 287.

# CHAPTER SEVEN

# Between Extremities

> Between extremities
> Man runs his course;
> A brand, or flaming breath,
> Comes to destroy
> All those antinomies
> Of day and night.
>       —'Vacillation', I.

I

An understanding of the Yeatsian 'theory of opposites' is central to our understanding. That echo of Platonism is apparent as early as *John Sherman* in 1891, but the dichotomy would have been emphasized by his studies for the edition of Blake. 'Without contraries is no progression.' His motto in the Golden Dawn had certified the paradox: *Demon Deus est inversus*, and here a passage from 'A.E.' is illuminating:

> There is, I think, some necessity for the descent of the spiritual into the bodily to gather strength, while the demoniac in us is for ever trying to make captive the spiritual beauty to sweeten its dark delights[1] . . . It is vain to say the demon does not worship the beautiful. That worship is in almost all art and literature. It is in those strange heads drawn by Da Vinci where spirit and sense co-exist in an almost sinister companionship in the same face . . .[2]

Antinomies and paradoxes were certified in all the 'sacred books', particularly in Heraclitus, Plotinus, Donne, Swedenborg, Nietzsche. From this comes his theory of the opposing psychological types,

---

[1] cf.                      I offer to love's play
                    My dark declivities. (*C.P.*, p. 312).
[2] *Song and its Fountains*, pp. 30–31.

'objective' and 'subjective'; two terms which can give rise to a great deal of confusion, since his usage is a special one. From it comes his cyclic theory, as in the gyres. The interlocking, counter-rotating cones of the gyres, though they point towards the qualities of the sphere and circle, move in contrary senses. They are the result of the descent of man into the corporeal world. So we have the antinomies of hot and cold, moist and dry (the alchemical theory of the humours with which he was familiar from many writings); male and female; water and fire; the Yin and Yang (yen and yin).[1] Thus man runs his course between spiritual and corporeal, between the fire of spirituality and the lush green leaf; the tree that is half-flame and half-green foliage is a compressed symbol of this.

Every action, even the smallest, moves towards its opposite, and then relapses into its first condition. Thus a physical act progresses from inertia to violence, and returns to inertia again.[2] A civilization passes from barbaric materialism to a search for its opposite, the spiritual, aesthetic and intellectual achievement which is symbolized in part by Byzantium. Athens, Greece, Alexandria, types of the rational, is destroyed by the impact of the irrational in *The Resurrection*; 'the heart of a phantom is beating'. Every personality desires its opposite. The cat and the moon, the earthbound and the heavenly body, are attracted and linked by material sympathy. Man not only seeks his opposite but 'always tries to become his opposite – to become what he would abhor if he did not desire it'. He desires it because he feels that he needs, not merely the fullness and roundness of personality, but the *dramatic* complement of those whose lack has given rise to frustration. So the Saint would become the swordsman, the scholar-recluse the soldier and lover. In the mutations of history the same principle is perceived. If the Greek civilization is fully subjective, the Hebrew which precedes it must be objective. And this principle holds good for all ages, even the present.:

> When a civilization ends, task having led to task, until everybody was bored, the whole thing turns bottom upwards, Nietzsche's 'transvaluation of all values'.[3]

[1] *W. & B.*, p. 103.

[2] This is the opening argument of the *Summa* of Aquinas.

[3] *On the Boiler*, p. 25. For a discussion of the debt to Nietzsche, see Engelberg's *The Vast Design*.

So it is in the supernatural world. Yeats accepted, wholly or partially, Plutarch's account of the Daemon, the guardian spirit; which is familiar from the dramatic presentation of that belief in *Antony and Cleopatra.* 'Plutarch's precepts have it that a strange living man may win for Daemon an illustrious dead man; but now I add another thought: the Daemon comes not as like to like but seeing its own opposite.'[1]

In this way the fighting hero Cuchulain has for his daemons 'convicted cowards'. Yeats' daemon in 'Byzantium' is death to his life, life to his death. It is another variant of the often repeated gnomic quotation from Heraclitus: 'Men and gods die each other's life, live each other's death.' These are the words with which 'The Greek' concludes *The Resurrection.*

On the initial premise of the antinomies most of Yeats' metaphysic is based. We can see the invocation of the complementary aspects, or their imagined subvention, as a step in the progression towards unity. So —

> By the help of an image
> I call to my own opposite, summon all
> That I have handled last, least looked upon.[2]

The image may take a multiplicity of forms. Imagined violence, leadership in war; horsemanship, in family tradition or in Robert Gregory; the fisherman; the roaring tinker or journeyman; Dante; Hector and Achilles; Swift and Berkeley in their assertion of the supreme intellect, sanctity without orthodoxy, that rejects Von Hügel, but speaks in favour of ancient heresies through Ribh the Hermit.

I do not think that any solution emerges in earthly being from this dialectic. The solution is in eternity, where we, and all lovers, are 'adrift on that miraculous sea'. The poems and plans that sharpen the opposing polarities grow more brutal and more violent as the physical solution recedes. 'Crown of gold and dung of swine' confront each other in *A Full Moon in March,* and

> . . . Love has pitched his mansion in
> The place of excrement.

[1] *P.A.S.L.,* p. 29.
[2] *C.P.,* p. 180.

The thought might be Swift's, or Villon's, or Odo's.[1] Resolution of the conflict on a woman's breast (as in 'The Wild Old Wicked Man') is momentary, a gesture or emblem of ultimate union. Even in 'Ribh at the Tomb . . .' the angelic marriage may be illusory;

> For the intercourse of angels is a light
> When, for *its moment*, both *seem* lost, consumed.

Only in the tiny fragment 'There'[2] is the assertion of this final unity in the classical symbol of the sphere:

> There all the barrel-hoops are knit,
> There all the serpent-tails are bit,
> There all the gyres converge in one,
> There all the planets drop in the Sun.

## II

At the centre of Yeats' view of the sexual act is the traditional one of both Hindu and Kabbalistic mythology. In it is symbolized the reconciliation of all opposites in the divine world. The lovers, the paired extremities, can achieve perfect unison only in the after-life; but earthly union may offer a Platonic shadow of the joy that is eternity. Perfect consummation would result in the cessation of time:

> Yet the world ends when these two things,
> Though several, are a single light,
> When oil and wick are burned in one.
> Therefore a blessed moon last night
> Gave Sheba to her Solomon.[3]

Oil, wick, candle, flame, torch are all traditional symbols, and for the antinomy we may remember *Hamlet*.

The same holds good in the relationships between men and women. 'Young, we discover an opposite through our love.' 'When a man loves a girl it should be because her face and character offer what he lacks, the more profound his nature the more should he realize the lack and the greater be the difference. It is as though he

[1] Of Cluny.
[2] *C.P.*, p. 329.
[3] 'Solomon and the Witch,' ibid., p. 199.

wanted to take his own death into his arms....'[1] Vacillation is implicit
in the act of love. 'The Three Bushes' concerns the Lady's attempt
at a compromise. She will think herself spirit; the Chambermaid will
provide the flesh:

> He shall love my soul as though
> Body were not all,
> He shall love your body
> Untroubled by the soul,
> Love cram love's two divisions
> Yet keep his substance whole.

So the woman in 'A Last Confession' is aware, without illusion as
to its spirituality, of the nature of the body:

> Flinging from his arms I laughed
> To think his passion such
> He fancied that I gave a soul
> Did but our bodies touch,
> And laughed upon his breast to think
> Beast gave beast as much.[2]

But her vision includes the final perfection of spiritual union in
death:

> I gave what other women gave
> That stepped out of their clothes,
> But when the soul its body off
> Naked to naked goes,
> He it has found shall find therein
> What none other knows.[3]

The wise man is aware of these antinomies, in himself and in the
great men of history. He finds a precedent for living cautiously in
obedience to the double thrust of mortality. Dante 'finds room
among his virtues for lechery'. There is ample justification from
philosophy and psychology.[4]

Opposites can only be resolved in the after-life; and this contrived
opposition is a necessary condition of life. 'Could these two impulses
... be reconciled all life would cease.' True love is only possible in
the divine world:

[1] *On the Boiler*, p. 22.
[2] *C.P.* p. 313.
[3] Ibid.
[4] See, *passim*. Martin's *Experiment in Depth*: and Jung's *The Secret of the
Golden Flower*, which Yeats had read.

And I that have not your faith, how shall I know
That in the blinding light beyond the grave
We'll find so good a thing as we have lost?[1]

– so that 'the intercourse of angels' is as important to Ribh as it was
to Milton and Swedenborg. The symbol of the divine world is, as
always, the sphere which stands for divine perfection, symmetry,
the mystery of completion:

> . . . I take
> That stillness for a theme
> Where his heart and my heart did seem
> And both adrift on that miraculous stream
> Where – wrote a learned astrologer –
> The Zodiac is changed into a sphere.[2]

This poem, 'Chosen', is one of the finest, and most complex, of the
sequence 'A Woman Young and Old'. The souls of the lovers are
on the 'miraculous stream' of the Milky Way, the *Via Lactea* of
the seventeenth-century imagination. It opens with Plato's Myth of
Er: the souls in heaven, resting between incarnations, 'choose' the
lots that represent their destinies in the after life. In it is embodied
Plotinus' essay, *The Heavenly Circuit*: the Zodiac-sphere is explained
in *A Vision*.[3] Yet none of the complexities could tarnish the magnificence of Yeats' rhetoric.

### III

The same antinomies pervade the material of the Celtic Revival.
Were the 'dusty deeds' ever capable of significant alignment with the
Irish political situation, in 1798 or in 1916? How forced were the
allegorical structures of, say, *Cathleen-ni-Houlihan* and *The Countess
Cathleen*? Was it merely good fortune that Oliver Sheppard's statue
should provide a credible link between Cuchulain and the Easter
Rising? The ancient legends on which so much Yeatsian theory
depended had even fewer roots in the Irish peasant memory than
had the Mabinogion in the Welsh. After the first excitement of
exploration the tensions were considerable. John Eglinton thought

---

[1] *C.P.* p. 102.
[2] Ibid., p. 311.
[3] (B) pp. 210, 240. See also 'Veronica's Napkin,' *C.P.*, p. 270.

E

that 'these ancient legends obstinately refuse to be taken up out of their environment and be translated into the world of modern sympathies': Jung and his archetypes were still unknown. The legends were, indeed, hardly familiar enough even for satire, though an attempt had been made by Eimar O'Duffy in *King Goshawk and the Birds*; the great field of traditional Irish satirical writing was hardly opened by the ploughs of the Abbey.[1] I suspect that George Moore's wish was an empty one:

> Art may rest for a space in this forlorn Atlantic island . . . re-knitting herself to the tradition which existed before England was in many tales of chivalry.[2]

And, always, there was the real or potential conflict of the Celtic Revival with the Church; mainly because of the Protestant background of those that wrote of it. 'A.E.''s worship of the Elder Gods was regarded with a slightly suspicious tolerance; his eccentricities no more than an embroidery on his very real services to the Department of Agriculture. Heresy had been found in *The Countess*, and it is difficult to appreciate the suspicion which Yeats had aroused. MacKenna wrote to 'A.E.' of the hostile review of the Collected Edition, 1908–9 which the Editor of *The Freeman's Journal* wanted to arrange:

> . . . he would have given it to a good fellow who, I don't know why, honestly thought W.B. raised up by the devil to corrupt and humiliate holy Ireland, and himself raised up by God and I think the Virgin Mary to save and protect her.[3]

[1] See, in particular, Vivian Mercier's *The Irish Comic Tradition*.
[2] Preface to *The Bending of the Bough*.
[3] *Memoirs and Journals*, p. 38.

# CHAPTER EIGHT

# The Development of Style

I persuaded myself that I had a passion for the dawn, and this passion, though mainly histrionic like a child's play, an ambitious game, had moments of sincerity. Years afterwards when I had finished *The Wanderings of Oisin*, dissatisfied with its yellow and its dull green, with all that overcharged colour inherited from the romantic movement, I deliberately reshaped my style, deliberately sought out an impression as of cold light and tumbling clouds. I cast off traditional metaphors and loosened my rhythm, and recognizing that all the criticism of life known to me was alien and English, became as emotional as possible but with an emotion which I described to myself as cold. – *Autobiographies*, p. 74.

I said, 'A line will take us hours maybe;
Yet if it does not seem a moment's thought
Our stitching and unstitching has been naught.'
'Adam's Curse'.

Yeats completed 'The Wanderings of Oisin' in the late summer of 1888. The beginning of the change in style is usually ascribed to the period 1910–12, though there are signs of self-criticism as early as 1904; his phrase 'years afterwards' is deliberately vague. It should be linked to what he called the 'Body of Fate', physical circumstance, such as the friendship with Synge, the political embroilments of 1909–14, the reading of metaphysical poetry, the love and bitterness from his affair with Maud Gonne, as much as to any deliberate assumption of a new role; although in view of his highly conscious artistry this aspect cannot be overlooked. But statements such as these are of interest in considering his conception of style. He insists again and again on its difficulty, and the perpetual revisions of the early work are an indication of the importance of the *labor limae*:

It was many years before I understood that I had surrendered myself to the chief temptation of the artist, creation without toil.

Metrical composition is always very difficult to me, nothing is done upon the first day. . . . At that time I had not formed a style. . . .[1]

As examples of this revision, that results at times in something approaching Shakespearean 'continuous copy', *The Rose* poems of 1892 were revised and reprinted in 1895 and 1899. Further revisions were carried out in 1925 (*Early Poems and Stories*) and in *Poems of 1927.*[2] In the Dedication to the former, Yeats wrote:

> . . . The Irish form of Victorian rhetoric [this is presumably Davis, Mangan, Ferguson, Allingham, and derives ultimately from Macaulay, modified by Tom Moore] had declined into a patriotic extravagance that offended all educated minds . . . But Victor Hugo and Swinburne had so delighted our schooldays that we distrusted our habitual thoughts. I tried after the publication of *The Wanderings of Oisin* to write of nothing but emotion, and in the simplest language, and now I have to go through it all, cutting out or altering passages that are sentimental from lack of thought. Are we not always doomed to see our world as the Stoics foretold, consumed alternately by fire and water? Upon the other hand, I cannot have altogether failed in simplicity, for these poems, written before my seven and twentieth years, are still the most popular that I have written. A girl made profound by the first pride of beauty, though all but a child still, once said to me, 'Innocence is the highest achievement of the human intellect', and as we are encouraged to believe that our intellects grow with our years I may be permitted the conviction that – grown a little nearer innocence – I have found a more appropriate simplicity.

The 'Irish form of Victorian rhetoric', which still persists among the books of verse used by schoolchildren, was remarkable for its chauvinism, sentimentality, mock-heroics, and general bad taste. There are many anthologies of it. Yeats was familiar with one of the better selections, *Irish Minstrelsy*, edited by Halliday Sparling, and there are some echoes of this in his own verse. And as regards the place of the intellect, we may quote from an early letter to W. T. Horton:

> I hold as Blake would have held also, that the intellect must do its utmost 'before inspiration is possible'. It clears the rubbish from the mouth of the sybil's cave but it is not the sybil.[3]

[1] *Autobiographies*, p. 202.
[2] These are some of the years under which I have found some printed emendations to some at least, and often to many, of the poems in *The Rose*, 1890–91–92–95–99, 1900–01–04–06–07–12–13–20–23–25–27 (Allt).
[3] Wade, *Letters*, p. 262.

In 1927 he wrote:

> This volume contains what is, I hope, the final text of the poems of my youth; and yet it may not be, seeing that in it are not only the revisions from my *Early Poems and Stories*, published last year, but quite new revisions on which my heart is greatly set. . . .

And the revisions were integral with the growth of his own personality:

> The friends that have it I do wrong
> Whenever I remake a song,
> Should know what issue is at stake:
> It is myself that I remake.

There are several points of interest in these two extracts. Yeats conceives his own dramatic progress to be from the emotional to the intellectual. Emotion that has not simplicity becomes sentimental, and is dead wood to be cut away. Simplicity is equated with innocence, towards which he is progressing; it is not the innocence of Blake, but a return to a bare and cold style, in which symbols rather than verbal rhetoric carry the necessary complexity. Revision itself is a matter of both leisure and 'mood'; but the process is, clearly, continuous. James Stephens offers an interesting explanation.[1] 'There was a delayed knowledge in his mind. The back of his mind was not satisfied, and it harried him and worried him, so that he had to do it again and again, but at the last he got it.' I am inclined to question this last phrase. The decrease in revising activity after 1927 suggests a lack of concern with the earlier work in comparison with the new and absorbing phase of creative activity, rather than a sense of final achievement.

Yeats insists on the 'difficulty' of verse as of life, for this difficulty is proper to the second quadrant of the waxing moon:

> But while the moon is rounding towards the full
> He follows whatever whim's most difficult. . . .[2]

Style was, paradoxically, something that drew from life, yet had to be carefully cherished, since it was an aspect of the Anti-Self, and therefore to be built objectively, critically: 'Style, personality – deliberately adopted and therefore a mask – is the only escape from

[1] *The Observer*, July 1948.
[2] 'The Phases of the Moon,' *C.P.*, p. 183.

the hot-faced bargainers and the money-changers.'[1] It was, in consequence, viewed a little self-consciously, still in the Pater-Symons manner. 'I often wonder if my talent will ever recover from the heterogeneous labour of these last few years.'[2] The 'heterogeneous labour' was that of the Abbey Theatre, the quarrels with George Moore, the conflict with the Irish newspapers over *The Playboy*, and the incessant financial troubles of the theatre; the full story is in Ellis-Fermor's *The Irish Dramatic Movement*, and the emotional repercussions are to be seen in Lady Gregory's *Journals*. 'I cry out vainly for liberty and have ever less and less inner life. Evil comes to us men of imagination wearing as its mask all the virtues . . . I thought myself loving neither vice nor virtue, but virtue has come upon me and given me a nation instead of a home. Has it left me any lyrical faculty?' The gap had been a long one. *The Wind Among the Reeds* was published in 1899, *In the Seven Woods* in 1903, and *The Green Helmet* in 1910. The first dramatic period is at its peak between 1904 and 1906, under the stimulus of his Abbey Theatre work.

The dramatic poem *Mosada* (1886) has not, perhaps, received the attention it deserves as a specimen of early technique. It is, in fact, almost a copy-book specimen of the work of a young but potentially distinguished poet with an admirable ear for the music of his verse. The plot, and some of the language, is clearly in debt to Thomas Moore. The verse owes much to Shelley; *Alastor* was archetypal, in several ways, for the young poet in the nineteenth century:

> There in a dell
> A lily-blanchèd place, she sat and sang
> And in her singing wove around her head
> White lilies, and her song went forth after
> Along the sea . . .

The shadow of Tennyson is there too, transposed into Sligo memories:

> Oh! swallows, swallows, swallows will ye fly
> This eve, tomorrow, or tomorrow night
> Above the farmhouse by the little lake

---

[1] *Autobiographies*, p. 461.
[2] Ibid, p. 484.

That's rustling in the reeds with quiet pushes,
Soft as a long dead footstep whispering through
The brain.

The ineptitudes are clear – the clumsy first and second lines, the insufficient word *pushes*. But there is this same desire for safety and escape: so Elremar to the dying Mosada:

Dear heart, there is a secret way that leads
Its parent length towards the river's merge,
Where lies a shallop in the yellow reeds.
Awake, awake, and we will sail afar
Afar along the fleet white river's face –
Alone with our own whispers and replies –
Alone among the murmurs of the dawn.

The third and last lines of the extract show the conscious and subtle patternings, on the Tennysonian model, that are to be exploited later with endless tone-variations.

'The Wanderings of Oisin' was traditional. The 'yellow and dull green' are of the pre-Raphaelite formula, working on a myth that lacked the strength and ferocity of the Norse which had brought out the best in Morris; its tapestry-effects were changed by that luminous softness of a rain-filled countryside and the nostalgia that it brings. The West of Ireland is a country of ruins, of traces of old faiths, of legends, and of a great reverence for the dead. To its peasantry the supernatural is vivid and real, but in the main spasmodic and without continuity in narrative. The connected legends are literary, not popular; and yet fragments of the peasantry's beliefs could be seen as part of the great mythology. 'A.E.' could write to Yeats:

Ballyglass is a haunted place. I heard lots of faery tales while there, very much like the tales you gathered at Gort; one curious belief I never heard before. They will not weep at a death, but sit grim and silent, and if grief overpower them they go far away and sob in some lonely place, for they believe that to weep over the dead would attract the phantom hounds to chase the soul newly gone from the body. So until it has passed into the other world they maintain their silent sorrow.[1]

Given the material, the brotherhood of the Rhymers' Club, and the

[1] *Letters*, 'A.E.' to W. B. Y., 1 February 1898.

poetic diction of Wardour Street – faint but perceptible, and persisting far into the twenties – the elements of 'Oisin' can be recognized immediately. Later its sentimentality is plain to Yeats: 'My very remorse' – that is, before his defection from orthodox Christianity – 'helped to spoil my early poetry, giving it an element of sentimentality through my refusal to permit it any share of an intellect which I considered impure.'[1] In 'Oisin' there is sentimentality, occasional clumsiness of technique, and a private symbolism. 'Under disguise of symbolism I have said several things to which alone I have the key. The romance is for my readers. They must not know that there is a symbol anywhere.'[2] So:

> I know not if days passed or hours,
> And Niamh sang continually
> Danaan songs, and their dewy showers
> Of pensive laughter, unhuman sound,
> Lulled weariness, and softly round
> My human sorrow her white arms wound.
> We galloped; now a hornless deer
> Passed by us: chased by a phantom hound
> All pearly white, save one red ear. . . .[3]

The symbols demand elucidation: they occur in a short poem with a long title, 'He Mourns for the Change that has come upon Him and His Beloved, and Longs for the End of the World.'[4] 'My deer and hound are properly related to the deer and hound that flicker in and out of the various tellings of the Arthurian legends, leading different knights upon adventures, and to the hounds and to the hornless deer at the beginning of, I think, all tellings of Oisin's journey to the country of the young. The hound is certainly related to the Hounds of Annwoyn or of Hades, who are white, and have red ears, and were heard and are, perhaps, still heard by Welsh peasants, following some flying thing in the night winds. . . .'[5]
It was such writing as this that provoked 'A.E.':

> Your detestable symbols too get a reflected light from the general twilight luminousness and beauty which does not belong to them by

[1] *Autobiographies*, p. 188. Cf. 'When such as I cast out remorse . . .' and 'Repentance keeps the heart impure . . .'
[2] Quoted by Hone, *Life*, p. 61.
[3] *C.P.*, p. 413.
[4] Ibid., p. 68.
[5] Ibid., Note, p. 525.

right, just as moonlight makes an ugly scene beautiful. I suppose you calculated on this.[1]

Later, the utmost simplicity will suffice; subtlety of music and stress made one with the bare evocation of legend which is now European:

> Sleep, beloved, such a sleep
> As did that wild Tristram know
> When, the potion's work being done,
> Roe could run or doe could leap
> Under oak and beechen bough,
> Roe could leap or doe could run.[2]

Sometimes the manner is more Keats than Morris – Keats, with the trisyllabic modulations that are so apparent in *The Countess Cathleen*:

> ... Wars shadowy, vast, exultant; faeries of old
> Who wedded men with rings of Druid gold;
> And how those lovers never turn their eyes
> Upon the life that fades and flickers and dies,
> Yet love and kiss on dim shores far away
> Rolled round with music of the sighing spray.[3]

Sometimes it is derived from Morris' technique, with the *Sigurd*-metre alternately rhymed, and the Wardour Street diction, and a certain clumsiness of idiom:

And over the limbs and the valley the slow owls wandered and came,
Now in a place of star-fire, and now in a shadow-place wide;
And the chief of the huge white creatures, his knees in the soft star-flame,
Lay loose in a place of shadow: we drew the reins by his side.[4]

But this imitation and 'invention' is a normal phase of the youth of a poet. Looking back, Yeats' own justification has in it something of an assured pride of aristocracy in his traditionalism:

> Perhaps it was because of Pater's influence that we, with an affecta-
> tion of learning, claimed the whole past of literature for our authority

[1] *Letters*, 'A.E.' to W. B. Y., p. 19.
[2] 'Lullaby', *C.P.*, p. 300. Note the extreme subtlety of the vowel tones; there are at least four separate values of the *o*-sound.
[3] Ibid., p. 423.
[4] Ibid., p. 434. I am aware of the attempt recently made by Mr Peter Faulkner to minimize Morris's influence; but I do not think that the subject has yet been sufficiently explored.

... that we preferred what seemed still uncrumbled rock, to the still unspotted foam; that we were traditional alike in our dress, in our manner, in our opinions, and in our style.[1]

*The Shadowy Waters* in its final version is more closely knit; the dialogue is derivative, sometimes Jacobean, sometimes Browningesque; more economical, but still lacking in stability except over the lyric 'peaks'. There are hints of Synge in the diction:

> FIRST SAILOR.   She will be like a wild cat; for these queens
> Care more about the kegs of silver and gold
> And the high fame that come to them in marriage,
> Than a strong body and a ready hand.
> SECOND SAILOR.   There's nobody natural but a robber,
> And that is why the world totters about
> Upon its bandy legs.[2]

There is nothing of this passage in the 1900 version.

The desire for 'cold light and tumbling clouds' is not to achieve an effect of atmosphere, but rather an economy of technique, a discipline of art. It is part of the deliberate striving towards the Anti-Self. The image was but part of Yeats' own background, and of the Gregorys at Coole Park:

> We dreamed that a great painter had been born
> To cold Clare rock and Galway rock and thorn,
> To that stern colour and that delicate line
> That are our secret discipline. . . .[3]

The landscape of the Burren in North Clare, that country of limestone outcrop and low thorn trees (of which Cromwell is reported to have said that 'there was not enough timber to hang a man, water to drown him, or earth to bury him') is a new symbol of reality and of the common speech:

> My country is Kiltartan Cross,
> My countrymen Kiltartan's poor . . .[4]

This sense of contact with the Irish countryside, of 'cold light and

---

[1] *Autobiographies*, p. 303.
[2] *C.P.*, p. 483.
[3] 'In Memory of Major Robert Gregory,' ibid., p. 148. There is a picture in the Municipal Gallery that exactly fits this description. I have no doubt that Yeats knew it well.
[4] 'An Irish Airman foresees His Death,' ibid., p. 152.

tumbling clouds', leads to the creation of a further image of himself, and this association appears to be deliberate, a rejection of the brain-spun image of the Twilight:

> And as I look backward upon my own writings, I take pleasure alone in those verses where it seems to me I have found something hard and cold, some articulation of the Image, which is the opposite of all that I am in my daily life, and all that my country is; yet man or nation can no more make this Mask or Image than the seed can be made by the soil into which it is cast.[1]

The revisions in pursuit of this 'articulation' are a fascinating and instructive lesson in technique; they may be studied in the Variorum Edition, and in Parkinson, Stallworthy and others.

It is instructive to see Yeats in competition with William Allingham, and to see the infinitely greater metrical subtlety that emerges even in the stock treatment and the simplesse of the younger poet:

*Allingham*

| | |
|---|---|
| High on the hill-top | Where the wave of moonlight glosses |
| The old King sits; | The dim grey sands with light, |
| He is now so old and gray | Far off by farthest Rosses |
| He's nigh lost his wits. | We foot it all the night, |
| With a bridge of white mist | Weaving olden dances, |
| Columbkill he crosses, | Mingling hands and mingling glances |
| On his stately journeys | Till the moon has taken flight; |
| From Slieveleague to Rosses; | To and fro we leap |
| Or going up with music | And chase the frothy bubbles, |
| On cold starry nights, | While the world is full of troubles |
| To sup with the Queen | And is anxious in its sleep.[3] |
| Of the gay Northern Lights.[2] | |

It is also interesting to compare the work of Yeats with that of Eva Gore-Booth: both working in a common country background, both with the same ideals of Irish nationalism. He says that he underrated her poems, 'because the dominant mood in many of them is one I have fought in myself to put down. In my *Land of Heart's Desire*, and in some of my lyric verse of that time, there is an exaggeration of sentiment and sentimental beauty which I have come to think unworthy.'[4] As early as 1904 there is this break with

---

[1] *Autobiographies*, p. 274.
[2] 'The Fairies.' He had written an article on Allingham early in 1888. (Wade, p. 85 *fn.*)
[3] 'The Stolen Child,' *C.P.*, p. 20.
[4] Wade, p. 434.

the Danaan shore:

> I cannot probably be quite just to any poetry that speaks to me
> with the sweet insinuating feminine voice of the dwellers in that
> country of shadows and hollow images. I have dwelt there too long
> not to dread all that comes out of it.[1]

But in other letters to George Russell there is the highly conscious
artist at work in the old tradition: 'I send you, as I said I would,
two modifications of the little poems. In the first verse of the first
poem I have changed "king of all the world" to "master of the
world", & "gold light", which the verse puts out of the usual
accentuation, to "music" which gives a full sound. In the second
place I have got rid of the needless passing from "scarlet" to "red"
and of the commonplace "richest", & in the last line of the fourth
verse (a very fine verse) I have got rid of the strained accentuation
of "grey light" (which is accentuated as if to rhyme with "daylight"!) and of the abbreviation "ere" which is a conventional bit
of poetic diction.'[2] Yeats is always critical of loose diction: 'I avoid
every kind of word that seems to me either "poetical" or "modern"
and above all I avoid suggesting the ghostly (the vague) idea about
a god, for it is a modern conception. All ancient vision was definite
and precise.'[3]

The first and final versions of *The Shadowy Waters*, when read
side by side, are almost unrecognizable. But in between them lie
three separate versions of the work. There is the A-text, quasi-
dramatic, quasi-narrative in form, designed to be read rather than
acted. Five years after its completion we have the first draft of the
B-text, the narrative version, and the first drafts of the C-text, the
acting version. From this point onwards the B- and C-texts each
undergoes a continuous process of change, excision, and growth.[4]
The early draft is full of exotic symbolism such as 'a red hound
running from a silver arrow'. The whole provides a highly complex
and interesting commentary on Yeats' method of approach. As an
extreme example, we may put side by side two passages:

[1] Wade, p. 434.
[2] Ibid., 1898 (?).
[3] Ibid., p. 343.
[4] I am indebted to Peter Allt for this.

| *1900* | *Collected Poems, 1934* |
|---|---|
| No man or woman has loved otherwise | But he that gets their love after the fashion |
| Than in brief longing and deceiving hope | Loves in brief longing and deceiving hope |
| And bodily tenderness; and he who longs | And bodily tenderness, and finds that even |
| For happier love but finds unhappiness, | The bed of love, that in the imagination |
| And falls among the dream the drowsy gods | Had seemed to be the giver of all peace, |
| Breathe on the burnished mirror of the world | Is no more than a wine-cup in the tasting, |
| And then smooth out with ivory hands and sigh. | And as soon finished.[1] |

It is a new philosophy that has called love in doubt, and found words to quicken the rhythm to that bitterness.

*The Countess Cathleen* passed through numerous revisions. One passage is of peculiar interest for what Yeats cut out: remembering that the play was dedicated to Maud Gonne. The scene is the sale of souls.

1892.[2]

> KEVIN [*a young man, who carries a harp with torn wires*].
> Here, take my soul, for I am tired of it;
> I do not ask a price.
> FIRST MERCHANT [*reading*].
> A man of songs —
> Alone in the hushed passion of romance,
> His mind ran all on sheogues, and on tales
> Of Finian labours and the Red-branch kings,
> And he cared nothing for the life of man:
> But now all changes.
> KEVIN.          Aye, because her face,
> The face of Countess Cathleen dwells with me.
> The sadness of the world upon her brow —
> The crying of these strings grew burdensome,
> Therefore I tore them – see – now take my soul.

In the second version the symbolism of the harp with torn wires is foregone. Kevin has become Aleel. The gain is obvious, both in

[1] *C.P.*, p. 479. The thought is Shakespearean: as in 'A Woman Young and Old.'

[2] Except for punctuation unaltered in the 1899 version.

the excision of the allusions to Celtic legend, and the greater fluency
of the verse.

> ALEEL.   Here, take my soul, for I am tired of it.
>             I do not ask a price.
> SHEMUS.                    Not ask a price?
>             How can you sell your soul without a price?
>             I would not listen to his broken wits;
>             His love for Countess Cathleen has so crazed him
>             He hardly understands what he is saying.
> ALEEL.   The trouble that has come on Countess Cathleen,
>             The sorrow that is in her wasted face,
>             The burden in her eyes, have broke my wits,
>             And yet I know I'd have you take my soul.

But there is a further reason why the verse should become tightened.
The Countess is, by now, more closely identified with Maud Gonne;
who is also Beatrice, 'the saint with the sapphire eyes'. For since
the earlier version history had drawn Yeats' images more closely
together; Maud Gonne's struggles in the West[1] on behalf of the
starving peasantry must have seemed like prophecy fulfilled.

> The people starve, therefore the people go
> Thronging to you. I hear a cry come from them
> And it is in my ears by night and day.

It is significant that the poems of *The Green Helmet* have been
considered by certain critics as a retrograde step in Yeats' development because of their obscurity. What is in fact happening is that
the vague historical symbols of the Celtic world are replaced by a
more personal set of images, sometimes set in a grammatical compression of language which is new. Two central experiences lie
behind the verse. Yeats is tired of the public theatre; Synge is dead.
There is the first hint of old age, for he is now forty-five, and later
he was to write:

> And from your fortieth winter by that thought
> Test every work of intellect or faith —

Maud Gonne is divorced from MacBride, but the flame is burning
still; Dante for Beatrice, Michelangelo for Vittoria Colonna. The
bitterness that went to make *Responsibilities* has not yet been
experienced, but Yeats is thinking of himself as in control of his
destiny and his poetry. This I take to be the symbol of the steering-

[1] See *A Servant of the Queen.*

·oar in the first poem, 'His Dream'.[1] His love is justified as the inspiration of his writing, even though Maud Gonne has not understood:

> . . . That every year I have cried, 'At length
> My darling understands it all,
> Because I have come into my strength,
> And words obey my call';
>
> That had she done so who can say
> What would have shaken from the sieve?
> I might have thrown poor words away
> And been content to live.[2]

Here is a new simplicity, a new restraint and tautness. There is a
new 'attack' in the openings. Yeats is rid of Shelley's Italian light;
words are obeying his call. I cannot trace whether or not he was
reading Homer in translation about this period; but Homer appears
three times in the score of poems. Maud Gonne is 'a woman Homer
sung'. Her beauty is celebrated with that dignity and simplicity
with which, in *Last Poems*, he was to write of Dorothy Wellesley;
both women seen processionally in the stream of time, and so reconciled and celebrated in the verse:

> What could have made her peaceful with a mind
> That nobleness made simple as a fire,
> With beauty like a tightened bow, a kind
> That is not natural in an age like this,
> Being high and solitary and most stern?
> Why, what could she have done, being what she is?
> Was there another Troy for her to burn?[3]

The rhythm is the index to the integrity and restraint of emotion:
beside it we may set, for comparison, a passage from 'The Rose
of the World':

> Who dreamed that beauty passes like a dream?
> For these red lips, with all their mournful pride,
> Mournful that no new wonder may betide,
> Troy passed away in one high funeral gleam,
> And Usna's children died.[4]

---

[1] Saul disagrees: but I still think there is an 'underlay' in this poem from
Arthurian sources.
[2] 'Words', *C.P.*, p. 100.
[3] 'No Second Troy,' Ibid., p. 101.
[4] Ibid., p. 41.

There is a new economy in epigram, as 'On hearing that the Students of our New University have joined the Agitation against Immoral Literature'. Other poets are irritating him, and a contempt akin to Blake's is stirring:

> But was there ever dog that praised his fleas?

Twice the thought of aristocracy, its gift to that civilization, and the present danger are treated in a manner that reminds us of 'Coole Park and Ballylee' and 'Ancestral Houses'. Here again the language is economical, the images simple and self-sufficient:

> How should the world be luckier if this house,
> Where passion and precision have been one
> Time out of mind, became too ruinous
> To breed the lidless eye that loves the sun? . . .[1]

And, with the same thought:

> These are the clouds about the fallen sun,
> The majesty that shuts his burning eye:
> The weak lay hand on what the strong has done,
> Till that be tumbled that was lifted high
> And discord follow upon unison. . . .[2]

I suggest that the period from 1909–14 is both a breathing space in which Yeats is considering the relationship between the theatre and poetry, speculating on the choice between 'perfection of the life or of the work', and attempting to solve the problem of contemplation through passion. There was precedent for this in the great poets:

> They and their sort [Dante, Villon] alone earn contemplation, for it is only when the intellect has wrought the whole of life to drama, to crisis, that we may live for contemplation, and yet keep our intensity.[3]

His own life story is coming into alignment with the lives of the poets. Biography is becoming a myth and myth biography, as he pointed out in *A Vision*. Intensity and passion are fed on Maud Gonne's obduracy —

---

[1] 'Upon a House Shaken by the Land Agitation,' *C.P.*, p. 106. The eagle image is to become a dominant later.

[2] 'These are the Clouds . . . ,' ibid., p. 107.

[3] *Autobiographies* pp. 273–4. The last phrase lived with him. In a personal letter to me he expressed the wish that, in old age, he might 'keep his intensity'.

... for the passionate feed their flame in wanderings and absences, when the whole being of the beloved, every little charm of body and of soul, is always present to the mind, filling it with heroical subtleties of desire.[1]

The keyword is *heroical*: the myth of Maud Gonne is almost complete. Within the next ten years Yeats was to have a series of experiences more intense and varied than even he would have imagined. There followed the affair of the Lane Pictures, the 1916 Rebellion, the death of Major Robert Gregory over Italy in 1918; the meeting with Iseult Gonne, and his proposal and rejection; the Troubles from 1917 to 1923; his marriage and his wife's 'automatic writing', the raw material of *A Vision*, the building of the Tower, all provided complexities of mire and blood, a ruin that must be straightened out in verse. He had learnt his lesson from the affairs of the Abbey Theatre. Between 1915 and 1920 there was time to observe.

They [the Rhymers] had taught me that violent energy, which is like a fire of straw,[2] consumes in a few minutes the nervous vitality, and is useless in the arts. Our fire must burn slowly, and we must constantly turn away to think, constantly analyse what we have done, be content even to have little life outside our work, to show, perhaps, to other men as little as the watch-mender shows, his magnifying glass caught in his screwed-up eye. Only then do we learn to conserve our vitality, to keep our mind enough under control and to make our technique sufficiently flexible for expression of the emotions of life as they arise.[3]

These statements, taken together, form a sufficiently clear picture of the ideal that Yeats had set himself. The debt to Pater's *Renaissance* is obvious. It remains to see the further development.

Technically the influence of his study of metaphysical poetry first becomes apparent about 1912,[4] when he was reading Donne. The thought is to be condensed, the rhythms brought closer to

[1] Introduction to *Spenser*, p. xxx. Compare 'The only legitimate passivity is that which follows exhaustion of the intellect.' (I am indebted for this to L. A. G. Strong.)
[2] This image is a familiar one; see 'In Memory of Major Robert Gregory'.
[3] *Autobiographies*, p. 318.
[4] Austin Clarke has suggested a general emotional rediscovery of major English poetry in Yeats' mature life. (*Dublin Magazine*, April/June 1939.)

common speech. Trisyllabic feet are largely abandoned; the checks and extra-metrical syllables are becoming integral with the verse; the half-rhymes and the false, and the injection of homely idiom, are acquiring a kind of insolence bred of certainty of technique. Words are 'obeying his call'. Individual phrases stand out in 'Major Robert Gregory':

> ... And solid men, for all their passion, live
> But as the outrageous stars incline
> By opposition, square and trine. . . .[1]

or

> Could share in that discourtesy of death

or

> What made us dream that he could comb grey hair?

There is speech from 'the book of the people':

> That lady and that golden king
> Could like a brace of blackbirds sing.[2]
>
> We have gone round and round
> In the narrow theme of love
> Like an old horse in a pound.[3]

There is the mature and certain accent, the accent of *Words for Music Perhaps* and of *A Woman Young and Old* in the verses to Iseult Gonne, 'To a Young Girl'. In the celebratory kind of verse he is, I think, moving towards that 'aristocratic esoteric Irish literature which has been my chief ambition.'[4]

But the two most interesting poems that show the new dignity and restraint are 'Shepherd and Goatherd', and 'Ego Dominus Tuus'. The first, a somewhat stilted and contrived poem, is for Robert Gregory:

> He had thrown the crook away
> And died in the great war beyond the sea —

---

[1] *C.P.*, p. 148. Trine – the 'aspect' of two heavenly bodies while on the third part of the zodiac; i.e. at 120° from each other. 'Opposition' and 'square' – when they are 180° and 90° apart respectively.
[2] 'Under the Round Tower,' ibid., p. 154.
[3] 'Solomon to Sheba,' ibid., p. 155.
[4] Wade, *Letters*, p. 286.

and is modelled on Spenser's *Astrophel.*[1] The poem has much that is autobiographical: the Shepherd is Yeats in youth, the Goatherd himself in age,

> That found when I had neither goats nor grazing
> New welcome and old wisdom at her fire . . .

The Shepherd's Song about the Cuckoo is designed to catch something of the early manner: it is of the 'natural life'. But the Goatherd has become (a little pompously) the sage and magician:

> They say that on your barren mountain ridge
> You have measured out the road that the soul treads
> When it has vanished from our natural eyes;
> That you have talked with apparitions.

In the Goatherd's reply there is something Yeats himself, seen with a new irony and a new humour of self-criticism:

> . . . Because of what he had dreamed,
> Or the ambitions that he served,
> Much too solemn and reserved.
> Jaunting, journeying
> To his own dayspring,
> He unpacks the loaded pern
> Of all 'twas pain or joy to learn,
> Of all that he had made.[2]

Women have now fallen into a dramatized perspective:

> All the wild witches, those most noble ladies,
> For all their broom-sticks and their tears,
> Their angry tears, are gone.
> The holy centaurs of the hills are vanished;
> I have nothing but the embittered sun.[3]

The poem 'On Woman' is at once exultant and clear-sighted; looking forward to the sexual imagery of *A Woman Young and Old*:

> . . . Harshness of their desire
> That made them stretch and yawn,
> Pleasure that comes with sleep,
> Shudder that made them one.[4]

[1] Wade, *Letters*, pp. 696–8.
[2] *C.P.*, p. 159. It is, of course, about Robert Gregory's 'return to innocence'.
[3] 'Lines Written in Dejection,' ibid., p. 163.
[4] Ibid., p. 164. See also 'Three Things', and 'Leda and the Swan'.

The quarrels of 1910 are partly reconciled in 'The People', and the thought is of Maud Gonne, who, in spite of all she had suffered from them, had never complained of the people. Confronted with this magnanimity, Yeats falls back on the antithesis between thought and action presented by the pair:

> All I could reply
> Was: 'You, that have not lived in thought but deed,
> Can have the purity of a natural force,
> But I, whose virtues are the definitions
> Of the analytic mind, can neither close
> The eye of the mind nor keep the tongue from speech.'
> And yet, because my heart leaped at her words,
> I was abashed, and now they come to mind
> After nine years, I sink my head abashed.[1]

'Ego Dominus Tuus' sums up the conflict between Self and Anti-Self, between perfection of life and work. Yeats is himself in the procession of the symbols: his love story is that of Dante. Every line is important for our understanding of his struggle in this phase. He is building the picture of the mysterious one, the Fisherman, realizing that it can never be himself.

He is conscious of the loss of strength and artistic vitality in his world:

> We are but critics, or but half create,
> Timid, entangled, empty and abashed,
> Lacking the countenance of our friends . . .
> What portion in the world can the artist have
> Who has awakened from the common dream
> But dissipation and despair?[2]

He must reject the style that is found by toil and imitation of the masters. Revelation will come through his Anti-Self.

> I call to the mysterious one who yet
> Shall walk the wet sands by the edge of the stream
> And look most like me, being indeed my double,
> And prove of all imaginable things
> The most unlike, being my anti-self,
> And standing by these characters disclose
> All that I seek . . .[3]

---

[1] *C.P.*, p. 169.
[2] Ibid., p. 180. 'Ego Dominus Tuus' was written in 1915, not 1917, as is usually held (Mrs Yeats).
[3] Ibid.

The myth of 'The Phases of the Moon' provides a half-deterministic pattern into which the experiences can be fitted.

By 1919 Yeats is recollecting the best of his past emotions in something approaching tranquillity. The language in which they find expression appears to be striving continually towards simplicity, with speech-rhythms which give place at will to lyric, the whole moving easily and gracefully. Image and symbol are used more sparingly; the 'luminous' or rhetorical Celtic symbols have been rejected; he is concentrating on a relatively small number of symbols, moving round them in poem after poem, establishing and enlarging their significance. Love is falling into perspective. There is a clarity of double vision (apart from Michael Robartes) which reflects on every page his faith in his own control of words. The other two great central experiences – the Rebellion and the historical systems of *A Vision* – provide material for the mature period, 1921–34. The Mask, the image of soldier, fulfilled lover, fisherman, horseman, scholar, hermit, the inheritor of aristocracy and the Ireland of the eighteenth century – all these will disclose what he seeks, while taking from him nothing of his own identity. But the disclosure will still be half-secret, for the love of mystery is strong, and the poet must separate himself from the profane; the Anti-Self must

> whisper it as though
> He were afraid the birds, who cry aloud
> Their momentary cries before it is the dawn
> Would carry it away to blasphemous men.

The dawn is, perhaps, a kind of Apocalypse, the Second Coming.

# CHAPTER NINE

# Image and Symbol

Plato thinks all things into Unity and is the 'First Christian'.
*A Vision* (B), p. 262.

Day after day I have sat in my chair turning a symbol over in my mind, exploring all its details, defining and again defining its elements, testing my conventions and those of others by its unity, attempting to substitute particulars for an abstraction like that of algebra.
*A Vision* (B), p. 301.

My main symbols are Sun and Moon (in all phases), Tower, Mask, Tree (Tree with Mask hanging on the trunk), Well.
*Letters*, Sturge Moore, p. 38.

I must leave my sights and images to explain themselves as the years go by, and one poem lights up another. – Preface to the 1899 Poems.

## I

A poet can establish his symbolism, and suggest its values, by one of three methods. He can relate it, directly, or obliquely, or sometimes negatively, to such myths or history as already command a reasonable measure of acceptance; weighing the readiness of response against the loss that changes in cultural background may, in the future, impose upon his work. So long as the background is constant, he can be assured of an immediate response. When, for example, Yeats sees Maud Gonne in terms of Helen, there is acceptance, but the full significance of the lines

> Another Troy must rise and set,
> Another lineage feed the crow . . .[1]

is, perhaps, only apparent when we are aware of the reference to Virgil's *Fourth Eclogue*,[2]

[1] 'Two Songs from a Play,' *C.P.*, p. 239.
[2] IV, 1.35. Yeats read the *Fourth Eclogue* in translation, with Samuel Palmer's illustrations (Mrs Yeats).

Alter erit tum Tiphys et altera quae vehat Argo
Delectos heroas: erunt etiam *altera bella*,[1]
Atque iterum ad Trojam magnus mittetur Achilles,

a reference that is pointed by Yeats' own reference to it: '. . . for
has not Virgil, a knowledgeable man and a wizard, foretold that
other Argonauts shall row between cliff and cliff, and other fair-
haired Archæans sack another Troy?'[2] So there is built up a kind
of image-cluster in which Troy serves to illuminate the beauty of
Maud Gonne —

– Was there another Troy for her to burn?

and to form a stable recurring point for the revolution of the gyres
of history in terms of 'The Second Coming'. Much classical history
can be so ordered and recombined to produce this recognition of
its basic symbols, and to suggest still more complex values through
other combinations of them.

Or he can use the so-called archetypal symbols, water, fire,
cavern, arrow, horse, and so on, relying on the constancy of human
experience of dream and fantasy and vision in which such symbols
appear. The penumbra of light thrown round the focal point of
such a symbol will be usually deeper and more complicated than
that supplied by history or myth; and the poet may achieve an
inner conviction of the validity of his symbols through observing
a constancy, or recurrence, or 'dispersed coincidence' in dream or
vision.[3] His work will suffer, perhaps, in communication; because,
while simpler symbols such as

What's water but the generated soul?

are reasonably (though not entirely) clear without further explanation,[4] the interpretation tends to grow conventional, as when the

[1] 'Send war in our time, O Lord!'
[2] *P. & C.*, p. 99.
[3] See, for example, Yeats' own account of the Archer-star vision, pp.
164 *infra*.
[4] This line from 'Coole Park and Ballylee' is related to Note I in *A Vision*
(B), p. 220: 'I think it was Porphyry who wrote that the generation of
images in the mind is from water.' Water, for any Neoplatonist, is the
traditional symbol of generation, and of the emotion and passion into
which the soul descends at birth.' cf. 'That dolphin-torn, that gong-tormented
sea'.

audience is an order of initiates; or unduly imprecise, as in much later Romantic poetry.

The third method is to create a personal mythology and a related symbolism, partly in the manner of Blake; and here success will depend on a gradual building up of determinant points of meaning through the use of the symbols in varying contexts. This most difficult task will be hampered still further if the meanings themselves vary from context to context, and still more if the symbols give no traditional clue by their derivation or sound. Thus Blake's arbitrary use of Oothoon, Enion, Athania or Orc forms a considerable obstacle; and, if the labour involved in the necessary study appears likely to be incommensurate with the result in the significance it proposes to establish, the myth will fail.

Yeats used all three methods; I do not think the Celtic mythology commanded sufficiently wide acceptance to be other than personal. P. C. Ure in his book, *Towards a Mythology*, has traced the growth of Yeats' mind in the matter, and the rejection of the Celtic material. His early discovery of the French Symbolists through Arthur Symons had taught him to admire them, but he was aware of their limitations:

> . . . there must always be a certain monotony in the work of the Symbolist, who can only make symbols out of the things that he loves.[1]

His use of the term is extremely wide; it appears to be used interchangeably with 'emblem' and, on certain occasions, with 'image'. Symbols are of two kinds, the emotional and the intellectual:[2] the second evoking 'ideas alone, or ideas mingled with emotions'. There is 'the continuous indefinable symbolism which is the substance of all style':[3] so that the word symbol appears, at moments, to denote little more than an intensified and noteworthy metaphor with a greater emotional potential than usual. 'Metaphors are not profound enough to be moving, when they are not symbols.'

The choice and the value of the symbol are, ultimately, mystical in character: 'When a man writes any work of genius, or invents some creative action, is it not because some knowledge or power

---

[1] Horton, *A Book of Images*, p. 15.
[2] *E. & I.*, p. 160.
[3] Ibid., p. 155.

has come into his mind from beyond his mind? It is called up by an image, as I think . . . but our images must be given to us, we cannot choose them deliberately.'[1] But sometimes they were chosen very deliberately:

'I wonder if *Per Amica* designs with a new emblem would do – a torch, a candle in waves, a hawk, a phoenix, a moon, a butterfly, a hunchback?'[2] Sturge Moore's sketch for a bookplate for his daughter Anne is relevant: 'It represents a girl, younger or older according to choice, dancing in a single half-transparent garment on a rocky islet in an animated but not a rough sea. The shape of the moon sets the tune for those of the child's dress, the light on the rocks and for the waves of the sea; the tower rocks in the same way, [to] keep time with the frame.'[3]

At the same time there is a firm distinction between Imagination and Fancy, although the approach is curious. 'The imaginative deals with spiritual things symbolized by natural things – with gods and not with matter. The fantasy has its place in poetry, but it has a subordinate place.'[4]

In the essay on 'Symbolism in Painting' he is acutely aware of the complex emotions which are liberated thereby and his quotations from Blake, Nashe and Shakespeare show a curious response to the half-rational: as when he quotes with approval (in 'The Symbolism of Poetry') Blake's

The gay fishes on the wave when the moon sucks up the dew.[5]

His approval of that image may go back to a childhood experience in Sligo Bay:

When a child I went out with the herring fishers one dark night, and the dropping of their nets into the luminous sea and the drawing of them up has remained with me as a dominant image.[6]

He would also have seen the hauling of the seine-nets for salmon in the Sligo river, close to his grandparents' house; an image even

---

[1] *Autobiographies*, p. 337.
[2] Letters to T.S.M., p. 33.
[3] Ibid., p. 90. See 'Long-Legged Fly,' *C.P.*, p. 381. But in the next letter Yeats tells Sturge Moore to 'make the dancing girl about eighteen'. The poem itself is dated 1937, eleven years after the letter.
[4] Wade, p. 343.
[5] *E. & I.*, p. 156.
[6] *A Vision* (A), p. 251.

more appropriate than the herring drift-nets for the closing of fate. That can become

> Out-worn heart, in a time out-worn,
> Come clear of the nets of wrong and right . . .

or

> Shakespearean fish swam the sea, far away from land;
> Romantic fish swam in nets coming to the hand;
> What are all those fish that lie gasping on the strand?[1]

– in which the phrase 'coming to the hand' is technically precise for the cork and lead-lines being 'handed' together.

Both in theory and in practice these past experiences play a large part in his poetic theory.

> All sounds, all colours, all forms, either because of their pre-ordained energies or because of long association, evoke indefinable and yet precise emotions, or, as I prefer to think, call down among us certain disembodied powers, whose footsteps over our hearts we call emotions; and when sound and colour and form are in a musical relation, a beautiful relation to one another, they become as it were one sound, one colour, one form, and evoke an emotion that is made out of their distinct evocations and yet is one emotion.[2]

This passage is, in spite of its transcendental phrasing, of great importance in Yeats' poetry. Memory becomes a kind of reservoir, not merely of the poet's own experiences in the past, but ultimately of all human thought and experience; since this lives on and can be called down, as it were, into the present by dream, vision, or image; which in their turn can be definitely cultivated. The emotions are 'indefinable and yet precise' which is the highest art of the symbolist poet, and which he achieved in the great period and after. The phase of Celtic symbolism is what Blake called 'a dark mystery': it lightens and clears until he relies on a few dominant images, closely linked to his own life, and established by repetition, or by recognition in other cycles of history, other civilizations. It is through symbols that Yeats thinks: for the symbol becomes the means by which the reality which is no more than guessed at can be indicated and perhaps defined, though in a broken light. And through the

[1] *C.P.*, p. 271.
[2] *E. & I.*, pp. 156–7.

symbol he can satisfy his instinct for the dramatic moment, the crystallization of the historical element in a dramatic irrational world.[1]

But besides the mystical view, there is a practical aspect of symbolism. It is a political activity. '... Nations, races and individual men are unified by an image, or bundle of related images.' Therefore the new mythology will be justified as a force that will serve at once to stimulate and order Irish nationalism. At first the symbol might be the sentimental image of Cathleen-ni-Houlihan;[2] then, perhaps the new *Prometheus Unbound*; then, as violence came on the roads, it grew into the terrible beauty that was born in 1916, and the red rose tree watered by blood; till that dream of a country fired by a poet becomes fragmentary, falling back on half-remembered or foreshortened ballads of Parnell, or Roger Casement, or Wolfe Tone, the legendary heroes.

II

Yeats' use of the symbol may be approached in a variety of ways; but it is perhaps best to consider only the 'dominants', and, by examining their implications, to suggest how they develop and fuse with the minor symbols. Of them all the Tower is perhaps the most widely and effectively used. Ireland is a land of towers, square and round; his own rebuilding of Thoor Ballylee was at once a practical gesture and the embodiment of a dream that had enchanted him.[3] It fitted so many things. First, there was the old emblem of the poet, the spiritual security of the tower, and the winding stair. That stair suggested Jacob's Ladder, as seen by Blake.[4] In the dream world it served to align him with the past of Ireland, and with the growth of the great philosophies which imaged that country's greatness in the past, and, perhaps, in the future:

[1] It will be remembered that this was explained by Jung in his theory of the collective unconscious. In particular, the chapter on 'Wit and Art' in Herbert's *The Unconscious Mind* throws a good deal of light on the process.
[2] 'Red Hanrahan's Song about Ireland,' *C.P.*, p. 90.
[3] It is apparent from his Preface to the translation of *Axël* that he attached great importance to the symbolism of that castle. Perhaps he was aware that it is the central point of *The Shepherd of Hermas*.
[4] T.S.M., *Letters*, p. 199.

I declare
This winding, gyring, spiring treadmill of a stair is my ancestral stair;
That Goldsmith and the Dean, Berkeley and Burke have travelled there.[1]

It becomes an image of past conflicts, a frame or translucent screen
for the processional evocation of the past:

> Before that ruin came, for centuries,
> Rough men-at-arms, cross-gartered to the knees
> Or shod in iron, climbed the narrow stairs,
> And certain men-at-arms there were
> Whose images, in the Great Memory stored,
> Come with loud cry and panting breast
> To break upon a sleeper's rest
> While their great wooden dice beat on the board.[2]

For a moment he is identified – the Mask and Anti-Mask again –
with the 'bloody, arrogant power'[3] that rose from it. The Tower
dominates the cottages around it; it is thus an emblem of aristocracy.
In the Troubles, when he feared it would be burnt, it serves to
foreshadow violence and disintegration; remembering, perhaps,
that the Lightning-Struck Tower is the sixteenth card of the Tarot
Pack. It is bound to the cycle of history, and its values of action
and war are seen, bitterly, against the decadence and confusion of
the present:

> Odour of blood on the ancestral stair!
> And we that have shed none must gather there
> And clamour in drunken frenzy for the moon.[4]

But the thought-rings widen on the water. The battlements are
crumbling; the butterflies – the human souls (*l'angelica farfalla* of
Dante) – and moths haunt the stairs. It is 'half-dead at the top.'[5]
The poet in his tower is part hermit, part sage, part fool, inheriting
the empty attributes of the man of action, conscious of the past, yet
powerless.
The complexities of related or self-begetting images cluster

---

[1] 'Blood and the Moon,' ii, *C.P.*, p. 268.

[2] 'The Tower,' ii, ibid., p. 218.

[3] 'Blood and the Moon,' i, ibid., p. 267.

[4] Ibid., iii, ibid., p. 269: 'We that have shed none . . .' Compare 'The
Stare's Nest by My Window'.

[5] See p. 13; and, for the butterfly-symbols, Yeats' Note at ibid., pp. 449–50.

thickly. An important instance is 'The Stare's Nest by My Window';
we may quote the final stanza:

> We had fed the heart on fantasies,
> The heart's grown brutal from the fare;
> More substance in our enmities
> Than in our love; O honey bees,
> Come build in the empty house of the stare.[1]

Yeats had read Porphyry while he was working on Blake:

> The ancients called souls not only Naiads but bees, 'as the efficient
> cause of sweetness'; but not all souls proceeding into generation are
> called bees, but those who live in it justly and who after having per-
> formed all things as are acceptable to the gods will return to whence
> they came. For this insect loves to return to the place whence it came, and
> is eminently just and sober.

The honey bees are the subject, then, for the invocation; the just
souls, the symbolism of unity (as opposed to the chaos of the
Civil War). The stare (Anglicé starling) is perhaps the poet,
lonely and subjective man: he prays that future generations may
bring sweetness and enlightenment to Ireland. And as to the
'fantasies', we may think of 'I am worn out with dreams' ('Men
Improve with the Years')[2] and Renan's *The Poetry of the Celtic
Races*, echoed by Arnold. The Celtic imagination 'has worn itself
out in mistaking dreams for realities'.[3]

But it is also the scholar's tower:

> He has found, after the manner of his kind,
> *Mere* images;

(the *Selbst-ironie* is typical)

> – chosen this place to live in
> Because, it may be of the candle-light
> From the far tower where Milton's Platonist
> Sat late, or Shelley's visionary prince.
> The lonely light that Samuel Palmer engraved,
> An image of mysterious wisdom won by toil;
> And now he seeks in book or manuscript
> What he shall never find.[4]

[1] *C.P.*, p. 230.
[2] Ibid., p. 152.
[3] *E. & I.*, p. 173.
[4] 'The Phases of the Moon,' *C.P.*, p. 183.

The linking of the symbols, first treated in an expanded form in
'A Dialogue of Self and Soul', is shown in microcosm in these
couplets:

> A storm-beaten old watch-tower,
> A blind hermit rings the hour.
>
> All-destroying sword-blade still
> Carried by the wandering fool.
>
> Gold-sewn silk on the sword-blade,
> Beauty and fool together laid.[1]

Those symbols are expanded in the 'Dialogue' into a system
carefully balanced with an almost intellectual precision to establish
the inter-relations of meaning. The tower is the emblem of the night
of war, of violence, of man's aspirations to philosophy, of the decay
of civilization, of ancient ceremony, disintegrating in the face of
the world – 'the broken crumbling battlements'. The tower is night;
but its stability is only apparent. Behind it is the cosmic universe,
permanent only in 'the star that marks the hidden pole'. The tower
becomes astronomical, the departure-point for man's thought
facing the universe. Set against it is the objective man, clinging, in
old age, to the emblem of love and war, the sword and the embroidery.

The Japanese sword was given him by Junzo Sato, to whom
the play *The Resurrection* is dedicated. The primary symbolic
meaning is obvious, though perhaps it is also 'the destructive sword'
of Blake, which is 'a portion of eternity too great for the eye of man'.
But it was particularly appropriate in other ways. Symons writes
of 'Students of magic, who have the sharp and swift swords of the
soldier'.[2] The scabbard-connections are emphasized by the royal
attributes of the silk and gold upon it and we remember, perhaps,
Byron's lyric. The sword is *consecrated*, carrying the heavy accent,
for the Japanese warrior is holy like the magician and the hermit.

---

[1] *C.P.*, p. 270. In a letter to Olivia Shakespear he records the origin of 'A
Dialogue': 'I am writing a new Tower poem . . . which is a choice of rebirth
rather than deliverance from birth. I make my Japanese Sword and its silk
covering my symbol of life' (Wade, p. 729).

[2] Symons, *The Symbolist Movement in Literature*, p. 54: of Villiers de
l'Isle-Adam. Note that the 'fool' introduces yet another dimension; v. *On
Baile's Stand.*

Its blade is like a looking-glass, the mirror of objective man: it is 'unspotted by the centuries'. It is also, perhaps, a symbol of the will. 'We possess nothing but the will and we must never let the children of vague desires breathe upon it nor the waters of sentiment rust the terrible mirror of its blade.'[1] The embroidery is 'flowering', with a double value in the word, for the significance of past love is continued in the present: it

> Can, tattered, still protect, faded adorn.

And there may be a further contrast between the *wooden* scabbard, (the intermediary, as it were, between the steel and the embroidery) and the steel. The tower is archetypal: the 'gyring spiring *treadmill* of a stair', carries key-stresses in the second movement of 'Blood and the Moon'. The tower, like the sword-blade, is 'unspotted by the centuries':

> Seven centuries have passed and it is pure,
> The blood of innocence has left no stain.[2]

At the outset, then, the two opposing symbols have an intimate connection in purity, independence of human repentance that 'keeps the heart impure'.[3] There is the water-fountain image, that seems closely linked to Blake's 'The cistern contains, the fountain over-flows. One thought fills immensity'; for there is evidence that at this period Blake was very much in his mind.[4]

But another passage might assist in determining this fountain-significance. 'Hidden, except at rare moments of excitement or revelation, even then shown but in symbol, the stream set in motion by the Galilean Symbol [i.e. the development of Christianity as a miraculous, irrational force] has filled its basin, and seems motionless for an instant before it falls over the rim. In the midst of the basin stands, in motionless contemplation, blood that is not His blood upon His Hands and Feet, One that feels but for the common lot,

---

[1] Wade, pp. 434–5.
[2] *C.P.*, p. 269.
[3] 'Stream and Sun at Glendalough,' ibid., p. 288.
[4] When Yeats was living at Oxford, Blake's illustrations to *Job* were hung all up the staircase. His concern with them, as evidenced by his collection of slides, is discussed later.

and mourns over the length of years and the inadequacy of man's fate to man.'[1]

This is such a moment of excitement or revelation.


III


Sometimes the values of the symbol are partly traditional, partly dependent on the recognition of their cumulative significance in a number of poems. The image of the swan is common enough in other poetry and its normal connotations are clear; strength, purity, fidelity, immortality, with overtones of the soul (for loneliness and mystery as embodying a human soul) and the ecstasy of death (for its song). It is the song of the last Romantic

> When the swan must fix his eye
> Upon a fading gleam . . .[2]

and the symbol of a civilization that is passing. It takes on a further mystic humanity from the Leda legend which moved Yeats so powerfully, perhaps because of its symbolic importance as the First Annunciation of history or myth. It was not merely 'an image out of Spenser and the common tongue' (he refers to another such in 'The Municipal Gallery Revisited'[3]) which he borrowed and made his own; but the place of the Leda legend in Greek mythology and its significance as producing the eggs from which were hatched love and war. 'I imagine the annunciation that founded Greece as made to Leda.' I have suggested elsewhere that the original image may have its source in a picture. In such treatment there is an ever-growing complexity, but without loss of definition. The technique seems to be justified, but at the price that all Yeats' symbols must be taken together, each affecting and modifying each, so that no single poem, in isolation, gives up its full significance.

A note to *Calvary* is relevant here:

> Certain birds, especially as I see things, such lonely birds as the heron, hawk, eagle and swan, are the natural symbols of subjectivity, especially when floating upon the wind alone or alighting upon some

[1] *A Vision* (B), p. 285.
[2] 'The Tower,' iii, *C.P.*, p. 218. All white birds seem to be emblematic of the soul.
[3] Ibid., p. 368. The reference is to the death of the Earl of Leicester.

pool or river, while the beasts that run upon the ground, especially those that run in packs, are the natural symbols of objective man. Objective men, however personally alone, are never alone in their thought, which is always developed in agreement or in conflict with the thought of others and always seeks the welfare of some cause or institution, while subjective men are the more lonely the more they are true to type, seeking always that which is unique or personal.[1]

The heron, with the hunchback appearance as he strides in a stream fishing, has human qualities:[2] there is a legend of a fowler who stalked and shot one of a company of herons; and found a dead man there.[3] Heron, gull, eagle and swan form a sort of counter-pointed pattern to *Calvary*: being as it were the dissociation of the lonely man from the act of the Crucifixion:

> Take but His love away
> Their love becomes a feather
> Of eagle, swan or gull,
> Or a drowned heron's feather
> Tossed hither and thither
> Upon the bitter spray
> And the moon at the full.[4]

Twelve years later the symbol is woven in, with every thread drawn tight, and with a preoccupation that is totally different:

> At sudden thunder of the mounting swan
> I turned about and looked where branches break
> The glittering reaches of the flooded lake.
>
> Another emblem there! That stormy white
> But seems a concentration of the sky;
> And, like the soul, it sails into the sight
> And in the morning's gone, no man knows why;

[1] *P. & C.*, p. 459.
[2] Compare:

> Nor can he hide in holy black
> The heron's hunch upon his back.
> 'Crazy Jane and the Bishop.'

and Dylan Thomas' 'heron-priested shore'.

[3] 'Old Men of the Twilight'; *Stories of Red Hanrahan* (1927). A white heron used to fly over the Yeats's garden in Riversdale, probably from the heronry at Rathfarnham Castle; and Yeats himself seemed particularly pleased at the appearance of such symbols in physical form (Mrs Yeats).

[4] *C. Plays*, p. 453.

F

> And is so lovely that it sets to right
> What knowledge or its lack had set awry,
> So arrogantly pure, a child might think
> It can be murdered with a spot of ink.[1]

The complexity is intense. The swan recedes under its load: it becomes a tiny remote picture, which a flick of the wrist can blot out. But is this certain? 'Did not M. Trebulet Bonhommie discover that one drop of ink would kill a swan?'[2] The spot of ink, its distinctiveness may be the mere act of writing 'about' the swan. Are there two literal senses, besides the third implication? Are both poems to be thought of in relation to Leda and the Swan, where the symbol becomes 'processional', that is, a component of the pattern of events in time?

> A shudder in the loins engenders there
> The broken wall, the burning roof and tower
> And Agamemnon dead.
>                    Being so caught up,
> So mastered by the brute blood of the air,
> Did she put on his knowledge with his power
> Before the indifferent beak could let her drop?[3]

The Leda-story, then, is seen as an annunciation, emphasizing the repetitive pattern of two cycles of time.

> The threefold terror of love; a fallen flare
> Through the hollow of an ear;
> Wings beating about the room;
> The terror of all terrors that I bore
> The Heavens in my womb.[4]

So the complexity grows; Leda and Jupiter, the Virgin and the falling flare, the shooting star, Parnell's Funeral, the archer on the

---

[1] 'Coole Park and Ballylee, 1931,' *C.P.*, p. 275.

[2] 'The Irish Dramatic Movement'; *P. & C.*, p. 25. But the allusion must be to Villiers de l'Isle-Adam's satiric novel, *M. Triboulat Bonhomet* (1887). Dr. Bonhomet is a hunter of swans.

[3] *C.P.*, p. 241. Yeats clearly owes something to T. Sturge Moore's poem of 'Leda'. Compare with the above

> . . . Sounds that made thee know, Troy must be burned,
> Helen be loved, and blamed;
> Ay, distant, 'neath thy closed lids, were discerned
> Those shriek-pulsed towers that flamed.

A similar debt was acknowledged over 'The Tower', III. (*C.P.*, p. 533, Notes).

[4] 'The Mother of God,' ibid., p. 281.

Cretan coin. The whole cluster swings back to the arrow, the bow, the reading of Ulysses' fight with the suitors in the *Odyssey*; and this was an incident that affected Yeats most powerfully. The psychological values of that symbol, the conflict of the One with the Many, require no emphasis.

The value of the symbol may, as Yeats pointed out, contain something of an allegory: as in his use of the Blind Man, the Lame Man, the Hunchback, and Saint and the Fool. The Blind Man is the body, the Lame Man the soul.[1] Hunchback and Saint and Fool belong to the last three crescents of the Phases of the Moon. The Hunchback appears to stand for Pure Mind which is no longer concerned with the Body, and as such is equated with 'the aged man' or woman, constrained to perceive the inwardness and unity of things. The Fool is the Lear-type, the licensed commentator on events: the simplicity of the child; the poet freed from the conventions of poetry and civilization to criticism of religion, or love, or politics: so that the beggar can criticize the king. There is a note to *On Baile's Strand* that is relevant: 'The Fool in both plays is perhaps the Fat Fool of Folk-lore who is "as wide and wild as a hill" and not the Thin Fool of modern romance.' (I cannot trace the reference.) Man in old age can be in turn all of these, and the character-types are integrated with myth and history.[2]

As the work grows more mature, the symbols, without losing their processional character, become more closely associated in time. It is a natural step in the perception of unity: myth and legend emerge out of the past to acquire a validity in the present: '... when I prepared "Oedipus at Colonus" for the Abbey Stage I saw that the wood of the Furies in the opening scene was any Irish haunted wood.'[3] Greek myth and Irish legend and the Civil War mingle in this foreshortening of time into the unity of vision:

> When Pearse summoned Cuchulain to his side
> What stalked through the Post Office?[4]

---

[1] 'When I had finished I found them in some medieval Irish sermon as a simile of soul and body, and then that they had some like meanings in a Buddhist Sutra' (Introduction to *The Cat and the Moon, W. & B.*, p. 138.)

[2] Enid Welsford's *The Fool* is relevant here.

[3] *On the Boiler*, p. 28.

[4] 'The Statues,' *C.P.*, p. 375. Note the *Hamlet*-word, 'stalked'.

> Man-picker Niamh leant and sighed
> By Oisin on the grass;
> There sighed amid his choir of love
> Tall Pythagoras.[1]

Sometimes Yeats seizes a phrase from his casual reading, ponders it, and weaves it into verse. The 'choir of love' appears twice: once in this passage and once in 'The Delphic Oracle upon Plotinus'.

> Behold that great Plotinus swim,
> Buffeted by such seas;
> Bland Rhadamanthus beckons him,
> But the Golden Race looks dim,
> Salt blood blocks his eyes.
> Scattered on the level grass
> Or winding through the grove
> Plato there and Minos pass,
> There stately Pythagoras
> And all the choir of Love.[2]

The source-material appears to be the following from the *Oracle* of Apollo:

> . . . where Minos and Rhadamanthus dwell, great brethren of the golden race of mighty Zeus; where dwells the just Aeacus, and Plato, consecrated power, and stately Pythagoras and all else that form the Choir of Immortal Love, there where the heart is ever lifted in joyous festival.[3]

But the whole passage is puzzling, until we turn to Henry More's 'The Oracle',[4] and to MacKenna's translation of Porphyry:

> How oft, when bitter wave of troubled flesh,
> And whirl-pool-turnings of the lower spright,

---

[1] 'News for the Delphic Oracle', *C.P.*, p. 376.

[2] 'The Delphic Oracle upon Plotinus', ibid., p. 306. It was natural that oracles and prophecies should fascinate Yeats.

[3] This quotation is from MacKenna's translation of Plotinus, Vol. I, p. 23, and is from Porphyry. Yeats had read this translation in 1918 (Mrs Yeats). But the passage is also quoted, though in a different translation, in G. R. S. Mead, *Select Works of Plotinus* (1921). Mead was Secretary of the Theosophical Society. The first two lines appear to be suggested by: '. . . The Oracle also adds, that while Plotinus was wandering [on the sea of life] the Gods frequently directed him into the right path.' Minos, Rhadamanthus and Aeacus are the 'judges of immortal souls'.

[4] The Oracle, or *A Paraphrasticall Interpretation of the answer of* APOLLO, *when he was consulted by* AMELIUS *whither* PLOTINUS' *soul went when he departed this life.* Philosophical Poems of Henry More, ed. Bullough, pp. 160–1.

Thou stoutly strov'st with, Heaven did thee refresh . . .
While thou in tumbling seas did strongly toyl . . .
Here Rhadamanthus, and just Æacus,
Here Minos wonnes, with those that liv'd of yore
I' th' golden age; here Plato vigorous
In holy virtue, and fair Pythagore.
These been the goodly Off-spring of Great Jove,
And liven here, and whoso filled the Quire
And sweet assembly of immortal Love
*Purging their spirits with refining fire.*

We can perhaps show a further complexity. Yeats was interested in the various artists who had illustrated Dante. Among them he describes the work of Stürler, 'very poor in drawing, very pathetic and powerful in invention . . . There are admirable and moving figures who, *having set love above reason*, listen in the last abandonment of despair to the judgement of Minos . . .'[1] The poem portrays the landscape of heaven or perfection towards which Plotinus journeys through the familiar image of the 'buffeting' seas.[2]

Another fragment from Plotinus may be picked up and pondered over, and we can watch, as it were, the process of defining the symbolic values. A passage quoted in *Per Amica Silentia Lunae* is found in Plotinus:

> There are two realities, the terrestrial and the *condition of fire*. All power is from the terrestrial condition, for there all opposites meet and there only is the extreme of choice possible, full freedom. And there the heterogeneous is, and evil, for evil is the strain one upon another of opposites; but in the condition of fire is all music and all rest.[3]

This explains, perhaps, the image in 'Vacillation' vii:

THE SOUL.    Seek out reality, leave things that seem.
THE HEART.   What, be a singer born and lack a theme?
THE SOUL.    Isaiah's coal, what more can man desire?
THE HEART.   Struck dumb in the simplicity of fire![4]

[1] *E. & I.*, p. 143.
[2] W. Y. Tindall, *The Permanence of Yeats*, p. 276, quotes some of the Latin of Ficino which Yeats had read in MacKenna. Tindall calls it 'a gay, preposterous and very successful poem, filled with mysterious overtones . . .' One such overtone may be the connection of Dante and Plotinus.
[3] *P.A.S.L.*, p. 70.
[4] 'Daemon and man are opposites; man passes from heterogeneous objects to the simplicity of fire' (*P.A.S.L.*, p. 79).

THE SOUL.    Look on that fire, salvation walks within.
THE HEART.    What theme had Homer but original sin?[1]

The allusion in Isaiah vi is well known, but is worth quoting in full, for the less-known verses that follow may have some relevance:

> Then flew one of the seraphims unto me, having a live coal in his hand which he had taken with the tongs from off the altar; and he laid it upon my mouth and said, Lo, this hath touched thy lips, *and thine iniquity is taken away, and thy sin purged.*

(Consider,

Measure the lot, forgive myself the lot

and

When such as I cast out remorse.)

Also I heard the voice of the Lord saying, Whom shall I send, and who will go for us? Then said I, Here am I; send me. And he said, Go and tell this people, Hear ye indeed, but understand not; and see ye indeed, but perceive not.

The hidden significance of Isaiah's message would have appealed to Yeats, who speaks in several prefaces, as well as in 'The Phases of the Moon', of his prophetic 'riddles'. The fire image may have many origins; the normal conversion symbol, the *Upanishads*, the passage from More quoted above, or Plotinus again: 'Hence it is that fire, unlike all material things, is beautiful in and by itself alone . . . itself admitting no other to itself, all the others penetrated by it.' It is linked to Berkeley's philosophy too: 'The American Samuel Johnson and his Irish disciples will understand that this light, this intellectual Fire, is that continuity which holds together 'the perceptions', that it is a substitute for the old symbol god'.[2]

The same passage underlies the thought in the fourth stanza of 'Byzantium':

> Dying into a dance
> An agony of trance
> An agony of flame that cannot singe a sleeve.

We can see the complexity of the death-imagery. 'One remembers the girl in the Japanese play whose Ghost tells a Priest of a slight sin

---

[1] *C.P.*, p. 285. Hence the 'unchristened heart' of Homer in the following poem to von Hügel. Homer seems to signify for Yeats the violent, heroic and lonely attributes of the poet. Wilde had praised his early work as Homeric.

[2] *Explorations*, pp. 324–5.

which seems a great sin because of its unforeseen and unforeseeable consequences, and that she is persecuted by flames. If she but touch a pillar, she says, it bursts into flames, and the Priest who knows that these flames are but her own conscience made visible, tells her that if she cease to believe in them they must cease to exist. She thanks him, but the flames return, for she cannot cease to believe, and the play ends with a dance which is the expression of her agony.'[1] Behind this we may think of the Stoic quotation in *A Vision*, 'the fire where all the Universe returns to its seed',[2] *Purgatorio* XXVII; and particularly (in view of the *singe* and a reference to 'the form of the fourth' in the Fiery Furnace) to Daniel iv.

### IV

The imagery of 'The Second Coming', 'this much atomized poem', has presented difficulties which are largely of our own making. The *falcon* was originally *hawk*,[3] and the hawk is familiar as one of Yeats' favourite emblems. The spirit of man has lost contact with tradition, wisdom, control; a civilization is passing, and the antithetical or subjective age is at hand. The *widening gyre* is appropriate to the mounting of the hawk in spirals; we may quote Blome:[4]

> . . . then let fly your *Hawk*, and the Kite perceiving the surprize, doth endeavour to preserve her selfe by mounting up and winding the most she can. And here the Combat begins, *but oft-times none can see where it ends*, both mounting out of sight . . .

If Yeats had in mind the Bolshevik revolution, *mere anarchy* is appropriate: but it would be relevant also to 'The Troubles' in Ireland.[5] *Loosed* and *blood-dimmed tide* have Shakespearean precedents, and we may think also of 'the drowning of the dykes';

[1] *A Vision* (A), p. 225. This is a recurrent thought. But see Kermode's *Romantic Image* for Loie Fuller and her fire-dance; and Wilson's discussion of the Nōh *Motomezuka* as a source. (*Iconography*, p. 214.)

[2] (B), p. 247.

[3] v. Stallworthy, op. cit. pp. 17–18. But we may suggest that Yeats attached less emphasis to the long-winged hawk than to the needs of metre. Stallworthy also points out the world events which prompted the sense of disintegration.

[4] *Hawking or Faulconry*, 1686.

[5] But hardly, as Hone suggested, to the threat that The Tower might be burned.

*ceremony* is much in his mind now, as in 'A Prayer for My Daughter'. Behind this may be Castiglione, and Chapman's continuation of *Hero and Leander*, doubly impressive because of the Pythagorean reference:

> Thus Time and all-states-ordering Ceremony
> Hath banish'd all offence: Time's golden thigh
> Upholds the flowering body of the earth
> In sacred harmony, and every birth
> Of men and actions makes legitimate;
> Being us'd aright, the use of time is fate.[1]

'The best lack all conviction' is perhaps a Shelley echo:

> The good want power, but to weep barren tears.
> The powerful goodness want . . .[2]

But it is over the second movement that controversy has raged. The mysterious sphinx-like figure, always enigmatic, suggests evil, violence, an antithetic religious movement:

> . . . It [the approaching antithetical influx] must reverse our era and resume past eras in itself; what else it must be no man can say, for always at the critical moment the *Thirteenth Cone*, the sphere, the unique intervenes.[3]

Ellmann was, I think, the first to point to the reference in *Autobiographies*:

> . . . there rose before me mental images that I could not control: a desert and a black Titan raising himself up by his two hands from a heap of ancient ruins.[4]

It is, as Ellmann says, a male or Egyptian sphinx. A reference to the Preface in *Wheels and Butterflies* is relevant:

> Had I begun *On Baile's Strand* or not when I began to imagine, as always at my left side just out of range of the sight, a brazen winged beast that I associated with laughing, ecstatic destruction?[5]

The 'indignant desert birds' have the usual ominous significance; they occur in *Calvary*:

[1] *The Third Sestiad.*
[2] *P.U.* 11. 625–8: also cit. Weeks and Stallworthy.
[3] *A Vision* (B), p. 263.
[4] p. 185. Many critics have noted the possible reference to 'Ozymandias'.
[5] *Explorations*, p. 392.

Another cries,
'Call on your father now before your bones
Have been picked bare by the great desert birds.'

I would not go as far as Wilson in relating them specifically to bird-daemons, 'precipitated into action' 'at that subjective rebirth'.[1] The possibilities of the *rough beast* are endless; they do not add to the poem. It may be a vision based on any or all the quotations given above; or a Blake illustration: or the man-headed sphinx drawn by Sturge Moore for Friberg's translation of Villiers de l'Isle Adam; or the brazen wingéd beasts in Ricketts' illustrations for Wilde's *Salome*. The Books of *Daniel* and *Revelation* are full of such apocalyptic and cyclic invasions: it is sufficient to quote from the former:

And the rough goat is the king of Grecia: and the great horn that is between his eyes is the first king.

And in the latter time of their kingdom, when the transgressors are come to the full, a king of fierce countenance, and understanding dark sentences, shall stand up.

And his power shall be mighty, but not by his own power: and he shall destroy wonderfully, and shall prosper, and practise, and shall destroy the mighty and holy people.[2]

The general meaning is clear. The premonition of a new era causes the stirring of the inexorable historical power that is latent in the desert ('Do not all religions come from the desert?'). Christianity has brought in the Irrational.[3] Now the period of two thousand years is drawing to a close. The new order will be powerful (the Black Titan), inscrutable (the Sphinx). It will be in opposition to Christianity; *beast* against the holy child; *rough*[4] against tenderness; *slouches* with the overtones of casual arrogance and cruelty (as of a killer), yet beginning the new antithetical cycle from the traditional Bethlehem. There is a conversation recorded by Lady Gregory which is pertinent:

[1] *Iconography*, p. 200.
[2] Daniel viii, 21–?4.
[3] *v.* the ending of *The Resurrection*.
[4] *cf.* 'What from the forest came? What beast has licked its young' (*C.P.*, p. 331), and his introduction to *The Ten Principal Upanishads*: 'These forest sages began everything; no fundamental problems of philosophy, nothing that has disturbed the schools to controversy, escaped their notice.' (pp. 10–11.)

Yeats talking of his work and of the consciousness outside ourselves
from which knowledge comes, and which he believes will lead to
another revelation, perhaps not for another two hundred years, he
thinks will not be so spiritual, so outside the world as Christ. I say
perhaps more like Buddha and he says, 'Yes. That is the antithesis
"they" use, Christ and Buddha.'[1]

It is of interest that the animal and bird symbolism is steadily
reduced as Yeats grows older. Irish myth is foreshortened, discarded
unless it can be made relevant to the present: the reading and travels
from 1922 are reflected in his choice, the Byzantine marbles, Greek
and Roman statuary, the scraps from Plotinus and Plato, the Tower
and the Sword. It is as if the range of symbols were being deliberately reduced to include only those which presented a series of
links with other symbols; which could be seen as facets of a relatively
few dominant experiences, and, being purged of all extraneous
significance, could give that sharp definition which there was in
his own mind. Among the most frequent charges made by his
contemporaries against his work, up to 1916, is that he had forsaken
the earlier lyricism for a pedantic obscurity. These judgements read
ironically enough now.

v

Critical attacks on the image and the symbol are familiar. They
include accusations of ambiguity, contradiction, imprecision,
arbitrary selection, 'private' significance; and finally, contradiction.

It is perhaps helpful to think of each symbol as a many-sided
crystal which has grown slowly from the solutions of tradition, from
the dissolved thought of many minds. The process of growth does
not stop. As the symbol is revolved in the hands of the poet new
facets take fire and light; or fail to illumine if the imaginative power
drops to that of the mere artificer. But the whole remains many-
faced, and time may turn the symbol a little. 'Symbol endeavours,
as it were, to *be* that of which it speaks, and imitates reality by the
multiplicity of its significance'.[2] ('The mirror-scaled serpent is
multiplicity'[3] contains at least five submerged images.)

[1] *Journals*, p. 261. 'They' are the Instructors of *A Vision*.
[2] Austin Farrer, *A Rebirth of Images*, p. 19.
[3] 'Ribh denounces Patrick,' *C.P.*, p. 328.

The facets of the crystal continue to shed and radiate their meanings. It is in the nature of the whole complex form that some of these faces should appear to offer contradictions, or contradictory meanings that can co-exist. A further dimension has been added by the unconscious; which is why poets, questioned as to what they meant or intended, refuse to give an explicit answer. All that criticism or exegesis may dare to do is to gesture towards interpretations, making due allowance for the refractions of subjective judgement. Our basis for these attempted gestures is, first and always, the poem itself, and especially its rhythmic integrity. Next in relevance comes the biographical pattern, the state of mind at the time of writing, the ancillary reading, the poet's established stylistic usage elsewhere; and, if there are esoteric depth-meanings, delicate or unconscious, these are relevant. The difficulties have been put concisely by Austin Farrer:

> The purpose of symbols is that they should be immediately understood, the purpose of expounding them is to restore and build up such an understanding. This is a task of some delicacy. The author had not with his conscious mind thought out every sense, every interconnection of his imagery. They had worked in his thinking, they had not themselves been thought. If we endeavour to expose them, we shall appear to over-intellectualize the process of his mind, to represent an imaginative birth as a speculative construction. Such a representation not merely misrepresents, it also destroys belief, for no one can believe in the process when it is thus represented. No mind, we realize, could *think* with such complexity, without destroying the life of the product of thought. Yet, if we do not thus intellectualize, we cannot expound at all; it is a necessary distortion of method, and must be patiently endured by the reader. Let it be said once for all that the convention of intellectualization is not to be taken literally. We make no pretence of distinguishing between what was discursively thought and what intuitively conceived in a mind which penetrated its images with intelligence and rooted its intellective acts in imagination.[1]

[1] Farrer, op. cit.

CHAPTER TEN

# Myth and Magic

I need some mind that, if the cannon sound
From every quarter of the world, can stay
Wound in mind's wandering
As mummies in the mummy-cloth are wound.
                                    'All Souls' Night'.

That we may believe that all men possess the supernatural powers, I
would restore to the philosopher his mythology. – *A Vision.*

It is the effort to prove the myth, century after century, that has made
civilization.[1]

I

There is a mass of legend, often malicious ('the mirror of malicious
eyes') concerning Yeats' view of magic, and his practices. Rosicrucianism, his association (though it seems to have been slight)
with Madame Blavatsky, 'the low comedian of the world to come';
his incursions into the Christian kabbala and the hermetic philosophies; his miscellaneous reading of Swedenborg, Blake, the Neo-
Platonists, Indian and Arabian mystics; all these go to form the
initial stock of the 'rag-and-bone shop of the heart'. It is typical
of the man that his reading was desultory and unsystematic: 'I have
read somewhere that . . .' is a common phrase in his essays; and
'sometimes the more vivid the fact the less do I remember my
authority. Where did I pick up that story of the Byzantine bishop
and the singer of Antioch, where learn that to anoint your body with
the fat of a lion ensured the favour of a king?'[2] The acquisitive poetic

---

[1] Yeats, in conversation with Myles Dillon.

[2] *Explorations*, p. 291. He picked it up in 'The Life of St Pelagia the
Hermit', in Helen Waddell's *The Desert Fathers*, pp. 178–80. 'A certain
Byzantine Bishop had said upon seeing a singer of Antioch, "I looked long

instinct appears to be always at work, and his taste for the recondite as source-material may well have been another device to achieve a certain remoteness, a defended position. All this can be twisted into a picture of the amateur of magic, the member of the Ghost Club, half in earnest, half charlatan: taking himself and his occult world too seriously and allowing it to cloud and distort his judgement. And, since the whole matter raises the question of a poet's use of his material, it is well to attempt some analysis of this magic.

I suggest that the key to it may be found in the opening stanza of a bad but interesting poem:

> Because there is safety in derision
> I talked about an apparition,
> I took no trouble to convince,
> Or seem plausible to a man of sense,
> Distrustful of that popular eye
> Whether it be bold or sly.
> *Fifteen apparitions have I seen;*
> *The worst a coat upon a coat-hanger.*[1]

Now the fifteen apparitions were in reality only seven: *fifteen* was brought in (much as Keats altered the 'score' of kisses in *La Belle Dame Sans Merci* to 'four') in deference to the demands of metre. 'The Apparitions' are a series of death-dreams that occurred after his illness in Majorca, and were of special significance in relation to Lady Gregory's death, and to his own.[2] Two readings are possible. It may be that the worst of the apparitions was quite literally, the worst, too terrible to be contemplated, linked perhaps to the image of himself as an 'old scarecrow'; suggesting, too, the complex speculations over the nature of matter and his readings of Bertrand Russell, Whitehead, G. E. Moore and the prolonged arguments

---

upon her beauty, knowing that I would behold it upon the day of judgement, and I wept to remember that I had taken less care of my soul than she of her body'." (*A Vision* (A) p. 157; (B), p. 285.) But it would have been typical of Yeats' associative thinking to have transmuted Byzantine material to illuminate, say, 'Crazy Jane and the Bishop'. He seems to have collected unusual scraps of information at an early date; as in John Sherman's comment on his fiancée: 'It is clear she did not know that a French writer on magic says the luxurious and extravagant hate frogs because they are cold, solitary and dreary.' (*John Sherman*, p. 49.)

[1] 'The Apparitions,' *C.P.*, p. 386
[2] I am indebted to Mrs Yeats for this information.

on the nature of reality with T. Sturge Moore.[1] Alternatively (but not exclusively) we may consider that 'there is safety in derision' is a key phrase. It involves what Yeats called 'scrutiny by the intellect', born of the knowledge that the visions, which 'A.E.' had taught him to see, were not to be accepted at their face value. By 1922 he had adopted the maxim, 'the thing seen is never the vision, nor the thing heard the message'.[2] Further, if mystery or magic became certain, wholly believed, it was no longer magic or mystery; and to himself as well as to his audience his own Sibylline stature would have been diminished through that certainty. Jack Yeats' image of his brother's position is worth considering: 'he was like a man on a moving staircase, perpetually putting one foot off the staircase on to the ground'. It is true that this ambiguous attitude can be countered by assertions so definite in their implied beliefs that they must be taken seriously: 'I have again and again tested the visibility and audibility of mind-created forms,'[3] or 'The experiments made by J. Ochorowicz in photographing images of the mind were made with the medium Stanislava Tomsczyk (now Mrs Everard Fielding) at Warsaw and are well known.'[4]

I do not know the nature of these 'tests' and 'experiments', but Yeats was obviously concerned to check and verify them so far as he thought possible, and so far as his temperamental inclinations to a partial belief allowed; and was prepared to admit failure, distortion and delusion in these phenomena. Some of them, on the edge of consciousness, were phantasmagoric, but still, perhaps, capable of generating images for poetry. Early magical experiences are stored, modified and re-combined in memory, and are then recalled when some event, personal or political, appears to assert their validity. The white fowl that sat on the highest bough of the Tree of Life[5] might become the golden cock of 'Byzantium'; the great love stories, like that of Baile and Aillinn, renewed themselves perpetually (there was Blake's word for it) in the present.

It is clear that from the first Yeats wished to create a rhetorical

[1] See *T.S.M. Letters*, in particular pp. 58–108.
[2] This is a note taken down by L. A. G. Strong, to whom I am indebted, from W. B. Y.'s conversation.
[3] *T.S.M. Letters*, p. 82.
[4] Ibid., p. 69.
[5] *E. & I.*, pp. 44–45.

and processional mythology, a framework of events which would allow to these past memories their full significance and continuity in relation to the past. He was enough of a Victorian to be implicated in the religious controversy. 'I was unlike others of my generation in one thing only. I am very religious, and deprived by Huxley and Tyndall, whom I detested, of the simple-minded religion of my childhood, I had made a new religion, almost an infallible church of poetic tradition, of a fardel[1] of stories, and of personages, and of emotions, inseparable from their first expression, passed on from generation to generation by poets and painters with some help from philosophers and theologians.[2] I wished for a world, where I could discover this tradition perpetually. . . . I had even created a dogma: "Because these imaginary people are created out of the deepest instinct of man, to be his measure and his norm, whatever I can imagine those mouths speaking may be the nearest I can go to truth." '[3]

This material, part traditional, part personal, and part to be acquired by study, is to be fused into a system; not a philosophical system but one which should have its roots among the people and their folk-lore:

> Might I not, with health and good luck to aid me, create some new *Prometheus Unbound*; Patrick or Columbkil, Oisin or Fion, in Prometheus' stead; and, instead of Caucasus, Cro-Patric or Ben Bulben? Have not all races had their first unity from a mythology, that marries them to rock and hill?[4]

In all this there was support from 'A.E.', whose belief in the Otherworld, reincarnation and the earth gods was held simply and tenaciously. 'A.E.' could cite Kant in support of Yeats' views on communication with the supra-natural:

> I am much disposed to assert the existence of immaterial natures in the world and to place my own soul in the class of these beings. It

[1] Fardel: the Autolycus-word is interesting. The rapid and violent association of images from 'the old rag-and-bone shop of the heart' becomes more pronounced as the technique matures and 'patterns' become clear.

[2] Cf. the allusions to Plato, Plotinus, Vico, Henry More, McTaggart, von Hügel. The history of the Trinity, and heretical modifications of that 'abstract-Greek absurdity', seems to have been one of his obsessions.

[3] *Autobiographies*, pp. 115–16. ('Where got I that truth? Out of a medium's mouth.')

[4] Ibid., pp. 193–4.

will hereafter, I know not where or when, yet be proved that the human
soul stands even in this life in indissoluble connection with all immaterial natures in the spirit world, that it reciprocally acts on these and
receives inspiration from them.[1]

'A.E's' vision was as definite as Blake's: 'He has made drawings
since he came here of quite a number of supernatural beings.'[2]
His theory of Anima Mundi was in substance that of Yeats and it,
too, depended on reincarnation:

> I do not think I could say of any of my earlier poems that I had
> learned in experience or suffering here what was transmuted into song.
> Indeed I would reverse the order and say that we first imagine, and
> that later the imagination attracts its affinities, and we live in the body
> what had first arisen in soul. I had the sense that that far-travelled
> psyche was, in this and other waking dreams, breathing into the new
> body it inhabited some wisdom born out of its myriad embodiments.[3]

There were other grounds for believing that Ireland might
provide him with the necessary material. Long before he had foreshortened history in *A Vision* he found confirmation of his cycle-
theories in the world of the peasant: '. . . I have noticed that
clairvoyance, pre-vision, and allied gifts, rare among the educated
classes, are common among peasants. Among those peasants there
is much of Asia, where Hegel has said every civilization begins.
Yet we must hold to what we have that the next civilization may
be born, not from a virgin's womb, nor a tomb without a body, but
of our own rich experience.'[4]

This first mythology, then, is to be at once historical, pantheistic
and prophetic (like *Prometheus*); and at the same time local and
patriotic. The final result was to be profoundly mystical: '. . . I
delighted in every age where poet and artist confined themselves
gladly to some inherited subject-matter known to the whole people,
for I thought that in man and race alike there is something called
"Unity of Being", using that term as Dante used it when he compared beauty in the *Convito* to a perfectly proportioned human
body.'[5] We have here a further stage: this 'Unity of Being' is linked

[1] *Song and Its Fountains*, p. 41.
[2] Wade, p. 287.
[3] *Song and Its Fountains*, p. 29.
[4] *On the Boiler*, p. 27.
[5] *Autobiographies*, p. 190.

to the realization, or the discovery by the great artist, of formal
perfection of the body: and becomes later the symbolism which he
finds in measurement.[1]

Unity of being is attained through the projection into consciousness of men's common ancestral memories. The thought is faintly[2]
of Shelley. It is a difficult process.

> . . . Nations, races, and individual men are unified by an image,
> or bundle of related images, symbolical or evocative of the state
> of mind, which is of all states of mind not impossible, the most difficult
> to that man, race, or nation; because only the greatest obstacle that
> can be contemplated without despair rouses the will to full intensity.[3]

The mythology was at hand in the Celtic legend. From the point
of view of a young man in the Nineties, the founder of literary
societies in London and in Dublin, it held great promise. If Ireland
could be awakened to her natural heritage of the heroic ages of
Cuchulain, Finn, Conchubor, Deirdre and the rest, if the people of
Ireland could really see their country as Cathleen-ni-Houlihan,[4] a
unity both spiritual and political would follow. Cathleen-ni-Houlihan might serve as the symbol of beauty and womanhood and
a romantic Ireland. The quarry was a rich one: Hyde, Martyn,
Lady Gregory with her *Gods and Fighting Men* and *Cuchulain
of Muirthemne* were all working it. There were sufficient memories

[1] See pp. 206–7.

[2] I say faintly; for he had striven to rid himself of Shelley's influence,
because 'his system of thought was constructed by his logical faculty to satisfy
desire, not a symbolical revelation received after suspension of desire.' At
the same time, there are many verbal echoes of Shelley, particularly from
*Prometheus* and *The Witch of Atlas*. And there seems to be some relevance in

> The Magus Zoroaster, my dead child,
> Met his own image walking in the garden.
> That apparition, sole of man, he saw.
> For know there are two worlds of life and death . . .
>                                                      *P.U.*, 192.

to the second verse of 'Byzantium', where *image* is used in Shelley's sense.

[3] *Autobiographies*, pp. 194–5. It is of interest that Yeats wanted the Irish 'to
unite literature to their great political passion, to live as the men of '48 by
by the light of noble books and the great tradition of the past'.

[4] 'One night I had a dream almost as distinct as a vision, of a cottage
where there was well-being and firelight and talk of a marriage, and into the
midst of that cottage there came an old woman in a long cloak. She was
Ireland herself, that Cathleen-ni-Houlihan for whom so many songs have
been sung. . . .' (*Plays*, 1931. Notes, p. 419.)

in place-name and legend, and dramatic episodes at his very door. 'I have a story of a Sligo stable boy who was dismissed by his employer because he had sent her late husband's ghost to haunt a weatherbeaten lighthouse, far out in the bay'.[1] There were vivid Elizabethan phrases from 'The Book of the People', as in the conversation recorded in Lady Gregory's *Visions and Beliefs*:

> 'How did you know you were damned?'
> 'I saw my own thoughts going past me like blazing ships.'[2]

At times the imagined or recorded tales seem to possess a curious quality as if a pre-Raphaelite vision had mingled with the Celtic legend. '"Sometimes at night", said the boy, "when you are reading with a stick of mountain ash in your hand, I look out of the door and see, now a great man driving swine among the hazels, and now many little people in red caps who come out of the lake driving little white cows before them. . . And I fear the tall white-armed ladies who come out of the air, and move slowly hither and thither, crowning themselves with the roses or with the lilies, and shaking about them their living hair, which moves, for so I have heard them tell the little people, with the motion of their thoughts, now spreading out and now gathering close to their heads."'[3]

This theory of the common myth, its peculiar symbolism, and its undoubted power, gave him grounds for belief that this consciousness of the past might yet unify the people. There should be pride in that national heritage that could lead to a new flowering of art and national life; much as the eighteenth century, for a few brief years, hoped for a new Homeric epic of the North from Macpherson's *Ossian*, or as Morris sought a rejuvenating simplicity and strength in the Norse saga. The pattern was to include traditional mystic symbolism fused with the common beliefs of the people; the folk-lore of Lady Gregory's *Visions and Beliefs* could amalgamate, in a poet's mind, with classical Irish legend. The poetry would take full advantage of the genius of place, using the numinous associations of the great pilgrimages: 'I think I would go – though certainly

---

[1] *A Vision* (A), p. 239.
[2] The phrase lived with him, as such memorable things were apt to do; it is quoted again in *If I were Four and Twenty*, p. 63.
[3] *Stories of Red Hanrahan* (1927), p. 134.

I am no Catholic and never shall be one – upon both of our great pilgrimages, to Croagh Patrick and to Lough Derg. . . . . In many little lyrics I would claim that stony mountain [Croagh Patrick] for all Christian and pagan faith in Ireland, believing, in the exultation of my youth, that in three generations I should have made it as vivid in the memory of all imaginative men among us, as the sacred mountain of Japan is in that of the collectors of prints: and I would, being but four-and-twenty and a lover of lost causes, memorialize bishops to open once again that Lough Derg cave of vision once beset by an evil spirit in the form of a long-legged bird with no feathers on its wings.'[1]

This bird, or its kin, recurs in 'The Pilgrim', and may well be linked to the mysterious birds in Margaret Clarke's picture, 'St Patrick Climbs Croagh Patrick', in the Municipal Gallery. It recurs in verse:

> A great black ragged bird appeared when I was in the boat;
> Some twenty feet from tip to tip had it stretched rightly out,
> With flopping and with flapping it made a great display,
> But I never stopped to question, what could the boatman say
> *But fol de rol de rolly O.*[2]

The promise was kept in the little lyrics: 'The Dancer at Cruachan and Cro-Patrick':

> I, proclaiming that there is
> Among birds or beasts or men
> One that is perfect or at peace,
> Danced on Cruachan's windy plain,
> Upon Cro-Patrick sang aloud;
> All that could run or leap or swim
> Whether in wood, water or cloud,
> Acclaiming, proclaiming, declaiming Him.[3]

And again in 'The Pilgrim':

> Round Lough Derg's holy island I went upon the stones,
> I prayed at all the Stations upon my narrow-bones,

---

[1] *If I were Four and Twenty*, p. 5. For the 'evil spirit' Mrs Yeats has referred me to Lady Wilde's *Ancient Legends of Ireland*: 'In another lake there is a huge-winged creature, it is said, which escaped the power of St Patrick, and when he gambols in the water such storms arise that no boat can withstand the strength of the waves' (Vol. II, p. 124).

[2] *C.P.*, p. 360.

[3] Ibid., p. 304.

And then I found an old man, and though I prayed all day
And that old man beside me, nothing would he say
*But fol de rol de rolly, O.*

And this did not exclude the possibility of a greater complexity,
when legend blended into esoteric symbols:

> I thought that for a time I could rhyme of love, calling it *The
> Rose*,[1] because of the Rose's double meaning; of a fisherman who
> had 'never a crack' in his heart;[2] of an old woman complaining of
> the idleness of the young,[3] or of some cheerful fiddler,[4] all those things
> that 'popular poets' write of, but that I must some day – on that day
> when the gates began to open – become difficult or obscure.[5]

At the same time the age was ripe for a revelation, or a second
coming. Yeats was acutely aware of the breaking-up of the world.
In his essay on 'The Tragic Generation' there is already the thought
of the gyre, of the age moving towards its opposite:

> Why are these strange souls born everywhere today? with hearts
> that Christianity, as shaped by history, cannot satisfy. . . . Why should
> we believe that religion can never bring round its antithesis? Is it true
> that our air is disturbed, as Mallarmé said, by 'the trembling of the
> veil of the temple', or 'that our whole age is seeking to bring forth a
> sacred book'? Some of us thought that book near towards the end of
> last century, but the tide sank again.[6]

The thought of the Sacred Book, the book that the hermit-saint
may interpret, comes again in the last plays and in 'Supernatural
Songs'. There were exciting possibilities in 'scientific' spiritualism.
'If photographs that I saw handed round in Paris thirty years ago
can be repeated and mental images photographed, the distinction
that Berkeley drew between what man creates and what God
creates will have broken down.'[7] Recurrent visions, manifestations
of the superhuman, strengthened the possibility: 'When supernatural events begin, a man first doubts his own testimony, but when

[1] *The Rose*, 1893. See in particular 'The Secret Rose' (*The Wind among the
Reeds*, 1899) for the fusion of the Celtic legend, the Magi and pre-Raphaelitism.
[2] Cf. 'The Meditation of the Old Fisherman' (*Crossways*): 'When I was
a boy with never a crack in my heart.'
[3] Cf. 'The Song of the Old Mother'.
[4] Cf. 'The Fiddler of Dooney'.
[5] *Autobiographies*, p. 254.
[6] Ibid., p. 315.
[7] Introduction to Hone & Rossi, p. xxiv.

they repeat themselves again and again, he doubts all human testimony.'[1]

II

At this point it is important to stress the fact that Yeats' magical preoccupations were in no way peculiar to himself; and still less were they evidence (as certain critics have suggested) of perversity or mental abnormality. He was following a well-trodden road, which seems to have broadened suddenly in the later nineteenth century into a diffuse and esoteric mysticism that looked to magic for its support. And magic was more than a support; it provided a continuous sense of excited exploration. No doubt some of the excitement was in the knowledge that it was proscribed by the Churches, and that its evil lay close at hand. True mysticism would have become dispersed in its own rarefied essences. Magic fulfilled the desire for ritual, ministered to his own sense of importance; through it he could claim his position as the seer, the prophet, always withholding part of his secret; he could blur or define the symbols as the proto-thought required.

But this mysticism had a long and honourable history, although by the Nineties it had degenerated into what Auden calls 'lower-middle-class occultism'. All Neo-platonist interpretations of the doctrine of the Unity of Being had been re-affirmed, in many ways and in varying degrees, in Romantic literature. The Pythagorean souls of the star-world had been accepted by Plato; Newton considered that hypothesis plausible, and even Kant was not altogether sceptical.

All ancient nations believed in the re-birth of the soul and had probably empirical evidence like that Lafcadio Hearn found among the Japanese. In our time Schopenhauer believed it, and McTaggart thinks Hegel did, though lack of interest in the individual soul had kept him silent. It is the foundation of McTaggart's own philosophical system.[2]

Yeats was in the habit of grasping at any philosophical authority that might be wrenched to support him. He read into Berkeley too much, perhaps, of his own thought. But philosophy, however

[1] *Autobiographies*, p. 264.
[2] *Explorations*, p. 396.

much it might be adulterated by theosophy, gave him at least the assurance that he had tradition behind him; he would choose 'Plato and Plotinus for a friend'.

> I could not read philosophy till my big book was written. Those who gave me material forbid me to do so; they feared, I think, that if I did so I would split up experience till it ceased to exist. When it was written (though the proofs had yet to come) I started to read. I read for months every day Plato and Plotinus. Then I started on Berkeley and Croce and Gentile. You introduced me to your brother's work and to Russell, and I found Eddington and one or two others for myself. I am still however anything but at my ease in recent philosophy. I find your brother [G. E. Moore] extraordinarily obscure.[1]

Again he writes:

> That sentence of yours about Time, Space, and Experience, has abolished all the philosophers I have ever read – Plato, St Thomas, Kant, Hegel, Bergson and last and least the Bald One. However that very British brother of yours had already abolished the lot. Bye the bye, please don't quote him again till you have asked him this question: 'How do you account for the fact that when the Tomb of St Theresa was opened her body exuded miraculous oil and smelt of violets?' If he cannot account for such primary matters, he knows nothing.[2]

This throws some light on the thought of 'Must we part, Von Hügel' ('Vacillation', viii),[3] and there is a further letter to Mrs Shakespear[4] that is related both to it and to 'Stream and Sun at Glendalough'.

> That night before letters came I went for a walk after dark, and there among some great trees became absorbed in the most lofty philosophical conception I have found while writing *A Vision*. I suddenly seemed to understand at last, and then I smelt roses.[5] I realized the nature of the timeless spirit. Then I began to walk and in my excitement came – how shall I say – that old glory so beautiful with its autumn tint – the longing to touch it was almost unendurable. The next night I was walking in the same path and now the two

[1] *T.S.M. Letters*, p. 83.
[2] Ibid., p. 121.
[3] *C.P.*, p. 285.
[4] November 1931.
[5] Yeats was liable to these smell hallucinations, which are well known to psychologists. The experiences were sometimes shared by those present at the time. (L. A. G. Strong.)

excitements came together – the autumnal tinge incredibly spiritual remote erect delicate-featured, and mixed with it the violent physical image, the black man of Eden. Yesterday I put my thought into a poem which I enclose, but it seems to me a poor shadow of the intensity of the experience.[1]

The poem is the first of 'Vacillation':

> Between extremities
> Man runs his course;
> A brand, or flaming breath,
> Comes to destroy
> All those antinomies
> Of day and night;
> The body calls it death,
> The heart remorse.
> But if these be right
> What is joy?[2]

## III

It is a basic romantic conception that, instead of a correspondence between natural law and the logic of human thought, there is an entirely new relationship to be established by the artist or poet; the relationship between images or symbols – whether perceived in a wise passiveness, or in a state of trance, or in dreams – and the framework of external or objective existence. There is thus a free and creative life of the soul which develops in harmony with the spontaneous life of the world. Hence the language of dreams is not a series of abstract symbols consciously adopted by human beings for convenience of communication. The dream world is composed of images which are directly and intimately linked to reality. This explains the importance that Yeats attached to dreams and visions of all kinds.

But such symbols were linked to the 'ancestral memory' and were to be recognized as 'standard' components of mythology. Their recurrence in archetypal form strengthened that belief; and to Yeats and his circle the continuity of myth as shown in *The Golden Bough* was yet another proof of the fragmentary nature of

[1] I am indebted for this reference to Professor Jeffares.
[2] *C.P.*, p. 282.

Christianity.[1] The images are thus of immense though indeterminate significance, even if they cannot at once be recognized, or their meanings related to each other.

Qu'une image, retenue par le verbe d'un poète ou évoquée par l'arabesque d'un bas-relief, vienne infailliblement susciter en moi une résonance effective, je puis poursuivre la chaîne des formes fraternelles qui relie cette image aux motifs de quelque mythe très ancien: je ne connaissais pas ce mythe, et je le reconnais. Entre les fables des diverses mythologies, les contes de fées, les inventions de certains poètes et le rêve qui se poursuit en moi, je perçois une parenté profonde.[2]

In the Preface to *Fighting the Waves* Yeats seems to suggest that Jung had provided a scientific justification for the value of his symbols. 'Science has driven out the legends, stories, superstitions that protected the immature and the ignorant with symbol': his own wisdom, linked to the new sciences, might form part of 'that concrete universal which all philosophy is seeking'[3].

Yeats' interpretation was more complex than that of Jung. Yet the close similarity to Jung's habit of thought is once again emphasized by Jung's *Memories, Dreams and Reflections* (1963), and he appears to envisage a literal belief in various concepts which Jung treated as figurative. The problem of the perception of Unity demanded that occult sciences should be enlisted in its service. Once grant a sympathy between man and the universe, it becomes essential to see the destiny of man as linked to planets and stars. Man is the centre of creation, and a privileged being; he is the mirror of the universe. He will seek to explain his pilgrimage towards cosmic unity as a retracing of those steps through which unity was lost. Those steps belong to myth: and hence myth acquires a renewed importance:

> That I might hear if we should kiss
> A contrapuntal serpent hiss. . . .[4]

[1] 'When I was young we talked much of tradition, and those emotional young men, Francis Thompson, Lionel Johnson, John Gray, found it in Christianity. But now that *The Golden Bough* has made Christianity look modern and fragmentary we study Confucius with Ezra Pound, or like T. S. Eliot find in Christianity a convenient symbolism for some older or newer thought...' (Preface to *Upanishads*, p. 10).
[2] Béguin, *L'Âme Romantique et Le Rêve*, i, Introduction, p. xiii.
[3] *Explorations*, p. 376, 378.
[4] 'The Lady's Third Song,' *C.P.*, p. 345.

The heavy lingering stress on *contrapuntal* directs us towards its meanings in depth; the sound itself suggests a heavy, lithe, slack but powerful quality. The clue might rest with the dead and their traditional wisdom:

> For Hades' bobbin bound in mummy-cloth
> May unwind the winding path. . . .

The whole pursuit became exciting as the images expanded or contracted their significances, perhaps in obedience to some supernatural power:

> Quelque signe, image ou hiéroglyphe, étrangement ordonnés, parviennent à exprimer en peu d'instants ce qu'on emploierait des heures à dire en paroles.[1]

Now all these investigations, all the speculations on dream symbols, phantoms, the hidden philosophies, have a long history. Yeats could have found endless justifications for his thought in the work of Hugo, Rimbaud, Gérard de Nerval, Charles Nodier, Clemens Brentano, and a dozen others. The problem was to find one or more mythologies which would serve to link symbols in some kind of pragmatic framework, from which all else would develop.

The quest for a myth had therefore a multiple object. It was nationalist, prophetic, mystical; it provided continuity and meaning for experience; and it afforded a release for that dramatic nostalgia generated by the memories of the Sligo mountains as seen from his London surroundings. The 'Innisfree' mood lends itself easily to sentimentality;[2] and there was plenty of precedent in Mangan and Davis and T. W. Rolleston. And, above all, the myth gave him power; to shape a world in which the heroes were virile and violent, the women gentle and dreaming – all but one fierce woman whose image remained with him.

---

[1] Béguin, *op. cit.* i, p. 200.

[2] 'I think he hated all his early poems, and 'Innisfree' most of all. But one evening I begged him to read it. A look of tortured irritation came into his face and continued there until the reading was over' (*Letters to Dorothy Wellesley*, p. 192).

IV

But the limitations of the Celtic mythology were all too quickly apparent. In the first place, it had, I think, little or no connection with 'the book of the people'. Fragments of that heroic story lingered here and there among the Irish-speaking peasantry of the West: but the real body of folk-lore was built upon the knowledge and superstitions which lay everywhere to hand. Cuchulain and Oisin were remote, but banshee and leprechaun, the holy and the haunted place, the return of the dead, were close to everyday experience. In rath and wood and in the holy wells of saints there were traces of the Elder Faiths,[1] but those were less complex and more immediate in their implications than the Tuatha-da-Danaan and the Firbolgs.

Further, the 'significant actions' of that mythology, in Arnold's phrase, were few. There was the death of Deirdre, Cuchulain fighting the waves, and the epic of his death, with 'six mortal wounds', bound to the pillar, the scald-crow perching on his shoulder: an heroic image of Yeats himself that haunted him to the last, and which he used in 'Cuchulain Comforted'. But even *The Countess Cathleen* owes its source to a legend in French.

The battles and kings cannot be fitted into a coherent pattern: and they move in Yeats' verse and prose with that far-off embroidered stiffness of Spenser's or Morris' world. The long Swinburnian rhythms accentuate their remote fantastic 'beauty'; the term so constantly and aimlessly used in the critical writings of the time:

I am haunted by numberless islands, and many a Danaan shore,
Where Time would surely forget us, and Sorrow come near us no more;
Soon far from the rose and the lily and fret of the flames would we be,
Were we only white birds, my beloved, buoyed out on the foam of the sea![2]

[1] Cf. W. G. Wood-Martin, *Traces of the Elder Faiths of Ireland.*
[2] 'The White Birds', *C.P.*, p. 46. The whole poem is of interest for the Swinburne-Morris characteristics, and the pernicious influence of decadent romanticism, as well as for the faults of technique. Note the death image of the seabird that 'announced death or danger to a Pollexfen'.

The problem of Yeats was to link the Danaan shore to the peasantry.[1] He believed that Ireland could discover, from the beliefs and emotions of her common people, the habit of mind that created the religion of the Muses. But what the common people had to give was much more direct and violent and brutal than this trance-like world; only Synge, and perhaps O'Casey, could have found it. What remained, of course, when 'Helmets, crowns and swords' were thrown 'into the pit', when the circus animals had deserted, were two certainties: the dead return among the living, and there is an ancestral memory in the people as in the universe, into which the poet can send down roots and from which he can draw new vitality:

> I had as yet no clear answer, but knew myself face to face with the Anima Mundi described by Platonic philosophers, and more especially in modern times by Henry More, which has a memory independent of embodied individual memories, though they constantly enrich it with their images and their thoughts.[2]

Side by side with the development of the first mythology there is his own interest in the psychic: and the important figure is MacGregor Mathers, who initiated him into the Order of the Golden Dawn, an order of Christian kabbalists.[3] Yeats even speculated as to whether Blake had belonged to the same order. George Russell was also a visionary, but whereas he sought to reach that state through austerities, the practice of Mathers was ritualistic:

> My rituals were not to be made deliberately, like a poem, but all got by that method Mathers had explained to me, and with this hope I plunged without a clue into a labyrinth[4] of images, into that labyrinth that we are warned against in those *Oracles* which antiquity has attributed to Zoroaster, but modern scholarship to some Alexandrian poets. 'Stoop not down to the darkly splendid world wherein lieth continually a faithless depth and Hades wrapped in cloud, delighting in unintelligible images.'[5]

Mathers' method or symbolic system was to use cardboard or

---

[1] George Moore gives an amusing and malicious account of Yeats' incursion into Irish agriculture: *v. Salve*, pp. 81–84.
[2] *Autobiographies*, p. 262.
[3] Hone, *Life*, p. 71.
[4] See 'Byzantium', and the Theseus-image of the thread-clue
[5] *Autobiographies*, p. 255.

painted symbols to evoke a world beyond visible reality.[1] This
world and its symbols were fragmentary at first, but might, as Yeats
thought, ultimately cohere by association to form a new and more
deeply apprehended life. Further, one image had the power to
suggest another in a related train;[2] they can be communicated between individuals, or be shared by several people at some given point
of time, thus suggesting the possibility of some cosmic event. It
appears that revelatory images may be deliberately invoked:

> I knew a man once who, seeking for an image of the absolute, saw
> one persistent image, a slug, as though it were suggested to him that
> Being which is beyond human comprehension is mirrored in the least
> organized forms of life.[3]

In 'The Stirring of the Bones' he tells how, when staying with
Martyn at Tullyra, he decided that he must make his invocation
to the moon. After he had repeated the ritual for eight or nine nights,
he saw a galloping centaur,[4] and a moment later 'a naked woman of
incredible beauty, standing upon a pedestal and shooting an arrow
at a star'. The same night Symons, also staying at Tullyra, wrote
a poem of great beauty on this theme, but without the bow and
arrow. On Symons' return to London, he found a story, sent to
*The Savoy* by Fiona MacLeod, in which there was a vision of a
woman shooting an arrow into the sky; and later of an arrow shot at
a faun that pierced the faun's body and remained, the faun's heart
torn out and clinging to it, embedded in a tree. The child of one of
Mathers' pupils had come running in from the garden crying out:
'Oh, mother, I have seen a woman shooting an arrow into the sky

---

[1] The Tarot Pack can be used for this purpose.
[2]                Those images that yet
                Fresh images beget . . .
                        'Byzantium'
and '. . . those forms [among the leaves of Byzantine decoration] that represent
no creature eye has ever seen, *yet are begotten one upon the other as if they were
themselves living creatures*' (*A Vision* (A), p. 192).
[3] *A Vision* (A), p. 195. There is, perhaps, a suggestion of humour in
Yeats' description of this. Compare: '. . . I once visited a Cabbalist who
spent the day trying to look out of the eyes of his canary; he announced at
nightfall that all things had for it colour but no outline. His method of
contemplation was probably in error' (Introd. to Hone & Rossi, p. xxviii).
*cf.* also the episode at Madame Blavatsky's: 'A big materialist sat on the
astral double of a poor young Indian . . .' (*Wade*, p. 59).
[4] Perhaps stimulated by Sturge Moore's poem, 'The Centaur's Booty'.

and I am afraid that she has killed God.' A few months later, a little cousin dreamed of a man who shot a star with a gun and the star fell down; but 'I do not think', the child said, 'it minded dying because it was so very old', and presently the child saw the star lying in a cradle.[1]

This image of the archer and the star found on a Cretan coin, or in a Renaissance painting, became a dominant image: perhaps because it afforded such a striking instance of the cosmic validity of such a vision. He knew from Shelley that the same dream occurs again and again. Of its power upon his mind there can be no doubt. It could combine with his favourite 'Brightness falls from the air' to form the images of the first two verses of 'Parnell's Funeral' and take on strange overtones:

> . . . Brightness remains; a brighter star shoots down;
> What shudders run through all that animal blood?
> What is this sacrifice? Can someone there
> Recall the Cretan barb that pierced a star?[2]

To the memory it affords also an emblem of the artist, a justification of his historical cycles, and a re-affirmation of the workings of 'The Body of Fate':

[1] *Autobiographies*, p. 372. The inference was, of course, that some cosmic event had been recorded simultaneously and independently.

[2] *C.P.* p. 319. Yeats had read S. W. Grose's *Catalogue of Greek Coins in the Fitzwilliam Museum, Cambridge*, in which many such 'archer' coins are illustrated. There are possible instances in Vol. II, pl. 239.15 or 243.22. It is not unlikely that these illustrations suggested other images, or confirmed the sense of 'dominance' of them, e.g. of the Dolphin which occurs so frequently. There is also the Chinese poem about the archer Yi, who shot down nine suns (Waley). The image of the archer shooting at a star also occurs in Hannay's *Wisdom of the Desert*, but the source for the desert and saint imagery is the *Lausiac History of the Palladins*: and from this he seems to have derived his ideas of sainthood. It contains the source of 'Demon and Beast'.

It is quite in keeping with his methods that the *first* discovery of such symbols should be accidental: 'I suppose that I must have put hawks into the fourth stanza because I have a ring with a hawk and a butterfly upon it, to symbolize the straight road of logic, and so of mechanism, and the crooked road of intuition . . .' (Notes to *C.P.*, p. 534; of 'Meditations in Time of Civil War'.)

And there is, I think, some humour in the symbolism in *John Sherman*: "John", she said, "look at this brooch William gave me – a ladder leaning against the moon and a butterfly climbing up it. Is it not sweet? We are going to visit the poor" (p. 141).

Many years ago I saw, between sleeping and waking, a woman of incredible beauty shooting an arrow into the sky, and from the moment when I made my first guess at her meaning I have thought much of the difference between the winding movements of nature and the straight line, which is called in Balzac's *Seraphita* the 'Mark of Man', but comes closer to my meaning as the mark of saint or sage. I think that we who are poets and artists, not being permitted to shoot beyond the tangible, must go from desire to weariness and so to desire again, and live but for the moment when vision comes to our weariness like terrible lightning, in the humility of the brutes. I do not doubt those heaving circles, those winding arcs, whether in one man's life or in that of an age, are mathematical,[1] and that some one in the world, or beyond the world, has foreknown the event and pricked upon the calendar the life-span of a Christ, a Buddha, a Napoleon: that every movement, in feeling or in thought, prepares in the dark by its own increasing clarity and confidence its own executioner. We seek reality with the slow toil of our weakness and are smitten from the boundless and the unforeseen.[2]

The explanatory gloss as to the whole is in the notes to *Autobiographies* (1926), p. 473. It represents such classic examples of Yeatsian complexity, of richness of layered associations, in its relation to several poems that we may summarize it here.

The Child and the Tree are related to an apple-tree in Devonshire, which is in turn linked to an ancient Cretan hymn. But Bolder is the tree embodied; behind the myth is the Cretan Apollo who in old Cretan belief was a sun-god. But the symbolic tree is also Hebrew 'and the star at which the arrow was shot seems to have symbolized a Sephiroth attributed to the Sun'. The woman who shot the arrow is the Cretan mother-goddess, but she is also Artemis. The heart torn out refers to the Myth of the Child Slain and Reborn, which is also Cretan in origin. But all this converges, in the first of 'The Songs from a Play', on the Dionysian–Christ association, and the wounded side of Christ in *The Resurrection*.

The interest in dream-symbolism is perpetual:

When you write to me about the symbol please tell me the figures you saw as well as the conclusions you come to. I saw the white door today and the white fool. He was followed out of the door by a marriage procession who had flowers and green boughs. Last night I had a dream about two lovers, who were being watched over by a blackbird or a raven, who warned them against the malice and the slander of the

[1] *v.* the ending of 'The Gift of Harun Al-Rashid'.
[2] *Mythologies*, p. 340.

world. Was this bird a transformation of Aengus or one of his birds? You are perhaps right about the symbol, it may merely be a symbol of ideal human marriage. The slight separation of the sun and moon permits the polarity which we call sex, while it allows the creation of an emotional unity, represented by the oval and the light[1] it contains.[2]

(This may be the origin of

> a most ridiculous bird
> Tore from the clouds his marvellous moon.

in 'A Memory of Youth',[3] and of the 'miraculous strange bird' in 'Her Triumph'.[4])

In séance or in vision there was the exciting possibility that his own age had been deliberately blinded:

> Was modern civilization a conspiracy of the sub-conscious? Did we turn away from certain thoughts and things because the Middle Ages lived in terror of the dark, or had some seminal illusion been imposed upon us by beings greater than ourselves for an unknown purpose?[5]

Further, Yeats' theory of memory demanded a traffic with the dead. Memory and the ghost are only different aspects of the same experience; for

> our animal spirits are but as it were a condensation of the vehicle of *Anima Mundi*, and give substance to its images in the faint materialization of our common thought, or more grossly when a ghost is our visitor.[6]

After death we live our lives backward for a number of years, treading the halls that we have trodden, growing young, even childish again. The dead achieve a Donne-like exactness of being and desire:

> ... A ghost may come;
> For it is a ghost's right
> His element is so fine

[1] I do not understand the allusion and the grammar is obscure; but the kind of thing Yeats had in mind is shown from the note to *The Wind Among the Reeds*, quoted on p. 253.
[2] Wade, p. 324.
[3] *C.P.*, p. 137.
[4] See p. 58.
[5] *Autobiographies*, p. 264. This also is close to Jung's position.
[6] *P.A.S.L.*, p. 59.

Being sharpened by his death,
To drink from the wine-breath
While our gross palates drink from the whole wine.[1]

There is also a certain morbid excitement of the 'dark tomb haunter', and he quotes with approval (and remembering, as always, Job) Lake Harris on Shakespeare: 'Often the hair of his head stood up and all life became the echoing chambers of the tomb.'[2]

Yet is it not most important to explore continually what has been long forbidden and to do this not only 'with the 'highest moral purpose', like the followers of Ibsen, but gaily, out of sheer mischief, a sheer delight in that play of the mind. Donne could be as metaphysical as he pleased, and yet never seem as unhuman and hysterical as Shelley often does, because he could be as physical as he pleased; and besides who will thirst for the metaphysical, who have a parched tongue, if we cannot recover the Vision of Evil?[3]

'A sheer delight in that play of the mind.' I believe that, when all is said, Yeats half-believed in his world of séances, just as he half-believed (and more at one stage of his life than at another) his own world of *A Vision*: that pretexts for the play of the mind, the dramatic apprehension of the rapid and heterogeneous image, were what he sought and found. There is abundant evidence that, for him, the phenomena of the séance were real; but what was reality? There was safety in derision, or in the possibility that those phenomena were no more than the evidence for a new Berkleian Theory of Vision. The other half of the mind stands aside prepared to mock 'because there is safety in derision'. From another point of view, the tomb-haunting of the séance is the first step to the progression through ritualism and spiritualism towards certain of the traditional values to be found in death. Nathaniel Wanley's apostrophe to the Skull has at least validity in history:

... For if wee
Rightly define the true Philosophy
To be a Meditation of the Graue
Then while I hugge thee I am sure I haue
The best Philosopher. ... [4]

Yeats is redeemed from morbidity by this 'sheer mischief', the

[1] 'All Souls' Night,' *C.P.*, p. 256; and also as the epilogue to *A Vision*.
[2] *A Vision* (A), pp. 87–88.
[3] *Autobiographies*, p. 326.
[4] *Poems*, 'Good Friday'.

awareness of the physical that phrase and idiom harmonize completely in their opposition:

> 'The third thing that I think of yet',
> *Sang a bone upon the shore*
> 'Is that morning when I met
> Face to face my rightful man,
> And did after stretch and yawn':
> *A bone wave-whitened and dried in the wind.*[1]

But the passage quoted has a further significance; Donne avoids becoming inhuman or morbid 'because he could be as physical as he pleased'. Again and again Yeats pulls back his verse from the sentimental and morbid by the physical:

> O but there is wisdom
> In what the sages said;
> But stretch that body for a while
> And lay down that head
> Till I have told the sages
> Where man is comforted.[2]

Perhaps that is one justification for the 'sensuality' of the last phase.

The grave offers the possibility of a clue to the labyrinth. It is a symbol which can foreshorten human history, provide a framework for incantation, assert and stabilize Yeats' pre-occupation with ancestry (whether his own or that of the nation), and clarify and focus the problems of sensuality, old age, and death. The Christian synthesis is rejected: but that great poem to von Hügel will show the attitude clearly.

> Must we part, Von Hügel, though much alike, for we
> Accept the miracles of the saints and honour sanctity?
> The body of Saint Teresa lies undecayed in tomb[3]

[1] 'Three Things,' *C.P.*, p. 300.
[2] 'Consolation,' ibid., p. 310.
[3] This is St Teresa of Avila. 'Such a strong and wonderful perfume came from her sepulchre that it was resolved to exhume the sacred body. . . . It was found entire, incorruptible and flexible as though it had only just been laid in the tomb, and impregnated with a sweet-scented liquid such as God causes to flow from it until this day, thus attesting the sanctity of His servant by a perpetual miracle' (from the Bull of Gregory XV, 1622). St Teresa's heart was pierced by the dart of an angel, as the symbol of the heavenly love which transfixed her – the cosmic image again. I do not know whether there is a contrast suggested between the ponderous mystic utterances of von Hügel and the practical common-sense precepts of the Saint.

G

Bathed in miraculous oil, sweets odours from it come,
Healing from its lettered slab. Those self-same hands perchance
Eternalized the body of a modern saint that once
Had scooped out Pharaoh's mummy. I – though heart might find relief
Did I become a Christian man and choose for my belief
What seems most welcome in the tomb – play a predestined part.
Homer is my example and his unchristened heart.
The lion and the honeycomb, what has Scripture said?
So get you gone, Von Hügel, though with blessings on your head.[1]

The reference to Homer, standing for epic strength and virility,
occurs frequently; sometimes grouped in opposition to Horace,
and in counterpoint with Plato, as in *Mad as the Mist and Snow*.
Against this we have the homeliness of the Anglo–Irish phrases –
*unchristened* heart, *blessings on your head*. The ideas play between
saint and mummy, for *those self-same hands* are of the ghosts of
Egyptian embalmers.[2] The lion and the honeycomb is a reference
to Judges xiv, but I am still doubtful about the image; unless, as
Ellmann suggests,[3] Yeats has some private meaning. The lion is
obviously strength and energy: honey for sweetness of word, the
contrast to bitterness. So in 'The Gift of Harun Al-Rashid':

> ... To show how violent great hearts can lose
> Their bitterness, and find the honeycomb.[4]

But honeycomb can also stand for the sexual act ('Honey of generation has betrayed.')[5] and, rather strangely, for longevity.

The tomb and the ghost make possible that peculiar dispassionate
elegiac strain which is typical of the later work. There were many
dead: the 'companions of the Cheshire Cheese', Mathers, Synge,
Major Robert Gregory; O'Leary: the men who fell in the 1916
Rising; and all 'those renowned generations'. Belief in the ghost, in
the trickery of the séance, were very minor properties of the play

---

[1] 'Vacillation', viii, *C.P.*, p. 285. There is, in the eighth and ninth lines, a
thought which seems to be an echo from Shelley's *Prince Athanase*, which
Yeats had read carefully:

> Nor what religion fables of the grave
> Feared he ...

[2] Wade, p. 790.
[3] *Identity*, p. 274.
[4] *C.P.*, p. 513.
[5] A classic instance in iconography is Kranach's *Venus and Cupid*.

in which he was Lear or Timon.[1] Perhaps some impish humour lit up from time to time his belief or unbelief:

> Mathers is much troubled by ladies who seek spiritual advice, and one has called to ask his help against phantoms who have the appearance of decayed corpses, and try to get into bed with her at night. He has driven her away with one furious sentence, 'Very bad taste on both sides.'[2]

But when all this is weighed up, and all that is irrelevant, or subsidiary, or half-believed has been set aside, we can see Yeats' mind moving steadily towards certain propositions:

1. Both the practice of magic and the history of myth led Yeats to the point at which the recurrence of symbols or emblems leaves no doubt as to their validity in human psychology and religion.

2. This in turn confirmed the belief in some kind of cyclic or repeating pattern in history.

3. Both these propositions suggested a common reservoir of thought, the 'Great Memory', on which we can draw, either unconsciously or by 'controlled' dream or vision.

4. The correspondence between the symbols of myths, and those of individual and group psychology, suggested that through their use the poet may express a more profound sense of reality than is possible by abstract thought; and that this expression may be justified *after* the event by philosophical and scientific inquiry.

> I feel that an imaginative writer whose work draws him to philosophy must attach himself to some great historical school. My dreams and much psychic phenomena force me into a certain little-trodden way but I must not go too far from the main European track, which means in practice that I turn away from all attempts to make philosophy support science by starting with some form of 'fact' or 'datum' . . .[3]

5. Myth was therefore important for three reasons:
   (*a*) it could effect the philosophical, religious and political unification of national life,
   (*b*) it could restore the richness of imaginative life of which

---

[1]       Myself must I remake
          Till I am Timon and Lear
          Or that William Blake . . . *C.P.*, p. 346.
[2] *Autobiographies*, p. 346.
[3] *T.S.M. Letters*, p. 149.

the people had been robbed as a result of nineteenth-century materialism,

(c) it might provide the key to the interpretation of history, and therefore to prophecy.

6. Magic rituals and the experience of spiritualism had supplied evidence that appeared to be converging towards empirical justification. The dream stone that he had watched a seer lift from the ground 'with an obvious sense of its weight' had an existence of its own. Berkeley and G. E. Moore might yet embrace; and the poet, having thus obtained a justification for what he had expressed in verse, would be justified as not only of Homer's lineage but also as the prophet or the saint.

*A Vision* is the rough draft towards a system by which myth and magic and philosophy might be related; but this too will be seen to be a kind of poetry, to be justified after the event. Before considering its implications it is convenient to consider a single component of the system, 'The Phases of the Moon'.

# CHAPTER ELEVEN

# The Phases of the Moon

I

You must be won
At a full moon in March, those beggars say.
That moon has come, but I am here alone.
*A Full Moon in March.*

Any consideration of 'The Phases of the Moon' must be linked ultimately to the whole philosophy of *A Vision*, but this single aspect of Yeats' belief is so important a source of imagery that it is convenient to consider it under a separate heading. The most convenient starting-point is from Chaucer's 'The Frankeleyn's Tale':

> He him remembered that, upon a day,
> At Orliens in studie a book he say
> Of magik natural, which his felawe,
> That was that tyme a bacheler of lawe,
> Al were he ther to lerne another craft,
> Had prively upon his desk y-laft;
> Which book spak muchel of the operaciouns,
> Touchinge the eighte and twenty mansiouns
> That longen to the mone, and swich folye,
> As in our dayes is not worth a flye;
> For holy churches feith in our beleve
> Ne suffreth noon illusion us to greve.[1]

Yeats knew this, and used the corresponding passage in Skeat's notes.[2]

'I here quote from my Preface to Chaucer's "Astrolabe" (F.E.T.S.), p. lix: "The twenty-eight 'moon stations' of the Arabs are given in Ideler's *Untersuchungen über die Bedeutung der Sternnamen*, p. 287. He gives the Arabic names, the stars that help to fix

[1] Skeat: 1.1122.
[2] I am indebted to Mrs Yeats for this information.

their positions, etc. . . . For the influence of the moon on these mansions, we must look elsewhere, viz., in lib. i, cap. 11 and lib. iv, cap. 18 of the *Epitome Astrologiae* of Johannes Hispalensis.[1] Suffice it to say that there are twelve temperate mansions, six dry ones, and ten moist ones. The number 28 corresponds with the number of days in a lunation."' Skeat has a further note on the passage, to which Yeats does not appear to have paid much attention: he quotes from Chaucer's 'Astrolabe':

> Natheles, thise ben observances of iudicial matiere and rytes of payens, in which my spirit ne hath no feith.

Another source is that richest of mines, Cornelius Agrippa: *e.g.* 11 Ch. xxxii of *Occult Philosophy:*

> The sun is the lord of all elementary virtues, and the moon by virtue of the sun is the mistress of generation, increase or decrease . . . but the moon, the nighest to the earth, the receptacle of all the heavenly influences, by the sweetness of her course is joined to the sun and the other planets and stars, every month, and being as it were the wife of all the stars[2] and receiving the beams and influences of all the other planets and stars as a conception and imaging them forth to the inferior world as being next to itself, is the parent of all conceptions.

There is no need to labour the implications of moon-symbolism throughout poetic history; but to Yeats, for reasons both of life and genius, that emblem had a particular value. The period from *Responsibilities* onwards is marked by a complete revaluation of the experiences before 1914, and in particular of those events which followed the 'Estrangement' of 1909. It was necessary to impose an order upon that experience, to attempt to re-shape the 'cosmic dance' to suit his own purpose. There was plenty of precedent in the astrologers, in Chaucer, Dante, the Elizabethans, Swedenborg, Blake.

In this dance the moon had special values. It could become an emblem, set against the Tower, of the antithesis of contemplative and active man, as in 'Blood and the Moon', iv:[3]

---

[1] I have not been able to find the reference, but Hispalensis may have been part of the assorted reading in the Bodleian in 1919–20.

[2] Is this the reference in 'The Crazed Moon'? – *v.* p. 186 *infra.*

[3] *C.P.*, p. 269.

No matter what I said,
For wisdom is the property of the dead,
A something incompatible with life; and power,
Like everything that has the stain of blood,
A property of the living; but no stain
Can come upon the visage of the moon
When it has looked in glory from a cloud.

He could make it serve his strange capacity for irradiating his world
from within, for communicating that 'dance-like glory', which
might be borrowed in part from Shakespeare or from Shelley.
He was familiar with its manifestations in the pastoral landscapes of
Blake, Calvert, Palmer. But above all the moon was the woman-
principle. He was to see the golden cock 'by the moon embittered'
in 'Byzantium'. In 'Lines written in Dejection'[1] there is a classic
instance of the mother-aspect of moon-symbolism, the significance
of which Miss Bodkin has described so fully.[2]

The holy centaurs of the hills are vanished;
I have nothing but the embittered sun;
Banished heroic mother moon and vanished,
And now that I have come to fifty years
I must endure the timid sun.

Here every image carries its psychological implications; and this
is 1915, a critical year. To impose an order on circumstances, to find
an order in the inconstancy of the woman-principle, would be to
'divine an analogy that evades the intellect',[3] and at the same time
to bring his own circle of destiny into line with the wheel of eastern
mysticism, the circles of Dante and Blake. The system would explain
'why there is a deep enmity between a man and his destiny'.[4] It had
astrological precedent, and there were the Instructors to answer, in
part at least (for they were not quite certain whether the wheel was
divided into twelve parts or ten), the questions that arose out of
complication and contradiction. It could produce 'a sudden luminous
definition of form which makes one understand almost in spite of
oneself that one is not merely imagining'.[5]

[1] *C.P.*, p. 163.
[2] See in particular Chapter IV ('The Image of Woman') in *Archetypal Patterns*.
[3] *P.A.S.L.*, p. 31.
[4] Ibid.
[5] Ibid., p. 48.

II

The explanatory diagram in *A Vision* is in the form of the Great Wheel of the lunar phases. It is closely associated with the cones and gyres, but the geometrical complexities set up by this are not of great interest in the interpretation of the poetry. The wheel symbolizes 'every *completed* movement of thought or life' (that is, it is applicable equally to a millennium or to a single life-span) or to 'a single judgement or act of thought'.[1] In the anti-clockwise revolution, man, starting from Phase 1, seeks his opposite at Phase 15, and then returns to his original starting-point.

In this progress, the circle is further resolved into a system of interlocking cones, symbolizing, in their oppositions and tensions, the four Faculties. 'When the Will predominates, and there is strong desire, the Mask or Image is sensuous, but when Creative Mind predominates, it is abstract. When the Mask predominates, it is idealized, when the Body of Fate, it is concrete, and so on.'[2]

The main division of the circle is between Primary and Antithetical. This dichotomy persists through the book; the egoist is opposed to the saint, artist to business man or politician, and so on. It is all-important, and on it depends Yeats' conception of personality which I have suggested in the chapter 'Self and Anti-Self'. In brief:

(a) All unity is derived from the Mask. The 'antithetical Mask' is 'the form created by passion to unite us to ourselves'.[3]

(b) Personality, *no matter how habitual*, is a constantly renewed choice, varying from 'an individual charm, in the more *antithetical* phases, to a hard objective dramatization. . . .'[4]

(c) The variations or oscillations between aspects of personality are subject both to choice and to external circumstance. Man may be in or out of phase, according to the success or

---

[1] *A Vision* (B), p. 81.
[2] This belief seems a possible rationalization of Yeats' own practice or an explanation of it. The early poet would idealize. Caught in the net of practical affairs, the Troubles, marriage, politics, the Mask would be concrete. (The resemblance of this psychology to Blake's Four Zoas, as expounded, by *e.g.*, W. P. Witcutt, has been pointed out before.)
[3] (B), p. 82.
[4] (B), p. 84. Yeats often speaks of the deliberate 'assumption of charm'.

# "THE PHASES OF THE MOON"

Based on the poem of that name,
The two versions of A Vision & references in other poems

This diagram is much simplified, & includes only those aspects of Yeats theory
that appear to be of special interest in the consideration of his life & poetry.

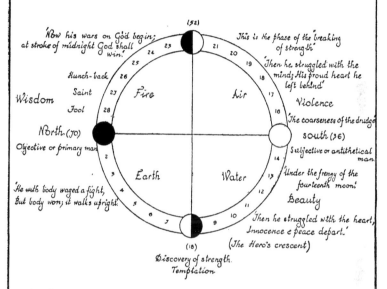

(52)

'Now his wars on God begin;
at stroke of midnight God shall win.'

This is the phase of the "breaking
of strength"

Hunch-back

'Then he struggled with the
mind; His proud heart he
left behind'

Saint

Violence

Fool

'The coarseness of the drudge

Wisdom

Fire    Air

North (70)

south (36)

Objective or primary man

Subjective or antithetical man

Earth    Water

'Under the frenzy of the
fourteenth moon.'

Beauty

'He with body waged a fight,
But body won; it walks upright.'

'Then he struggled with the heart,
Innocence & peace depart.'

(18)

(The Hero's crescent)

Discovery of strength.
Temptation

1   The quotations in couplets are taken from 'The Four Ages of Man.'
2   Other quotations are from 'The Phases of the Moon'.
3   The figures in brackets opposite each of the main quarters show Yeats
    own age at those phases, assuming a seventy years span. On this basis
    there seems to be a fairly close correspondence with the phases of his life
    as he saw them.

otherwise of his struggle with the various 'false' attributes in his psychology.

(*d*) Phases 1 and 15 are opposites – 'the superhuman phases' in which chance and choice coincide.

(*e*) Each phase is characterized by two major attributes, *Will*, and *Body of Fate*, or circumstance: and by two other attributes, the *Mask* or the *Creative Mind*, either of which may be true or false. These are shown in a complex and not altogether consistent table.

(*f*) Each phase has also special 'characters': the Four Perfections; Four Types of Wisdom; Four 'Contests' (conflicts), which are the Moral, Emotional, Physical and Supersensual; with a further Four which are placed under the curious headings of 'Rage', 'Phantasy', etc.

(*g*) There are a large number of other headings – 'General Character of Created Mind', 'General Character of Body of Fate', and a 'Table of the Quarters' giving other attributes. It is of interest to note that the poem 'The Four Ages of Man'[1] is taken directly from the first of these. There is also a number of unclassified attributes.

One day the full correlation of these phases and attributes may be worked out; it is obvious that there is a general correspondence with his own biography. I am concerned at present only with the direct bearing of the system on the interpretation of certain poems.

In the figure shown on the previous page, I have re-drawn from *A Vision* a simplified diagram of the wheel. The astrological signs have been disregarded, and relevant quotations from 'The Phases of the Moon'[2] and elsewhere have been inserted, together with comments selected from the texts of *A Vision*. Much is omitted that does not appear to me relevant to the interpretation of the poetry. But if the life-span is taken at seventy years, and the quadrant plotted in relation to Yeats' own life, the correspondence is striking. At the same time, it is clear to me that there is a conflict in *A Vision* itself: for there appears to be both a progression through the

---

[1] *C.P.*, 332. The poem is in fact a rhymed version of the statement: see *A Vision* (A), p. 160.
[2] *C.P.*, p. 183.

'stations', and a static aspect in which every station is listed as characteristic of specific human types.

The fullest explanation is in 'The Phases of the Moon'. The meaning of the poem is far from clear; so far as it can be isolated from the poetic statement, we have a pattern in which it is convenient to think of this circle of twenty-eight points; starting with the crescent moon.

The first quarter, Points 1–6, is given up to adventure and sensuous happiness, a time not unlike Keats' Chamber of Maiden Thought.

The initial period of animal happiness is followed by the phase of experience, in which 'he follows whatever whim's most difficult. . . .'

> and though scarred
> As with the cat-o'-nine-tails of the mind,
> His body moulded from within his body
> Grows comelier.[1]

Nos. 11–12 are periods of violent heroic action: with the peculiar phrase (to which Yeats frequently recurs and which appeared to have a special significance for him: 'Athena takes Achilles by the hair'[2]). Phase No. 13 sees the

> soul at war
> In its own being.

This is followed by a period of quiescence and contemplation and knowledge at the full moon, when

> The soul begins to tremble into stillness,
> To die into the labyrinth of itself.

The fifteenth phase is of great importance. Thought and will, effort and attainment, become indistinguishable. During the previous stage all the images and 'cadences of the mind' – a peculiar phrase – have been converging towards this state where 'contemplation and desire, united into one, inhabit a world where

---

[1] The usual Neo-platonic view.

[2] As, for example, 'When the goddess came to Achilles in the battle she did not interfere with his soul, she took him by his yellow hair' (*The Resurrection, W. & B.*, p. 121). The incident is in *Iliad*, i. 197. It impressed Yeats deeply: elsewhere he refers to it as 'one of those more trivial supernatural benedictions'.

every beloved image has bodily form, and every bodily image is beloved'.

This may be in part the explanation of

> Paul Veronese
> And all his sacred company
> Imagined bodies all their days
> By the lagoon you love so much,
> For proud, soft, ceremonious proof
> That all must come to sight and touch.[1]

Compare with this:

> All that the being has experienced as thought is visible to its eyes as a whole, and in this way it perceives, not as they are to others, but according to its own perception, all orders of existence.[2]

This and the preceding sentence are referred to in the lines:

> ROBARTES. All thought becomes an image and the soul
> Becomes a body: that body and that soul
> Too perfect at the full to lie in a cradle,
> Too lonely for the traffic of the world:
> Body and soul cast out and cast away
> Beyond the visible world.
> AHERNE.                                All dreams[3] of the soul
> End in a beautiful man's or woman's body.
> ROBARTES. Have you not always known it?
> AHERNE.                                The song will have it
> That those that we have loved got their long fingers
> From death, and wounds, or on Sinai's top,
> Or from some bloody whip in their own hands.
> They ran from cradle to cradle till at last
> Their beauty dropped out of the loneliness
> Of body and soul.

I do not understand these last lines. It is possible, as Jeffares has suggested, that they may allude to an affair with 'Diana Vernon' in 1896. He saw her as one who had known in her life much passion (and suffered greatly). His idea of doomed beauty is, of course, recurrent: as, for example, in the 'Crazy Jane' poems. Perhaps a key to the interpretation of the whole passage is contained in a note

---

[1] 'Michael Robartes and the Dancer,' *C.P.*, p. 197. But there may be a visual image behind it also. See p. 254.
[2] (B), p. 136. (The thought is Blake's.)
[3] *v. The Only Jealousy of Emer*, *C. Plays*, p. 185.

on *The Only Jealousy of Emer*. "The invisible fifteenth[1] incarnation is that of the greatest possible bodily beauty, and the fourteenth and sixteenth that of the greatest beauty visible to human eyes. Much that Robartes has found might be a commentary on Castiglione's saying that the physical beauty of women is the spoil or monument of the victory of the soul, for physical beauty, only possible to subjective natures, is described as the result of emotional toil in past lives."[2] Past suffering, therefore, has produced this present beauty. But such beauty is doomed, recognizing that it must soon vanish:

> It must be that the terror in their eyes
> Is memory or foreknowledge of the hour
> When all is fed with light and heaven is bare.

This would be the last phase of the circuit; the one immediately preceding it being that of the Saint, when the heavenly light is still broken.

Phase 16 is one of excitement and 'aimless illusion', with "an element of frenzy, and almost always a delight in certain glowing or shining images of concentrated force: in the smith's forge . . . in the solar disc; in some symbolical representation of the sexual organs; for the being must brag of its triumph over its own incoherence."[3]

There is some illumination here of other aspects of imagery; such as the recurrent sword metaphor in relation to the 'glowing or shining images'; and the thought of the smith's forge suggests an enrichment of meaning in 'Byzantium' —

> The golden smithies of the Emperor.

It is perhaps significant that this phase is also one of illusion; 'in it the soul may surround itself with some fairyland, some mythology of wisdom or laughter'.[4] On the suggested time-scale of the wheel this would correspond to the early 1900's.

In a superb passage he describes the loneliness of the phase, the fifteenth, under the full moon:

---

[1] The fifteenth phase is the 37th year of Yeats 'life, and is 1903; the year of Maud Gonne's marriage.
[2] *P. & C.*, pp. 433, 444.
[3] (B), pp. 138, 139.
[4] (B), p. 138.

> When the moon's full those creatures of the full
> Are met on the waste hills by country men
> Who shudder and hurry by: body and soul
> Estranged amid the strangeness of themselves,
> Caught up in contemplation, the mind's eye
> Fixed upon images that once were thought;
> For separate, perfect, and immovable
> Images can break the solitude
> Of lovely, satisfied, indifferent eyes.

Perhaps the image is of *The Countess Cathleen* and Maud Gonne, and the hope that the solitude of those eyes would be broken by an image; for Aherne, with his aged, high-pitched voice (that will one day be the voice of Ribh 'that ninety years have cracked') laughs at the thought. The moon crumbles, and then

> The soul remembering its loneliness
> Shudders in many cradles; all is changed,
> It would be the world's servant, and as it serves,
> Choosing whatever task's most difficult[1]
> Among tasks not impossible, it takes
> Upon the body and upon the soul
> The coarseness of the drudge.

The period of the drudge, and its coarseness, is that of the Abbey Theatre. It is followed by a phase which picks up the past piece by piece:

> Reformer, merchant, statesman, learned man,[2]
> Dutiful husband, honest wife by turn,
> Cradle upon cradle, and all in flight and all
> Deformed because there is no deformity
> But saves us from a dream.

There may be anticipation of desire here. Yeats' children were born in 1919 and 1921:

> Bring the soul of man to God,
> Make him fill the cradles right.[3]

---

[1] This thought of choosing the 'most difficult/Among tasks not impossible' recurs frequently, and appears to be his self-justification in terms of his theory of the Will.

[2] Perhaps corresponding to the Nationalist, the 'merchant' of the Abbey Theatre, the Senator (though that is yet to come), and the hermit-scholar.

[3] 'Under Ben Bulben', *C.P.*, p. 397.

The deformity is that of the Mask, the Anti-Self, the practical man, who will later develop into the Hunchback: the phase in which Yeats will be the 'sixty-year-old smiling public man', now possessed of power.

Hunchback and Saint and Fool are the last crescents. The end of the poems lingers on them. Aherne ponders over the words:

> I'd stand and mutter there until he caught
> 'Hunchback and saint and fool', and that they came
> Under the three last crescents of the moon,
> And then I'd stagger out. He'd crack his wits
> Day after day, yet never find the meaning.
>
> *And then he laughed to think that what seemed hard*
> *Should be so simple. . . .*

This most important transition between the Hunchback and the Saint is expressed concisely in the poem of that name.[1]

HUNCHBACK. Stand up and lift your hand and bless
A man that finds great bitterness
In thinking of his lost renown.
A Roman Caesar is held down
Under this hump.
SAINT.                    God tries each man
According to a different plan.
I shall not cease to bless because
I lay about me with the taws
That night and morning I may thrash[2]
Greek Alexander from my flesh,
Augustus Caesar, and after these
That great rogue Alcibiades.
HUNCHBACK. To all that in your flesh have stood
And blessed, I give my gratitude,
Honoured by all in their degrees,
But most to Alcibiades.[3]

[1] *C.P.*, p. 189.
[2] Compare 'Among School Children':
Solider Aristotle played the taws
Upon the bottom of a king of kings.
[3] Yeats, like 'Longinus', was attracted by sonorous words, such as Delacroix and Alcibiades. But the symbol fits well enough, for Alcibiades had beauty, charm, great capacity, and a love of debauchery. He was the friend of Socrates, was banished by the Athenians, then recalled, and subsequently became Commander-in-Chief. After a defeat he went into voluntary exile, but was killed in a dramatic fashion by assassins.

The system of the Phases of the Moon is not without its significance in Yeats' own life. He was capable both of perceiving his own life in terms of that cycle, and of adjusting his own life and thought to fit the framework, remembering his father's advice that he should control his fantasies; though we can never be certain whether he was rationalizing his own emotions in terms of the myth, or explaining the myth in terms of himself. That the two were closely related is plain from *A Vision*: 'Upon the throne and upon the cross alike the myth becomes a biography'.

The three aspects of personality are, I believe, of immense importance in Yeats' poetical development. The Hunchback is the 'Multiple Man'. Yeats seems perplexed in his attempt to define his true significance, for this is 'the first of those phases for which one can find few or no examples from personal experience'. 'One must create the type from the symbols without the help of experience'.[1]

The Hunchback is 'the most completely solitary of all possible men'. 'Without personality he is forced to create its artificial semblance'. His hump symbolizes the 'ambition that thwarts what seems to be the ambition of a Caesar or of an Achilles. He commits crimes, not because he wants to . . . but *because he wants to feel certain that he can*. . . . If he live amid theologically minded people, his greatest ambition may be to defy God, to become a Judas, who betrays, not for thirty pieces of silver, but that he may call himself creator.'[2] 'If the man of this phase seeks, not life, but knowledge, of each separated life in relation to supersensual unity . . . he will, *because he can see lives and actions in relation to their source and not in their relations to one another*, see their deformities and incapacities with extraordinary acuteness. His own past actions also he must judge as isolated and *each in relation to its source*. . . .'[3] It is worth noting that the 'Body of Fate', or circumstance, proper to the Hunchback is 'enforced disillusionment'.

It will be seen that these phases can be related to specific poems in the late period:

[1] *A Vision* (B), p. 177. It is obvious, from the very few examples given, that Yeats was hard put to it in finding concrete instances in support of what the 'Instructors' had said.

[2] Ibid., p. 178. Compare the death of Cuchulain, for twelve pennies, at the hands of a fool; as well as Judas' apologia in *Calvary*.

[3] *A Vision* (B), p. 179.

> I am content to follow to its source
> Every event in action or in thought.[1]

and

> All that I have said and done,
> Now that I am old and ill,
> Turns into a question till
> I lie awake night after night
> And never get the answers right.
> Did that play of mine send out
> Certain men the English shot?[2]

And I think there is something of the perversity, the paradoxical renunciation of

> Hatred of God may bring the soul to God[3]

in the self-justifications, the 'enforced disillusionment', of this phase.

I do not wish to press this argument too far, and exact chronological correspondences are obviously impossible; but the resemblances are so close that a consideration of them increases very greatly the coherence of the last poems.

So, too, the correspondence with the Saint. Examples of this are Socrates, and, strangely enough, Pascal. 'Thought and action have for their object display of zeal or some claim of authority. . . .' '. . . the man asserts when out of phase his claim to faculty or to supersensitive privileges beyond that of other men; he has a secret that makes him better than other men.'

This suggests something of Keats' 'negative capability'. '. . . the total life has suddenly displayed its source.' 'If he possesses intellect he will use it but to serve perception and renunciation. His joy is to be nothing, to do nothing, to think nothing; but to permit the total life, expressed in its humanity, to flow in upon him and to express itself through his acts and thoughts.'[4] 'He will, if it be possible, not even touch or taste or see: "Man does not perceive the truth; God perceives the truth in man."'[5] The paradox of Ribh and his renunciation is again emphasized.

---

[1] 'A Dialogue of Self and Soul,' C.P., p. 265.
[2] 'The Man and the Echo,' ibid., p. 393.
[3] 'Ribh considers Christian Love insufficient,' ibid., p. 330.
[4] A Vision (B), p. 180.
[5] Ibid., p. 181.

The Fool of the last crescent is natural man, 'a straw blown by the wind . . . and is sometimes called "The Child of God". . . . The physical world suggests to his mind pictures and events that have no relation to his needs or even to his desires; his thoughts are an aimless reverie; his acts are aimless like his thoughts; and it is in this aimlessness that he finds his joy.'[1] He is in part the Shakespearean Fool, in part the fool of folk-lore 'who is as wide and as wild as a hill'. He is the fool of the play *The Hour Glass*, natural man whose wisdom may save humanity.

### III

The richness and depth of the normal moon-symbolism is greatly magnified by the myth of the phases. In the short and difficult poem 'The Crazed Moon'[2] there is, I think, a double symbolism at work. In this the moon is womanhood,

> Crazed through much child-bearing
> The moon is staggering in the sky. . . .

Mankind seeks for the 'children born of her pain', the events that arise from her predestined round. But in the next there is virginal womanhood:

> When she in all her virginal pride
> First trod on the mountain's head
> What stir ran through the countryside
> Where every foot obeyed her glance!
> What manhood led the dance!

which stands both for an earlier, more rich age, and – the accent of the two pieces is similar – for the memory of Constance Gore-Booth.

> When long ago I saw her ride
> Under Ben Bulben to the meet,
> The beauty of her countryside
> With all youth's lonely wildness stirred . . .[3]

In the third verse, woman and circumstance both unite in the symbol:

[1] *A Vision* (B), p. 182.
[2] *C.P.*, p. 273. This was written in 1923 and then lost.
[3] 'On A Political Prisoner,' ibid., p. 206. See also p. 62.

> Fly-catchers of the moon,
> Our hands are blenched, our fingers seem
> But slender needles of bone;
> Blenched by that malicious dream
> They are spread wide that each
> May rend what comes in reach.

In 'The Cat and the Moon', the pupils of the cat's eyes change with the phases of the moon. The cat is 'the nearest kin of the moon', most sharply affected by its sensuality:

> For, wander and wail as he would,
> The pure cold light in the sky
> Troubled his animal blood.[1]

For the cat is also the emblem of man, and also his antitype; in the Preface[2] to the play he wrote: '. . . [I] allowed myself as I wrote to think of the cat as the normal man and of the moon as the opposite he seeks perpetually, or as having any meaning I have conferred upon the moon elsewhere.' What follows is of special interest: 'Doubtless too, when the lame man takes the saint upon his back, the normal man has become one with that opposite, but I had to bear in mind that I was among dreams and proverbs, that though I might discover what had been and might be again an abstract idea, no abstract idea must be present. The spectator should come away thinking the meaning as much his own manufacture as that of the blind man and the lamed man had seemed mine.' So the cat goes creeping through the grass, his eyes changing from round to crescent as the moon changes:

> Alone, important and wise,
> And lifts to the changing moon
> His changing eyes.

[1] *C.P.*, p. 188. Some light is thrown on this and the preceding passage by a passage from *John Sherman*:
   Crossing the river at Putney, he hurried homewards among the market gardens. Nearing home, the streets were deserted, the shops closed. Where King Street joins the Broadway, entirely alone with itself, in the very centre of the road, a little black cat was leaping after its shadow. 'Ah!' he thought, 'it would be a good thing to be a little black cat. To leap about in the moonlight and sleep in the sunlight, and *catch flies*, to have no hard tasks to do or hard decisions to come to, to be simple and full of animal spirits' (pp. 65–66).
[2] *Explorations*, p. 403.

The application of the myth reaches what I take to be its greatest complexity in 'The Double Vision of Michael Robartes'.[1] In the first movement the poet is concerned with his own predestined obedience to 'some magical hidden breath'.

> When had I my own will?
> O not since life began.

In the second, there are two poles between which the mental conflict oscillates: the Sphinx on the grey rock of Cashel (related, I suggest, to Ingres' *Oedipus and the Sphinx*) and

> A Buddha, hand at rest,
> Hand lifted up that blest . . .

Both know the answer to the riddle of existence; the Sphinx in a kind of fierce exultation of intellect, the Buddha in love and sadness. It seems likely that Yeats in his own mind was the Oedipus whose task it was to solve the riddle of Ireland (linked always in his thought with Egypt) whose misfortunes of blood and suffering were not unlike those described at the opening of Sophocles' play. The Sphinx and the Buddha represent the two approaches to wisdom, from West and East. Between these two is the vision of the dancing girl, Iseult Gonne, or the girl dying into a dance in the Japanese play[2] ('That, it may be, had danced her life away'); the image of desire for the girl who sang on the sea-shore in Normandy

> Let all things pass away.

In the third movement the pattern becomes clearer. Iseult Gonne is linked in memory to her mother, who is Helen

> Who never gave the burning town a thought;
> To such a pitch of folly I am brought,
> Being caught between the pull
> Of the dark moon and the full . . .

The Sphinx with woman breast and lion paw is now both the oracle, and the woman, and the cat mysteriously linked to the moon with her expanding and contracting pupils; the tail is lashed, as by

[1] *C.P.*, p. 192.
[2] See p. 143.

a cat before it springs: and we are again confronted with the mysterious beast of the Second Coming, that symbolized 'laughing ecstatic destruction'[1] – woman, or cat, or Sphinx, or those strange winged lions in Ricketts' illustrations for *The Sphinx*. In contrast there is the Buddha:

> That other's moonlit eyeballs never moved,
> Being fixed on all things loved, all things unloved,
> Yet little peace he had,
> For those that love are sad.

So the two resolve themselves into symbols of action and contemplation; and this antithesis provides, I think, the explanation of the difficulty in 'The Statues'.[2]

> Empty eyeballs knew
> That knowledge increases unreality, that
> Mirror on mirror mirrored is all the show.
> When gong and conch declare the hour to bless
> Grimalkin crawls to Buddha's emptiness.

Sphinx, lion, woman, cat, have been, as it were, tamed in the contemptuous and homely epithet, with its overtones from the Witches in *Macbeth*.[3]

I have used this moon symbolism as offering a simple illustration of the need for sympathy in understanding Yeats' cosmic interpretation, so that we may realize the full complexity of his imagery. I have deliberately selected only a few aspects. When we come to consider *A Vision*, we have again an ordered cosmic dance, in which the gyres are the basis of the system, with some image of a shuttle or bobbin within these cones, interlocking or juxtaposed; and over all the moon's influence as a deterministic factor in virtue of which man oscillates between Choice and Chance. Man's life is a microcosm of the larger cycles of history. These are the essentials of *A Vision*. The very profusion of diagrams gives rise to limitless flexibility of application; so that, as we read, we feel that Yeats is juggling with his own beliefs in something approaching bewilderment. All this has to be applied – again in a desultory and arbitrary

[1] See p. 144.
[2] *C.P.*, p. 375. See also *Autobiographies*, p. 142.
[3] See Wilson's *Icocography*, pp. 209 *et. seq.* for the best exegesis of the poem at present available.

fashion – as a theory of history. But the theory is so important for the interpretation of the poetry that it is necessary to set out its main features. 'History seems to me a human drama, keeping the classical unities by the clear division of its epochs, turning one way or the other because this man hates or that man loves.'

# CHAPTER TWELVE

# A Vision and the Interpretation of History

> Civilization is hooped together, brought
> Under a rule, under the semblance of peace
> By manifold illusion; but man's life is thought. . . .
>        'Meru', *Supernatural Songs.*

I must create a system myself or be enslaved by another man's. – BLAKE.

I am the first to substitute for Biblical or mythological figures, historical movements and actual men and women – *A Vision* (A), p. xii.

I

Shortly after Yeats' marriage in 1917, he discovered that his wife produced automatic writing. The result appears in *A Vision* (1925); and he himself believed that it embodied the philosophy of the Unknown Instructors,[1] the Spirits: who yet came, not to give him a system of thought, but metaphors for poetry.[2] It is an exasperating book, as many reviewers have noted; astrology, Plato's *Timaeus*, confused geometry, and a partial and arbitrary application of a time scheme to a personal view of history – all these are yoked together to produce a kind of prophecy which is as much beyond criticism as, for instance, Blake's *The Four Zoas*; with which it has something in common. As for the bearing of *A Vision* on Yeats' poetry, I think it possible to approach the problem by setting out, as simply as possible, the elements of the system, and then to show its function in providing the scaffolding for his thought.

*A Vision* is of interest for three reasons. It gives us an idea,

---

[1] Cf. 'Gratitude to the Unknown Instructors,' *C.P.*, p. 287.
[2] *A Vision* (B), p. 8. But this was an understatement by the Instructors: they gave much more.

however fragmentary, of Yeats' view of history; and therefore of such divergent matters as the myth-value of Leda and the Swan, Greek sculpture, Byzantine mosaics, the painters of the Renaissance and the poetry of T. S. Eliot. It helps to explain the symbolic values he found in the work of the artists of his various 'eras', waxing and waning in their arts, repeating themselves in cycles, or seeking their opposites, according to the Phases of the Moon. And, finally, it offers an instance of the strange workings of his mind, that could select and sometimes distort so much historical fact to fit his theories; but which, having seen history in this arbitrary pattern, could use its symbols with such conviction. Perhaps this sense of conviction is more important, as the undercurrent of his working mind, than the diffuse and fragmentary philosophies that are evoked to strengthen it.

For all the exasperation it has produced, I do not think that it is possible to dismiss *A Vision* with contempt or to argue, as Kleinstück has done, for its entire irrelevance. It offers a broad and sweeping chronicle of those historical events that seemed important to Yeats. Its detail is often helpful and at times essential to our interpretation. A major difficulty in presenting a simplified version for this purpose is the discrepancy between the two versions, that of 1925 (the Werner Laurie edition) and the Macmillan edition of 1937.[1] The early version, which is noted for convenience as 'A', is more likely to represent the immediate result of the original automatic writings, the visit to Italy (the book was finished in Capri) and the stimulus resulting from pictures, statues and mosaics. The 1937 or 'B' version is heavily cut, toned down, and modified so as to admit, in parts, of a half-serious interpretation – perhaps

Because there is safety in derision.

A desire to seek safety in derision, or a certain love of mischief, may have been responsible for the machinery of disguise – the puppet figures of Robartes and Aherne, the drawing of the magician that looks like an authentic woodcut, but which was done by Dulac. (A beard was added to disguise the resemblance of the finished block to Yeats himself.)

There is a certain mystery about it all. 'I published in 1925 an

[1] Reprint 1962 by Macmillan.

inaccurate, obscure, incomplete book called "A Vision". It lies beside me now, clarified and completed after five years' work and thought.' But it was published in a limited edition of 600 copies in 1925; it was re-worked at Rapallo during 1929–30,[1] and this statement on its revision was made in 1931. It seems probable that Yeats did carry out exhaustive revision (he speaks of rewriting for the seventh time that part of it that deals with the future); then, knowing that its promise of a philosophical system could never be fulfilled, he abandoned it and returned to *The Tower*, until the 'corrected' version was published in 1937.

The 'B' version throws a good deal of light on Yeats' reading between 1925 and 1937, though it is not clear when the bulk of the revision took place. There is some evidence for the period of 1926–8. It is perhaps significant that in it there are a number of footnotes explaining his indebtedness to various sources. They include *An Adventure* (that of the Petit Trianon), Pierre Duhem's *Systéme du Monde*, Toynbee's *A Study of History*, Henry Adams' *History as Phase*,[2] and Flinders Petrie's *The Revolutions of Civilization*.[3] All such references are omitted in the first edition; it looks as if Yeats designed, with how much seriousness we do not know, to give the whole credit to the mysterious 'Instructors' and to excuse some of the obscurities and inconsistencies by the work of the equally mysterious 'Frustrators'. These 'Instructors' and 'Frustrators' deserve a special note in the light of Jung's latest work. Under these somewhat pompous titles they seem to derive from certain normal experiences in Indian mysticism, towards which Yeats was attracted throughout his life. The *Guru* who guides the mystic in his progress towards enlightenment may be the spirit of some long-dead sage; other 'influences' may convey enlightenment in dreams or visions. But evil or malicious spirits may seek to confuse or intervene or mislead, and this was familiar in the séances, and dramatized in

[1] Hone, *Life*, pp. 412–13. But the 'vision scripts', the raw material of the system, went on at intervals from 1926–34, and, at rarer intervals, up to the date of the second publication in 1937 (Mrs Yeats). Much of the note-material was never used.

[2] 'I have read Adams & find an exact agreement even to dates with my "law of history"' (Wade, *Letters*, p. 666). This is dated 14 March 1921. Compare Yeats' later discovery of Spengler.

[3] The last was read in 1923.

*The Words upon the Window Pane*. It is possible to regard both 'Instructors' and 'Frustrators' as a dramatic and startling method of denoting that which provided, through his own Blakean practices of vision and dream, the material which was revealed. Whether the sources are archetypal dreams, ancestral memories, 'cosmic' visions of the type of the Archer and the Star, or emotion recollected and transformed in the dream state, it is impossible to decide. But it seems likely that, having once been familiar with such 'systems' as were afforded by the Golden Dawn, the writings of G. R. S. Mead, and his reading in astrology, the images multiplied and adjusted themselves in a steady and elaborate progression. Later he refers to the complex and recondite sources that he has used. It is clear from the Prologue in 'A', addressed to Vestigia (who is Mrs Mathers), that much of the reading goes back to theosophical days. There are allusions to Husserl, to Arabian astrological manuscripts, Frobenius, Josef Strzygowski ('the most philosophical of archaeologists'); and there is, I think, evidence of a more commonplace debt to H. G. Wells' *Outline of History*.

As usual, the net of desultory reading has been flung wide. The 'gyres' – the conical spirals of determined events in which man and events move – are from Plato: 'The first gyres clearly described by philosophy are those described in the *Timaeus* which are made by the circuits of "the Other" (creators of all particular things), of the planets as they ascend or descend above or below the equator. They are opposite in nature to that circle of the fixed stars which constitutes "the Same" and confers upon it the knowledge of Universals.'[1] But there is also a Chinese aspect: 'I have a Chinese painting of three old sages sitting together, one with a deer at his side, one with a scroll open at the symbol of yen and yin, those two forms that whirl perpetually, creating and re-creating all things.'[2]

The origin and development of the gyres has been discussed at length by A. N. Jeffares, and, lately, by H. H. Vendler. They derive, through many ramifications, from Plato, Heraclitus, Descartes, Swedenborg, Boehme, Blake. A gyre is 'a combination of line and plane, and as one tendency or the other must always be stronger, the gyre is always expanding or contracting'. Therefore

[1] *A Vision* (B), p. 68.
[2] *Explorations*, p. 396.

two cones are used to symbolize the double effect of the normal tensions set up in life: i.e. soul and self, man and nature, heart and head.

In the sketch at page 196, the manner in which Yeats used the gyre as the basis of a symbol-group is suggested. The figure of the interlaced double triangle used in *A Vision* has been simplified to show two expanding cones, each formed by a sphere moving onward in space. Within the cones moves the 'perne', a spool which unwinds the thread spirally as the sphere moves onward: spool and thread having in part connotations of the Three Fates, in part those of the exploration of the labyrinth, 'Hades' bobbin' of 'Byzantium'. As each age reaches its catastrophic climax it disintegrates, 'things fall apart': yet within, as it were, the new age starts its growth, 'unwinding the thread the previous age has wound'. But the movement is not merely circular and spiral, but oscillatory, like the shuttle, and thus provides an image for the antithetical aspects of personality. 'Gyre' and 'perne' are also associated with bird-flight, and the failure of the falconer, God, to control the falcon,[1] the human mind in its spiral ascent; so that we have an association with the winding stair and the whole range of images from *The Tower*, linked to Blake's 'A Design of Circular Stairs' (*Paradiso*, xix).

Any attempt at a detailed analysis of *A Vision* is likely to be unprofitable. But it is possible to extract from the book what appear to be Yeats' central *poetic* beliefs, isolating them from any attempts to consider them as components of a system; and then to show the forms which those beliefs assume in the fabric of his verse. The important points are perhaps these:

1. History can be interpreted as a series of expanding cones; each age, as it wears on, generating a centrifugal tendency, which finally produces decadence or disintegration.

2. But the symbol is in reality that of a *double* cone, since each age unwinds what its predecessor has wound. Thesis and antithesis are in progress simultaneously.

3. The gyre is applicable to each man's life, as well as to history.

4. Man and history are further governed by twenty-eight phases of the moon.

[1] Taken, as Jeffares has noted, from *Inferno*, xvii.

5. These phases are shown symbolically (and appear to be superimposed both *vertically and horizontally* on the gyres) as quadrants of a circle, one quadrant symbolizing each of the Four Faculties.

6. The Four Faculties are:

    (*a*) Volition or Will.

    (*b*) Reasoning power or Creative Mind.

    (*c*) The Mask ('the image of what we wish to become, or that to which we give our reverence').

    (*d*) The Body of Fate, including

        (i) physical and mental environment.

        (ii) the changes in the human body – e.g. the coming of old age.

        (iii) the stream of phenomena (e.g. the Easter Rising) as these affect a particular individual.

The basis of the time-scheme is the Platonic Great Year; the period at the end of which all the planets would, in theory, return to their original positions. This is the so-called *thema mundi*. The time taken for this cycle was variously estimated from 6,000 years to 24,000, 72,000 or even more. Yeats appears to accept the estimate of 26,000 years for the cycle.

Christ's life and death are images of the Great Year. According to tradition the world and the sun were created in the Vernal Equinox, the moon two days later. His Crucifixion and Conception took place two days after the Vernal Equinox. Hence the explanation of the lines

> And then did all the Muses sing
> Of Magnus Annus at the spring,
> As though God's death were but a play.[1]

The date of Conception changed from year to year, but that of the Birth did not.

The Great Year is split up into twelve cycles corresponding to the twelve lunar months. At the First Cycle the first new soul comes into the world; at the end of the Twelfth Cycle there will be born a New Fountain. (This is, in another form, the Second Com-

---

[1] 'Two Songs from a Play,' *C.P.*, p. 239. But in *A Vision* the Crucifixion, and the assassination of Julius Caesar, are seen in some sort of alignment as miraculous events [(B), p. 254].

# THE GYRE & ITS IMAGES

The cones are traced by the revolving spindle which carries the thread. As the gyre disintegrates a new cone starts in a reverse direction. The spiral is associated with the winding stair

'Things fell apart, the centre cannot hold'.

'Turning & turning in the widening gyre The falcon cannot hear the falconer'

'The loaded pern.'
"Hades' bobbin."
"Perne in a gyre."
"Though I had long perned in a gyre."
"There the loves a-circle go,
The flaming circle of our days,
Gyring spiring to and fro
In those great ignorant leafy ways."

"An age is the reversal of an age."
"Each age unwinds the thread
the previous age had wound."
"For love is but a skein unwound
Between the dark and dawn."

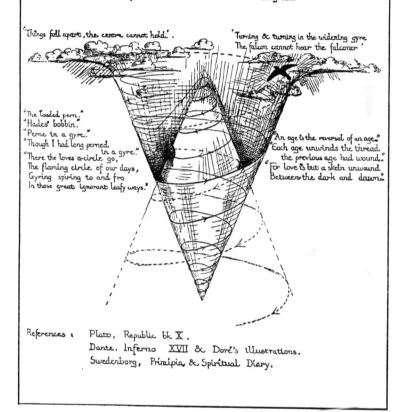

References :   Plato,  Republic  bk X .
Dante. Inferno  XVII  &  Doré's Illustrations.
Swedenborg, Principia, & Spiritual Diary.

ing.) 'Then there will come the first of a new series, the Thirteenth Cycle which is a Sphere and not a cone.'[1] I suggest that this is the origin of the obscure cosmic image in 'Chosen' of *A Woman Young and Old*:

> ... Where his heart my heart did seem
> And both adrift on the miraculous stream
> Where – wrote a learned astrologer –
> The Zodiac is changed into a sphere.[2]

Each of the Twelve Cycles lasts, in theory, approximately two thousand years; but, since history is seen as a series of interlaced expanding and contracting cones, there is no break in continuity. This series of cones or gyres is also perceived in terms of wheels, which are used to interpret not only each complete era, but also each half of it, thus complicating its astrological explanation. Since I am concerned only with the light that the system sheds on the poetry, I shall disregard this complication and others connected with psycho-astrological theories such as that of the 'tinctures'. What is important at this stage is Yeats' idea of a 'millennium' – 'the symbolic measure of a being that attains its flexible maturity and then sinks into rigid age'.[3] 'The loss of control over thought comes towards the end; first a sinking in upon the moral being, then the last surrender, the irrational cry, revelation, the scream of Juno's peacock.'[4]

## II

The symbolic figure that Yeats used is an interlaced, double cone, divided by horizontal bands which show the correspondences, in terms of the lunar phases, between the different ages. (For example, the period A.D. 1005–1180 corresponds to the Homeric period.) The resultant geometry is difficult to follow, not wholly consistent, and not very profitable. For the present purpose I have simplified the cones, and left out the less significant aspects, in the following

---

[1] (A), p. 170. See also Ellmann, *Yeats, The Man and the Masks*, p. 286.
[2] *C.P.*, p. 311. The 'learned astrologer' is Macrobius; *C.P.*, p. 536. Compare: 'According to Simplicius, a late commentator upon Aristotle, the Concord of Empedocles fabricates all things into "an homogeneous sphere"' (*A Vision* (B), p. 67).
[3] *A Vision* (A), p. 180.
[4] Ibid.

The Chronology of *A Vision* set out in simple form
to show its relationship to certain poems. Phases of
the moon are shown but not the Gyres.

| Time Scale | Moon Phase | Notes | Some Poems and Plays Concerned |
|---|---|---|---|
| 2000 to 500 B.C. | 10 | Babylonian Mathematical Starlight 'Fabulous Darkness.' 'Myth of Leda and the Swan.' The First Annunciation. Egyptian Sculpture. Homer and the Trojan legend.<br><br>Pythagoras. | 'Two Songs from a Play.'<br><br>'Chosen.'<br><br>'Under Ben Bulben', 'His Bargain'; and all poems that use the Troy-Helen symbol. 'Among School Children', 'Leda', 'Nineteen Hundred and Nineteen', 'The Tower'. |
| 500 B.C. to A.D. I | 13 14 22 | Phidias. Plato. The 'Growing Solitude of the Soul'. Aristotle. Scopas. 'Greek Civilization loses itself in Asia.'<br><br>The Annunciation. The Nativity. The Magi. End of the First Wheel. Break-up of Alexander's kingdom. Salome. | 'The Statues', 'Demon and Beast'.<br><br>'Supernatural Songs.' 'The Mother of God.' 'A Stick of Incense.' 'A Nativity.' 'The Magi.' *A Full Moon in March*, etc. |
| A.D. I to 250 | 2 to 7 | The 'Galilean Turbulence'. Outbreak of 'Irrational Force' seen against 'an antithetical aristocratic civilization'. Decay of Rome. Symbolism of Roman Statues contrasted with those of Greece. | 'The Second Coming.' *Calvary. The Resurrection.*<br><br>[OVERLEAF] |

## The Chronology of *A Vision* – *continued*

| Time Scale | Moon Phase | Notes | Some Poems and Plays Concerned |
|---|---|---|---|
| 250 to 500 | 9 10 11 12 | Rise of Byzantine Empire. Statues & Mosaic – Height of Byzantine Achievement. 'Religious Aesthetic & Practical Life are One.' | 'Sailing to Byzantium.' 'Byzantium.' |
| 500 to 800 | 13 to 18 | Justinian becomes Emperor, 527. Building of St. Sophia. | |
| 800 to 1005 | 19 to 28 | Phase 22 is the break-up of Charlemagne's Empire; as in previous cycle, Alexander's was destroyed in this Phase. *End of First Millennium.* | 'Whence Had They Come?' ('Supernatural Songs.') |
| 1005 to 1180 | 2 to 7 | Corresponds (apparently) to Homeric Period. Arthurian Tales and Romanesque Architecture. Gothic Architecture. 'The Church grows secular that it may fight a new-born secular world.' | |
| 1250 to 1300 to 1380 | 8 9, 10 11 13 | The Schoolmen (as again in 1875–1927). Giotto & Fra Angelico. Froissart. 'Gentleness and Violence' of the Gyres. Masaccio, Chaucer, Villon. | |
| 1450 to 1550 | 15 | The Renaissance: Botticelli, Crivelli, Mantegna. Da Vinci. Dürer. Breaking of the Christian Synthesis, corresponding to era of Phidias. 'Element of Strain & Artifice.' Attempted reconciliation of Paganism & Christianity. | 'Wisdom.' 'Her Vision in The Wood.' |

## The Chronology of *A Vision* – *continued*

| Time Scale | Moon Phase | Notes | Some Poems and Plays Concerned |
|---|---|---|---|
| 1550 to 1650 | 16 17 | Raphael. Titian. Michelangelo. Rabelais. Aretino. 'Awakening of Sexual Desire.' Sistine Chapel. Shakespeare. 'Human personality bursts like a shell.' Milton. Attempted return to Synthesis like that of Sistine Chapel. Belief dies out. | 'Under Ben Bulben.' 'Long-legged Fly.' 'An Acre of Grass.' |
| 1650 to 1875 | 18 19 20 21 | Newton. Locke, Swift, Berkeley, Goldsmith. Napoleon. 'Mechanical force will in a moment become supreme.' Rodin; creating his Art from 'The Hell of Baudelaire, not of Dante'. | 'The Seven Sages.' |
| (1815) 1875 to 1927 | 22 23 24 & 25 | Period like that of 1250–1300. Popularization of Physical & Economical Science. (Abstraction began at Phase 19 & will end at Phase 25.) 'Hatred of the Abstract, when the intellect turns on itself.' Pound, Eliot, Joyce, Pirandello, Wyndham Lewis, Spengler. 'What if there is always something that lies outside knowledge, outside order? What if the irrational return? What if the circle begin again?' 'We may be about to accept the most implacable authority the world has known.' | 'Statistics. 'The Gyres.' 'The Second Coming.' 'Meru.' |

H

account, which is shown chronologically on pages 199–201.
The first era is 2000 B.C.–A.D. 1. Greek civilization drives out an
older one. Yeats is but dimly conscious of the first period to 500 B.C.,
though he speaks of 'some corner of the mathematical Babylonian
starlight' – mathematical because of the Babylonian eminence in
astronomy. There is, however, a First Annunciation, the myth of
Leda and the Swan, bird and woman, corresponding to the Second
Annunciation, giving birth to Greece; hence

> A shudder in the loins engenders there
> The broken wall, the burning roof and tower
> And Agamemnon dead.[1]

By 1000 B.C. the Jewish religious system was complete, and the
Jews themselves grown barbaric and Asiatic. The progress is
through Homer, the development of civil order, to a phase of independence and solitude. In the sixth century B.C. 'personality begins,
but there is as yet no intellectual solitude'. The discovery of solitude[2]
brings with it 'the visible art that interests us most today'. After the
Persian wars the 'Doric vigour' suggests a deliberate turning away
from all that is Eastern, or a moral propaganda like that which turned
the poets out of Plato's Republic. In Phidias Ionic and Doric
influences revive again. Persia falls before Phidias and his 'westward-
moving art' just as Rome gave way to the glory of the Byzantine
Empire, and the Byzantine to the Renaissance. The end of the
millennium comes with the birth of Christ. The Annunciation and
Birth are in some degree astrological events, linked to older civilizations – aspects of the same myth repeating itself. The date of 6
January for Christmas has been received 'from the learned men of
an older civilization, from the Greeks and Chaldeans perhaps,
perhaps even from those worshippers of Korê at Alexandria who
upon that day carried up from the Temple Crypt a wooden figure
marked upon head and hands and knees with a Cross and a Star,
crying out "The Virgin has given birth to the God".' (This explains
the *fabulous* darkness in 'Two Songs from a Play':

> The Roman Empire stood appalled:
> It dropped the reins of peace and war

[1] *C.P.*, p. 241.
[2] Cf. 'I would be . . . solitary as the dawn'; and the whole symbol of the
hermit-scholar in 'The Tower'.

> When that fierce virgin and her Star
> Out of the fabulous darkness called.[1])

The star-conception image is frequent —

> Another star has *shot* an ear

— perhaps linked in association with the vision of the arrow shot at a star, and therefore another aspect of this world-image.[2] With this dominant the Magi are continually associated; Mantegna's *Adoration of the Magi* (though it cannot be related specifically to any one description) may be thought of as illuminating his image of them. The same painter's *Apollo and Diana* shows Apollo standing on a star-covered sphere, and shooting an arrow into space, a symbol that occurs on Cretan coins, and in Blake, as well as in Chinese poetry and painting.

It appears that 2000 B.C.–A.D. 1 is, arbitrarily, Phase 1 of the millennium. At its end there is the 'Galilean turbulence': 'the Roman Empire stood appalled'. The Christian church is in sharp antithesis to the realization of divinity through the discovery of formal perfection that Yeats finds in Greek sculpture. 'It follows that it must be idolatry to worship that which Phidias and Scopas made. . . .' 'Night will fall upon man's wisdom now that man has been taught that he is nothing. . . .' The gyre is widening at its end. Man is 'stirred into a frenzy of anxiety and so to moral transformation. . . .' (There was to be something of this kind when the last gyre ended, round about 1927.) 'The mind that brought the change, if considered as man only, is a climax of whatever Greek and Roman thought was most a contradiction to its age; but considered as more than man He controlled what Neo-Pythagorean and Stoic could not — irrational force. He could announce the new age, all that had not been thought of, or touched, or seen, because He could substitute for reason, miracle . . . We say of Him because His sacrifice was voluntary, that He was love itself, and yet that part of Him which made Christendom was not love but pity,[3] and not pity for intellectual despair, though the man in Him, being *antithetical* like His age, knew it in the Garden, but *primary* pity, that for the common

---

[1] *C.P.*, p. 240.

[2] See p. 164. *Shot* also contains the idea of intense physical or spiritual effort.

[3] Cf. 'In pity for man's darkening thought. . . .'

lot, man's death, seeing that He raised Lazarus, sickness, seeing that He healed many, sin, seeing that He died.'[1]

I have quoted this passage at length because I believe that it contains several important clues to Yeats' thought. Christianity casts out the rational for the miraculous:

> Odour of blood when Christ was slain
> Made all Platonic tolerance vain
> And vain all Doric discipline.[2]

It is in part (for there is also the thought of the Irish Troubles) the explanation of the line in 'The Gyres':

> Irrational streams of blood are staining earth[3]

– an irrationality that is associated with the coming of Christianity, and hence with the 'rough beast' and the 'uncontrollable mystery' of 'The Second Coming'. The 'Two Songs' are taken from the beginning and end of *The Resurrection*.

> THE GREEK. O Athens, Alexandria, Rome, something has come to destroy you! The heart of a phantom is beating! Man has begun to die. Your words are clear at last, O Heraclitus. God and man die each other's life, live each other's death.[4]

Further, this reference to Christ's Agony in the Garden is the only one that I can find in all the poetry and prose. We know that Yeats was strongly affected by Mantegna ('A thoughtless image of Mantegna's thought'). We know that he visited the National Gallery in London. There is no conclusive evidence that he had seen Mantegna's 'Agony'. But the possibility that he knew it is a strong one. There is the peculiar marble quality of the rock, the pity, bewilderment, and a hint of fanaticism in the face:

> Nobody before him had so pitied human misery. He preached the coming of the Messiah because he thought the Messiah would take it all upon himself. Then some day when he was very tired, after a long journey perhaps, he thought that he himself was the Messiah. He thought it because of all destinies it seemed the most terrible.[5]

[1] *A Vision* (B), p. 275.
[2] 'Two Songs from a Play', *C.P.*, p. 239.
[3] Ibid., p. 337.
[4] Note the correspondence with the characteristic movement of the gyres.
[5] *The Resurrection, C. Plays*, p. 579.

I do not think it can be accidental that the image of the white
heron occurs as a dominant symbol in *Calvary*. In Mantegna's
'Agony' two white herons are fishing in the stream that winds at
the foot of the Mount. They are dispassionate, apart, symbols of the
'subjective':

> God has not died for the white heron.

It is plain elsewhere that the heron stands for the lonely, self-
sufficient man, perhaps linked to the other lonely image of the
Fisherman. It is objective life, dissociated from mental conflict;
graduated downwards, the fifth plane of activity in the picture.
Mantegna is far more concrete, more concerned with the symbols
of ordinary life, than El Greco. Herons, rabbits, birds, the minute
life of plant and bush and tree, and the armed party led by Judas
emerging from the city – all these are set in a most moving and
dramatic rhythm. On the bough of the sparse and dying tree a bird,
half-vulture and half-raven, is sitting watching Christ. It may be
kin to the image in 'Byzantium', or to the 'miraculous strange bird'
of the love poems. But I suggest that there is a kinship with that
black bird which, in Oliver Sheppard's statue, watches the dying
Cuchulain from the stump of a tree.

### III

The Phases of the Moon are superimposed upon history in accordance with a system which is not clear to me. The first millennium
appears to be Phase 1, for Phases 2–7 cover the period A.D. 1–250,
and include the decay of the Roman Empire. This is followed, in
Phases 9, 10, 11, by the rise of the Byzantine state. In his account
of the contrast between the Greek and Roman civilizations, Yeats
is much affected by the symbolism of their statues, and his treatment
of them is of special interest. 'The Greeks painted the eyes of marble
statues and made out of enamel or glass or precious stones those
of their bronze statues, but the Roman was the first to drill a round
hole to represent the pupil, and because, as I think, of a preoccupation with the glance characteristic of a civilization in its final phase.'[1]

The significance that Yeats sees is more than an artistic decadence,
for the statue both represents man's vision of the image of God,

[1] *A Vision* (B), p. 275.

in his mathematical proportions (the Greeks had found the secret of perfect man) and a potential embodiment of the soul. He had read Plotinus:

> I think, therefore, that those ancient sages, who sought to secure the presence of divine beings by the erection of shrines and statues, showed insight into the nature of the All; they perceived that, though this Soul is everywhere tractable, its presence will be secured all the more readily when an appropriate receptacle is elaborated, a place especially capable of receiving some portion or phase of it, something reproducing it, and serving like a mirror to catch an image of it.[1]

The statue was more than a representation of man.

He stresses the delineation by the Romans of character revealed in the face and hands alone; the head being screwed or dovetailed on to a 'stock' body made in the workshop. (This is the age becoming 'rigid'.) 'When I think of Rome I see always those heads with their world-considering eyes, and those bodies as conventional as the metaphors in a leading article, and compare in my imagination vague Grecian eyes gazing at nothing, Byzantine eyes of drilled ivory staring upon a vision. . . .'[2]

This interest in statuary is partly the result of the visit to Sicily and Rome, but he seems to have studied plaster casts with some care in order to substantiate a theory that the depth of the eye-socket had some connection with the state of a given civilization. The thought occurs in 'A Bronze Head' – that of Maud Gonne, illustrated in Hone's *Life*:

> Here at right of the entrance this bronze head,
> Human, superhuman, a bird's round eye,
> Everything else withered and mummy-dead.[3]

In 'Beautiful Lofty Things' she is seen in terms of statuary:

> . . . Maud Gonne at Howth station waiting a train,
> Pallas Athene in that straight back and arrogant head.[4]

Yeats may have had in mind any one of a dozen different statues, but Phidias, to whom he refers so often, had made a head of Athena (Copenhagen) superbly arrogant, and the Lemnian Athena. Either

---

[1] *On the Nature of the Soul*, Fourth Ennead, iv. 3, 11 (transl., Mackenna).
[2] (A), p. 188.
[3] *C.P.*, p. 382.
[4] Ibid., p. 348.

could have fittingly expressed Maud Gonne's poise. The values of statuary were linked in a curious manner to the formal qualities of the Nōh plays:

> . . . Statues full of an august formality that implies traditional measurements, a philosophic defence.[1]

The measurements refer not only to the 'divine perfection' achieved by the Greeks, but also to the rules of proportion which the Egyptians followed for their human figures. The figure was first divided by a vertical line passing through nose, navel and genitals, making of the body two symmetrical halves. The figure was then further divided by twenty-two horizontal lines ruled at regular intervals; the mouth was invariably placed on the twentieth parallel and so on with the other features. In the sixth century the Greeks obeyed the first part of the system:[2] hence

> Measurement began our might:
> Forms a stark Egyptian thought,
> Forms that gentler Phidias wrought.

Egyptian statues are always architectural decorations, and hence there is no reason to show action. The proportions are a 'philosophic defence', perhaps as representing constancy in the changing world, perhaps merely from Yeats' own obsession with symmetry. It is pertinent to quote Béguin again:

> Et le grand mystère, qu'ils poursuivaient par tant de voies diverses, était une formule capable d'exprimer à la fois le rhythme du Tout et le rythme analogue de chacune de ses parties vivantes. De là leurs speculations mathématiques: le nombre seul peut rendre compte d'une réalité conçue comme essentiellement rhythmique.[3]

The reign of Justinian (527–565) should coincide with Phase 15, though the chronology is confused; and the building of St Sophia precedes the 'moment of climax'. It appears, so close is the correspondence with parts of *A Vision*, that Yeats had been reading H. G. Wells' *Outline of History*, which had been published in 1920. For an example:

---

[1] *E. & I.*, p. 225.

[2] 'There are moments when I am certain that art must once again accept the Greek proportions . . .' (*On the Boiler*, p. 37.)

[3] Béguin, op. cit., i, p. 101. Compare also Blake: 'Mathematic Form is Eternal in Reasoning Memory'.

One characteristic of its [Byzantine] decoration is a peculiar rigidity; all the flexibility of Greek and Roman painting and sculpture has gone, and in its place we have mosaics shewing flat, symmetrical, erect figures in full face. Hardly ever is there a profile or any stir of foreshortening. It is as if that natural body which the Greeks idolized had become reprehensible, a thing of fear.[1]

Justinian is followed by a blank period, including Phases 17–21. The next date that Yeats feels, though somewhat vaguely, to be significant, is 'the break up of Charlemagne's Empire', which is equivalent to Phase 22, and which explains the image in 'Whence Had They Come?'

> Whence had they come,
> The hand and lash that beat down frigid Rome?
> What sacred drama through her body heaved
> When world-transforming Charlemagne was conceived?[2]

This brings us to about the end of the tenth century, and the 'sinking down of Christendom into the heterogeneous loam'. The gyre breaks up into 'Asiatic and anarchic form'.

IV

The period A.D. 1005–1180 corresponds to the previous Homeric period of the first millennium and is significant for the Arthurian Legend and Romanesque architecture. Then follows 1250–1300, or Phase 8: though it is not clear exactly when this new phase-system started. 1300–80 is the period of the Fourth gyre, and Phases 8–13 of the Moon, the last covering the age of Masaccio, Chaucer, Villon. 1450–1550 is the centre of the Italian Renaissance, and here Yeats' selection of representative figures is interesting. Botticelli, Donatello, Crivelli, Mantegna, Leonardo da Vinci exhibit 'intellectual beauty' in this, the fifteenth phase.

The next period is 1550–1680 which covers Phases 16, 17 and 18. The important artists are Raphael, Michelangelo, and Titian: its achievements are the Sistine Chapel and the Camera della Segnatura. Then for a moment intellect and emotion are unified, but the phase dies with the 'noble ineffectual faces' of Van Dyck. In Milton's 'On

---

[1] *The Outline of History*, Eighth Revision, p. 559.
[2] *C.P.*, p. 332.

the Morning of Christ's Nativity', the two elements, sacred and profane, which had been unified in the Sistine Chapel, fall apart: and the Chapel remains throughout several poems a most significant symbol. It seems to me that Yeats linked it with all the Creation and Annunciation relics, perhaps with Pater's most suggestive phrase in mind:

> Not the Judgement but the Resurrection is the real subject of his last work in the Sistine Chapel; and his favourite subject is the legend of Leda, the delight of the world breaking from the egg of a bird.[1]

In the period 1680–1875 'the world begins to long for the arbitrary and accidental, for the grotesque, the repulsive and the terrible, that it may be cured of desire'.[2] Gainsborough's women recall Egyptian faces. Rodin is a typical figure of Phase 21; 'creating his powerful art out of the fragments of those Gates of Hell that he had found himself unable to hold together – images out of a personal dream'. 1875–1927 is Phase 22, the last crescent before the Second Coming, and the beginning of the third millennium. Phase 23 is the first where there is hatred of the abstract (although in other writings Yeats had found this hatred in Swift and Berkeley too). 'The intellect turns upon itself'.[3] Pound, Pirandello, Joyce, Eliot, Wyndham Lewis, Brancusi, are figures of this phase. So, in some curious way, is Shaw; Yeats liked to insert his friends or enemies into 'the System':

> Shaw, as I understand him, has no true quarrel with his time, its moon and his almost exactly coincide. He is quite content to exchange Narcissus and his Pool for a signal-box at a railway junction, where goods and travellers pass perpetually upon their logical glittering road.[4]

But there is perhaps salvation:

> I agree about Shaw, he is haunted by the mystery that he flouts. He is an atheist who trembles in the haunted corridor.[5]

In the Preface to *Fighting the Waves*, he includes Virginia Woolf as a typical figure. It is of special interest that all reference to contemporary figures, and the discussion of their significance, is cut

[1] *The Renaissance*; 'The Poetry of Michelangelo'.
[2] (A), p. 206.
[3] (A), pp. 211 *et seq.*
[4] *Autobiographies*, p. 294. Cf. Wilson, *Axel's Castle*, pp. 59, 60.
[5] Wade, *Letters*, p. 671.

out of the 1937 edition: in which the chronology proper follows, word by word, that of the early version. In outline, Yeats believes that myth and fact have now fallen apart: and for that reason man is calling up myth 'which now but gropes its way out of the mind's dark, but will shortly pursue and terrify'. This is another reference to 'The Second Coming'. The new era will be like the beginnings of Christianity, bringing its stream of irrational force. Phase 24 may offer peace, but it will be followed first by a kind of passive obedience, and after by decadence.

> I foresee a time when . . . a ceaseless activity will be required of all; and where rights are swallowed up in duties, and solitude is difficult, creation except among avowedly archaistic and unpopular groups will grow impossible. Phase 25 may arise, as the code wears out from repetition, to give new motives for obedience. . . . Then with the last gyre must come a desire to be ruled or rather, seeing that desire is all but dead, an adoration of force spiritual or physical, and society as mechanical force be complete at last.

> > Constrained, arraigned, baffled, bent and unbent
> > By those wire-jointed jaws and limbs of wood
> > Themselves obedient,
> > Knowing not evil or good.[1]

A new period, that of the Eleventh gyre, will commence in 1927. Yeats has observed, in the poets and artists to whom he has referred, a 'falling in two of the human mind'. This may be a preparation for the last phase. 'Perhaps now that the abstract intellect has split the mind into categories, the body into cubes, we may be about to turn back towards the unconscious, the whole, the miraculous'.[2] The cultivated classes will be separated from the community. A new philosophy will arise, concrete in expression, established by immediate experience, personal. It will teach individual immortality and the re-embodiment of the soul. The ecstasy of the saint and mystic will recede: 'Men will no longer separate the idea of God from the human genius, human productivity in all its forms.' The new era will be different from Christianity; the 'new thought must find expression among those that are most subtle, most rich in memory'. It is to be the product of an aristocracy, the learned and

---

[1] (A), p. 212; and in 'The Double Vision of Michael Robarts', *C.P.*, p. 192; which reads *and* for *or* in the last line.

[2] Introduction to *The Cat and The Moon*; *W. & B.*, p. 140.

the rich — 'and the best of those that express it will be given power, less because of that they promise than of that they seem and are. This much can be thought because it is the reversal of what we know, but those kindreds once formed must obey irrational force and so create hitherto unknown experience, or that which is incredible.'[1]

v

One of the strangest features of *A Vision* was its justification, in Yeats' view, after its composition. Spengler's *Decline of the West* came out at this time, and gave Yeats the opportunity to emancipate himself from the surfaces of history:

> I was writing my notes in Galway and drawing my historical diagrams while his first Edition was passing through the press in Germany. I had never heard his name and yet the epochs are the same, the dates are the same, the theory is the same. Even some of my examples, such as the drilling of the eyes in the Roman statues, and the screwing on of Roman portrait-heads to ready-made conventional bodies, and these examples are used to prove the same things.[2]

At Rapallo Yeats was reading Spengler in the mornings and writing verse in the afternoons.

Wyndham Lewis also provided confirmation:

> I have read *Time and Western Man* with gratitude, the last chapters again and again. It has given, what I could not, a coherent voice to my hatred. You are wrong to think that Lewis attacks the conclusions of men like Alexander and Russell because he thinks them 'uncertain'. He thinks them false. To admit uncertainty into philosophy, necessary uncertainty, would seem to him to wrong the sovereignty of intellect, or worse, to accept the hypocritical humility of the scientific propagandists, which is, he declares, their 'cloak for dogma'. He is a Kantian, with some mixture of older thought, Catholic or Greek, and has the vast Kantian argument behind him, the most powerful in philosophy. He considers that both 'space and time are mere appearances', whereas his opponents think that time is real though space is a construction of the mind.[3]

[1] (A), p. 215.
[2] *T.S.M. Letters*, p. 105. For the significance of the Roman statues, see *A Vision* (B), pp. 18 and 276.
[3] Ibid., p. 122.

It is essential to realize this intense and perpetually growing interest in philosophy, and to watch the emotion receiving sanction, as it were, so that images are reborn, not as refractions of second-hand opinions, but in a state of intense excitement arising from the central certainty that his previous intuition had been just, even to the smallest detail. The very myths were now stabilized:

> He [Ezra Pound] is sunk in Frobenius, Spengler's German source, and finds him a most interesting person. Frobenius suggested the idea that cultures (including arts and sciences) arise out of races, express those races as if they were fruit and leaves in a preordained order and perish with them; and the two main symbols, that of the Cavern and that of the Boundless.

Compare

> And haughtier-headed Burke that proved the State a tree,
> That this unconquerable labyrinth of the birds, century after century,
> Cast but dead leaves to mathematical equality.[1]

> He [Frobenius] has confirmed a conception I have had for many years, a conception that has freed me from British Liberalism and all its dreams. The one heroic sanction is that of the last battle of the Norse gods, of a gay struggle without hope. Long ago I used to puzzle Maud Gonne by always avowing ultimate belief as a test. Our literary movement would be worthless but for its defeat. Science is the criticism of Myth. There would be no Darwin had there been no Book of Genesis, no electron but for the Greek atomic myth; and when the criticism is finished there is not even a drift of ashes on the pyre. Sexual desire dies because every touch consumes the Myth, and yet a Myth that cannot be so consumed becomes a spectre.[2]

> I am reading William Morris with great delight, and what a protection to my delight it is to know that in spite of all his loose writing I need not be jealous for him. He is the end, as Chaucer was the end in his day, Dante in his, incoherent Blake in his. There is no improvement: only a series of sudden fires, each though fainter as necessary as that before it. We free ourselves from obsession that we may be nothing. The last kiss is given to the void.[3]

I suggest that there are matters of profound importance emerging

[1] 'Blood and the Moon,' ii, *C.P.*, p. 268.
[2] I do not know what this means, unless it be the Phoenix-image. Or perhaps the key is in 'Baile and Aillinn': 'Where for its moment both seem lost, consumed'; or again it may be that Yeats is thinking of Blake's Spectre, the symbol of the critical reason which is antagonistic to vision.
[3] *T.S.M. Letters*, p. 154. There are further references to Frobenius and the symbolism of the Cavern in *A Vision* (B), pp. 258–9.

here. *A Vision* was coming into its own, and all the preceding thought that had been given to it was being shown, at least in part, to be valued. Hatred was justified:

> I study hatred with great diligence,
> For that's a passion in my own control,
> A sort of besom that can clear the soul
> Of everything that is not mind or sense.[1]

Science, the 'opium of the suburbs' is the enemy, its criticism of myth an indispensable adjunct of its own growth; so that, logically, new myths might later win their justifications as foreshadowing proved reality. Only the mind is certain; Spengler and Berkeley meet, the two representatives of their disintegrating gyres. From the pessimism of Schopenhauer – 'Schopenhauer can do no wrong in my eyes, I no more quarrel with his errors than with a cataract',[2] – comes the sense of joy in defeat:

> They know that Hamlet and Lear are gay;
> Gaiety transfiguring all that dread.[3]

The reading of Spengler explains much of the 'fascism' of *On the Boiler*. Yeats is aware of the change in Europe. 'But Europe is changing its philosophy. Some four years ago the Russian Government silenced the mechanists because social dialectic is impossible if matter is trundled about by some limited force.'[4] The prophet of the new age must believe in the return of the 'unfashionable gyre'; he must abandon the straight-line evolutionary Darwinian thinking of Western Civilization; he must follow Toynbee in adopting, as the proper unit of history, a culture or a civilization, the age of Phidias or of Byzantium. Both Spengler and Toynbee have a strong tendency to mysticism, the one romantic, the other religious. So, in the pattern of history, Yeats must consider, with Swift, the factor of growth and disintegration, the problem of the dominant minority, the impact of new forces on old institutions, the barrenness of the soul because mythology has died.

---

[1] 'Ribh considers Christian Love insufficient,' *C.P.*, p. 330.
[2] *T.S.M. Letters*. p. 117
[3] 'Lapis Lazuli,' *C.P.*, p. 338. L. A. G. Strong points out that he owes this remark to Lady Gregory: 'All true tragedy is a joy to him who dies.' The thought is of Nietzsche, as are many of the preceding quotations.
[4] Introduction to *Fighting the Waves*, *W. & B.*, p. 73.

I suggest, too, that Yeats received confirmation from this study of much of his previous interest in Balzac; through whom I think he saw the possibility of fusing the religious elements in Ireland. That he was profoundly interested in this writer is apparent from various essays and *The Herne's Egg*: 'Balzac is the only modern mind which has made a synthesis comparable with that of Dante. . . .' 'I might set some exceptional young man, some writer of Abbey plays, to what once changed all my thought: the reading of the whole *Comèdie Humaine*.'[1] Unity might yet be possible, Neo-platonism and Catholicism and folk-lore finding common ground. 'Then, too, I would associate that doctrine of purgatory, which Christianity has shared with Neo-platonism, with the countryman's belief in the nearness of his dead "working out their penance" in rath or at garden end; and I would find in the psychical research of our day detail to make the association convincing to intellect and emotion. I would try to create a type of man whose most moving religious experience, though it came to him in some distant country, and though his intellect [were] wholly personal, would bring with it imagery to connect it with an Irish multitude now and in the past time.'[2]

## VI

Those portions of *A Vision* that deal with 'the nearness of the dead' have not perhaps received the attention they deserve; we might suggest many possible reasons, sociological and philosophical. All esoteric cults deal with the return of the dead, and the commerce of the dead with the living, the progress of the soul. Yeats was in some sense a 'dark tomb-haunter'. As a young man he had lived through the great age of spiritualism, and seen a second wave rise and break as a consequence of the First War. Many sources and authorities offered material, in all ages, to confirm the stories of spirit gathered in his boyhood at Sligo, and in his maturity in North Clare: Plotinus, Agrippa, More, Cudworth: Swedenborg and Boehme: Rosicrucianism and the Kabbalistic learning refracted

---

[1] *Explorations*, p. 269.
[2] Ibid., p. 267. Many of these aspects are incorporated in *The Dreaming of the Bones*.

through *The Golden Dawn*: Plutarch and *The Book of the Dead*; the great falcon that hovers over the God Horus; Ochorowicz and Conan Doyle. In the background are the Nōh plays and their characteristic ghosts; below all, the lush and tangled undergrowth of Celtic myth.

Myers had documented the subject with great elaboration in his *Human Personality and its Survival after Death*;[1] Conan Doyle had shown his photographs of ectoplasm to packed audiences, Strzygowski[2] had shown mysterious photographs and wax mouldings of spirit limbs, Sir Oliver Lodge's *Raymond* was widely known. Behind all was Christian doctrine, out of which might be chosen

> What seems most welcome in the tomb[3]

and perpetually supported from the text

> Wherefore seeing we also are compassed about with so great a cloud of witnesses . . .[4]

We may isolate Yeats' apparent beliefs under a few broad headings:

(1) Reincarnation. (We should remember that this is Celtic as well as Eastern.) It is one of the more satisfying ways in which a poet may contemplate immortality.

(2) The 'Great Memory' stored with accumulated memories of race and personality, and on which the living could draw by means of symbols, dreams, visions. 'For wisdom is the property of the dead . . .'

(3) The dead may appear as phantasms; they can make contact with the minds of the living in order to attain to a realization of themselves, they may haunt the living in order to procure the completion of some action in which they themselves have failed.

(4) The progress of the spirit after death is on a backward path through time. It relives its past life, and sometimes encounters a kind of 'knot' at which it is forced to re-enact (as in *Purgatory* and in the Nōh plays) some violent action or emotion.

---

[1] F. W. H. Myers; London, 1903. The author died in 1901.
[2] *If I were Four and Twenty*. See, especially Section VI–end.
[3] 'Vacillation', VIII, *C.P.*, p. 285.
[4] Hebrews xii, 1.

(5) This 'dreaming back', which is related to the all-pervading phases of the moon, is a progress towards self-knowledge and the recovery of 'radical innocence'.

(6) The souls, being thus purified, become 'blessed spirits', with whom earthly communion was once possible through contemplation. But communion with other spirits is normal while in this state.

(7) The soul is then ready for re-birth, after its katharsis in the period after death, which is normally three generations in time. In certain cycles it can choose the form which it will take on reincarnation.

(8) The apparently deterministic cycle of death, dreaming-back, re-birth, is not deterministic; 'at the critical moment the Thirteenth Cone, the sphere, the unique, intervenes.'[1]

Yeats' account of the events after death is made more difficult because of an astrological complication imposed on its progress, in addition to its relationship to the historical cycles and to a total reincarnation cycle of some two thousand years. To attempt to précis and synthesize the accounts in the two versions of *A Vision* would be onerous and not very profitable. I propose only to select some of the more dramatic episodes which are directly related to the work.

The experience of death is not separation from the body, but from exclusive association with one body. The Daimon is a kind of inclusive and eternal soul, it

> contains within itself, co-existing in its eternal moment, all the events of our life, all that we have known of other lives.

At the moment of death the experiences of life pass rapidly before the soul. The body lies for a time while the soul disengages itself: this I take to be the meaning of

> Ah, when the ghost begins to quicken,
> Confusion of the death-bed over . . .[2]

The first stage is one of darkness and sleep, in which the dead may have a vision of their 'Blood Kindred', either as simulacra or as spirits awaiting reincarnation. At this stage it may appear to the

[1] *A Vision* (A), p. 262.
[2] 'The Cold Heaven', *C.P.*, p. 140.

living; Myers' account of the frequency and time-appearances is relevant.[1]

Three aspects of the dead then begin to emerge. The Spirit first floats horizontally within the dead man's body, but later rises till it stands at his head. So with the Celestial Body, which subsequently assumes an opposite position at the feet.[2] The 'Passionate Body', which rises from the genitals, and stands upright; thereafter to vanish.

The Spirit must then explore its past life on the road to self-knowledge; much as a man in old age may review his own living progression —

> I am content to follow to its source
> Every event in action or in thought . . .[3]

In this search the Spirit encounters all those who have influenced the man, or whom he has influenced: 'But if he has belonged to some faith that has not known rebirth he may explore sources that require symbolical expression'.[4] On the 'Return' the Spirit exhausts the good and evil of past life by re-enacting it. In the 'Dreaming Back' the Spirit is attracted to the Passionate Body, and at this stage may re-enact (and in the process appear as a phantasm), significant events, whether painful or happy. A murderer 'may be seen committing the murder night after night'[5] or 'the seer but meets the old huntsman once more amid a multitude of his friends and all his hounds'.[6]

The dream may be long or short or intermittent, 'but the man must dream the event to its consequence as far as his intensity permits'. 'The more complete the exploration the more fortunate will be its future life . . .' '. . . the dream is as it were a smoothing out or an unwinding'. ('He unpacks the loaded perne' . . .) and the labyrinth of 'Byzantium'.

When the Spirit is freed from pleasure and pain by re-living the experiences which caused them, it now enters upon 'a state of

---

[1] Op. cit, especially Chapters I, VII – 'Phantasms of the Dead'.
[2] See 'A Prayer for My Son' (C.P., p. 238) and *The Only Jealousy of Emer*.
[3] 'A Dialogue of Self and Soul' (C.P., p. 265).
[4] *A Vision* (A) p. 225.
[5] *Purgatory*.
[6] This is one version of the universal 'Wild Hunt'. v. E. A. Armstrong, *The Folklore of Birds*. Cf. 'The Ballad of the Foxhunter' and 'Hound Voice'.

intellect' in which it is also set free from good and evil. It is a state of equilibrium, but in it there is neither emotion nor sensation. But here men and women meet, and seek to supplement, in each other, the defects they experienced in life. Only in death, and in this final state of equilibrium, is unity possible.

## VII

I believe that future studies of the two versions of *A Vision* will show very clearly its importance in Yeats' poetical development as well as in his poetry. It will always remain an exasperating book to read. Research will establish its sources and piece together many unconscious recollections. Yeats was drawing on a long-accumulated store of miscellaneous reading; and the value of the book lies in the manner in which it shows us the ferment in process. In the 1930 *Diary* he gives what I think is the simple truth:

> When my instructors began their explanation of the Great Year all the history I knew was what I remembered of English and Classical history from schooldays, or had since learned from the pages of Shakespeare or the novels of Dumas. When I had the dates and diagrams I began to study it, but could not so late in life, and with so much else to read, be a deep student. So there is little in what follows but what comes from the most obvious authorities.[1]

But once the excrescences can be cut away to show the simple pattern of *A Vision* the work takes on a new complexion. In the simplified presentation of its main features, I have omitted the psychology of the Four Faculties, the Twenty-Eight Embodiments, the Zodiacal references, the geometry of the interlocking cones, and the long mysterious analysis of Souls and Spirits, with its curious terminology of 'covens' and 'shiftings'. In these rejections I am aware that there may be some loss in detailed explanation of at least two poems. What remains shows his sense of the continuity both of history and of myth; it explains the dramatic interest which he found in certain figures and events; and the plausibility of it all is sufficient to account for the increasing certainty of unified thought from 1926 onwards. T. Sturge Moore has commented aptly upon it. '. . . *A Vision* maps out a frame of thought more capacious than

---

[1] *Explorations*, p. 291.

most poets have had at hand, though no doubt as difficult to use and as full of gaps as any other.'[1] It is unlikely that future poets will ever use such source-material. No one without Yeats' dramatic and esoteric inclinations would dare to exploit it. *A Vision* remains the product of his own idiosyncracies, intensely valuable to him as a offering a perpetually expanding and dramatically ordered universe. Its 'arbitrary, harsh, difficult symbolism' seems to have retained the power to stimulate him until the end of his life.

[1] In *English*, Vol. II, No. 11, 1939. And there is a notable passage in Arland Ussher's *The Twilight of the Ideas*: 'The doctrine of antiquity that everything which the mind of man can conceive has happened and will happen again in eternal cycles seems to me (besides being metaphysically cogent) to satisfy certain religious aspirations of our nature in a less objectionable manner than Christian or Eastern supernaturalism – those namely for the *marvellous*, for *congruence*, and for *return*' (p. 46).

# CHAPTER THIRTEEN

# Byzantium

And therefore I have sailed the seas and come
To the holy city of Byzantium.

Yes, I have decided to call the book Byzantium. I enclose the poem,
from which the name is taken, hoping that it may suggest symbolism for
the cover. The poem originates from a criticism of yours. You objected
to the last verse of 'Sailing to Byzantium' because a bird made by a
goldsmith was just as natural as anything else. That showed me that the
idea needed exposition . . .

I wrote the poem last spring; the first thing I wrote after my illness.

Letter to T. Sturge Moore.

I

'I think if I could be given a month of Antiquity and leave to
spend it where I chose, I would spend it in Byzantium a little before
Justinian opened St Sophia and closed the Academy of Plato. I think
I could find in some little wine shop some philosophical worker in
mosaic who could answer all my questions, the supernatural des-
cending nearer to him than to Plotinus even, for the pride of his
delicate skill would make what was an instrument of power to
Princes and Clerics and a murderous madness in the mob, show as a
lovely flexible presence like that of a perfect human body.'[1]

The city became the central symbol of two of the most important
poems – 'Sailing to Byzantium' of *The Tower* (1928) and 'Byzantium' of *The Winding Stair* (1933).[2] It is more than the mere meeting-
point of East and West, or the point on which his philosophy of art

---

[1] *A Vision* (A), p. 190; (B), p. 279. The mass of critical and exegetical
writing on these two poems is already of formidable size. For a beginning,
Saul's *Prolegomena* and Unterecker's *Guide* may be consulted; Stallworthy's
*Between the Lines* is essential.

[2] Dated in MS. Sept. 1926 and Sept. 1930 respectively.

coheres.[1] His description of it in *A Vision* must be read in the light of his conception of the cycles of history, and of his own journeyings under the Phases of the Moon.

I think that in early Byzantium, maybe never before or since in recorded history, religious, aesthetic and practical life were one,[2] that architect and artificers – though not, it may be, poets, for language had been the instrument of controversy and must have grown abstract – spoke to the multitude and the few alike. The painter, the mosaic worker, the worker in gold and silver, the illuminator of sacred books, were almost impersonal, almost perhaps without the consciousness of individual design, absorbed in their subject-matter and that the vision of a whole people.[3]

This desire for an art which should be the 'vision of the people' is fundamental in Yeats.[4] It is the antithesis of the 'dissipation and despair' that he found in the modern world. He had seen the gold and enamel work at Ravenna in 1908: but it was the visit to Italy and Sicily in 1925 that produced this sense of excitement at the revelation of mosaic's qualities. But Byzantium seems to be much more than Rome approached from the east, as Hone suggests,[5] or a peculiar kind of heroic vision,[6] or even a sort of Grecian Urn round which Yeats can crystallize the thought of the permanence of art in a world of mutability. It was linked to his theory of perfection in measurement:

This reconciliation [of Paganism and Christianity], which to Pope Julius meant that Greek and Roman antiquity were as sacred as that of Judea, and like it 'a vestibule of Christianity', meant to the mind of Dürer – a visitor to Venice during the movement of the gyre – that the human norm, discovered from the measurement of ancient statues, was God's first handiwork, that 'perfectly proportioned human

[1] Cf. Sacheverell Sitwell: *The Hunters and the Hunted*. 'The slow growth of centuries must have permeated the workshops of the palace . . . [a view of them] would be among the highest aesthetic experiences ever possible to human beings.'
[2] Cf. Synge's remark to him: 'We should unite stoicism, asceticism and ecstasy. Two of them have often come together, but the three never'. *Autobiographies*, p. 509.
[3] *A Vision* (B), pp. 279, 280.
[4] '[An article in the *Yale Review*] . . . commends me above other modern poets because my language is "public". That word which I had not thought of myself is a word I want' (*Letters to Dorothy Wellesley*), p. 179.
[5] *Life*, p. 367.
[6] Mrs Yeats.

body', which had seemed to Dante Unity of Being symbolized. The ascetic, who had a thousand years before attained his transfiguration upon the golden ground of Byzantine mosaic, had turned not into an athlete but into that unlabouring form the athlete dreamed of: the second Adam had become the first.[1]

But there is further possibility as to the associations of Byzantium in Yeats' mind. It had been a province of the Roman Empire; it had suffered from the rigidity, bureaucracy, and lack of imaginative treatment of its own ancient and complex traditions. There were parallels to be drawn between Rome and England as imperialistic powers; and Byzantium might well symbolize a new Ireland breaking away from its masters so that it might develop, or rather return to, its own philosophical, religious and artistic destiny. As for the past, both Byzantine and Gaelic Christendom might be judged to stand for a similar interpenetration of religion and art, the Hebraic and Hellenic held in perpetual synthesis. And the destruction of both came, not from within by gradual decline, but by a series of shocks, catastrophically, from without.[2] The first drafts dealt with Ireland, and later shifted to Byzantium. Material for the parallel is to be found in Dalton:

> When the power of Rome declined, in all the distant regions subjected to her rule there was a revival of native sentiment in *revolt against an imposed and alien art*. Everywhere the signs of this recrudescence are apparent; from Gaul to Egypt there is a reassertion of indigenous taste.[3]

There is apparent in Yeats' thought a hatred and contempt of Latin culture. In 'A Letter to Michael's Schoolmaster' the very anguage is to be avoided: 'Do not teach him one word of Latin. The Roman people were the classic decadence, their literature form without matter. They destroyed Milton, the French seventeenth and our own eighteenth century, and our schoolmasters even to-day read Greek with Latin eyes.' (To judge from *A Vision*, 'Latin eyes' suggested emptiness, rigidity, the hardness of a formalized mind.) 'Greece, could we but approach it with eyes as young as its

[1] *A Vision* (B), pp. 291–2. p. 207
[2] I owe this thought to Peter Allt.
[3] Dalton: *Byzantine Art*, p. 12. The italics are mine. Precisely the same indictment had been framed by Yeats and by Synge.

own, might renew our youth. . . . If he wants to read Irish after he is well founded in Greek, let him – it will clear his eyes of the Latin miasma.'

Byzantium, then, has a multiple symbolic value. It stands for the unity of all aspects of life, for perhaps the last time in history. It has inherited the perfection of craftsmanship, and more than craftsmanship, perhaps, the 'mystical mathematics' of perfection of form in all artistic creation. That culture is the inheritor of Greek tradition, in philosophy and handiwork. The disintegration of the 'Galilean turbulence' has not yet begun. But because it is in the past, it contains in itself, like Egypt to which it is linked, the mysteries of the dead. Memory may think back, with or without the aid of the shade, into the past and learn its secrets, the 'wisdom of the dead'.

The dance on the marble pavement is one of expiation; the refining fire, as in the Nōh play *Motomezuka*, is the lower or purgatorial fire, in contrast to the fire of inspiration, the 'simplicity of fire' of 'Vacillation', VII, the fire of Pentecost. The flames are dreamed or imagined; they are set against the material flames of martyrdom. Yeats refers to them constantly.

> The inflowing from their mirrored life, who themselves receive it from the Condition of Fire, falls upon the Winding Path called the Path of the Serpent, and that inflowing coming alike to man and to animals is called natural[1].

The relevance to the poem is obvious. Again 'Daemon and man are opposites; man passes from heterogeneous objects to the *simplicity of fire*, and the Daemon is drawn to objects because through them he obtains power, the extremity of choice.'[2]

The dolphin in 'Byzantium' is the escort of the dead, the rescuer of man from the complexities of mire and blood: compare 'News for the Delphic Oracle' in *Last Poems*:[3]

> Straddling each a dolphin's back
> And steadied by a fin,
> Those Innocents re-live their death,
> Their wounds open again.

[1] *P.A.S.L.*, p. 78. Cf. also Plotinus on Fire, *Enneads*.
[2] Ibid., p. 79. See 'Vacillation', VII, *C.P.*, p. 285
[3] *C.P.*, p. 376.

> The ecstatic waters laugh because
> Their cries are sweet and strange,
> Through their ancestral patterns dance. . . .[1]

There were many reasons for the attractiveness of the Dolphin. Arion won the musical prize in Sicily (Yeats was awarded the Nobel Prize) and had been flung overboard with his lyre, by the seamen of his ship. 'While he struggled in the waves, a Dolphin offered him his back, and carried him mounted thereon safe to shore. At the spot where he landed a monument of brass was afterwards erected upon the rocky shore, to preserve the memory of the event.' But there are other resemblances; far-fetched, perhaps, but of the kind in which Yeats delighted. His friend Oliver St John Gogarty had been captured in Dublin, escaped by plunging into the Liffey on a winter's night, swam to land amid the fire of his captors, and made a dramatic vow to give two swans to the river if he came safe to land. Both Dolphin and Swan were complex emblems.

II

It is now possible to examine more fully the texture of the two poems in relation to their symbolism.

> That is no country for old men. The young
> In one another's arms, birds in the trees,
> – Those dying generations – at their song,
> The salmon-falls, the mackerel-crowded seas,
> Fish, flesh, or fowl, commend all summer long
> Whatever is begotten, born and dies.
> Caught in that sensual music all neglect
> Monuments of unageing intellect.

The ironic reference to the 'Ode to the Nightingale' contributes to the tension, and has a parallel in the second poem. The salmon-falls are a visual memory: Sligo River drops through the town in a series of shallow falls where the fish run up to Lough Gill, and the memory is that of spring and the magnificent strength and grace of the leaping fish, itself magical and a symbol of strength in Celtic

---

[1] I discuss later a pictorial origin. The literary origin in Mrs Strong's book is considered by Jeffares, op. cit., p. 52.

literature.[1] The mackerel has special associations;[2] the appearances of the shoals out in the Bay roused a particular excitement which infected the whole fishing-village with the prospect of the net-harvest. *Commend*: the word carries the key-stress, set off by the arrogant use of the 'popular' fish, flesh or fowl. They commend their life-cycle and their death, the Spenserian mutabilitie; compare —

> All that could run or leap or swim
> Whether in wood, water or cloud,
> Acclaiming, proclaiming, declaiming Him.[3]

Man is *caught* – again a keyword – as in a net of that sensual music; but for an old man there is nothing still but the great achievements of the past: But he is now old – 'Sailing to Byzantium' was written in 1928; and there is the persistent nostalgia for the strength and vitality of the 'young in one another's arms', yet tempered by some acceptance of age with its compensations in poetic achievement. The voyage is itself a magical one, as in Malory and Shelley; the scarecrow image is double, and we recall *A Coat*:[4]

> An aged man is but a paltry thing,
> A tattered coat upon a stick, unless
> Soul clap its hands and sing, and louder sing.[5]
> For every tatter in its mortal dress.
> Nor is there singing school but studying

[1] At Galway, Yeats took George Moore to see 'the salmon lying in the river, four and five deep, like sardines in a box . . . Yeats is a bit of an individualist, and in an indolent mood it is pleasant to listen to him telling of the habits of the salmon which only feed in the sea . . .' (*Salve*).

[2] There is, for example, that strangely moving rhyme:

> The herring loves the salt moonlight
> The mackerel loves the wind:
> But the oyster loves the dredging-sang
> For they come of a gentler kind.

[3] 'The Dancer at Cruachan and Cro-Patrick,' *C.P.*, p. 304.

[4] *C.P.*, p. 142.

[5] L. A. G. Strong suggested that this image is derived from Blake's vision of his brother's soul flying up to heaven and clapping its hands.

> Monuments of its own magnificence;
> And therefore I have sailed the seas and come
> To the holy city of Byzantium.

Yeats was a traditionalist, in the peculiar sense that each great poet re-casts his style within that tradition. The 'singing school' is important. He was aware always of how much he had owed to what he took to be the technical perfection of the members of the Rhymers' Club. In a letter to Dorothy Wellesley:

> This difficult work, which is being written everywhere now . . . has the substance of philosophy and is a delight to the poet with his professional pattern; but it is not your road or mine, and ours is the main road, the road of naturalness and swiftness and we have thirty centuries upon our side. We alone can 'think like a wise man, yet express ourselves like the common people.'[1]

The monuments for his study might be verse, pictures, any artistic creation:

> I have prepared my peace
> With learned Italian things
> And the proud stones of Greece,
> Poet's imaginings. . . .[2]

The old have only their minds. They are fastened to a 'dying animal', but the mind can yet be supreme; 'men improve with the years', to attain

> A mind Michael Angelo knew
> That can pierce the clouds,
> Or inspired by frenzy
> Shake the dead in their shrouds;
> Forgotten else by mankind,
> An old man's eagle mind.[3]

Michaelangelo is one of the archetypal creators – see 'Long-legged Fly' – and a Magus also: poet, soldier, scholar, painter. So in this third verse there is the invocation:

> O sages standing in God's holy fire
> As in the gold mosaic of a wall,

[1] *Letters*, p. 64.
[2] *C.P.*, p. 222.
[3] Ibid., p. 346.

> Come from the holy fire, perne in a gyre,
> And be the singing-masters of my soul.
> Consume my heart away; sick with desire
> And fastened to a dying animal
> It knows not what it is; and gather me
> Into the artifice of eternity.

The consummation of fire[1] appears again in 'Byzantium'. The perne is the bobbin of the spinning-mill: he recounts in *Autobiographies* how, looking from the window of the Sligo house, he had seen smoke rising in the distance, and had been told it was the perne-mill. Perhaps the word struck him then, as it might well do, for its resonance and remote, faintly menacing quality; here the image seems to be that of the shuttle revolving round and up the walls of the cone of time,[2] leaving behind it that traditional thread as a clue (compare the second verse of 'Byzantium') by which the depths may be explored again. It is worth while to notice the deliberate clash of the internal rhyme and the repetition of *holy fire* (for the sages are not only the gold-set saints in any church – it might be those in St Appollinare in Classe – but also those in the burning fiery furnace): and the rhythm is broken deliberately on *artifice of eternity*[3] to hold the mind for an instant before the paradox comes home.

Then he chooses the form of his reincarnation, and there was a precedent in Marvell's *The Garden*:

> Casting the Bodies Vest aside,
> My Soul into the Boughs does glide:
> There like a Bird it sits and sings,
> And, till prepared for longer flight
> Waves in its Plumes the various light.

So in the last verse:

> Once out of nature I shall never take
> My bodily form from any natural thing,
> But such a form as Grecian goldsmiths make

[1] The reference is both to 'Isaiah's coal' and to Plotinus.

[2] He uses this to show the interconnection of succeeding gyres; the two poems have the image in common.

[3] Perhaps a thought of Browne, with whom he was familiar: 'In brief all things are artificial, for nature is the art of God'. Cf. also Bowra, *The Heritage of Symbolism*, p. 209, quoted by Jeffares.

> Of hammered gold and gold enamelling
> To keep a drowsy Emperor awake;
> Or set upon a golden bough to sing
> To lords and ladies of Byzantium
> Of what is past, or passing, or to come.

Yeats' note on this is familiar: 'I have read somewhere that in the Emperor's palace at Byzantium was a tree made of gold and silver, and artificial birds that sang.'[1] The ghost can return, and take what shape its imagination allows: but nothing less than that perfection of the artificer's form will suffice for his embodiment. It is well to stress again that this achievement of art is more than the arrested beauty of the 'Grecian Urn': it is the embodiment of long striving after mathematical perfection of form, and as such has contact with God.

### III

In 'Byzantium' the system of tensions is more complex, the overtones more significant. The most interesting clue to it is given in the *1930 Diary*.

*Subject for a poem. April 30th.*
Death of a friend. To describe how mixed with one's grief comes the thought, that the witness of some foolish act or word of one's own is gone.[2]
Describe Byzantium as it is *in the system* towards the end of the first Christian millennium. A walking mummy. Flames at the street corners where the soul is purified, birds of hammered gold singing in the golden trees, offering their backs to the wailing dead that they may carry them to paradise.
These subjects have been in my head for some time, especially the last.[3]

'The system' is, of course, that of *A Vision*. 'The walking

---

[1] Note, *C.P.*, p. 532. For a full discussion of the origin of the image, see Jeffares, *R.E.S.*, Jan. 1946. It is probable that Yeats had seen in Dalton (op. cit., p. 692) the gorgeous 'golden bird' in a silk textile.

[2] Compare, 'Only the dead can be forgiven' of 'A Dialogue of Self and Soul', and

> Some stupid thing that I had done
> Made my attention stray.
> 'Stream and Sun at Glendalough'.

[3] *Explorations*, p. 290.

mummy' represents, perhaps, the Egyptian element in Byzantine art; it also becomes permanent in the 'mummy-cloth' of the final version. In the poem itself the birds that bear the dead on their backs have been replaced by the dolphins. The poem falls into five divisions; the city which is the background with its violent contrasts; the exploration of death and the wisdom of the past: the goldsmith's art which can give that permanence and significance in life unattainable by flesh; and the mosaics which depict the spiritual experience, stabilized by the knowledge and technique of the artist. At the last the spirits unified, and made triumphant by the art of goldsmith or worker in mosaic, triumph over the limitations of the body, the Dolphin's mire and blood.

> The unpurged images of day recede;
> The Emperor's drunken soldiery are abed;
> Night resonance recedes, night-walkers' song
> After great cathedral gong;
> A starlit or a moonlit dome disdains
> All that man is,
> All mere complexities,
> The fury and the mire of human veins.[1]

'Images' are, I think, used not in the psychic, but rather in the Neo-platonic sense; they are the dross-covered reflected shapes of reality that fade as night approaches and mind grows strong again.[2] They recede, with the long closing stress, growing fainter in the distance. The soldiers of the great Emperor are drunken, and that is the ironic paradox of empire. But they are also the drunken *soldiery* (the word has overtones of contempt) that

> . . . can leave the mother, murdered at her door,
> To crawl in her own blood and go scot-free. . . .

of 'Nineteen Hundred and Nineteen'. This incident, a murder by a burst of machine-gun fire from a passing lorry of Black and Tans near Kiltartan, affected Yeats profoundly, and the same incident recurs in the second 'Irish Airman':[3]

> Half drunk or whole mad soldiery
> Are murdering your tenants there. . . .

[1] *C.P.*, p. 280.
[2] Here 'A Dialogue of Self and Soul' is relevant.
[3] First published, under the title of 'Reprisals', in the Ulster periodical *Rann*, by permission of Mrs Yeats; now in the *Variorum*, p. 791.

The drunken soldiery are *abed* – and that false rhyme jars for an instant (as it is meant to) with the homely half-contemptuous word. *Resonance* – the dark heavy word also becomes fainter in the distance as *recedes*; the night-walkers are, as it were, a later parallel to the '*drunken soldiery*'. The *great cathedral gong* reverberates back over the first movement, symbolizing perhaps in its violent conjunction the meeting of the religions of the East and West. There is a quotation from 'Nineteen Hundred and Nineteen' that is relevant, since the gyres are involved in the gong-association:

> So the Platonic Year
> Whirls out new right and wrong,
> Whirls in the old instead;
> All men are dancers and their tread
> Goes to the barbarous clangour of a gong.[1]

The tone grows lighter and more peaceful. The dome is the symbol of Byzantine achievement, the image of heaven, the only canopy for God. It disdains – and the purity and *scorn* of moonlight is picked up later – not mankind, but the comparative simplification of his complexities. The Shelley memory[2] is clear; but in the Cuala Press Edition (which often has misprints or mispunctuations, but was presumably set up from a manuscript) the word appears as 'distains'. In all four manuscript versions that I have seen it is spelt thus, though Yeats' spelling is at its best unreliable. That new image with its ambiguities is not without attractions: perhaps one day it may be an accepted variant. The accent falls with a heavy stress on *mere* complexities, for there are spiritual complexities beyond them. *Fury* has its overtones: The Psalms ('. . . my fury it upheld me') and the poet's spirit, the fury and the mire, fire and earth, clay and water, the paradox of the contending elements stressed to destruction. (So in

> What matter though numb nightmare ride on top,
> And blood and mire the sensitive body stain?[3])

[1] *C.P.*, p. 232. Jeffares points out that the relevant passage is noted in W. G. Holmes: 'At the boom of the great *semantron*, a sonorous board suspended in the porch of each church, and beaten with mallets by a deacon. . .' *R.E.S.*, op. cit., p. 50. But see *T.S.M. Letters*, p. 164.

[2]      Life like a dome of many coloured glass,
        Stains the white radiance of eternity. . . .
The descriptions of the building of the dome would be familiar from many sources, including Gibbon and Dalton.

[3] 'The Gyres', *C.P.*, p. 337.

The second stanza gives the incantation-element:

> Before me floats an image, man or shade,[1]
> Shade more than man, more image than a shade;
> For Hades' bobbin bound in mummy-cloth
> May unwind the winding path;[2]
> A mouth that has no moisture and no breath
> Breathless mouths may summon;
> I hail the superhuman;
> I call it death-in-life and life-in-death.

This most difficult verse concerns the invocation of the dead to discover their wisdom. Some light is thrown on it by a quotation from 'All Souls' Night':

> ... Nothing can stay my glance
> Until that glance run in the world's despite
> To where the damned have howled away their hearts,
> And where the blessed dance;
> Such thought, that in it bound
> I need no other thing,
> Wound in mind's wandering
> As mummies in the mummy-cloth are wound.[3]

There are two other prose passages that are of interest:

> ... In making the penance of Dermot and Dervorgilla last so many centuries I have done something for which I had no warrant in these papers or from that source but warrant there certainly is in the folklore of all countries. At certain moments the Spiritual Being, or rather that part of it which Robartes calls 'the Spirit', is said to enter into the Shade, and during those moments it can converse with living men, though but within the narrow limits of its dream.[4]

*Shade*, then appears to be incorporeal spirit, but with certain properties of communication. *Image* would seem to be the shade in a more or less materialized condition.

[1] We need not, I think, go to the Egyptian theurgy to explain *shade*; the usage is Shelleyan, and the *shade* is the similacrum or phantasm of the body, as in Dante.

[2] Cf. also:

> Have not old writers said
> That dizzy dreams can spring
> From the dry bones of the dead?
> *The Dreaming of the Bones, C. Plays*, p. 433.

[3] *C.P.*, p. 256.

[4] Note to *The Dreaming of the Bones, P. & C.*, p. 458.

It may be that More but copies Philoponus who thought the shade's habitual form, the image that it was as it were frozen in for a time, could be again 'coloured and shaped by fantasy', and that 'it is probable that when the soul desires to manifest it shapes itself, setting its own imagination in movement, or even that it is probable with the help of daemonic co-operation that it appears and again becomes invisible, becoming condensed and rarefied'.[1]

*Hades' bobbin* suggests the image of the labyrinth and the minotaur or of Orpheus and Eurydice; but it is also limited to his other image of the thread wound and unwound by the revolving gyres: perhaps taken, as Jeffares suggests, from the Vision of Er in Plato, or from Mead's *Echoes from the Gnosis*. The mummy-cloth suggests his own 'dark tomb-haunting'. In one manuscript there is '*Breathing* mouths may summon' for 'breathless' mouths; a thought that produces a more vivid antithesis between the living and the dead, while 'breathless' carries with it both the excitement of haste or exhaustion, as well as the ambiguity. The superhuman seems to carry memories of 'The Ancient Mariner':

> The Nightmare Life in Death was she,
> Who thicks man's blood with cold.

This image may well be of himself, in a trance or dream; it may in that state summon the breathless mouths. But the ghost, in its coming and going, is linked by association to the cock.

> Miracle, bird or golden handiwork,
> More miracle than bird or handiwork,
> Planted on the star-lit golden bough,
> Can like the cocks of Hades crow,
> Or, by the moon embittered, scorn aloud
> In glory of changeless metal
> Common bird or petal
> And all complexities of mire or blood.

It is one of the 'forms' of the Grecian goldsmiths in 'Sailing to Byzantium'. *Starlit* picks up the 'starlit dome' of the first stanza,

---

[1] Lady Gregory: *Visions and Beliefs*, Vol. II, p. 330. Essay on *Swedenborg, Mediums and the Desolate Places*, by W. B. Y. Also in *If I were Four and Twenty*, p. 59. For 'condensed and rarefied', see Donne, 'Aire and Angels'. Yeats refers to 'the shade of Achilles in the Odyssey drawing its bow as though still in the passion of battle, while the true spirit of Achilles is on Olympus with his wife Hebe' (*Explorations*, p. 330).

W. B. Yeats
from the frontispiece to *Mosada*, 1886

Poussin: Acis and Galatea
(formerly the Marriage of Peleus and Thetis)
'*Slim adolescence that a nymph has stripped, Peleus on Thetis stares*'

and we contrast the constancy of starlight with the inconstancy of
the moon, though both are reflected lights. The golden bough
needs no annotation, though there may be an image from Turner's
painting here. The bird belongs both to the world of the dead, and
to that of immortality; it can serve as sentinel to the underworld and
to the earth. It is above all change: the moon – symbol of womanhood and of flux or instability[1] – leaves it *embittered* in the light which
shines pale on the gold. The cock, the dominant untiring male, is
*embittered*, scorned by the moon. But is, perhaps, a spirit also; compare *The King's Threshold*:

> It's out of a poem I made long ago
> About the Garden in the East of the World,
> And how spirits in the images of birds
> Crowd in the branches of old Adam's crab-tree.[2]

The image-cluster contracts and tightens; the cock is linked to the
hawk, the ghost to Egyptian mythology, the tree in the garden
to the apple tree that grew from Baile's tomb: the tree is the crab-
tree with its sour fruit. The cock knows all mutability, but transcends
all change. It scorns *common* – the stress falls heavily with the arrogant trick again – 'common bird or petal',[3] and with the craftsman's
flower the thread of association returns to the bough, and the
flower-image calls up the overtones of arrested beauty and decay.

From the craftsman in the garden we pass to the mosaics, the
other summit of achievement. We catch up the background again:
it is the *Emperor's* pavement, and the violence of his drunken soldiery
has no place here:

> At midnight on the Emperor's pavement[4] flit

[1] For Yeats it had also the overtones of phase-development, and the
inexorability of that process.

[2] *C. Plays*, p. 105. And, also in *K.T.*, 'the moon's daughter, that most
whey-faced metal'.

[3] Birds are 'the natural symbols of subjectivity . . . while the beasts . . .
are the natural symbols of objective man' (Note to *Calvary*, *P. & C.*, p. 459).
See p. 129. I am aware of the arguments for birds other than the cock, but I
do not find them convincing; particularly in view of 'Solomon and the Witch',
*A Full Moon in March*, and the correspondence with Sturge Moore on this
point.

[4] Jeffares points out that Yeats marked the descriptive passage in Holmes.
(*R.E.S.*, op. cit., p. 51.)

I

Flames that no faggot feeds, nor steel has lit,
Nor storm disturbs, flames begotten of flame,
Where blood-begotten spirits come
And all complexities of fury leave,
Dying into a dance,
An agony of trance,
An agony of flame that cannot singe a sleeve.

*Flames* and *faggot* suggest martyrdom, or the devastation of a countryside by the soldiery: steel has its double sense of the flint or the sword. In one of the manuscripts it is

A flame that no faggot feeds nor taper lights.

The flames of the mosaic are born of spiritual intensity and they have also the purifying function. The spirits that come there, for instruction or purification, are *blood-begotten*.[1] Again the complexities appear, like a thread running through the fabric of the poem, but now they are complexities of fury: which can be resolved in the final ritual dance, perhaps of expiation.[2] It cannot singe a sleeve; and, half contemptuously (for he does this often) there is the Biblical reference to the fiery furnace. The rescuers of humanity, the dolphins, are themselves mortal.

Astraddle on the dolphin's mire and blood,
Spirit after spirit! The smithies break the flood,
The golden smithies of the Emperor!
Marbles of the dancing floor
Break bitter furies of complexity,
Those images that yet

[1] Cf. Donne:
As our blood labours to beget
Spirits, as like soules as it can,
Because such fingers need to knit
That subtile knot which makes us man.
('The Extasie'.)

[2] See p. 200 above. It is pertinent to quote from Jeffares' reference to Miss Murphy's comment (*R.E.S.*, op. cit.): 'Blood-begotten spirits are probably human ghosts who, haunting the flame-mosaic pavement, are purged of their complexities of fury by its grandeur. The phrase describing them is a parenthesis, so that the account of the flames begotten of flames continues as "Dying into a dance".'
I do not agree: the spirits are surely purged by the natural acts of the dance and of the spiritual fire. The pavements might have a maze-pattern to assist the *lusis;* there are vases which depict this.

Fresh images beget,
That dolphin-torn, that gong-tormented sea.

The sea has the normal symbolic values of life and sex; it is 'the
drifting indefinite bitterness of life'. It is torn by the two forces of
sex and religion; for the dolphin is also the love-beast. The quick
pattering of the dactyls, *spirit after spirit* lets the words burst on
the triumphant paradox. *The smithies break the flood*: the flood
symbolizes the irrational, the confusion, the pattern, perhaps a
consequence of the 'Galilean turbulence': against this the formal
ceremonious art of Byzantium, the art of the goldsmith, *hammered*
work linked with the idea of *breaking*, complete the paradox of that
opposition of fire and water. Yet they are the *smithies of the Emperor*;
*golden* for the price and value of the Emperor's power, *golden*
because of their handiwork, smithies of the Emperor whose power
is founded on the drunken soldiery. The mosaics, with their formal
geometrical patterns, impose a second order, this time of measurement, proportion, upon the 'irrational stream'. The marbles (which
stand for coldness and durability as well as pattern) share with the
smithies the reflected *break*. They belong to the pattern and rhythm
of the dance: *marbles of the dancing floor*. *Flood* and *bitter furies of*
*complexity* – water and fire – are linked again as aspects of life
resolved by art. There is even a different kind of complexity
modified by *bitter*[1] (frustration or disappointment) and *furies*
(energy) that grows out of the irrationality of fate. The bitterness
throws back to 'by the moon embittered', for the frustration is, at
least in part, a sexual frustration.

What follows is more difficult. Smithies[2] and marbles break not
only the flood and the furies, but the skein of images to which they
give rise. 'Has not Porphyry said the generation of images

---

[1] 'Bitter' is a keyword in Yeats' self-dramatization. His working towards
the finality of this line is of special interest:
                    Break bitter black stupid furies.
                                aimless
Cf.: 'Plucked bitter wisdom that enriched his blood'
                                        ('Parnell's Funeral'.)

[2] We may remember this traditional image for the re-making of
language, the labour of composition; it is used in the Preface to the Authorized
Version.

in the mind is from water?'[1] We are carried back to the first stanza, and its 'unpurged images', before art and measurement come into their own at night. They break '*that dolphin-torn, that gong-tormented sea*': or perhaps the line is in apposition to 'those images'? The sea is torn by the love-beast, the dolphin, and tormented by the gong, the religions that have met in the Cathedral of St Sophia, East and West. I think it is likely that this line embodies the nature of the images that haunt him perpetually, love and religion. But because of this very obscurity I feel that the resolution, both from the meaning and rhythm, is incomplete, and the poem the less thereby.

Yet I have sometimes thought that the two Byzantine poems have been buried under a great mass of exegetical rubble, and that we may lose sight of what they are. It may be well to attempt some simplification. They are great rhetorical poems of a traditional kind,[2] which lament the passing of youth, virility, strength, and which seek to establish, by symbols which are part traditional, part personal, an imagined defence against Time's decay. They are linked by the theme of Byzantium and the golden bird or cock. The second poem (which I now think wears less well than the other) seems to me more cerebral, less spontaneous, even a little disjointed as regards the second stanza. Let us stand back a little.

The poet is old, and he is concerned with the real or imagined loss of sexual power. We know this from many sources. At death he will undergo reincarnation; the thought of this, as we know from *A Vision*, may have to be stated in symbolical language. The nightingale is clearly the traditional symbol of permanence. The dead in 'Cuchulain Comforted' 'had changed their throats and had the throats of birds'. But it seems possible that one aspect of the generalized bird image is the cock; and there is no reason why it

---

[1] *A Vision* (B), p. 220. Note the use of the river-image in 'Coole Park and Ballylee'. Cf. also 'Those forms [i.e. among the leaves of Byzantine decoration] that represent no creature eye has ever seen, yet are *begotten one upon the other* as if they were themselves living creatures' (*A Vision* (A), p. 192).

[2] Jeffares, who has provided the best summary so far of the construction of these poems, has indicated the rhetorical devices. The pattern may be summed up as: the arrival of the spirits at the City: the invocation of their ghostly guide; the description of the bird into which he is about to be embodied; the entry of the spirits into their ritual purgation; the assertion of the final *lusis*.

should not exist coterminously (as it were) with other birds. One thinks of 'Solomon and the Witch'[1] and of the 'bird of day' in 'A Last Confession'[2]; and it would not be alien to Yeats' method to combine the supernatural and sexual images. The Cock, which combines many attributes, is the sentinel of the world of ghosts; it is mysteriously linked to Christianity in the Betrayal as well as to other events of the spring solstice (see *A Full Moon in March*). But above all the cock (together with its supposed enemy the lion) has, uniquely, the gift of unwearied vitality in copulation. The supreme achievement of the artificer's skill can 'keep a drowsy emperor awake': it scorns the mutabilities of love associated with the moon, by which it is *embittered*; it proclaims its superiority over common bird or *petal*, which is again the symbol of woman. This third stanza forms as it were a peak. The second is perhaps of the dream state that follows immediately on death. The fourth returns to the patterns of the ritual dance that are such a constant memory, and whose mazes may be seen on Greek vases. The fifth brings in the dolphin and the sea to help to round the poem; and 'News for the Delphic Oracle' is relevant here. In draft after draft[3] the lines are brought back to the forge for shaping to the rhetorical perfection of the final version; yet I remain a little uneasy. Perhaps James Stephens is right when he suggests that one day Yeats might have written his third and last Byzantium, but yet could never have done so. As Alexander has pointed out,[4] it was a transcendental phase which had to be left behind in his progress towards the 'passionate'. I find a finer and more satisfying resolution in 'Ribh at the Tomb of Baile and Aillinn', discussed in the chapter, 'The Achievement of Style'.

[1] *C.P.*, p. 199.
[2] Ibid., p. 313.
[3] See the admirable and most illuminating account in Stallworthy's *Between the Lines*. The golden bird originally 'muttered/What the cocks of Hades know'.
[4] 'Valèry and Yeats', *Scottish Periodical*, i, 1, Summer 1947.

# CHAPTER FOURTEEN

# Painter and Poet

He thought Keats a greater poet than Shelley, because less abstract, caring little, I think, for any of that most beautiful poetry which has come in modern times from the influence of painting.

W. B. of his father: *Autobiographies.*

Those unperturbed and courtly images . . .

. . . Those images that yet
Fresh images beget . . .

I

Much has been written, since the first edition of this book, on Yeats' debt to painting. There is Giorgio Melchiori's important study of *The Whole Mystery of Art*, Professor Kermode's *Romantic Image*, and his Reading Exhibition catalogued under the title *Images of a Poet*. Wind's *Pagan Mysteries of the Renaissance* is also very relevant. I have therefore recast this chapter. At the outset it is desirable to review the whole problem, with some of its attractions and dangers.

Yeats was the son of a pre-Raphaelite painter; he himself had some artistic training, and did a little pastel work. To the end of his life he visited galleries whenever he had the opportunity. He was the friend of contemporary artists of importance: in particular, Shannon, Ricketts, 'A.E.', Dulac, Sturge Moore. His early selections from Spenser had been illustrated, in the decadent pre-Raphaelite manner, by Jessie M. King. He was an admirer of Wilde's *Salome*, which had been illustrated both by Ricketts and Beardsley. He mentions in his poetry and prose some fifty painters and sculptors.[1]

[1] The list given in the first edition omitted Jacopo della Guardia and Piero di Cosimo.

Certain reproductions were continually beside him. And there is a special interest in Blake and his illustrations.[1]

The significance which he found in painting and sculpture can be considered under several headings:

(1) Painters and sculptors are symptomatic of the great movements of civilization, both as types and as personalities. Yeats uses them constantly in his characterization of historical epochs; and there are occasions when his choice seems forced.

(2) They are ordained to provide instances of physical perfection of form, 'so that instinct may find its lamp'.

(3) They possess supra-natural insight into the order or essence or 'inscape' of the world.

(4) Their repetition or recurrence, particularly in widely-separated civilization and epochs, suggests the continued validity of such representations. They come to be regarded as archetypal. And if in addition there were at hand familiar physical and concrete manifestations,[2] so much the better.

(5) Whenever the pictures appeared to offer Baudelairian *correspondances* (however metaphysical in kind) his imagination was prepared to seize on them.[3]

## II

We must be aware of the dangers of speculating upon Yeats' use of the pictures he had seen. The subject raises of course the question of 'extrinsic' knowledge, to which I have referred elsewhere.[4] We can divide the possible instances into three broad groups:

(1) Those for which the correspondence or debt is verifiable from external sources.

(2) Resemblances so close as to leave no reasonable ground for doubt.

(3) Resemblances which are no more than probable: having

---

[1] We can assume a knowledge of most of Blake, in view of the Ellis-Blake Edition; as well as of the illustrations to Dante and to Blair's *The Grave*.

[2] *e.g.* the Swan and the Heron at Coole and Ballylee.

[3] *e.g.* the supposed resemblance between Egyptian portraiture and Gainsborough's faces.

[4] *v.* p. xx–xxi.

regard to the galleries in which the paintings are, or were at the times he saw them, the dates of composition in relation to the visits, and his *general* view of the significance of the artists or work concerned.

It is necessary to give some accounts of Yeats' journeys which he made to particular galleries, though we must remember that the dates are not necessarily conclusive, since he may well have seen the works in reproduction at some earlier date, or found descriptions in Vasari, Ruskin, Pater, Burkitt, Reinach or Salzmann. Where he discusses specific works, as at Florence, Rome, Ravenna, Naples, it is reasonable to infer that he studied the work at those galleries of other artists whom he mentions. On the other hand, having regard to the fact that he does *not* mention Poussin and other sources in the Dublin National Gallery, we may expect to find other work which has no overt reference or acknowledgement. Yeats' memory, though abundant, was like Shakespeare's reading, 'desultory and unsystematick'. Finally we can never exclude the possibility of composite or 'overlay' imagery, or the products of visual *plus* verbal memory.

The Italian journeys were as follows:

| | |
|---|---|
| 1907 (with Lady Gregory) | Florence, Milan, Ferrara, San Sepulchio, Urbino, Venice, Ravenna. |
| 1924–5 | Rome, Naples, Syracuse, Palermo, Monreale, Cefalu – this last 'in such bad weather that we could not see the great mosaics'.[1] |

The United States visits are listed by Hone: 1903, 1911, 1916, 1919–20, 1932–3.

I do not know for which of the American journeys he prepared the collection of slides – Blake's *Book of Job*, Blake's Illustrations to Thornton's *Virgil*, and the Calverts and Palmers, which were given to me by Mrs Yeats. I am told that Yeats spent much time in the Isabella Stuart Gardner Museum at Boston. This is of particular relevance, since it is the only collection in which the pictures and their positions are unchanged since its inception; and the 'aristocratic and wasteful virtues' which are apparent there are likely to have been of special interest to him.

[1] Information from Mrs Yeats.

## III

It is convenient to begin with Yeats' own description of his manner of contemplating pictures:

> All art that is not mere story-telling, or mere portraiture, is symbolic, and has the purpose of those symbolic talismans which medieval magicians made with complex colours and forms, and bade their patients ponder over daily and guard with holy secrecy; for it entangles, in complex colours and forms, a part of the Divine Essence.[1] A person or a landscape that is part of a story or a portrait, evokes but so much emotion as the story or the portrait can permit without loosening the bonds that make it a story or a portrait; but if you liberate a person or a portrait from all bonds of motives and their actions, causes and their effects, it will always change under your eyes, and become a symbol of an infinite emotion, a perfected emotion, a part of the Divine Essence; for we love nothing but the perfect, and our dreams make all things perfect, that we may love them.[2]

This suggests a general debt to the *Upanishads*, and 'A.E.' takes much the same position in *Song and its Fountains*.

Later, Yeats' approach is more concrete:

> Wagner's dramas, Keats' odes, Blake's pictures and poems, Calvert's pictures, Rossetti's pictures, Villiers de l'Isle Adam's plays, and the black and white art of Mr Beardsley and Mr Ricketts, and the lithographs of Mr Shannon, and the pictures of Mr Whistler, and the plays of Mr Maeterlinck, and the poetry of Verlaine, in our own day, but differ from the religious art of Giotto and his disciples in having accepted all symbolisms, the symbolisms of the ancient shepherds and star-gazers, that symbolism of bodily beauty[3] that seemed a wicked thing to Fra Angelico, the symbolism in day and night,[4] and winter and summer, spring and autumn, once so great a part of an older religion than Christianity,[5] and in having accepted all the Divine Intellect, its anger and pity, its waking and its sleep, its love and its lust, for the substance of their art.[6]

In many essays, notably those on Shelley and Blake, these ideas

---

[1] We may compare the account of this given by Aldous Huxley in *The Doors of Perception*.
[2] Preface to W. T. Horton, *A Book of Images*, London 1898 (p. 10). Reprinted in *Ideas of Good and Evil*, omitting all references to Horton.
[3] *v.* (e.g.) 'The Living Beauty', *C.P.*, p. 156.
[4] *v.* (*e.g.*) 'Michael Robartes and the Dancer', *C.P.*, p. 197.
[5] *v.* Wind, op. cit.: and Austin Farrer, *A Rebirth of Images*, passim.
[6] *E. & I.*, p. 149.

are elaborated. He was a constant visitor to galleries. The Nativity in particular had most vivid associations. 'When I close my eyes and pronounce the word "Christianity" and await its unconscious suggestions, I do not see Christ crucified, or the Good Shepherd from the catacombs, but a father and mother and their children, a picture of Leonardo da Vinci most often. While Europe had still Christianity for its chief preoccupation men painted little but that scene.'[1]

## IV

This desire for pictorial symbolism is apparent even in the designs of the book-covers. In 1922 C. R. Ricketts wrote to him:

> The cover is quite abstract decoration in which you can detect (by the eye of faith alone) roses and sprays of yew with their berries. I found your preferences in fauna, caves, fountains, etc., beyond the range of an end-paper, so I have combined most of them in a sort of book-plate design which is placed inside the cover, like an ordinary book-plate. On this I have represented a Unicorn couching on pearls before a fountain, backed by a cave full of stars. On the crest of the cave is what I believe to be a hawk contemplating the moon.[2]

Other cover-designs carried various emblems. The cover of *The Winding Stair* carries the magic cock of Byzantium and the dolphin, on which there is a seated figure beating a drum; with other symbols that I do not recognize. The dust cover of *Selected Poems*, 1938, has three stylized butterflies round a blossom.[3]

Yeats developed his beliefs in the essay on 'Symbolism in Painting'. '. . . Symbolism said things which could not be said so perfectly in any other way, and needed but a right instinct for its understanding; while Allegory said things which could be said as well, or better, in another way, and needed a right knowledge for its understanding. The one thing gave dumb things voices, and bodiless things bodies; while the other read a meaning – which

---

[1] *If I Were Four and Twenty*, p. 12.

[2] *Self Portrait*: Letters and Journals of Charles Ricketts; p. 341. Ricketts also wrote a book on Titian, which may account for some of Yeats' interest in that painter. The plate can be seen in several volumes, e.g. *P. & C.*, 1923.

[3] Sturge Moore, who designed the dust cover of the 1940 Edition of *Last Poems*, has a most elaborate pattern of symbols.

had never lacked its voice or its body – into something heard or seen, and loved less for the meaning than for its own sake.'[1] This opinion is put into the mouth of a German symbolist painter in Paris, but it appears to represent substantially Yeats' own views. Allegory and Symbolism may at times melt into each other; but it is clear that Allegory is a lower and more obvious form of art. Symbolism is expansive, mystical: 'symbols are the only things free enough from all bonds to speak of perfection', and he goes on to quote with approval Blake's 'The world of imagination is the world of eternity. . . .' This most important essay is dated 1898, and we can again see in it the influence of 'A.E.'. But it is important to remember that the expanding, resonant, and complicated nature of the symbols, and their continual approximation to a world order perceived in this manner, remains a feature of his poetry. The expansion is from the particular outwards and upwards. . . . 'Their thought wanders from the woman who is Love herself, to her sisters and her forebears, and to all the great procession; and so august a beauty moves before the mind, that they forget the things which move before the eyes.'[2]

He had received some training as a painter, and had shown promise: but . . . 'the work I was set to bored me. When alone and uninfluenced, I longed for pattern, for pre-Raphaelitism, for an art allied to poetry, and returned again and again to our National Gallery to gaze at Turner's 'Golden Bough'. Yet I was too timid, had I known how, to break away from my father's style and the style of those about me. I was always hoping that my father would return to the style of his youth, and make pictures out of certain designs now lost, that one could still find in his portfolios.'[3] But he retained a certain interest, and wrote to George Russell from Coole: 'I have started pastels by and by and done much better than I expected. I hope to be able to draw sacred places on my own account.' His brother has spoken highly of his potential ability as an artist.

Later he recognized the defects of his father's technique:

'My father began life a Pre-Raphaelite painter; when past thirty he fell under the influence of contemporary French painting. Instead of finishing

[1] *E. & I.*, p. 147.
[2] Ibid., p. 150. Note the words *great procession*.
[3] Quoted by Hone, *Life*, p. 42.

a picture one square inch at a time, he kept all fluid, every detail dependent upon every other . . . the more anxious he was to succeed, the more did his pictures sink through innumerable sittings into final confusion.[1]

But Yeats mentioned specifically two of his father's drawings which seem to me to be of profound psychological interest:

> There was one of an old hunchback in vague medieval dress, going through some underground place where are beds with people in the beds; a girl half rising from one has seized his hand and is kissing it. and one . . . an old ragged beggar in the market place laughing at his own statue.[2]

Both pictures are suggestive of the imagery of the later verse: the first is a typical compensation image, the second a paradox of the wild gay type in which Yeats the poet delighted. The Hunchback and the Beggar are standard images. His imagination 'was stirred by a visit' to Dulac's studio, where the mask prepared for Cuchulain had 'this noble, half Greek, half-Asiatic face,' which 'will appear perhaps like an image scene in reverie by some Orphic Worshippers', (Several poems are concerned here – 'The Statues', 'Troy Passed Away', and those from *The Resurrection*).

v

The influence of the work of Jack Yeats is also worth consideration. Poet and painter draw largely upon childhood memories of Sligo and of Rosses Point, of Ballisodare and Kilvarnet. 'I am constantly reminded of my brother, who continually paints from memory the people and houses of the village where he had lived as a child.' In those early naïvely violent paintings, especially in the spirited illustrations done for the Broadsheets of 1912–14, there is an impression most vividly conveyed of the smell and laughter ('porter-drinkers' randy laughter') and dust and horses of fair and race-meetings: of a world in which each animal and horse stands out in a foreshortened, distorted, living picturesqueness, but surrendering personality through stylized form into a sardonic gaiety of living. It is very like the world of Crazy Jane, of Red Mannion, and of the balladry of *Last Poems*. Both have something of the coarse-

[1] *Autobiographies*, p. 436.
[2] Ibid., pp. 81–82.

ness, energy and clarity of a Breughel picture. In particular, the 'Peasants' Wedding' in the Dublin National Gallery seems to offer some analogies.

His father's influence is a vast subject, and will no doubt be developed in subsequent studies;[1] but it appears to have been psychological and literary rather than concerned with the aesthetics of painting. J. B. Y. approved highly of *The Celtic Twilight*,[2] of Blake and Landor, and disapproved of the vulgarity and 'aristocratic insolence' of Byron and Swinburne:[3] of the latter in a memorable phrase – 'His roots strike nowhere, he grows in light soil.' Kipling is 'all tinsel and vulgarity and both elaborated'.[4] We are continually encountering literary opinions that are echoed in W.B. The father was obsessed with the idea of the great artist as 'solitary' man: Coleridge, Landor, Hardy.[5] Facts and dreams are related closely; and facts that may harm or distort dreams are to be handled and controlled so as to deprive them of their power to do mischief. Phantasy is to be scientifically cultivated with 'conscious purpose and a great ambition'.[6] He commends the reading of Homer, following him in 'untrammelled flight'.[7] 'The poet is not primarily a thinker, but incidentally he is a thinker, and a stern thinker, since the source of his magic is his personal sincerity.'[8] The process of artistic creation is, first, intensity, whether of impression or emotion: he must then '*work with cold logic and resolute purpose, till he has created his work of art – the work of art completed, all the fire will be in it for ever....*'[9] It is interesting that this letter is concerned with the work of Turner, whose fire and fluidity obviously appealed both to father and son.

The poet was interested in many aspects of painting, and, so far as one can gather from the references, at all periods of his life. L. A. G. Strong writes[10] of his excitement over a painting by 'A.E.' in which a man standing on a crag gazed at his shadow flung by the drifting clouds; an image peculiarly fitted to reinforce the theory of the Mask. At Woburn Place the sitting-room was hung with Blake's

[1] This was written before the publication of Richard Ellmann's *The Man and the Masks*, which deals at length with this question. It is possible that its importance has been over-rated.
[2] *Letters*, p. 72.    [3] Ibid., pp. 92–93.    [4] Ibid., p. 167.
[5] Ibid., p. 207.    [6] Ibid., p. 216.    [7] Ibid., p. 185.
[8] Ibid., p. 210    [9] Ibid., p. 152.    [10] *Cornhill*, July 1937.

'Whirlwind of Lovers', 'The Ancient of Days' and 'Dante striking Bocca degli Abbati's Head'.[1] In 1913 he was working with a Gauguin over his breakfast table; at the Bodleian in 1920 his table was covered with Blakes and Calverts.

He often alludes to Corot, whose luminous greys and greens suggest some analogy with the early period. Yeats was always interested in light, 'cold', 'grey', with 'tumbling clouds'. He wrote a Preface to the strange visions of W. T. Horton. Horton, who seems to have specialized in mystical images based on Blake's general symbolism recast in a crude Aubrey Beardsley technique, also wrote a book called *The Way of the Soul*, with a number of symbolical illustrations.

At this stage there is a transcendental view of symbolism:

> A person or a landscape that is a part of a story or a portrait, evokes but so much emotion as the story or the portrait can permit without loosening the bonds that make it a story or a portrait; but if you liberate a person or a landscape from the bonds of motives and their actions, causes and their effects, and from all bonds but the bonds of your love, it will change under your eyes, and become a symbol of an infinite emotion, a perfected emotion, a part of the Divine Essence.[2]

VI

At this stage all correlation becomes uncertain and speculative; and we must first consider what definite ground there is for identifications of the poetry with particular authors or paintings:

1. The image "O Sages standing in God's holy fire"[3] is related to Blake's illustrations for Dante, Plate 84. The reference was given to him by a medium. 'When I went to London I had just finished a poem in which I appeal to the Saints in "the holy fire" to send death on their extasy. In London I went to a medium called Cooper and on the way called to my people for their especial wisdom. The medium gave me "a book test". Third book from R bottom

---

[1] Masefield, *Some Memories of W. B. Yeats.*
[2] *E. & I.*, p. 148. I am inclined to think that this passage explains the attention which he gave to Calvert and Palmer. There seems to have been a strong pastoral element, at least in his imagination, during his life at Riversdale.
[3] 'Sailing to Byzantium', *C.P.*, p. 217.

shelf – study – Page 48 or 84. I have only this morning looked it up. The book was the complete Dante designs of Blake. It is not numbered by pages but by plates. Plate 84 is Dante entering the Holy Fire (*Purgatorio*, Canto 27). Plate 48 is "The serpent attacking Vanni Fucci". When I looked them up in Dante I found that at the serpent's sting Vanni Fucci is burned to ashes and then recreated from the ashes and that this symbolizes "the temporal Fire".'

Hone refers to the letter (*Life*, p. 373), which is to Olivia Shakespear, 27 October 1927.[1]

The next line, 'As in the gold mosaic of a wall' might come from any mosaic.[2] But Blake's next Plate, 85, is an equally possible source of the whole image: 'Dante at the moment of entering the fire'. The reference is to *Purgatorio*, xxvii. These two fire-images may have begotten others. But there is much in Plotinus, Berkeley, and the *Upanishads* to account for them.

2. The lines 'Another star has shot an ear',[3] and

> . . . a fallen flare
> Through the hollow of an ear[4]

are certainly based on an Annunciation, presumably Crivelli's, in which the falling ray seems to pass behind her head and unite the Word to the ear, the Virgin's head. There is a perpetual interest in all Annunciation images, and Claudel's 'L'Annonce Faite à Marie' had concerned him greatly.

3. The twice-repeated dolphin image:

> A-straddle on the dolphin's mire and blood
> ('Byzantium')

and

> Straddling each a dolphin's back
> And steadied by a fin,
> Those Innocents relive their death
> Their wounds open again.

[1] Also quoted in Jeffares, *Yeats: Man and Poet*, p. 246. Wade, *Letters*, pp. 730–1.
[2] See the chapter 'Byzantium'.
[3] *C.P.*, p. 387.
[4] Ibid., p. 281.

> The ecstatic waters laugh because
> Their cries are sweet and strange . . .
>     ('News for the Delphic Oracle')

has many visual precedents. I have reproduced the Ostia Mosaic, but it is only one of many which Yeats might have seen. A cupid rides a dolphin in Titian's *Europa and the Bull*, to which I have alluded elsewhere. There are two ancient carvings on a pillar in the Square of Ravenna. And there is in the Boston Museum of Fine Arts a drawing by Shannon of a turbulent sea, with cherubs floating on it: there are red roses scattered on the sea and on the bodies of some of the cherubs. An interesting cross-reference is suggested by a footnote in *A Vision* (B): . . . 'I read . . . of a custom . . . of washing new-born children in a bath "made wholesome . . . with red roses" of rolling them in salt and roses, and of sprinkling them, when the parents could afford it, with oil of roses.'[1] The Dolphin is met with in several Emblem Books, e.g. *Andrea Alciati*, No. 146, but without a rider. Other Emblems have the rider, but none (to my knowledge) who could be termed *Innocents*. A picture of 'Arion Riding a Dolphin', attributed to Michele di Verona, is in the Ashmolean. I have since been told[2] that the dolphin ridden by a cherub which Yeats actually saw was a plaster cast now in the Victoria and Albert Museum, but this appears also in the next picture to be considered.

4. I had previously thought that the lines at the end of 'News for the Delphic Oracle' suggested a Botticelli or Crivelli painting.

> Slim adolescence that a nymph has stripped,
> Peleus on Thetis stares.
> Her limbs are delicate as an eyelid,
> Love has blinded him with tears;
> But Thetis' belly listens.
> Down the mountain walls
> From where Pan's cavern is
> Intolerable music falls.
> Foul goat-head, brutal arm appear,
> Belly, shoulder, bum,
> Flash fishline; nymphs and satyrs
> Copulate in the foam.

---

[1] pp. 229–30.
[2] By Oliver Edwards.

But Poussin's 'The Marriage of Peleus and Thetis', reproduced facing page 228, offers such startlingly exact correspondence that there can be no doubt as to the source. The picture has an interesting history. It is No. 814 in the Catalogue of the National Gallery of Ireland, and originally had the title of 'Acis and Galatea'. Then it became 'The Marriage . . .', and was thus known when Yeats knew it. After the first edition was published the picture reverted to its original title, this being a result of the *Colloque Poussin* in 1958.[1] It is, perhaps, the classical instance of a word-for-word transposition.

5.       In this altar-piece the knight,
Who grips his long spear so to push
That dragon through the fading light,
Loved the lady.[2]

This is very like Tintoretto's 'St George and the Dragon' (National Gallery). Of many such pictures (*e.g.* Crivelli's) this seemed at first the most probable by reason of the fading light and the Lady fleeing from the encounter. Ingres' 'Ruggiero liberating Angelica' is also a possible origin. Rossetti wrote a sonnet on this painting.

But the actual source is in the Dublin National Gallery. (The confirmation for this is from Mrs Yeats,[3] as also the information that 'the lady' is Iseult Gonne.) It is 'Saint George and the Dragon', ascribed to Bordone (1558–1623), and is part of the Lane Bequest. All the features are here – dragon, lady, fading light: in each case the dragon is thrust towards the left-hand edge of the picture. The fact that none of these pictures appear to be, strictly, altar-pieces, is not relevant.

The Perseus–St George image appears in its most interesting form in 'A Woman Young and Old':

And then you stood among the dragon-rings.
I mocked, being crazy, but you mastered it
And broke the chain and set my ankles free,
Saint George or else a pagan Perseus;

[1] I am grateful to the Director of the National Gallery, Mr. Thomas MacGreevy, for this and other information.

[2] 'Michael Robartes and the Dancer', *C.P.*, p. 197.

[3] Mrs Yeats also tells me that Yeats saw Cosimo Tura's 'St George and the Dragon' in the cathedral at Ferrara in 1907. This would explain 'this altar-piece'.

> And now we stare astonished at the sea,
> And a miraculous strange bird shrieks at us.[1]

6. The symbol of the white heron, used as a 'dominant' in *The Resurrection*, has been discussed previously in relation to Mantegna's 'Agony in the Garden'. It appears in a mosaic in a dome at Ravenna, and in Piero di Cosimo's mysterious painting (the so-called 'Mythological Subject') there appears to be a heron fishing on the margin of the lake. Another possible source, though without the contextual significance of this painting, is the frontispiece to Binyon's book, showing a 'Lotus, White Heron and Kingfisher' of the Sung Dynasty.

7. To these I would add two lines from 'The Double Vision of Michael Robartes' —

> On the grey rock of Cashel I suddenly saw
> A Sphinx with woman breast and lion paw . . .[2]

— which seems to be too close to Ingres' 'Oedipus and the Sphinx'[3] to admit of any reasonable doubt, particularly when we consider his concern with the whole episode, and his reading of Oscar Wilde, for whose *Sphinx* Ricketts did the illustrations, as Aubrey Beardsley did for *Salome*. It is worth noting that Ingres, 'the modern who proves the oneness of past and present'[4] has much in common with Yeats' view of mythology, and the juxtaposition of the Sphinx with the holy rock, and its relics of early Christianity, would have appealed to the self-dramatization of the solver of the Irish riddle, who was to translate both the Oedipus plays.[5]

The next step would seem to be to list other images which fulfil the following conditions:

(a) They should not be explicable without a pictorial origin or reference.

---

[1] 'Her Triumph', *C.P.*, p. 310. Compare also 'Solomon and the Witch', ibid., p. 199.

[2] Ibid., p. 192. The complexity of the poem is discussed elsewhere.

[3] The reproduction shown is from the Louvre: there is another version in the National Gallery, where Yeats is more likely to have seen it.

[4] Sickert: *Artists on Art*, ed. Goldwater and Trevor, p. 395.

[5] There is further evidence for this in *A Vision* (B), p. 28, where Oedipus is 'a man of Homer's kind' . . . 'I think he lacked compassion, seeing that it must be compassion for himself, and yet stood nearer to the poor than saint or apostle'.

(*b*) Their qualities should offer analogies with other known instances of painting – poetry connection, whether of Yeats or not.

(*c*) There should be some evidence of a relationship of that image *either* to pictures (or statues or images) seen at that time, or remembered for some special reason, or of the relationship of the poem concerned to a particular age or event, of which the artist in question was representative.

Identification will be more reasonable if we can, for example, relate visits to specific galleries to the dating of poems arising from them, or poems to friendships with particular painters, as, for example, C. R. Ricketts who, in his *Self Portrait*, has much of interest to say about Yeats. In *A Vision* Ricketts is noted as 'my education in so many things. How often his imagination moves stiffly as though in fancy dress, and then there is something – Sphinx, Danaides – that makes me remember Callimachus' return to Ionic elaboration and shudder as though I stared into an abyss full of eagles.'[1] Such a collection as *Sixty-Five Illustrations*, which has a preface by T. Sturge Moore, suggests many possible sources for pictorial images, a possibility that is emphasized when we remember the debts to Sturge Moore and the common friendship with Shannon. In particular the oil painting of 'Don Juan and the Statue' (which cannot be directly related to any of the variants of the legend, since the statue is one of a horseman) may be related to the final 'Horseman, Pass By!' There are a number of curious illustrations to Oscar Wilde's *Sphinx* which have great purity of line and a lyric quality of imagination. One of them in particular, called 'Rose Up the Painted Swathéd Dead', with a winged lion figure and a pyramid background, may perhaps be related to the line in 'The Black Tower':

> There in the tomb stand the dead upright.

though this is as likely to be an allusion to the heroic burial on the summit of Knocknarea.[2] But there is no certainty; equally, knowing their common interest in parables, there may be other originals in

[1] *A Vision* (B), p. 298: and see 'Lapis Lazuli'.
[2] See Chapter 1. But the vertical burial is not uncommon elsewhere. Cf. Myles Dillon, *The Cycles of the Kings*, and Wood-Martin, *History of Sligo*.

Ricketts' portfolios. All we can do is to notice a certain community of outlook; the 'intimate felicity' in Christian symbolism, the common troubled concern with scenes from the Passion; the significance he attached to the legend of Don Juan, as a rebel or saint; the contrast between woman's beauty and her fanatical cruelty suggested by the Salome story,[1] and treated in two notable pictures, 'The Head of Orpheus' and 'Judith returning with the Head of Holofernes'; and Ricketts' place, as Sturge Moore points out, as the third in the line from Raphael through Delacroix.

The images that offer some obscurity, and at the same time suggest a possible pictorial origin, appear to me to be as follows. For convenience of setting out, I have noted suggestions from painters or paintings below each quotation.

1.           Thy great leaves enfold
       The ancient beards, the helms of ruby and gold
       Of the crowned Magi. . . .[2]

An Italian Primitive? or perhaps based on Botticelli's 'Adoration of the Magi', with a pre-Raphaelite overlay. (I owe this last suggestion to Mrs Yeats.)

2.   When the flaming lute-thronged angelic door is wide;
     When an immortal passion breathes in mortal clay;
     Our hearts endure the scourge, the plaited thorns, the way
     Crowded with bitter faces, the wounds in palm and side,
     The vinegar-heavy sponge, the flowers by Kedron stream;
     We will bend down and loosen our hair over you. . . .[3]

This may be a *Via Crucis* of the Flemish School. It may well be composite.

3.   The Powers whose name and shape no living creature knows
     Have pulled the Immortal Rose;
     And though the Seven Lights bowed in their dance and wept,
     The Polar Dragon slept,
     His heavy rings uncoiled from glimmering deep to deep:
     When will he wake from sleep[4]

Perhaps a Rosicrucian or Hermetic image? But it may not be pictorial after all; there is a note to *The Wind Among the Reeds*.

[1] *A Full Moon in March*; cf. the discussion in Chapter 15.
[2] 'The Secret Rose,' *C.P.*, p. 77.
[3] 'The Travail of Passion,' ibid., p. 78.
[4] 'The Poet pleads with the Elemental Powers,' ibid., p. 80.

'I have made the Seven Lights, the constellation of the Bear, lament for the theft of the Rose, and I have made the Dragon, the constellation Draco, the guardian of the Rose, because these constellations move about the pole of the heavens, the ancient Tree of Life in many countries, and are often associated with the Tree of Life in mythology.'[1]

4. Now as at all times I can see in the mind's eye,
In their stiff, painted clothes, the pale unsatisfied ones
Appear and disappear in the blue depth of the sky
With all their ancient faces like rain-beaten stones,
And all their helms of silver hovering side by side,
And all their eyes still fixed, hoping to find once more,
Being by Calvary's turbulence unsatisfied,
The uncontrollable mystery on the bestial floor.[2]

See No. 1. It may well be a Primitive Nativity, except for the 'helms of silver' which may be pre-Raphaelite. Or it may be a composite image, the key to be found in a passage from the *1930 Diary*: 'When I was in my twenties I saw a drawing or etching by some French artist of an angel standing against a midnight sky. The angel was old, wingless, and armed like a knight, as impossibly tall as one of those figures at Chartres Cathedral, and its face was worn by time and innumerable battles . . . that image remained and I imitated it in the old angels at the end of *The Countess Cathleen*.[3]

5. When have I last looked on
The round green eyes and the long wavering bodies
Of the dark leopards of the moon? . . .[4]

An image from Horton or Dulac? But the poem may have, in whole or in part, a literary source in Ferguson's translation of 'Deirdre's Lament for the Sons of Usnach', in Yeats' *A Book of Irish Verse*. (I am indebted for this suggestion to Peter Allt.)

6. The lonely light that Samuel Palmer engraved, . . .

and

---

[1] Note to *The Wind Among the Reeds*, Third Edition, p. 77. Compare also: 'The word seven throws the imaginative strength to the time when the planets were god,' *Letters to 'A.E.'* (1900) (*Dublin Magazine*, July/Sept. 1939).
[2] 'The Magi,' *C.P.*, p. 141. See Yeats' note, ibid., p. 531.
[3] Page 19.
[4] 'Lines written in Dejection,' *C.P.*, p. 163.

> The burning bow that once could shoot an arrow
> Out of the up and down. . . .[1]

Many of Palmer's pictures embody this 'lonely light', *e.g.* 'The Magic Apple Tree'. But I am certain he is thinking of 'The Lonely Tower', chosen for his collection of lantern slides, and which I have used as a frontispiece.

The second image is universal: but the context of this suggests a source in an illustration of Blake's 'Jerusalem'. But perhaps it is another memory of the Coin-image, 'the Cretan barb that pierced a star'.

7.
> Paul Veronese
> And all his sacred company
> Imagined bodies all their days
> By the lagoon you love so much,
> For proud, soft, ceremonious proof
> That all must come to sight and touch;
> While Michael Angelo's Sistine roof,
> His 'Morning' and his 'Night' disclose
> How sinew that has been pulled tight,
> Or it may be loosened in repose,
> Can rule by supernatural right
> Yet be but sinew.[2]

I do not know the reference. It may be to Veronese's four pictures in the London National Gallery: 'Unfaithfulness', 'Happy Lovers', 'Scorn', 'Respect'.

Michelangelo is an important figure in Yeats' procession of artists: standing at that point of time where 'the forms, as in Titian, awaken sexual desire'. The Sistine Chapel is the last attempt to synthesize paganism and Christianity. 'The soul's unity has been found and lost'. But Yeats may have had in mind the passage from Pater: 'The titles assigned traditionally to the four symbolical figures, *Night* and *Day*, *Twilight* and *The Dawn*, are far too definite for them; for these figures . . . concentrate and express, less by way of definite conceptions than by the touches, the promptings of a piece of music, all those vague fancies, misgivings, presentiments which shift and mix and are defined and fade again, whenever the

---

[1] 'The Phases of the Moon', *C.P.*, p. 183.
[2] 'Michael Robartes and the Dancer', ibid., p. 197.

thoughts try to fix themselves with sincerity on the conditions and surroundings of the disembodied spirit.'[1]

8. Their legs long, delicate, and slender, aquamarine their eyes,
   Magical unicorns bear ladies on their backs.[2]

The key to this passage appears in *Letters to Dorothy Wellesley*[3] (Nov. 8, 1936).

> ... On the other wall are drawings, paintings or photographs of paintings of friends & relatives, & three reproductions of pictures, Botticelli's 'Spring', Gustave Moreau's 'Women and Unicorns', Fragonard's 'Cup of Life', a beautiful young man and girl running with eager lips towards a cup held towards them by a winged form. The first & last sense, & the second mystery – the mystery that touches the genitals, a blurred touch through a curtain.

Botticelli's 'Spring' is well known. The Fragonard is 'La Fontaine d'Amour' (Wallace Collection). The Gustave Moreau is less often seen. It is obvious from the last comment that the symbolic appeal is both complex and powerful; and note should be taken of the final phrase. It is first used in *John Sherman* ... 'for poetry is essentially *a touch from behind a curtain.*'

9.     A sudden blow: the great wings beating still
       Above the staggering girl, her thighs caressed
       By the dark webs, her nape caught in his bill,
       He holds her helpless breast upon his breast.[4]

Melchiori has developed at length the intricate background of the poem: how Pater had discussed the parallel between Helen and St Anne, and how the complexities include Madame Blavatsky's *The Secret Doctrine*, the relationship to an illustration of Blake's 'Jerusalem', the two-fold debt to Spenser, Shelley's translation of the 'Homeric' Hymn to the Dioscuri, Gogarty's *An Offering of Swans*,

---

[1] *The Renaissance*: 'The Poetry of Michelangelo'.
[2] 'The Tower', vii, *C.P.*, p. 231.
[3] Page 109.
[4] 'Leda and the Swan', *C.P.*, p. 241. For the link between Leda and Helen, consider the following from Todhunter's *Helena in Troas*, which Yeats admired:

> O pitiless mischief! Thee no woman bore
> Wooed by the billing of the amorous swan.
> Yea, Leda bore thee not but Nemesis
> To be the doom of Troy and Priam's house.

Gustave Moreau's *Leda*. He has discussed in detail all (I think), the possible sources, including some of the suggestions which I had made in the first edition of this book. To this it would be presumptuous to add: except to note that among the Ricketts drawings is the scene of the winged angel in a narrow cell, the terrified half-naked girl clasping his feet: that a Cretan coin shows the union of the dove ('Dove or Swan') with Dictynna, the Cretan Diana[1], and the Swan may be a phallic symbol.[2] Raymond Lister has drawn my attention to the possible relevance of the woman-swan figure in Plate 11 of 'Jerusalem'. But since Melchiori's book was published a further dimension has been given by Wind,[3] who points out the connection of Leda with Death, and confirms the link with Michelangelo's *Night*. Through this there is the connection with the Neo-Platonic conception of the 'Eros funèbre' and the kiss of death.

The poem is perhaps the test case for the extent to which we may, if we wish, pursue meanings in depth. Let us take the poem first in its simplicity.

Two Annunciations form a pattern in history: Leda and the Virgin. The Virgin is linked, mistakenly, to St Anne, *via* Pater's Essay. Both events concern the union of godhead and woman. Both produce momentous births. The eggs of Leda give rise to the fall of Troy; from them emerge the legend of two destined women Helen and Clytemnestra. Helen has long been a personal symbol for Maud Gonne. The swans are archetypal, everywhere; in Spenser, emblems, paintings, Celtic myth, and concretely on the Lakes at Coole. The swan stands for power, phallic strength, purity, spirit and spirits (as all white birds), fidelity; fire and air (as the dove); the ineffable Godhead. In the act of congress the *loosening thighs* and the *white rush* are antithetical aspects. Into the softness and whiteness is concentrated all the sensuality of touch. The outcome of the union is further history or myth, pagan or Christian, Love and War. But what of the woman? Yeats speculates continually on the emotions of woman in such a crisis.[4] Did Leda or Mary by that act

[1] R. Payne Knight: *A Discourse on the Worship of Priapus*; London, 1865. p. 85 and Plate III.

[2] Ibid., Plate XXV, 3.

[3] Op. cit., Ch. X.

[4] See 'The Mother of God', 'A Nativity'.

become half or wholly divine? Did a god share with beast the lassitude that overcomes all animals, save only the lion and the cock?[1] *Shudder* is of the sexual act, the moment of orgasm, as all husband-men know; but it is also anticipation in fear.

The verbal tensions are everywhere. The *white rush* is perhaps not only from Spenser, but the wind of Pentecost. The *beating* heart is the assurance of incarnation, not of the immaterial or ghostly. The *dark webs* (which replaced the earlier, and ridiculous, *webbed toes*), give a paradox of bleak cold to cut across the finger associations of the sensual caress.[2] Behind the poem, its phonetic subtlety, its changes of speed, what do the depth references add? Many pictures, coins, emblems, confirm the centrality of the myth. Two world events converge, compress, in a paradox of cosmic implications, in a synthesis of virility, sensuality, and of the traditional and necessary domination. To embrace the monstrous fact strains all imagination; Semele, Danaë, the faintly comic Europa are thin or insignificant by comparison.

Behind again (but I think faintly) may be the Leda-Leto equation, the ironic questioning of the permanence of the supreme sexual act, the relation of male to female, god to mortal, god to woman. Dove or Swan; and behind them standing lonely and a little sardonically, the image of the White Heron.

10. 'On a Picture of a Black Centaur by Edmund Dulac.' This, which should have been the most obvious example of the pictorial debts, is, in fact, a composite image. The poem was started in relation to Dulac's picture but was altered to correspond to a picture of Cecil Salkeld's. (My authority is again Mrs Yeats.[3])

11.          Miracle had its playtime where
             In damask clothed and on a seat
             Chryselephantine, cedar-boarded,
             His majestic Mother sat
             Stitching at a purple hoarded . . .[4]

This is, almost beyond doubt, based on a poorish seventeenth-century painting, formerly hung in the Dublin National Gallery,

[1] See Gogarty's poem in the *Oxford Book of Modern Verse*, No. 165.
[2] Donne: *On His Mistress Going to Bed*.
[3] See Hone, p. 328; though his account of the incident differs as to the sequence of composition. The reference of the poem is *C.P.*, p. 242.
[4] 'Wisdom', *C.P.*, p. 246.

then stored in its cellars, and now on view again. It was originally labelled 'The Annunciation', though Our Lady is obviously *enceinte* and there are two angels. A more possible title is 'The Seamless Garment'. It shows precisely this scene. Two angels attend the Virgin, a basket containing the sewing materials beside her. The painter is unknown.

12.     The threefold terror of love; a fallen flare
Through the hollow of an ear;
Wing beating about the room;
The terror of all terrors that I bore
The Heavens in my womb.[1]

I had thought this to be some remembered Primitive association I now think it likely that there were two possible sources, both of which Yeats knew. One is the tempera drawing, Blake's 'Annunciation' (in which Gabriel stands with massive eagle wings on the left of the picture): and Ricketts' drawing[2] of which the title is 'Eros leaving Psyche'. Here the departing winged god stands beside the bed: the naked Psyche clutches his feet in the turmoil.

13.     A tree there is that from its topmost bough
Is half all glittering flame and half all green,
Abounding foliage moistened with the dew;
And half is half and yet is all the scene;
And half and half consume what they renew,
And he that Attis' image hangs between
That staring fury and the blind lush leaf
May not know what he knows, but knows not grief.[3]

The source of this image is from the *Mabinogion*:

. . . The ancient religion is in that passage of the *Mabinogion* about the making of 'Flower Aspect' . . . and one finds it in the not less beautiful passage about the burning Tree, that has half its beauty from calling up a fancy of leaves so living and beautiful, they can be no less living and beautiful a thing than flame: 'They saw a tall tree by the

---

[1] 'The Mother of God', *C.P.*, p. 281. Cf. Yeats' note in *C.P.*, p. 450. I have not been able to trace the 'Byzantine mosaic picture'. It is not among the accessible illustrations of the mosaics in St Vitale at Ravenna – a possible source.
[2] Sturge Moore's edition, Plate XLIII.
[3] 'Vacillation', *C.P.*, p. 282.

side of the river, one half of which was in flames from the root to the top, and the other half was green and in full leaf.'[1]

This passage is also quoted by Arnold in his 'Study of Celtic Literature'.

The Attis reference is taken from Julian's 'Hymn to the Mother of God'.

14.           The mountain throws a shadow,
              Thin is the moon's horn . . .[2]

I suggested previously a memory of a Horton or a Calvert drawing. Yeats wrote a preface to Horton's *A Book of Images*: he meditated once a book on Calvert. It is a curious feature of this pastoral group – Blake, Calvert, Palmer – that a very thin crescent moon is a constant feature in these miniature landscapes.

15.           I dreamed as in my bed I lay,
              All night's fathomless wisdom come,
              That I had shorn my locks away
              And laid them on Love's lettered tomb:
              But something bore them out of sight
              In a great tumult of the air,
              And after nailed upon the night
              Berenice's burning hair.[3]

This looks like a dominant picture image – see No. 18 following – but I cannot find the source. Perhaps it is related to Ben Jonson's *The Forest*, xii (Epistle to Elizabeth, Countess of Rutland).

              Who heav'd Hercules
       Unto the starres? or the *Tyndarides*?
       Who placed Jason's Argo in the skie?
       Or set bright Ariadne's crowne so high?
       Who made a lampe of Berenice's hayre?
       Or lifted Cassiopea in her chayre?
       But only *Poets*, rapt with rage divine?

There are several memories of Jonson: e.g. the phrase, *the household spies* (a strange expression) is in *Volpone*, iii, 6.

16.       But the dark changed to red, and torches shone,
          And deafening music shook the leaves; a troop

[1] *E. & I.*, p. 176. But I have sometimes wondered whether Yeats did not have in mind Palmer's 'The Magic Apple Tree', or a Turner painting.
[2] 'Love's Loneliness,' *C.P.*, p. 298.
[3] 'Her Dream,' ibid., p. 299.

> Shouldered a litter with a wounded man,
> Or smote upon the string, and to the sound
> Sang of the beast that gave the fatal wound.

This suggests Adonis or Diarmuid, who met his death from the enchanted boar on the slopes of a Sligo mountain. The scene may be suggested by an account of the Attis ritual in the chapter of *The Golden Bough* referred to previously.

> All stately women moving to a song
> With loosened hair or foreheads grief-distraught,
> It seemed a Quattrocento painter's throng,
> A thoughtless image of Mantegna's thought.[1]

Perhaps this is a composite image. I can find no corresponding picture in Mantegna. Rossetti wrote a sonnet for an 'Allegorical Dance of Women' on Mantegna's picture in the Louvre.

> 17.          The Heavenly Circuit; Berenice's Hair;
> Tent-pole of Eden; the tent's drapery;
> Symbolical glory of the earth and air!
> The Father and His angelic hierarchy
> That made the magnitude and glory there
> Stood in the circuit of a needle's eye.
>
> Some found a different pole, and where it stood
> A pattern on a napkin dipped in blood.[2]

(See No. 16 above.) There is a picture of the Styrian School (No. 978) in the Dublin National Gallery showing the apostles setting forth. It bears on the reverse side a large and crude painting of St Veronica's napkin. The opening verses may refer to an Ascension of some kind, but I can find no clue. The image appears to be a dominant: compare

> All the stream that's roaring by
> Came out of a needle's eye;
> Things unborn, things that are gone,
> From needle's eye still goad it on.[3]

> 18.          What woman hugs her infant there?
> Another star has shot an ear.

[1] Her Vision in the Wood,' *C.P.*, p. 312.
[2] Veronica's Napkin,' ibid., p. 270.
[3] Supernatural Songs,' ibid., p. 333.

What made the drapery glisten so?
Not a man but Delacroix.

What made the ceiling waterproof?
Landor's tarpaulin on the roof.

What brushes fly and moth aside?
Irving and his plume of pride.

What hurries out the knave and dolt?
Talma and his thunderbolt.

Why is the woman terror-struck?
Can there be mercy in that look?[1]

This is an obscure and difficult poem, and the sources are complex. It is symmetrical in structure, the first and last couplets concerned with the Annunciation, as in No. 13, and the other four with violent men who are typical of the 'Ninth Gyre' – Phases 19–21 of the Phases of the Moon. Three of them are linked; both Landor and Delacroix knew Talma. I do not know what picture, if any, by Delacroix Yeats had in mind. There were many monographs written on him between 1928 and 1933, and an exhibition was held in 1930.[2] Perhaps the picture is 'The Death of Sardanapalus' or an illustration for Shakespeare; perhaps, as has been suggested, he merely liked the rotundity of Delacroix's name.[3] But Delacroix was the noblest and greatest of Romantic painters, the opponent of the classical David, the illustrator of *Faust*, the theorist of straight and crooked lines. There are passages by him which read curiously like Yeats:

> In life we preserve the memory of those feelings only that move us; all the rest becomes less even than what has actually occurred, because nothing any longer lends it colour in our imagination. . . . Solitude is far from weighing on me as much as does the cold rain of common-places that greets you in every salon. . . . As it is my imagination that peoples my solitude, I chose my company.[4]

Landor is the type of the physically violent man who is full of 'calm nobility' in his writings; coupled with Donne as the pair with whom Yeats would 'dine at journey's end'; and yet a man

[1] 'A Nativity,' *C.P.*, p. 387. Compare Baudelaire's *Les Phares*.
[2] For details, see Venturi, *Modern Painters*, p. 226.
[3] Mrs Yeats.
[4] Venturi, p. 109.

continually beset by every kind of domestic calamity. Perhaps, therefore, the tarpaulin; faintly ridiculous, the temporary cover against popular ridicule.

Talma is the great French actor, perhaps balancing Delacroix as a revolutionary in their respective arts: whose performance in *Charles IX* in Paris in 1789 is said to have had a profound influence on public opinion —

> (Did that play of mine send out
> Certain men the English shot?)

And in *The Death of Cuchulain* the old man of the prologue claims him as his kin: '. . . unless indeed I am, as I affirm, the son of Talma, and he was so old that his friends and acquaintances still read Virgil and Homer.'[1]

As to the fourth, 'Irving and his plume of pride', one would like to think that this is Henry Irving, the actor,[2] whose 'plume of pride' might be a remembered image of a costume portrait. But it has been suggested that it may refer to Edward Irving, the editor of Blake, a violent and powerful preacher, who quoted Shakespeare and was much concerned with the imminence of the Second Coming. All five men appear to be linked to a common source in Shakespeare – also a man of the Twentieth Phase of the Moon.[3]

19.    Through light-obliterating garden foliage what magic drum?
       Down limb or breast or down that glimmering belly move his
           mouth and sinewy tongue,
       What from the forest came? What beast has licked its young?[4]

---

[1] *C. Plays*, p. 693. Compare also *On the Boiler*, p. 15: 'Ricketts made pictures that suggest Delacroix by their colour and remind us by their theatrical composition that Talma once invoked the thunderbolt.'

[2] Mrs Yeats has confirmed that the reference is to Henry Irving the actor. Yeats met Irving, with his father, about 1882, and Irving said to J.B.Y.: 'If your son ever thinks of becoming an actor, send him to me.' Compare also: 'Even the forms of subjective acting that was natural to the professional stage have ceased. Where all now is sympathy and observation no Irving can carry himself with intellectual pride, nor any Salvini in half-animal nobility, both wrapped in solitude' (*P. & C.*, p. 215); and 'Irving, the last of the sort on the English stage . . . never moved me but in the expression of intellectual pride . . .' (*Autobiographies*, p. 125).

[3] I am indebted for many points in the above to an unpublished essay by A. L. Cloudsley.

[4] 'What Magic Drum?' *C.P.*, p. 331.

Perhaps from *Purgatorio*, viii, or one of the serpent illustrations by Blake?

Images that appear at first sight to have pictorial roots, but which can be explained otherwise, are:

> 20.  I would be ignorant as the dawn
>      That has looked down
>      On that old queen measuring a town
>      With the pin of a brooch. . . .[1]

The arms of the City of Armagh are the brooch and breast-pin of Emain Macha, a kind of Celtic Atalanta. The story is in the *Annals of Tigernach*.

> 21.  . . . Or climbed among the images of the past —
>      The unperturbed and courtly images —
>      Evening and morning, the steep street of Urbino
>      To where the duchess and her people talked
>      The stately midnight through until they stood
>      In their great window looking at the dawn. . . .[2]

This is directly from Castiglione: see *The Courtier*, particularly the opening of Book I. There are many references to the work; and it is clearly of importance in building up Yeats' philosophy of aristocracy.

> 22.  . . . yet should I dream
>      Sinbad the sailor's brought a painted chest,
>      Or image, from beyond the Loadstone Mountain,
>      That dream is a norm.[3]

This is not among the Dulac illustrations for the *Arabian Nights*. Mrs Yeats has told me that he was very much interested in painted chests of all kinds, and wished to have one at Ballylee. (Jack Yeats possessed a magnificent example.) The passage that appears relevant – its symbolism would have appealed powerfully to him – is in *Sinbad the sailor and other stories from the Arabian Nights*,[4] and may perhaps shed some light on the nature of the dream.

[1] 'The Dawn,' *C.P.*, p. 164.
[2] 'The People,' ibid., p. 169.
[3] 'A Prayer on going into my House,' ibid., p. 183.
[4] Illustrated by Dulac: Hodder and Stoughton. Yeats possessed a copy of Powys Mathers' *Arabian Nights* (*A Vision* (A), p. xiii.). See also *Autobiographies*, p. 53.

'Tell me', I said, 'what is the history of the mountain?'

'It is black, steep and inaccessible,' he replied. 'On its summit is a dome of brass, supported by ten pillars of brass; and on the dome is a brazen horseman, mounted on a brazen horse, bearing in his hand a spear of brass, and on his breast a plate of lead, engraven with mystic signs. Sirs, while that horseman sits upon his horse, the spell of the loadstone spares no ship in the surrounding sea, for without iron no ship is built.'

VII

But even when such relationships have been suggested or established, we must ask ourselves how far and in what manner they serve to enlarge our appreciation of Yeats' poetry, beyond the obvious, but rare, redemption from obscurity. I think the true answer is that we are helped to perceive the unifying principles of Yeats' use of symbols. Their apparent arbitrariness and confusion vanishes, and they can be seen as clearly related to his six great periods of human myth and history and thought; the 'Babylonian starlight', the Greeks at the time of Phidias, Byzantium, the Quattrocento, the Renaissance, Blake. Yeats had learnt his lesson from the failure of Blake's personal mythology.

His practice of allowing images to beget fresh images, to multiply in clusters round a single nucleus, or to range widely for possible analogies in time, thus becomes apparent; for always he must think in these images. The more clearly the basic image is established and accepted in his mind, the greater is the vitality that coheres about the subsidiary images.

Hawk and man are associated, not arbitrarily but historically: 'The men that Titian painted, the men that Jongsen painted, even the men of Van Dyck, seemed at moments like great hawks at rest.'[1] The effect is to deepen and extend our sense of the significance of such connected images, as, for example, the transplanting of the Sphinx to the Rock of Cashel (with Yeats as the Oedipus of Ireland?) or of the psychological significance of 'St George and the Dragon' in the Bordone, and the interpretation of that episode, or of the Perseus–Andromeda story, in relation to Maud Gonne. There are countless pictures of this latter subject: but it seems probable that

[1] *Autobiographies*, p. 292.

Ricketts: Don Juan and the Equestrian Statue

*'To stare Upon great Juan riding by'*

Ingres: Oedipus and the Sphinx

*'On the grey rock of Cashel I suddenly saw A Sphinx with woman breast and lion paw . . .'*

the one which first attracted Yeats was the wall-painting at Pompeii.[1] At Pompeii, too, there is a 'Europa and the Bull', though I prefer to think (in view of the comic context, in which the cherub on the dolphin parodies Europa's ridiculous and uncomfortable attitude) that he had in mind the great Titian in the Isabella Stuart Gardner Museum at Boston. It seems also likely that the response of many readers to visual aspects of poetry, a response which has perhaps become dulled of late, will be stimulated again with interesting results, as Dante and Milton are perpetually renewed by Blake's illustrations. Visual images in verse are apt to be faintly seen, or incompletely defined; if they can be referred to the norm of their original they gain in freshness. It is possible that, if a large number of pictures could be correlated, a common factor would emerge that would be of considerable interest. But more important even than the influence of painting upon Yeats was the influence of the criticism of that painting, and particularly of the work of Walter Pater. As we read *The Renaissance*, phrases start up continually that suggest counterparts in Yeats' prose or poetry. A dozen such can be found even in the Preface. In the essays on specific artists the debt is still more apparent, not merely in verbal resemblance but in obvious contributions to Yeats' exemplification, through art, of his philosophy of history. 'The beginnings of Venetian painting link themselves to the last, stiff, half-barbaric splendours of Byzantine decoration . . .'[2] Sometimes a phrase will suggest a series of parallels, as of the famous 'La Gioconda':

> She is older than the rocks among which she sits; like the vampire, she has been dead many times, and learned the secrets of the grave; and has been a diver in deep seas, and keeps their fallen day about her; and trafficked for strange webs with Eastern merchants: and, as Leda, was the mother of Helen of Troy, and, as Saint Anne, the Mother of Mary . . . The fancy of perpetual life, sweeping together ten thousand experiences, is an old one . . .[3]

– the passage that he printed as the first poem in the *Oxford Book of Modern Verse*.

I have noted, from Pater's essay on Michelangelo, the possible relevance of the quotation regarding the fire and ice;[4] there is

[1] *E. & I.*, p. 280.　　　　　　　　[2] 'The School of Giorgione.'
[3] 'Leonardo da Vinci'.　　　　　　[4] See p. 94, *supra*.

K

perhaps a clue to the line in von Hügel that contains the lion-honeycomb image, in that passage where Pater alludes to the artist's 'immense patriarchal age, till the sweetness it had taken so long to secrete in him was found at last. Out of the strong came forth sweetness, *ex forti dulcedo*.'[1] Pater may have led him to consider Phidias, since his eulogy expresses values very similar to those Yeats finds in the historical sculptor – 'that law . . . which prompted them constantly to seek the type in the individual, to abstract and express only what is structural and permanent, to abstract from the individual all that belongs only to him'. There is the germ of Yeats' view of the passing of Greek perfection into the 'Galilean turbulence':

> The longer we contemplate that Hellenic ideal, in which man is at unity with himself, with his physical nature, with the outside world, the more we may be inclined to regret that he should ever have passed beyond it, to contend for a perfection that makes the blood turbid, and frets the flesh, and discredits the actual world about us.[2]

Pater's account of Pico della Mirandola is applicable, almost word for word, to Yeats himself:

> Taught by them [the ancient philosophers] Pythagoras became so great a 'master of silence', and wrote almost nothing, thus hiding the words of God in his heart, and speaking wisdom only among the perfect. In explaining the harmony between Plato and Moses, Pico lays hold on every sort of figure and analogy, on the double meanings of words, the symbols of the Jewish ritual, the secondary meanings of obscure stories in the later Greek mythologists. Everywhere there is an unbroken system of correspondences. . . . There is the element of fire in the material world; the sun is the fire of heaven; and in the super-celestial world there is the fire of the seraphic intelligence. 'But behold how they differ! The elementary fire burns, the heavenly fire vivifies, the super-celestial fire loves.'

This 'unbroken system of correspondences' was of perpetual and exciting concern to Yeats. He speaks of 'Bernini's big altar in St Peter's with its figures contorted and convulsed by religion as

---

[1] 'The Poetry of Michelangelo.' The image is used again in 'The Gift of Harun Al-Rashid':
> To show how violent great hearts can lose
> Their bitterness and find the honeycomb.
> *C.P.*, p. 513.

[2] 'Winckelmann.'

though by the devil'.[1] He looks at Botticelli's 'Nativity' in the National Gallery in London, and perceives that the thatch of the stall has been projected so as to form a sort of cave, which immediately begets the thought of Porphyry's cave and his own visit to Capri.[2] And so another resemblance is built up between the Oracle and Christianity. The Renaissance is credited with a significant mysticism in which time is bent into a pattern:

> Did da Vinci, when he painted a St John that seemed a Dionysus, know that St John's father begot him when the grape was ripe, and that his mother bore him at the Mediterranean ripening of the corn?[3]

But the explanation of the apparently obscure passage is to be found in the Louvre, where da Vinci's two pictures of Bacchus and St John hang on either side of 'The Virgin of the Rocks'. The same youth has served as a model for both.

There was a further and most important function for the artist, and this time positive and sociological:

> If, as these writers [Balzac, Péguy] affirm, the family is the unit of social life, and the origin of civilization which but exists to preserve it, and almost the sole cause of progress, it seems more natural than it did before that its ecstatic moment, the sexual choice of man and woman, should be the greater part of all poetry. A single wrong choice may destroy a family, dissipating its tradition or its biological force —

> > (And what if my descendants lose the flower
> > Through natural declension of the soul,
> > Through too much business with the passing hour,
> > Through too much play, or marriage with a fool?)[4]

– and the great sculptors, painters and poets are there so that instinct may find its lamp.[5]

[1] *A Vision* (B), p. 296.
[2] Ibid. (A), pp. 202–3.
[3] Ibid. (A), p. 164. Consider also the following: 'Does one not discover in the faces of Madonnas and holy women painted by Raphael or da Vinci . . . a condition of soul where all is still and finished, all experience wound up upon a bobbin?' (Preface to *The Holy Mountain*, p. 40.)
[4] 'Meditations in Time of Civil War,' iv, *C.P.*, p. 228.
[5] *Explorations*, p. 274.

VIII

> Calvert and Wilson, Blake and Claude
> Prepared a rest for the people of God
> Palmer's phrase, but after that
> Confusion fell upon our thought.

Yeats' collection of slides included six of Blake's illustrations to Thornton's *Virgil*, four Palmers and six Calverts. He had once planned a monograph on Calvert. The whole sixteen form a homogeneous group: the seventh of the Blake slides, 'A Rolling Stone is ever bare of Moss' seems to me irrelevant. They might have been selected to show a vision of an idyllic pastoral in which a healthy sensuality is intricately blended with a cosmic but simple awareness of a Morrisian, or Celtic, Other World. We may quote from Palmer:

> I sat down with Mr Blake's Thornton's *Virgil* woodcuts before me . . . I happened first to think of their sentiment. They are visions of little dells, and nooks, and corners of Paradise; models of the exquisitest pitch of intense poetry. I thought of their light and shade, and looking back found no word to describe it. Intense depth, solemnity and vivid brilliancy only partially describe them. There is in all such a mystic and dreamy glimmer as penetrates and kindles the inmost soul . . . They are like that wonderful artist's work the drawing aside of the fleshly curtain, and the glimpse which all the most holy, studious saints and sages have enjoyed, of *that rest which remaineth to the people of God.*[1]

It is, I think, possible to see what Yeats had in mind. Calvert is influenced by Claude, but derives directly from Blake; the state of pastoral and spiritual blessedness, Blake's land of Beulah:

> a mild and pleasant rest
> Named Beulah, a soft Moony Universe, feminine, lovely,
> Pure, mild and gentle, *given in Mercy to those who sleep* . . .[2]

The countryside of Shoreham provided such a setting. Yeats' selection of slides suggest that he wanted to draw attention to some particular aspects of this rich pastoralism. The landscapes are secure, calm, intimate; cottage or woodland huts melt into the protection of woodland and forest. The earth is gracious and

[1] *Life and Letters*, pp. 15–16.
[2] *The Four Zoas*, Night, I. 11 86–89. I am much indebted here to Raymond Lister.

fruitful: Calvert's *The Brook* uses imagery from Virgil's *Georgics*. Man returns from his labour in the evening, and the symbols of earth's lavishness are stacked about him; in *The Chamber Idyll* he draws his half-naked bride towards him in Blake's unashamed sensual delight. In *The Ploughman* there is sheer exultation in energy, and Yeats would have found in the close-packed symbolism – the cut tree, the serpent smitten by lightning, the growing corn and the angelic choir in the background – the recurrent and masterful images that he delighted in.

But there are other curious aspects of his choice. Engraving No. VIII of the Blake series shows a river that seems to flow from a lake, over a waterfall; to separate, in the foreground, a pasture with sheep and lambs from a thatched cottage that seems to grow into the wood. The exact theme is repeated in Calvert's *The Sheep of His Pasture*, though with more elaborate detail and without the background lake. I do not think it fanciful to suggest a resemblance to the opening verse of 'Coole Park and Ballylee'.[1]

It is possible to suggest other aspects of these slides. Calvert's *The Return Home* has a shepherd, riding on a donkey, carrying a crook; plodding wearily along a path that leads to a woodland hut, where a woman waits for him in the doorway. Perhaps the Christ-like figure is related to a heresy like that of Ribh the Hermit in his opposition to St Patrick:

> An abstract Greek absurdity has crazed the man[2]

for we know that Yeats was obsessed at times, and sometimes blasphemously, with the doctrine of the Trinity.

All three painters have a fondness for soft moonlit landscape: the moons strong and friendly. 'The moon herself bore little resemblance to the pallid small reality we see above us now. She seemed to blush and bend herself towards men . . . casting a warm romantic glow over the landscape that slept at her feet.'[3]

[1] *C.P.*, p. 275.
[2] Ibid., p. 328.
[3] Palmer, *Life and Letters*, pp. 39–41: cit. Lister.

IX

But the impression left after visits to some thirty of the galleries, museums, mosaics which Yeats appears to have seen is a strange one. His symbolic usages and his perceptions of historical order cease to be arbitrary or capricious. They are sanctioned and confirmed, compressed and foreshortened, by their permanence or recurrence in time. In the Museum of the Church of St Vitale are fragments of stonework that might have come from Clonmacnoise or Glendalough, to confirm the link between Ireland and Byzantium. S. Apollinare in Classe is a forest of symbols; the Cabalistic Tau Cross with the serpent twined about it, the Candelabra of Seven Lights. Peacocks are carved on the sarcophagi in the churchyard of S. Vitale and near Dante's tomb; the cherub riding the dolphin is in the market place of Ravenna. In the Uffizi is Gherardo Starnino's *Thebaid* with its incredible presentation, among rivers, caves, animals of the Desert Fathers; to amalgamate, perhaps with the *Lausiac History* or Waddell's *Desert Fathers*.

Everywhere there are pictures of the Severed Head: Jael and Sisera, Judith and Holofernes, Salome and John, to confirm the *Bacchae* of Euripides and find room in *The Resurrection, On Baile's Strand, A Full Moon in March*. Countless annunciations show the arrow shooting the ear, the descent of the Logos: one remembers particularly Botticelli's Annunciation, or the Van Eyck in the National Gallery at Washington in which the dove descends in a form like that of a flexed bow.

One is tempted to speculate. Why does Bellini's *St. Francis in Ecstasy* contain, side by side, a donkey and a heron, important symbols in *The Herne's Egg*? What picture of Veronese had he in mind in

> . . . Paul Veronese
> And all his sacred company
> Imagined bodies all their days
> By the lagoon you love so much
> In proud self-ceremonious proof
> That all must come to sight and touch.

In Venice the greatest of Veronese's work is in the Church of San Sebastiano, where the painter is buried. While he was writing *The*

*Cutting of an Agate* he had two pictures before him, a Canaletto and a Frans Francken the younger. 'Neither painting could move us at all, if our thought did not rush out to the edges of our flesh, and it is so with all good art . . .'[1]

But there is another range of possible sources, as yet (I believe) untouched. A series of ballads, illustrated by Jack Yeats, were produced by the Cuala Press. When I saw the painter shortly before his death he was unwilling to let me reproduce any of them. But there are a few striking things: notably a sketch for *The Circus Animals' Desertion*, of a circus packing up to leave some Mayo town, with

> – those stilted boys, that burnished chariot
> Lion and woman and the Lord knows what.

– of which a memory would combine, so typically, with Ezekiel, Blake, and the symbology of the Golden Dawn. There is a picture that looks as if it had been made to fit 'The Three Beggars'[2] (the dates are close) of a stone cairn–as of Cruachan or Knocknarea – with a gloomy unshaven man crouching in a hollow of the stones, while a younger man with a keen exultant foolish face looks down from the wind-blown mountain. In their intense dramatic qualities, a violent romanticism of colour, Jack Yeats' later paintings suggest certain analogies which I think are useful. One would like to know more of 'A.E.'s' pictures which the poet knew; vision of the kind (though far from the quality) of Blake's.

[1] *E. & I.*, p. 292.
[2] *C.P.*, p. 124.

# CHAPTER FIFTEEN

# The Poetry of the Plays

> Not what it leaves behind it in the light
> But what it carries with it to the dark
> Exalts the soul.
>
> *The King's Threshold.*

An analysis of dates and subject-matter shows some interesting correspondences between the poems and the plays. In both there is the early exploitation of the Celtic legend, with the intention of providing the national mythology that was to unify the imagination of the people. The Abbey Theatre period produced little pure poetry: *In the Seven Woods* and *The Shadowy Waters* are slight compared to *Responsibilities*. There are attempts at topical comedy in competition with Lady Gregory, and *Deirdre* is a predecessor of Synge's more effective play. Then, under the stimulus of Ezra Pound, there is the development of the Nōh-type drama, with which he continues to experiment till the end; with a notable break in the two mystery plays, *Calvary* and *The Resurrection*, which are connected with *A Vision* and his views on the historical significance of Christianity. *The Words upon the Window-pane* is linked to the political importance attaching to Swift; and, through him, to the political events in Ireland in the period from 1928 onwards. If, as I have suggested, it is necessary to consider the whole of Yeats' poetry together, the poetry of the plays must also be taken together with the poems by reason of the light, though 'somewhat broken' by dramatic form, that each sheds on the other. The lyric impulse is always strong: 'Somebody, Dr Todhunter, the dramatic poet, I think, had said in my hearing that dramatic poetry must be oratorical and I think that I wrote partly to prove that false; but every now and then I lost courage, as it seems, and remembering that I had some reputation as a lyric poet wrote for the reader of lyrics.'[1] The use of symbol in each shows a parallel development.

It is curious to observe the unanimity of critical opinion that Yeats is not a dramatist. MacNeice stated triumphantly that Aristotle would not have recognized his plays at all: perhaps forgetting a more famous historical pronouncement on that critic if he had been confronted with Shakespeare. But before Yeats is dismissed, we must first, I think, consider precisely what he was trying to do; and whether, within that intention, he was successful. The structure of a short verse play is in any case peculiar, and calls for special handling by poet and judgement by critic. Character must be represented as complete, or almost complete, at the outset. Any large differentiation of character through dialogue, except in the transitions between verse and prose, is perhaps beyond the scope of the form, and was certainly beyond Yeats' skill. He could never write consistently good peasant dialect, nor could he imitate, in dialogue or anecdote, the accent and intonation; and this deficiency was a constant source of annoyance to him. But he did evolve a clear, lucid and altogether efficient prose in his plays, in particular in *The Resurrection* and *The Words upon the Window-pane*.

His theatre was first intended to be one of beautiful speech, of romance, of extravagance, that should at the same time stir into life the imagination of the people, remembering Synge's brave words in the Preface to the *Playboy*, so soon to be falsified by events:

> In Ireland, for a few years more, we have a popular imagination that is fiery, and magnificent, and tender; so that those of us who wish to write start with a chance that is not given to writers in places where the spring-time of the local life has been forgotten, and the harvest is a memory only, and the straw has been turned into bricks.

Yeats' plays were to be spoken by 'men who had music in their voices and a learned understanding of sound'. Speech and personages were to transcend common speech and action, as the golden cock and flower of 'Byzantium' were to transcend the common bird or petal.

> After all, is not the greatest play not the play that gives the sensation of an external reality but the play in which there is the greatest abundance of life itself, of the reality that is in our minds?[2]

[1] *P. & C.*, p. 300.
[2] 'The Irish Dramatic Movement', ibid., p. 120.

This reality is, of its essential quality, personal and (at least initially), remote; to be communicated through rhetoric, through contrasting values of symbols, through 'the emotion of multitude' in the manner of Maeterlinck, using 'vague symbols that set the mind wandering from idea to idea, emotion to emotion'.[1] As the plays are revised, this aspect of 'far off multitudinous things' grows less important; images narrow down to a comparatively few dominants, which build up their significance from the repeated contextual usage in both plays and poems. Even the 'heart's mysteries' with which we are confronted grow at least half-translucent through this double reading.

Yeats' desired a theatre of great speech, elimination of unnecessary action, and the stylization of what remained; in which dramatic tension is built up by the resonances of image and symbols. It owed much to Maeterlinck and more to Mallarme and Symons. Even before he had planned the translations of Oedipus it was to be Sophoclean in character: a 'pure' drama, mystical, incantatory:

> The theatre began in ritual, and it cannot come to its greatness again without recalling words to their ancient sovereignty.[2]

The final product was inevitably a salon drama, for a limited and sophisticated audience; secure from the religious or social improprieties that the Dublin audience might perceive in *The Countess Cathleen* or in the *Playboy*, or in *The Herne's Egg*. Nor was there the danger that disturbances might be caused in the theatre because the lines

> Sign with this quill.
> It was a feather growing on the cock
> That crowed when Peter dared deny his Master,
> And all who use it have great honour in Hell;

implied a reflection on the Pope.[3] Therefore

> I wanted an audience of fifty or a hundred, and if there are more. I beg them not to shuffle their feet or talk when the actors are speaking. I am sure that as I am producing a play for people I like, it is not probable, in this vile age, that they will be more in number than those

---

[1] *E. & I.*, p. 216.
[2] Ibid., p. 170.
[3] *Autobiographies*, p. 414.

who listened to the first performance of Milton's *Comus*. . . . If there are more than a hundred I won't be able to escape people who are educating themselves out of the Book Societies and the like, sciolists all, pickpockets and opinionated bitches.[1]

It was natural that his dramatic theory should tend from the wider vision of the national theatre to a drama that embodied these delicate and aristocratic qualities of ritual, symbol, music, dance, song. . . . 'I will teach them, if I live, the music of the beggar-man, Homer's music. . . . Emer must dance, there must be severed heads – I am old, I belong to mythology – severed heads for her to dance before.'[2] In such a setting crow- or cat-headed men, hawks, eagles, unicorns, the complex juxtapositions of the Fool, the Lame Man and the Blind Man to symbolize different aspects of personality, could alone touch the remote borders of the imagination. The values of the mask were also complex: 'If some fine sculptor should create for my *Calvary*, for instance, the masks of Judas, of Lazarus, and of Christ, would not this suggest other plays now, or many generations from now, and possess one cannot tell what philosophical virility? The mask, apart from its beauty, may suggest new situations at a moment when the old ones seem exhausted. . . .'[3] But this stage, which is closely linked to his poetical development, was the last one, and the complexity of it exceeds that which even a private and selected audience could receive. *The Herne's Egg*, written specially for a festival at the Abbey, proved incapable of production. The last plays must be considered as dramatic poems.

But against these apparent failures are to be set the views, on the earlier work at least, of Lennox Robinson, who as manager and producer at the Abbey, had a right to be heard. He was enthusiastic over the dramatic perfection achieved in *The Countess Cathleen*. It had been revised in 1895, 1899 and 1901; Aleel's song, 'Lift up the White Knees', is said to have been influenced by the visit of the Russian Ballet to London in 1912.[4] Oona's song, the famous 'Who will go drive with Fergus now?' had been cut out when the scene was re-written. A great deal of mythological cloudiness was cleared

---

[1] *The Death of Cuchulain, C. Plays*, p. 693.
[2] Ibid.
[3] *P. & C.*, p. 332.
[4] Lennox Robinson: *Curtain Up*, p. 51. But see Kermode, op. cit.

away. Lennox Robinson paid tribute to the speed and intensity of the final version of the play, the excellence of the last scene in the theatre, and to Yeats' 'power and invention in the portrayal of character'. All the evidence of those who worked with him at the Abbey suggests that Yeats took infinite trouble to learn stagecraft, to measure accurately the response possible within his given intention; and, without losing anything of the original themes, to make them effective. *On Baile's Strand* and *Deirdre* act well; *The King's Threshold* remains, in its fierce sincerity, a great and impressive piece of writing. *The Player Queen* is, I think, the most exciting. It is probable that this complexity and subtlety of verse could never have been appreciated in a commercial theatre, impatient of a native mythology that was half a laughing-stock, half the recreation of the scholars. The interest in the strange heroic passions, the conflicts in his own mind that were to be revealed in character-projections, his own re-firing and forging of a philosophy of love and hatred and death, were in the main outside the presumptions of the twentieth-century theatre. Miss Ellis-Fermor speaks with understanding of the 'tough matter-of-fact wisdom'[1] in all the later poetry; and it is the added intensity given by the heroic impetus and the resources of music, dance and mask that helps us to understand the alchemy of *Last Poems*.

The central themes of the plays seem to be the following:

1. The Cuchulain legend: with the perpetual image of that 'amorous violent man', contending with men, and women, and with an 'ungovernable sea'; which might represent 'the Many' in conflict with the hero.

*The Only Jealousy of Emer.*
*Fighting the Waves.*
*The Death of Cuchulain.*
*On Baile's Strand.*

2. The tragedy of love: the high tradition linked, always, to his own story; with a progressive reduction to its elements in the sexual act, but perceived always ambivalently; and with a constant preoccupation, in the later work, with old age and lost virility.

[1] *The Irish Dramatic Movement*, p. 112.

*The Countess Cathleen*, with himself as Aleel.
*The King's Threshold.*[1]
*Deirdre.*
*The Only Jealousy of Emer, At the Hawk's Well, The Death of Cuchulain.*
*A Full Moon in March* and *The King of the Great Clock Tower.*
*The Herne's Egg.*

3. The Soul and God: in particular the perversity of the 'irrational force', the problems of Chance and Choice, and the soul's 'war with God'.

*The Hour Glass.*
*Calvary.*
*The Resurrection.*
*The Herne's Egg.*

4. Ireland and the eighteenth-century tradition:

*The Words Upon the Window-pane.*
*Purgatory.*

Among the remaining plays *The Cat and the Moon* and *The Player Queen* are of importance; the former in particular for its complex lyric statement.

*The Countess Cathleen* offers an interesting example of Yeats' method:

In Christianity what was philosophy in Eastern Asia became life, biography and drama. A play passes through the same process in being written. At first, if it has psychological depth, there is a bundle of ideas, something that can be stated in philosophical terms; my *Countess Cathleen*, for instance, was once the moral question, may a soul sacrifice itself for a good end? but gradually philosophy is eliminated until at last the only philosophy audible, if there is even that, is the mere expression of one character or another.[2]

The compression of language achieved in this play is striking, with some last relics of the Nineties appearing beneath a new and violent tone:

> I have seen a vision under a green hedge,
> A hedge of hips and haws – men yet shall hear

[1] See the study of the play as Yeats' 'Defence of Poetry' by S. B. Bushriu, in *A Review of English Literature*, Vol. I, No. 3, July 1963.
[2] *Autobiographies*, p. 468.

> The Archangels rolling Satan's empty skull
> Over the mountain-tops.[1]

It seems that there are elements of Dante and Blake, a new *terribilità*
in the vision, but all a little forced, self-conscious still:

> First, Orchill, her pale, beautiful head alive,
> Her body shadowy as vapour drifting
> Under the dawn, for she who awoke desire
> Has but a heart of blood when others die;
> About her is a vapoury multitude
> Of women alluring devils with soft laughter;
> Behind her a host heat of the blood made sin,
> But all the little pink-white nails have grown
> To be great talons.[2]

These are experiments with blank verse, that almost break it under
the anapaests, and yet achieve a new accent:

> CATHLEEN.          You have seen my tears
> And I can see your hand shake on the floor.
> ALEEL.                    I thought but of healing.
> He was angelical.
> CATHLEEN. No, not angelical, but of the old gods,
> Who wander about the world to waken the heart —
> The passionate, proud heart – that all the angels,
> Leaving nine heavens empty, would rock to sleep.[3]

There is still much debt to Tennyson in the play, as there seems to
be in a great deal of the early verse; dying out, so far as can be
judged, by 1909 or so. *The Land of Heart's Desire* was not so
heavily revised, and, in spite of a certain stiffness, we can see Yeats
experimenting both with his technique and the problems of the later
poems:

> THE CHILD. But I can lead you, newly-married bride,
> Where nobody gets old and crafty and wise,
> Where nobody gets old and godly and grave,
> Where nobody gets old and bitter of tongue,
> And where kind tongues bring no captivity;
> For we are but obedient to the thoughts
> That drift into the mind at a wink of the eye.[4]

It includes the lyric

[1] *C. Plays*, p. 44.          [2] Ibid., p. 46.
[3] Ibid., p. 27.          [4] Ibid., p. 70.

> The wind blows out of the gates of the day,
> The wind blows over the lonely of heart . . .[1]

for the child dancing upon the level ground, as Iseult Gonne will later dance on the shore in Normandy, and there are thoughts that will recur again from *Job* or from *The Resurrection*.

> We must be tender to all budding things,
> Our Maker let no thought of Calvary
> Trouble the morning stars in their first song.[2]

There is a picture-image of the Magi,

> The adoring Magi in their coats of mail

(set in brackets, as are many passages that could be omitted in production). Yeats has a significant note on the play. 'Till lately it was not part of the repertory of the Abbey Theatre, for I had grown to dislike it without knowing what I disliked in it. This winter (1912), however, I have made many revisions, and now it plays well enough to give me pleasure.'[3]

The verse of *On Baile's Strand* is more level in tone, shows less of the strata of revision. The Women's Song – 'in a very low voice after the first few words so that the others all but drown their words' – is of interest for the technique of the four-foot line which became such a favourite metre after 1920, used with alternate rhymes. The ordinary four-stress couplet form is rare, though he returns to it in 'Under Ben Bulben'. The song —

> But the man is thrice forlorn,
> Emptied, ruined, wracked, and lost,
> That they follow, for at most
> They will give him kiss for kiss;
> While they murmur 'After this
> Hatred may be sweet to the taste.'
> Those wild hands that have embraced
> All his body can but shove
> At the burning wheel of love,
> Till the side of hate comes up.[4]

[1] *C. Plays*, p. 72.
[2] Ibid., p. 66.
[3] *P. & C.*, p. 327.
[4] *C. Plays*, p. 262. There is an illustration in Blake's *Vala*, a naked girl pushing at the rim of a wheel, that may have suggested this image. But see also the Titian reproduced by Wind, Plate 48, op. cit.

– is prophetic of the *Odi et Amo* theme, an early statement of the paradox that was to occupy Yeats so greatly. It appears again in *Purgatory*, but with greater depth:

> . . . she must live
> Through everything in exact detail,
> Driven to it by remorse, and yet
> Can she renew the sexual act
> And find no pleasure in it, and if not,
> If pleasure and remorse must both be there,
> Which is the greater?[1]

From *The Hawk's Well* onwards there is an intense interest in all aspects of virility and the contrast between young and old. The symbolism of the dry well, and the old man watching beside it, need not be stressed; nor that of the girl who turns into a hawk.[2] The two shadows in *The Only Jealousy of Emer* – the Ghost of Cuchulain and the Woman of the Sidhe – are symbols of the search for perfection in love.

WOMAN OF THE SIDHE. Could you that have loved many a woman
That did not reach beyond the human,
Lacking a day to be complete,
Love one that though her heart can beat,
Lacks it but by an hour or so?
GHOST OF CUCHULAIN. I know you now, for long ago
I met you on the mountain side,
Beside a well that seemed long dry,
Beside old thorns where the hawk flew.
I held out arms and hands; but you
That now seem friendly, fled away
Half woman and half bird of prey.[3]

*The Hour Glass* was first written in prose in 1902,[4] performed at The Abbey in 1912, and republished, after extensive revisions,

---

[1] *C. Plays*, p. 686.

[2] And there may be other associations. Moireen Fox wrote a poem 'To the Mountain Ben Bulben,' beginning

> I would I were a wide-winged hawk, belovèd
> With all the silence of thy peaks my own. . . .

[3] *C. Plays*, p. 291.

[4] The fable is in Lady Wilde's *Ancient Legends of Ireland*, vol. i; the story is called 'The Priest's Soul'. It is printed in full in the Shakespear Head Collected Edition.

in 1922. It is a simple play, with three main characters; the Wise Man, Bridget his wife (who is no more than a foil), Teigue the Chorus-Fool, and an angel: with the Wise Man's children and pupils. I think it deserves more attention than it has commonly received, for in it there is the groundwork, as it were, for part of the philosophy of the later poems, and in particular of 'Supernatural Songs'. It shows again, like strata on a cliff face, two different kinds of verse from the ten years' revision. Twice the Wise Man has dreamed the dream his pupils bring to him as a text for their lesson:

> There are two living countries, one visible and one invisible, and when it is summer there, it is winter here, and when it is November with us, it is lambing-time there.

And therefore:

> Twice have I dreamed it in a morning dream,
> Now nothing serves my pupils but to come
> With a like thought. Reason is growing dim;
> A moment more, and Frenzy will beat his drum
> And laugh aloud and scream;[1]
> And I must dance in the dream.
> No, no, but it is like a hawk, a hawk of the air,
> It has swooped down – and this swoop makes the third —
> And what can I, but tremble like a bird?

FOOL.    Give me a penny.[2]

This is the thought of the 'irrational force' of 'The Second Coming', the dance of agony and frenzy that is the background to 'Byzantium'. The dialogue develops against the *King Lear* pattern with the Fool. The Angel comes to sentence the Wise Man to die: and here the verse throws back to *The Countess Cathleen*:

> You have to die because no soul has passed
> The heavenly threshold since you have opened school,
> But grass grows there, and rust upon the hinge;
> And they are lonely that must keep the watch.[3]

The summons is deferred if the Wise Man can find but one human soul that still believes in God. But he has taught his pupils to disbelieve:

[1] Cf. 'What Magic Drum', *C.P.*, p. 331.
[2] *C. Plays*, p. 303.
[3] Ibid., p. 308.

Master, we all have learnt that truth is learnt
When the intellect's deliberate and cold,
As it were a polished mirror that reflects
An unchanged world; not when the steel dissolves
Bubbling and hissing, till there's naught but fume.

WISE MAN. When it is melted, when it all fumes up,
They walk, as when beside those three in the furnace[1]
The form of the fourth.[2]

All three pupils deny, as he has taught them, the existence of God. Meanwhile the sands of the Hour Glass that the Angel has set are running out. For a moment the fourth pupil makes as though he would believe, but then denies also. Bridget, the Wise Man's wife, is called in, but long ago he taught her to leave off her prayers, and she will not listen. There is a Faust-like speech:

I can explain all now,
Only when all our hold on life is troubled,
Only in spiritual terror can the Truth
Come through the broken mind – as the pease burst
Out of a broken pease-cod.

(*He clutches* BRIDGET *as she is going.*)

Say to them
That Nature would lack all in her most need,
Could not the soul find truth as in a flash,
Upon the battlefield, or in the midst
Of overwhelming waves, and say to them —
But no, they would but answer as I bid.

BRIDGET. You want somebody to get up an argument with.[3]

There is much of interest here. The 'spiritual terror' of 'The Second Coming', of 'Supernatural Songs'; The *Lear*-image of Nature; the truth found on a battlefield ('Under Ben Bulben', and *On the Boiler*) or in Cuchulain's fight with the sea; all these recur again as dominants. The sands run out; the Fool comes in with a dandelion, blowing upon it to find what hour it is. The Wise Man waits:

[1] Cf. 'An agony of flame that cannot singe a sleeve', and the dominant steel-sword-mirror images. Daniel iii, 25 and 27: 'the fire had no power, nor was an hair of their head singed, neither were their coats changed, nor the smell of the fire had passed on them.'
[2] *C. Plays*, p. 313.
[3] Ibid., p. 318.

> Will there be a footfall,
> Or will there be a sort of rending sound,
> Or else a cracking, as though an iron claw
> Had gripped the threshold stone?[1]

His *Oedipus Rex* is mainly of interest for the technique of compression. It is not, and does not purport to be, a translation. Much is omitted, foreshortened, selected as for a ritual. By all accounts it was effective on the stage. The dialogue is in a clear, tense prose; the Choruses are in a metre that suggests Elizabethan origins. Two contrasting extracts will serve to show the method; in each instance the first quoted passage is taken from Sir George Young's translation:

> O banish from our country! Drive him back,
> With winds upon his track,
> On to that chamber vast of Amphitrite,
> Or that lone anchorage, the Thracian main;
> For now, if night leave bounds to our annoy,
> Day levels all again;
> Wherefore, O father Zeus, thou that dost wield the might,
> Of fire-fraught light,
> Him with thy bolt destroy!

This is clumsy, complex in grammar, pedestrian, and close to the original. Beside it:

> Hurry him from the land of Thebes with a fair wind behind
> Out on to that formless deep where not a man can find
> Hold for an anchor-fluke, for all is world-enfolding sea;
> Master of the thunder-cloud, set the lightning free,
> And add the thunder-stone to that and fling them on his head
> For death is all the fashion now, till even Death be dead.

There is a sense of exhilaration in the rhythm, a declamatory beat, with a realization that the evocative names mean little to an audience now. The phrase

> where not a man can find
> Hold for an anchor-fluke

is far from the Greek, but it is speech that a Greek seaman would have known and valued. There is the outrageous effectiveness of the last line, with its Irish intonation. At the end of the play there is a

[1] *C. Plays*, p. 320.

similar drastic compression, a reliance on the unspoken. There is at least behind it the dignity and weight of speech that is required, contrasted with the pecking, jerking rhythm of the first version, which carries no conviction. Here is Young again:

> Dwellers in Thebes, behold this Oedipus,
> The man who solved the riddle marvellous,
> A prince of men,
> Whose lot what citizen
> Did not with envy see,
> How deep the billows of calamity
>     Above him roll.
> Watch therefore and regard that supreme day;
> And of no mortal say
> 'That man is happy,' till
> Vexed by no grievous ill
>     He pass Life's goal.

Beside this Yeats is vivid, direct:

> Make way for Oedipus. All people said,
> 'That is a fortunate man';
> And now what storms are beating on his head!
> Call no man fortunate that is not dead.
> The dead are free from pain.

The short play, *Calvary*, is of great importance. It is linked to three themes:

The symbol of the white heron, objective solitary man, is the symbol of Yeats himself; '. . . Your Daimon would have a bird's shape because you are a solitary man.'[1] It is staring

> Upon the glittering image of a heron,
> That now is lost and now is there

in the stream: the vision of another reality in the life-stream. But

> God has not died for the white heron.

It is the development of the conflict of Yeats' so-called anti-Christianity, to be stated from another angle in 'Supernatural Songs': but with a complication that I do not yet fully understand in the lines

> But that the full is shortly gone
> And after that is crescent moon,

[1] Note to *Calvary*, *P. & C.*, p. 459.

> It's certain that the moon-crazed heron
> Would be but fishes' diet soon.[1]

The sense may perhaps lie in an allusion to 'The Phases of the
Moon', of those 'whom the last servile crescent has set free', those
who are liberated from desire:

> And having no desire they cannot tell
> What's good or bad, or what it is to triumph
> At the perfection of one's own obedience. . . .[2]

I have connected this image with Mantegna's 'Agony in the
Garden',[3] partly because of the heron image, partly because of the
lines

> Good Friday's come,
> The day whereon Christ dreams His passion through.
> He climbs up hither but as a dreamer climbs.
> The cross that but exists because He dreams it
> Shortens his breath and wears away His strength.[4]

The second theme centres on the figures of Lazarus and Judas;
Lazarus claims Christ's death for the wrong that He has done him:

> For four whole days
> I had been dead and I was lying still
> In an old comfortable mountain cavern
> When you came climbing there with a great crowd
> And dragged me to the light.[5]

There are strange overtones in that – (*cavern* – *tavern*, set against
*mountain* and *comfortable*.) We may remember 'The Three Beggars'
and 'The Mountain Tomb'. There are two striking images in
Lazarus' complaints:

> You dragged me to the light as boys drag out
> A rabbit when they have dug its hole away. . . .

and

> make way,
> Make way for Lazarus that must go search
> Among the desert places where there is nothing
> But howling wind and solitary birds.

[1] *C. Plays*, p. 450.
[2] *C.P.*, p. 183.
[3] See pp. 204–5, *supra*.
[4] *C. Plays*, p. 450.
[5] Ibid., p. 451.

Judas has betrayed Christ because He seemed all-powerful; and if a man betrays God he is the stronger of the two. There is again the mysterious heron image; when Judas planned the betrayal —

> There was no live thing near me but a heron
> So full of itself that it seemed terrified.

This goes back to the heron of *The King's Threshold*, and forward to *The Herne's Egg*; a kind of projection of the natural mind, of the solitary man, opposing God. 'I have therefore represented in Lazarus and Judas types of that intellectual despair that lay beyond His sympathy, while in the Roman soldiers I suggest a form of objectivity that lay beyond His help.'[1] The Roman soldiers, playing at dice, dancing about the Cross, bring in the third theme, developed in the note. All things are divided into Chance and Choice:

> Some worship His Choice; that is easy . . . but I have spent my life in worshipping His Chance, and that moment when I understand the immensity of His Chance is the moment when I am nearest Him.[2]

With that saying we are in the last paradoxical world of 'Supernatural Songs', with a memory of Blake behind it; and this is the key to Ribh's saying

> Hatred of God may bring the soul to God.

*A Full Moon in March* and *The King of the Great Clock Tower* were both re-written from prose plays: both on the same theme, of a stranger who comes to court a Queen, is slain for his presumption and whose severed head sings. The symbolism is plain. It is that of the Mother-Goddess and the Slain God, the ultimate victory of man over perverse, even, vicious woman, obsessed with her 'virgin cruelty', the poet triumphant after death through his magical and enduring art. It is, I think, apparent that the transposition of the prose into verse is relatively lifeless, while the songs are vigorous, crude, 'processional' in the blending of history with the people's speech, echoing in their rhythm the country jigs and ballads:

> Every loutish lad in love
> Thinks his wisdom great enough
> *What cares love for this and that?*

[1] Note to *Calvary*, *P. & C.*, p. 460.
[2] Ibid., p. 461.

Tó make all his parish stare,
As though Pythagoras wandered there.
*Crown of gold or dung of swine.*[1]

This is the only passage I have found where Yeats uses an accent-stress to make the rhythm plain. It has something in common with the more concise

> Who talks of Plato's spindle;
> What set it whirling round?
> Eternity may dwindle,
> Time is unwound,
> Dan and Jerry Lout
> Change their loves about.[2]

The swineherd goes to his death: before his severed head is brought back there is the First Attendant's song, with the old themes handled again:

> O what innkeeper's daughter
> Shared the Byzantine crown?
> Girls that have governed cities,
> Or burned great cities down,
> Have bedded with their fancy-man
> Whether a king or clown.[3]

Byzantium – the 'topless towers' of 'Long-Legged Fly' – Maud Gonne and Helen: I suggest that here is the whole early love-story of the poet re-worked, seen with a new dramatic twist; and this is evidenced in the rhythm of the Queen's song to the severed head, a rhythm which is new to Yeats, but of which the origin – and therefore the ironic significance – is immediately apparent:

> Child and darling, hear my song.
> Never cry I did you wrong;
> Cry that wrong came not from me
> But my virgin cruelty.
> Great my love before you came,
> Greater when I loved in shame,
> Great when there broke from me
> Storm of virgin cruelty.[4]

[1] *C. Plays*, p. 622. Eric Bentley has written on the contrast values of the two opposing symbols, and their psychological significance (*The Kenyon Review*, Spring 1948).
[2] 'His Bargain,' *C.P.*, p. 299.
[3] *C. Plays*, p. 627.
[4] Ibid., p. 628.

Woman craves for, is obsessed by, the sexual act. Her dance before
the severed head ends as she takes it to her breast. The Chorus of
the Attendants wonder, and solve the riddle of her hate and love.
Woman is the moon, in its changing virginity:

> I cannot face that emblem of the moon
> Nor eyelids that the unmixed heavens dart,
> Nor stand upon my feet, so great a fright
> Descends upon my savage, sunlit heart.
> What can she lack whose emblem is the moon?

FIRST ATTENDANT. But desecration and the lover's night.[1]

Woman is eternally seeking this ravishment, within her very
being; because of the 'craving in her bones'. At the end, when
human love is purified by tragedy, its essence is found by Ribh at
the tomb of Baile and Aillinn. The thought goes and comes in the
mind from a dozen different sides; sometimes in the fierce singing
rhythm of the Head:

> Clip and lip and long for more,
> Mortal men our abstracts are;
> *What of the hands on the Great Clock face?*
> All those living wretches crave
> Prerogative of the dead that have
> Sprung heroic from the grave.
> *A moment more and it tolls midnight.*[2]

And the image of the severed head is, in some curious way, integral
with the Second Coming: 'When I think of the moment before
revelation I think of Salome . . . dancing before Herod and receiving
the Prophet's head in her indifferent hands, and wonder if what
seems to us decadence was not in reality the exaltation of the
muscular flesh and of civilization perfectly achieved.'[3]

The play of *The Herne's Egg* presents a problem that I cannot
solve to my satisfaction. It was written for a dramatic festival but it
was never performed, for it could not have succeeded on the stage.
An episodic plot is built round the central mystery figure, 'The
Great Herne', whose priestess Attracta is half prophetess, half
symbolic womanhood. (She does *not*, as current Dublin gossip

---

[1] *C. Plays*, p. 629. Note the recurrence (and complexity) of the Annunciation-image in *dart*.
[2] Ibid., p. 639.
[3] *A Vision* (B), p. 273.

once suggested, represent the Virgin Mary; nor do the seven men who rape her represent the Seven Sacraments.) But it is not difficult to detect heresy and blasphemy in the play.

Exegesis and criticism of this play have now reached a complicated and perhaps final stage; the most helpful explanations seem to me to be those of F. A. C. Wilson,[1] Professor Ure[2] and H. H. Vendler.[3] The following generalizations would probably command some measure of assent:

The play is 'about' a theme that was much in Yeats' mind; the frozen and unfulfilled quality of virgin womanhood, to whom sexual union is necessary before she can attain unity, but who is obsessed with a false image of the values involved in the act, and with the conflicting attraction and repulsion of the desired contact. It is also a play 'about the transmigration and reincarnation of the soul, in which Yeats' interest in Indian thought – its foundations laid long ago in the Nineties – resumes its common round under the influence of Shree Purohit Swami. It is, and is intended to be, darkly symbolic, and contains at the same time elements of the 'heroic farce'. It is linked to the Leda-legend, and hence to the Christian Annunciation:

> Being betrothed to the Great Herne
> I know what may be known: I burn
> Not in the flesh but in the mind;
> *Chosen out of all my kind*
> That I may lie in a blazing bed
> And a bird take my maidenhead,
> *To the unbegotten I return,*
> All a womb and funeral urn.[4]

The great Herne has been interpreted in various ways. He may be Yeats' Daimon, or bird-god. I think of him as a pagan and pre-Christian deity, the apex of Yeats' heron-symbolism, the anti-type of God, the killer of the fish. The offence which has to be expiated is the theft of the eggs. It is full of mocking overtones:

> This they nailed upon a post
> On the night my leg was lost
> *Said the old, old herne that had but one leg.*

[1] *W. B. Yeats and Tradition.*
[2] *Yeats' the Dramatist.*
[3] *Yeats Vision and the Later Plays.*
[4] *C. Plays*, p. 650.

> He that a herne's egg dare steal
> Shall be changed into a fool
> *Said the old, old herne that had but one leg.*[1]

Attracta is (by her very name) a thin abstraction, as from a Morality Play; again the essence of woman who, in her delusion, has refused sexual congress. Yet she is further deluded, for she thinks she has lain with the Great Herne, as the seven men think that they have lain with her. (Is sexual intercourse a real or imagined image? What of the traditional woman–god annunciations? 'Did she put on his knowledge with his power?')

It is 'about' man's war with God:

> Now his wars on God begin:
> At stroke of midnight God shall win.

A king commits hubris, and meets his death for a few pennies, at the hands of a fool, as did Cuchulain. But now the whole universe dissolves into a multitude of fools; as it were converging towards the last of the Phases of the Moon, and defeating the man of power who proceeds to the coming of wisdom through annihilation of self.

In the background is Ferguson's *Congal*. The traditional heroisms are burlesqued, blasphemed. In counterpart are the three country girls (rather like those in Synge's *Playboy*) who represent normality, and comment upon it. Leda or Danaë enter the verse with Jove:

> All I know is that she
> Shall lie there in his bed.
> Nor shall it end until
> She lies there full of his might
> His thunderbolts in her hand.[2]

And among the last of the lyrics (for the poetry in general is not distinguished) this:

> When beak and claw their work begin
> Shall horror stir the roots of my hair?[3]
> *Sang the bride of the Herne, and the Great Herne's bride,*
> And who lie there in the cold dawn

[1] *C. Plays*, p. 651.
[2] Ibid., p. 655.
[3] cf. 'The Mother of God.'

When all that terror has come and gone?
Shall I be the woman lying there?[1]

With chair-leg and kitchen spit the Cuchulain myth is parodied. King Congal will be reborn into the shape of a donkey – 'because we were not quick enough'. (Giraldus Cambrensis describes the intercourse of the Chief of an Ulster clan with a white donkey, as part of the ceremony of installation. The Chief afterwards drinks soup made of the donkey, which is the incarnation of the mother-goddess.) This is the final farcical moment of a savage, violent play, which has too many and too complex overtones to achieve significance. But I am still puzzled about Bellini's picture of St Francis in Ecstasy, the donkey and heron side by side on the plateau on which stands his cell. And I do not think criticism has yet investigated possibilities of depth-meaning in the egg-symbolism, though I do not think such a meaning could be made to appear effective. Melchiori's thesis – see his Chapter V, called 'The Mundane Egg' – is relevant, particularly in view of Yeats' Blake studies.

*Purgatory* is a simpler play to consider. The following quotation is relevant:

> When I went every Sunday to the little lecture hall at the side of William Morris' house, Lionel Johnson said to me, his tongue loosened by slight intoxication, 'I wish those who deny eternity of punishment could realize their own unspeakable vulgarity.' I remember laughing when he said it, but for years I turned it over in my mind and it always made me uneasy.[2]

It made him uneasy, and in 1938 all matters concerning death were important. *Purgatory* is the simple story of an old man and a boy before a ruined house and a bare tree. The old man's mother had married a groom in a training stable: she died in giving birth to him; the father had burned the house when drunk: the old man killed him with a knife, and thrust the body into the burning house. He was then sixteen years old. Now he and his own son, just sixteen also, have come back. They watch the house. Hoof-beats come up the grass-grown avenue, and the scene of the bridal night is re-enacted. The boy cannot at first hear or see, and attempts to slip away with his father's money-bag, while the father watches:

[1] *C. Plays*, p. 665.
[2] *Irish Statesman* (Hone Papers.)

> Do not let him touch you! It is not true
> That drunken men cannot beget,
> And if he touch he must beget
> And you must bear his murderer.
> Deaf! Both deaf! If I should throw
> A stick or a stone they would not hear;
> And that's a proof my wits are out.[1]

The boy threatens to kill him: then at last perceives the ghosts, and is horror-struck. So the father stabs his son, with the same knife he had used on his own father, so that the horrible re-enaction of the scene may cease:

*(He stabs again and again. The window grows dark.)*

> 'Hush-a-bye baby, thy father's a knight,
> Thy mother a lady, lovely and bright.'
> No, that is something that I read in a book,
> And if I sing it must be to my mother,
> And I lack rhyme.[2]

But it is useless; the hoof-beats return; there are many instances in the past of the use of that ominous sound:

> Her mind cannot hold up that dream.
> Twice a murderer and all for nothing,
> And she must animate that dead night
> Not once but many times!
>         O God,
> Release my mother's soul from its dream!
> Mankind can do no more. Appease
> The misery of the living and the remorse of the dead.[3]

The verse of the play has been marked out by T. S. Eliot's tribute to it:

> 'It was only in his last play *Purgatory* that he solved his problem of speech in verse, and laid all his successors under obligation to him.'[4]

I do not think that Yeats' technique in this play has, in the event, much prominence as a model, but it is remarkable for the subtlety and strength of the verse. The structure is that of a compressed Nōh; the theme, that of the 'dreaming back'.[5] It gains much through the simplicity of its symbolism, the fidelity of description:

[1] *C. Plays*, p. 686.
[2] Ibid., p. 688.
[3] Ibid., p. 689.
[4] *Poetry and Drama*, 1951, p. 20.
[5] *v.* p. 217

The floor is gone, the windows gone,
And where there should be a roof there's sky,
And here a bit of an egg-shell thrown
Out of a jackdaw's nest.[1]

He can use with subtlety the full rhetorical diapason (Coole Park is much in memory):

Great people lived and died in this house;
Magistrates, colonels, members of Parliament,
Captains and Governors, and long ago
Men that had fought at Aughrim and the Boyne. . . .
But he killed the house; to kill a house
Where great men grew up, married, died,
I here declare a capital offence.[2]

The incantations are delicately adjusted in the fourth and last lines. But the verse can shift its rhythms quickly, come alive with descriptive tension:

It's louder now because he rides
Upon a gravelled avenue
All grass today. The hoof-beat stops
He has gone to the other side of the house,
Gone to the stable, put the horse up.
She has gone down to open the door.
This night she is no better than her man
And does not mind that he is half drunk,
She is mad about him . . .[3]

The fall of the great houses, the memory of 'Castle Dargan's ruin all lit . . .'[4] fuses with the burnings in The Troubles. It seems likely that he thought of Dorothy Wellesley's poem 'Matrix', which he much admired:

A burnt-out house is the mind.
Or a house in building? A room,
Plaster wet on the floor,
Generations afoot, ghosts born,
When the first dweller enters the door?[5]

[1] C. Plays, p. 682.
[2] Ibid. p. 683.
[3] Ibid. p. 685.
[4] Ibid., p. 640. 'A brawling squireen lived there' – v. Autobiographies, pp. 53 et. seq.
[5] Selected Poems, p. 101.

*The Death of Cuchulain* served, as did 'Under Ben Bulben', to bring together many threads of past thought —

> Character isolated by a deed
> To engross the present and dominate memory.[1]

The dance before the severed head comes from *A Full Moon in March*; and behind are *Salome* and Mantegna. The protagonists are Cuchulain, his mistress Eithne, Aoife, the pale fierce woman whose son he had once begotten, but who is now erect and white-haired, whom he had met at the Hawk's Well, whose son he had killed on Baile's Strand; the Blind Man who had stood between Cuchulain and the sea at Baile's Strand, and Emer, Cuchulain's wife. And lastly, there is the Morrigu, the woman with a crow's head, the war-goddess. All of that mythology that has survived its testing, that can still decorate or explain a poet's heroic mask, is there on the stage.

The pattern works itself out swiftly. Cuchulain, who is the poet, and the hero of the Rebellion (remembering the statue by Oliver Sheppard in the Post Office) stands between these women, his mistress Eithne, and his son's mother, Aoife, and his wife. He goes out to the fatal battle and returns, mortally wounded, to fasten himself by his belt to the pillar lest he should be seen to fall. Aoife has wounded him and will kill him. To make certain of him she winds her veil about him. All the actions are symbolical. Before she can kill him, she must question him; but before she can do either the Blind Man of *On Baile's Strand* comes in. He has been advised to kill Cuchulain, for Maeve has promised him twelve pennies for a reward.

> CUCHULAIN. Twelve pennies! What better reason for killing a man?
>     You have a knife, but have you sharpened it?
> BLIND MAN. I keep it sharp because it cuts my food.[2]

The Blind Man cuts off his head: the Morrigu, the war-goddess, a woman with a crow's head, comes in to dance before the severed head. At the end of her dance there is the stage-direction:

> There is silence and in the silence a few faint bird notes.

(So in 'Cuchulain Comforted'[3] at the end of the vision

1 'The Circus Animals' Desertion', *C.P.*, p. 391.
2 *C. Plays*, p. 702.
3 *C.P.*, p. 395.

> They sang, but had nor human tunes nor words,
> Though all was done in common as before;
>
> They had changed their throats and had the throats of birds.

since this is the country of Tir-nan-ogue.)

Then the music changes to that of an Irish fair. The style brightens, leaving the three musicians; two with pipe and drum (for the play is both Mystery and Morality), the third as a street-singer, singing to a Dublin ballad rhythm, jerky, violent; all mythology, measurement, sexuality and the supernatural focused in a point:

> I meet those long pale faces,
> Hear their great horses, then
> Recall what centuries have passed
> Since they were living men.[1]
> That there are still some living
> That do my limbs unclothe,
> But that the flesh my flesh has gripped
> I both adore and loathe.
>
> *(Pipe and drum music.)*
>
> Are those things that men adore and loathe
> Their sole reality?
> What stood in the Post Office
> With Pearse and Connolly?
> What comes out of the mountain
> Where men first shed their blood,
> Who thought Cuchulain till it seemed
> He stood where they had stood?[2]

I do not wish to labour the possible analogies, though there is precedent enough in Yeats' habit of thought. But it is very clear that the plays must be studied at each stage with the poetry, since they interlock so closely; and that through them the pattern of the poet's concern with specific problems can be perceived. In this last work the man had

> . . . thought Cuchulain till it seemed
> He stood where they had stood. . . .

But Cuchulain was another self; the lover of the pale fierce woman;

[1] We may recall John Eglinton: 'There is no such race living now, none so fine-proportioned.' *The Literary Movement in Ireland*, p. 96.

[2] *C. Plays*, p. 704.

the fighter of the waves, perhaps, of popular misjudgement; the victim of the six mortal wounds; the stranger whose head is severed by virgin cruelty, and yet retains the power of speech for final consummation or revenge;

> What's prophesied? What marvel is
> Where the dead and living kiss?
> *What of the hands of the Great Clock face?*
> Sacred Virgil never sang
> All the marvel there begun,
> But there's a stone upon my tongue.
> *A moment more and it tolls midnight.*[1]

The Morrigu and the birds, the Great Herne, the king of the Great Clock Tower that will toll the stroke of midnight – all these appear to be symbols of God for the man who could not write of Him.

Behind all these, there should be remembered the speech of the Ghost of Cuchulain in *The Only Jealousy of Emer*, which, like the verse of 'Under Ben Bulben', gathers up many experiences:

> Old memories:
> A dying boy, with handsome face
> Upturned upon a beaten place;
> A sacred yew-tree on a strand;
> A woman that held in steady hand,
> In all the happiness of her youth
> Before her man had broken troth,
> A burning wisp to light the door;
> And many a round or crescent more;
> Dead men and women. Memories
> Have pulled my head upon my knees.[2]

---

[1] *C. Plays*, p. 640. Cf. 'But when I think of that my tongue's a stone'.

[2] *P. & C.*, p. 370. Compare the much-compressed version in *C. Plays*, p. 291.

## Mosaic at Ostia

*'Straddling each a dolphin's back*
*And steadied by a fin,*
*Those Innocents relive their death . . .'*

## Bordone (?): St George and the Dragon

*'In this altarpiece the knight,*
*Who grips his long spear so to push*
*That dragon through the fading light*
*Loved the lady . . .'*

'Miracle had its playtime where
In damask clothed and on a seat
Chryselephantine, cedar-boarded,
His majestic Mother sat
Stitching at a purple hoarded . . .'
(ITALIAN SCHOOL, PAINTER UNKNOWN)

# CHAPTER SIXTEEN

# The Achievement of Style

By the study of those impulses that shape themselves into words without context we find our thought, for we do not seek truth in argument or in books but clarification of what we already believe. – *1930 Diary*.

Second-rate poets attempt to reach mysticism through vagueness. Great poets use the compound or multiple symbol to reflect the image of their thought. – C. M. Bowra.

Pour le vrai poète, la langue n'est jamais assez particulière; il est obligé d'employer les mots en les répétant pour les délivrer de leur sens usuel, usé, trop général et pour leur conférer cette signification unique, évocatrice d'une seule réalité spirituelle trés concréte, à quoi il veut atteindre.

Béguin, ii, 114.

We have seen that in Yeats' poetic theory 'symbolism' is a wide term, and on its perfection of function all style depends. In certain contexts the symbol appears to be no more than a successful and emotion-charged metaphor.[1] One aspect of the growth of technique will therefore be measured by the contextual precision in the use of symbols, and by the meaning which he places upon them by repetition, modification, and rhythmic setting. The tower symbol is built up in half a dozen metres that each fulfil a specific function; from the deliberate dragging incantation of

I declare this tower is my symbol: I declare

with its loose Alexandrine, to the controlled nostalgia of

I climb to the tower-top and lean upon broken stone,
A mist that is like blown snow is sweeping over all. . . .[2]

[1] *E.g.* 'Metaphors are not profound enough to be moving, when they are not symbols'. *E. & I.*, p. 156.
[2] 'I see Phantoms of Hatred . . .', *C.P.*, p. 231. Cf. also, 'Mad as the mist and snow'.

L

In her book *Elizabethan and Metaphysical Imagery*, Miss Rosemond Tuve has praised many aspects of Yeats' style as traditional: in particular his adherence to decorum, to the division between the 'high, middle, and low styles': and in a footnote so comprehensive as to require quotation, 'One could not find better Elizabethan examples of decorum justly and delicately maintained in the character of images, and 'governing': absence or presence of tropes; their complexity, logical tautness, or emotional reach; amplifying or diminishing suggestions through epithet or detail; brevity of expansion; amount and character of rhetorical ornament; all adjusted by syntactical or metrical means, to tone.'[1] This aristocracy of style was wholly conscious,[2] and developed with his training: it is often lacking in the early period. Yeats' impatience with the early work, the continuous revision, suggest a high and fastidious taste. Perhaps it is to this that MacNeice referred when he spoke of him as 'using words with the precision of a dandy'.[3] Against it we may set Yeats' own statement: 'I have before me an ideal expression in which all that I have, clay and spirit alike, assist; it is as though I most approximate towards that expression when I carry with me the greatest possible amount of hereditary thought and feeling, even national and family hatred and pride.'[4]

One aspect of the traditional style was Yeats' fondness for the 'magnificence' of proper names and for enriched strongly-cadenced phrases. His ear delights in sonorities: Plotinus, Phidias, Salamis, Empedocles; Rhadamanthus, Smaragdine, Mareotic.[5] He lingers on, tastes, whole cadenced phrases and heavily-evocative names:

> Troy passed away in one high funeral gleam,
> And Usna's children died.

> Doomed like Odysseus and the wandering ships,
> And proud as Priam murdered with his peers.

> Men that had fought at Aughrim and the Boyne.

[1] Page 235.
[2] *v.* p. 122 *supra.*
[3] Op. cit., p. 20.
[4] 1930 *Diary*, p. 6.
[5] Gogarty's recent memoir tells of his pleasure on being diagnosed by a Spanish doctor: 'I would rather be called "cardio-sclerotic" than "Lord of Lower Egypt".'

Cuchulain fought the ungovernable sea.

And fought with the invulnerable tide.

. . . all that sensuality of shade . . .

A verse from Nashe or Browning lives with him, to be repeated often; sometimes it is difficult to see why, or even what a particular phrase meant to him:

> the scream of Juno's peacock

> When the goddess Athene came to Achilles in the battle,
> she took him by his yellow hair.

The high style can be counterpointed against the colloquial (Synge uses this technique effectively) and united in the robust and easy-going gait of the verse. As technique develops, the traditional devices are used more sparingly, more cogently, and in sharper definition; the syntax transmits Yeats' energy or 'intensity' through the abandonment of the slacker adjectives of the early period, and through the strong assertions of the verbs.

In Yeats' criticism of great poets, though not of his contemporaries, the taste appears to be exact; even though in the comment on the imagery of others he must have recourse to images of his own. '. . . or take some line that is quite simple, that gets its beauty from its place in a story, and see how it flickers with the light of the many symbols that have given the story its beauty, as a sword-blade may flicker with the light of burning towers.'[1]

The achievement of style is partly in this swift flashing of the images; the ease with which the correspondences are moved back and forth, juxtaposed mentally and pictorially and rhythmically. For a simple example:

> Things out of perfection sail,
> And all their swelling canvas wear,
> Nor shall the self-begotten fail
> Though fantastic men suppose
> Building-yard and stormy shore,
> Winding-sheet and swaddling-clothes.[2]

[1] *E. & I.*, p. 156. Note the convergence of two dominants, the Sword and the Trojan legend; with their submerged meanings.
[2] 'Old Tom Again,' *C.P.*, p. 306.

At first hearing it is effortless, controlled, precise: yet it is so tightly woven as to be difficult. The first line may mean either – 'Things are generated by perfection and move onward from it', or 'Things pass out of this state of perfection, forward into something that is not perfection, *yet* they are still noble and in their apparent full strength', for the interpretation depends on the tone given to *out*. The ship image is traditional – Shakespeare, Bridges, a dozen others – and yet new-minted here. *Wear* has a double or triple meaning: it is right, technically, for a ship's canvas set: she *wears* it, but it is only temporary, not integral with substance: and *wear* links up (actively) with the passive *swaddling-clothes* at the end. The *self-begotten* is both the human mind, and God; the mind is eternal, self-generating. Mind, for which alone the reality of things, in perfection or imperfection, exists, has no explicable origin in building-yard or Nativity. *Suppose*, carrying its heavy stress and forcing a voice-pause before the *b-* of the next line, is half-technical, the hypothesis of philosophy. In the last two lines the sequence reverses itself, as it were diagonally, so that the relationship is, rhythmically, 'building-yard – winding-sheet' and 'stormy shore – swaddling clothes', and time becomes in consequence a kind of cyclic movement. The final imperfect rhyme holds up the thought, with its easy violence, and forces the voice to drop.

So again the *terribilità* of the dragging, remote half-smothered rhythm in 'Oil and Blood':

> In tombs of gold and lapis lazuli
> Bodies of holy men and women *exude*

– the heavy word for oil-mill or grape, for richness, fertility, stressed deliberately against the beat:

> – Miraculous oil, odour of violet.

> But under heavy loads of trampled clay
> Lie bodies of the vampires full of blood;
> Their shrouds are bloody and their lips are wet.[1]

– where the lines are stripped bare of images, and only this sinister inexplicable thing remains. In the 'mechanical little poem' of 'Mad as the Mist and Snow'[2] this compressed suggestion reaches its height.

[1] *C.P.*, p. 270.
[2] Ibid., p. 301.

I think the opening lines may be deliberately a half-reminiscence of the formula for the Hand of Glory,[1] to set the tone of incantation; they also represent of course the normal protection of a house on the West Coast by the Atlantic, where windows are shuttered and buttressed with wooden bars from the inside. The night is mysterious, with the *Macbeth* thought in *foul*, reinforcing the suggestion of incantation:

> Bolt and bar the shutter,
> For the foul winds blow:
> Our minds are at their best this night,
> And I seem to know
> That everything outside us is
> *Mad as the mist and snow.*

The heavy accent falls on *seem*: even here, in the security of the house, no certainty is possible. Everything outside us – both in the storm and in that which lies beyond our minds (Berkeley again) – is mad: but mad without order, vague and chaotic. For the moment there is security in the mind. He glances at the books on the shelves:

> Horace there by Homer stands,
> Plato stands below. . . .

Epicurean poise and Stoic detachment meet in Horace, and the life of the 'last Romantic' is still possible in Homer; Plato, ordered rational wisdom, perhaps moral propaganda also,[2] stands *below* – with the word carrying the heavy stress, so that the meaning is more than that of mere physical position:

> And here is Tully's open page.
> How many years ago
> Were you and I unlettered lads
> *Mad as the mist and snow?*

He has been reading Cicero, for the page is open: perhaps at the *De Amicitia*, for friendship has been long, and is worth consideration now. *Unlettered* picks up the thought and kills every suggestion of a nostalgia such as Housman's; the mist and snow are changed to a new kind of madness, the kindly 'wildness of youth'. It moves on:

[1]         'Open lock, to the Dead Man's knock
            Fly bolt, and bar, and band. . . .'
[2] See *A Vision* (B), p. 270.

You ask what makes me sigh, old friend,
What makes me shudder so?

*Sigh* for the past, *shudder* in anticipation of what is to come: and
the two, past and present, are joined in the next line, to anticipate
the manner of locking home the three authors, and all their values,
with time:

I shudder and I sigh to think
That even Cicero —

with the stress falling, half-serious, half-ironic, on *even* Cicero —

And many-minded Homer were

with the epithet 'many-minded' thrown there in contempt of
'unlettered lads' before all are gathered up into yet another tonal
modification of the refrain:

*Mad as the mist and snow.*

For one of Yeats' strangest gifts is that of making the refrains of
certain poems carry (when read aloud) subtle shifts of meaning from
verse to verse. One can do no more than gesture towards them. In
the first stanza the line relates to the world outside the room, and
the accent dwells a little on *mist* and *snow*. In the second it picks
up, from *unlettered lads*, qualities of wildness, strength, vitality,
and the accent shifts forward to the opening *Mad*, with its Anglo-
Irish overtones. In the third the stresses carry equal weight; both
unifying the poem and completing a single level assertion. Something
of the same thing happens in 'Crazy Jane on God',[1] 'Her Anxiety'[2]
and above all in 'Three Things'.[3] There are striking tone-changes
in 'The Curse of Cromwell'[4] and in 'Long-Legged Fly'.[5] We do
not find these in the patriotic ballads ('The O'Rahilly' is a possible
exception), and the few refrains of the early ballads are no more than
musical patterns in the pre-Raphaelite manner.

The accumulative significance of past usage of language is
apparent in 'Stream and Sun at Glendalough'.[6] It is slight in its
first intention. 'Stream and gliding sun' in their 'intricate motions' –
the word *intricate*, bearing its stress, as it were, against the grain,
is typical, since even nature's patterning is complex. The joy of it

[1] *C.P.*, p. 293.        [2] Ibid., p. 297.        [3] Ibid., p. 300.
[4] Ibid., p. 350.        [5] Ibid., p. 380.        [6] Ibid., p. 288.

is only glimpsed as the poet returns to himself, for Yeats was never a nature poet, and his thought must seek the centre before it spreads outward again:

> Some stupid thing that I had done
> Made my attention stray.

The next line

> Repentance keeps my heart impure

is a more strident echo of 'A Dialogue of Self and Soul':

> When such as I cast out remorse
> So great a sweetness flows into the breast . . .

And the following lines, with a kind of humility, are set in this deliberately flat slowed rhythm to give the fall before the climax.

> But what am I that dare
> Fancy that I can
> Better conduct myself or have more
> Sense than a common man?

Everything is tentative still: in the first stanza the heart *seemed*, only seemed, gay; here it is 'dare fancy'. Then in the final stanza,

> What motion . . .

– picking up the *motions* of the opening stanza, but using it now with cosmic significance —

> What motion of the sun or stream
> Or eyelid shot the gleam
> That pierced my body through?
> What made me live like these that seem
> Self-born, born anew?

*Eyelid* would refer to the glance of a woman.[1] *Shot the gleam – pierced my body* is the Annunciation-Image, the star that shot an ear; Crivelli's Annunciation, perhaps, in a new setting; so that the next two lines, with the re-birth image, the assertion of unity with the world, fall into place with precision. But still it is *seem*: there is no certainty, the sense of unity is (as perhaps always)

[1] Cf.    'I cannot face that emblem of the moon
              Nor eyelids that the unmixed heavens dart.'

momentary. There is no Wordsworthian certainty like that inherent
in

> And then my heart with pleasure fills
> And dances with the daffodils.

The music of a remembered phrase could beget a new rhythm.
'I am of Ireland'[1] is based on *The Irish Dancer*.[2] In the original

> I am of Ireland
> And of the holy land
> Of Ireland.
> Good sir, pray I thee,
> For of sainte charite
> Come and dance with me
> In Ireland.

The opening verses became:

> '*I am of Ireland*
> *And the Holy Land of Ireland,*
> *And time runs on,' cried she.*[3]
> '*Come out of charity,*
> *Come dance with me in Ireland.*'

> One man, one man alone
> In that outlandish gear,
> One solitary man
> Of all that rambled there
> Had turned his stately head.
> 'That is a long way off,
> And time runs on,' he said,
> 'And the night grows rough.'

He had heard the ghost of his tune in the old poem; it is snatched
up, smoothed, and elaborated, to give harmony with what follows.
We can see the key-phrase 'And time runs on', played on, integrated,
in the next stanza. *Outlandish, gear, rambled* – the last two words
have in Anglo-Irish nuances a meaning not easy to define – are
used to set off, so truculently, the grotesqueness of the speaker;

[1] *C.P.*, p. 303.
[2] Bodleian MS. Rawlinson D.913. Sisam, *Fourteenth Century Prose and
Verse*, p. 166. Yeats found this in St John D. Seymour's *Anglo-Irish Literature,
1200–1582*, in whose spelling I have quoted it.
[3] 'It is of more interest to us, as it is placed in the mouth of an Irish girl,
and so presumably was composed by an Anglo-Irish minstrel' (Seymour,
p. 98).

and then we are confronted, suddenly, with *stately* head. That gives the meaning of the keyword *solitary*, and of the *outlandish gear*, and all falls into place, for this is Yeats himself: and the dance is of Ireland, of Irish Politics:

> 'The fiddlers are all thumbs,
> Or the fiddle-string accursed,
> The drums and the kettledrums
> And the trumpets all are burst,
> And the trombone,' cried he,
> 'The trumpet and trombone,'
> And cocked a malicious eye,
> 'But time runs on, runs on.'

The emblem of the trumpeter goes back to 'Nineteen Hundred and Nineteen', the army with its little casual wars to give it exercise:

> Parliament and king
> Thought that unless a little powder burned
> The trumpeters might burst with trumpeting
> And yet it lack all glory. . . .[1]

There is a similar remaking of an old tune in the phrase taken from *A Winter's Tale*:

> When you do dance, I wish you
> A wave o' the sea. . . .

caught up in 'The Fiddler of Dooney',[2] with its complex lilting rhythm:

> When I play on my fiddle in Dooney,
> Folk dance like a wave of the sea. . . .

Even when the subject might have been treated with banality, the sheer instinct for rightness of phrasing gives it this 'flashing brightness'

> Although the summer sunlight gild
> Cloudy leafage of the sky,

– where *gild* holds the attention by stress, and leads to the thought of its superficiality, and *cloudy leafage* is shock-enforced by *sky*, so that meaning is thrown back on *gild*.

[1] *C.P.*, p. 233
[2] Ibid., p. 82.

> Or wintry moonlight sink the field
> In storm-scattered *intricacy*,
> I cannot look thereon,
> Responsibility so weighs me down.[1]

Here the correspondence is perfect; not only for the visual image of the field made *intricate* by the storm in the moonlight, the clouds showing the landscape fitfully, but also for the tones of *gild* – *sink* – *intricacy*, related to the mood of depression. (So, perhaps, in Donne's 'Twicknam Garden'.)

This use of the strange, charged word is almost unerring. I confess the poem 'In Memory of Eva Gore-Booth and Con Markiewicz'[2] is spoilt for me, by the seeming-forced rhyme of Lissadell – gazelle; though indeed there is no other rhyme for that once-great house.[3] In the fifth line, technique returns:

> But a raving autumn *shears*
> Blossom from the summer's wreath —

while the violence and overtones of cruelty and casualness (as of the Blind Fury) give perfectly the destruction, as it were to nakedness, of both the beauty and the wisdom of the two girls: the *raving* autumn being the madness that came with political leadership in middle age, related to all that 'delirium of the brave' of 'September 1913'.[4]

Even in the poems of hatred there is the certainty of control, grammar and idiom continuing to give each word its full bitter value:

> They must to keep their certainty accuse
> All that are different of a base intent —[5]

where the levelling stresses on *their certainty*, emphasized by the pause after *certainty*, give the necessary ironic value to the 'leaders

[1] 'Vacillation,' V, *C.P.*, p. 284. The word was pronounced by Yeats 'intríc'acy'; compare 'In Memory of Major Robert Gregory', x:
> In all lovely intric‿acies of a house,
and 'fanatic' as 'fán-atic' in 'Remorse for Intemperate Speech'.

[2] *C.P.*, p. 263.

[3] Perhaps Yeats had different associations from T. Sturge Moore's poem, 'The Gazelles'.

[4] *C.P.*, p. 120.

[5] 'The Leaders of the Crowd', ibid., p. 207.

of the crowd', and weight and power of accent to *accuse*; which in
turn allows the momentum to carry forward to the next line:

> Pull down established honour; hawk for news
> Whatever their loose phantasy invent
> And murmur it with bated breath, as though
> The abounding gutter had been Helicon
> Or calumny a song.

*Hawk* is of the newsboy and is linked in the image-cluster to
*gutter* and *calumny*;[1] but, throwing back in the line, or modified
by what is before it, there seems an image of the hounds and the
deer in *pull down established honour*; and *loose* has in it immorality
as well as vagueness. The gutter is *abounding*;[2] again the extra
syllable holding up the stress to fall more heavily on the second
syllable.

> How can they know
> Truth flourishes where the student's lamp has shone,
> And there alone, that have no solitude?

where the central symbol is from 'The Phases of the Moon':[3]

> He has found, after the manner of his kind,
> Mere images; chosen this place to live in
> Because, it may be, of the candle-light
> From the far tower where Milton's Platonist
> Sat late. . . .
> And now he seeks in book or manuscript
> What he shall never find.

If it is objected that my emphasis on the repetition of images,
the echoing of phrases and rhythm, is overdone, I reply that Yeats
himself insists on the importance of this recognition of unity in the
body of a poet's imagery, and of the 'stitching and unstitching' of
the verse by which delicacy and complexity of rhythm is achieved.

[1] He uses this image again: cf.

> When all that story's finished, what's the news?

('The Choice', *C.P.*, p. 278.) This was originally a stanza of 'Coole Park and
Ballylee'.

[2] Cf.

> Blind and leaders of the blind
> Drinking the foul ditch where they lie . . .

and

> Or into that most *fecund* ditch of all. . . .

[3] *C.P.*, p. 183.

Yeats' sense of control is evident, too, in the violence of the grotesque; which above all modes, tests fidelity to an image. 'His Memories'[1] is an extreme example of integrity and compression:

> We should be hidden from their eyes,
> Being but holy shows[2]
> And bodies broken like a thorn
> Whereon the bleak north blows,
> To think of buried Hector
> And that none living knows.
>
> The women take so little stock
> In what I do or say
> They'd sooner leave their cosseting
> To hear a jackass bray;
> My arms are like the twisted thorn
> And yet there beauty lay . . .

All the tides of memory and emblem are meeting. Maud Gonne, and later, her daughter too, are Helen —

> Hector is dead, and there's a light in Troy. . . .
>
> Was there another Troy for her to burn?

With Horace and Villon and Wyat standing at his shoulder, the savage idiom of the first four lines is set against the restraint of the last two. The three stanzas interlock; the first and second through the thorn, with its own associations, and the first and third through Hector:

> The first of all the tribe lay there

— the three light accents before it brings the beat down contemptuously on *tribe* —

> And did such pleasure take —
> She who had brought great Hector down

---

[1] *C.P.*, p. 251.
[2] 'Shows' has, in the Irish usage, a half-contemptuous sense that may be intended here. It is worth remarking that Yeats quotes frequently, of himself and of other writers, Aristotle's 'To write well, express yourself like the common people, but think like a wise man'. Another passage of Aristotle is of interest in connection with this technique: 'For by deviating in exceptional cases from the normal idiom, the language will gain distinction; while, at the same time, the partial conformity with usage will give perspicuity' (*Poetics*, xxii, 4).

> And put all Troy to wreck —
> That she cried into this ear,
> 'Strike me if I shriek.'

I do not find (against the views of many critics) a falling off in technique in *Last Poems*; since I believe the disapproval that has been expressed of this group is based on a misunderstanding of the different range and tone. There is a fulfilment of the promise made in 'Sailing to Byzantium', that with the coming of infirmity

> Soul clap its hands and sing, and louder sing
> For every tatter in its mortal dress.

With old age, and the tomb near, and the phase of the Hunchback passing into that of the Saint and then the Fool, a poet might remember in his 'loose imagination' to be wild, and lustful, and a singer of street ballads, and a prophet, all in turn. But when the sudden widening of intention is understood, and the kinds of poetry separated out from one another, there is no falling off of technique. 'The Pilgrim' is as perfect in its mode as the lines 'To Dorothy Wellesley' are in theirs. The difficult and impressive 'Cuchulain Comforted', with its new *terza rima* metre, is Yeats himself, the Anti-Self:

> A man that had six mortal wounds, a man
> Violent and famous, strode among the dead;
> Eyes stared out of the branches and were gone.[1]

. . . 'You cannot give a body to something that moves beyond the senses, unless your words are as subtle, as full of mysterious life, as the body of a flower or of a woman.'[2] The poet who uses symbols is concerned with this movement beyond the senses; and even when the symbols are reckoned up, and their fusion or apportion perceived and valued, there still remains the problem of the 'mysterious life' of their rhythmic setting.

I have insisted throughout on the need for reading aloud all Yeats' poetry. Few possess the necessary sensitivity to tone, pitch, intonation to interpret it. Only then are we aware of the immense complexity of his manipulation of sound, of which he himself had written in the essay *The Symbolism of Poetry*.[3] These complexities

[1] *C.P.*, p. 395.
[2] *E. & I*, p. 164.
[3] Ibid., p. 153.

have been studied with admirable sensitivity by David Masson[1] and I know of no comparable work which applies to the poetry the work of Paget, Macdermot and Grammont. It seems probable that there is a large field of investigation here, particularly as regards the Anglo-Irish variations on the 'darker' vowel sounds, and probably of consonantal values also.

Almost any poem of the 'great period' – the post-1936 work seems to become coarser in this respect – will serve to illustrate this technique. We may glance at 'The New Faces'.[2] It is addressed to Lady Gregory; the scene is Coole Park:

> If you, that have grown old, were the first dead

the deep vowels of *grown old* balance the lighter ones of *first dead*, *first* set in tension against *old* both phonetically and semantically. The next line

> Neither catalpa tree nor scented lime

is as it were enclosed by the *n-m* sounds, and falls away from the arresting strangeness of *catalpa* to the gentle vowels of the last two words —

> Should hear my living feet, nor would I tread

is relatively 'neutral', picking up the rhyme-word but dwelling lightly on it, and providing an 'interlock' between *living, old.* And the *t-* of *t*read prepares us for the explosive arrogant consonants of the next line —

> Where we wrought *th*a*t* shall *b*reak the *t*ee*th* of *T*ime

which are hardened by the *voyelles claires* of the last three nouns. So the first question ends. The next line, carrying four full stresses and two half-ones, bridges the caesura with the *a*-vowels:

> *L*et the new faces ‖ play wha*t t*ricks they will

where the homeliness of the contemptuous idiom is emphasized again by the scorn of the *t*-sounds, and the lightening of the

[1] *ELH.*, Vol. 20. No. 2. June 1953.
[2] *C.P.*, p. 238. It was written in 1912, but not published until 1928. See Jeffares, *R.E.S.*, Oct 1947, pp. 349–53: *Man and Poet* (1963), p. 163.

vowels. Is there a suggestion of mere superficial appearance in *faces*? In the next line

> – In the old rooms: night can outbalance day

*old* picks up the first line, in a new context (venerable tradition), and the deep *o*-sounds reinforce the contempt for the preceding *play what tricks they will*. *Night can outbalance day* has overtones in Yeats' mind ('For wisdom is the property of the dead', 'Think of ancestral night' . . .): the poetic achievement of Coole remains. The *shadows* draw together *dead, old rooms, night*: the lengthening and deepening vowels of

> Our shadows rove . . .

culminate on the stress of *rove* (moving mysteriously, lightly, perhaps aimlessly, as a swan on the water); but we shift to the lighter harder sounds of

> – the garden gravel still

where the associations of *garden* are pulled back by *gravel*, which becomes more actual by contrast – sound against silence – under the feet of the ghosts.

For a last example of the achievement of style I take a late, complex, and little-known poem, 'Ribh at the Tomb of Baile and Aillinn'.[1] Its conception is described in a letter to Mrs Shakespear: 'I have another poem in my head where a monk reads his breviary at midnight upon the tomb of long-dead lovers on the anniversary of their death, for on that night they are united above the tomb, their embrace being not partial but a conflagration of the entire body – and so shedding the light he reads by.'[2] The fable may well have been a kind of correlative of an incident which had struck his imagination from the Japanese play *Nishikigi*, in which two lovers sorrow, as ghosts, lament for their unconsummated love, until the prayers of the priest whom they have brought to their tomb unite them in marriage and set them free. Ribh, who is, I think, yet another image, perhaps the last, and of the 'Saint Phase' of the Phases of the Moon, is 'an imaginary critic of St Patrick. His

[1] *C.P.*, p. 327.
[2] Hone, *Life*, p. 438.

Christianity, come perhaps from Egypt like so much early Irish
Christianity, echoes pre-Christian thought.'[1] The basic reference is
to the love story of Baile and Aillinn, on which Yeats had made a
poem of that name in 1903. The two were lovers, 'but Ængus,
the Master of Love, wishing them to be happy in his own land
among the dead, told to each a story of the other's death, so that
their hearts were broken and they died.'[2] They are changed into
white swans, linked by a golden chain. Where Baile's body lay
there sprang a yew tree, and a wild apple where Aillinn's was; and
love stories were written on tablets of thin board, 'made of the apple
and the yew', which are bound together, never to be disunited, in the
hands of art. There are already important associations with the
lovers' tomb: 'When Merlin in Chrestien de Troyes loved Ninian he
showed her a cavern adorned with gold mosaics and made by a
prince for his beloved, and told her that those lovers died upon the
same day, and were laid "in the chamber where they found delight".'[3]
There is also the story of 'The Three Bushes' in *Last Poems*. It is
of interest to watch the recharging of the symbols with an entirely
new emotion. The poem should, perhaps, be interpreted with much
of the previous poetry in mind:

> Because you have found me in the pitch-dark night
> With open book you ask me what I do.
> Mark and digest my tale, carry it afar
> To those that never saw this tonsured head
> Nor heard this voice that ninety years have cracked.
> Of Baile and Aillinn you need not speak,
> All know their tale, all know what leaf and twig,
> What juncture of the apple and the yew,
> Surmount their bones; but speak what none have heard.

The dramatic opening, the 'attack', is superbly phrased. *You*, the
reader of the poem, the discoverer of Ribh by the tomb, as mysterious as the Wedding Guest of 'The Ancient Mariner', runs through
this expository first stanza. The words are put in his mouth,
creating the tension of the unspoken – *you ask me what I do* – *you
need not speak* – leading up to the prophetic or liturgical *speak what
none have heard*. There is the urgent mystery of the *open* book in the

---

[1] *A Full Moon in March*, Preface, p. vi.
[2] *C.P.*, p. 459.
[3] *A Vision* (A), p. 197.

*pitch-dark night*: wisdom awaiting the symbolic light; *pitch-dark*, the homely idiom of the soft opaque dark with its overtones of defilement, to be caught up again and lifted, as it were, in the last stanza by the heavier, more mysterious *pitch-dark atmosphere. Mark and digest*, the insolence of the catechism phrase used for the disciple, throws forward to *my* tale, which becomes personal, mysterious; strengthened by the dragging unexpected dactyl of *carry it afar*. This *tonsured* head (there are no redundant words in this poem) is half-contemptuous; reinforced in tone by the next line —

> Nor heard this voice that ninety years have *cracked*.

where *cracked* carries its ambiguity of physical breaking of the body, of the prophetical faculty grown mad, as well as the breaking of the voice. So far, every word is from 'the book of the people': now the tone changes, as the proper names call up the great legend of the lovers. But it is not of *their* tale that he will speak. All know of the first symbolic miracle:

> – all know what leaf and twig,
> What juncture of the apple and the yew,
> Surmount their bones.

I do not know clearly what these lines mean. The *leaf* and *twig*, symbols of fertility, suggest the living tree set against the grave, and physical resurrection; the *juncture*, half-astrological from *conjunction*, half-softened, as by the touch of branches, by the lightening of the second *u*-sound in the word, of the apple[1] (youth and sex) and the yew (death), seems to be echoed and elevated in the sound by *surmount*: with its overtone of the two qualities that both endure beyond the bones, and rise physically above them beside the tomb. The joining

---

[1] With, of course, many references beside that of Eden. Compare, for example:

> A cockerel
> Crew from a blossoming apple bough
> Three hundred years before the Fall,
> And never crew again till now,
> And would not now but that he thought
> Chance being at one with Choice at last,
> All that the brigand apple brought
> And this foul world were dead at last.

'Solomon and the Witch', *C.P.*, p. 199.
Dürer's *Virgin with the Apple* is of interest in this connection.

·of two trees above a grave, or the growth of bushes to symbolize
the union of the lovers, is in the Ballads and in 'The Three Bushes'
·of *Last Poems*; but this goes far beyond. It is, in his own words,
·'the indefinable conscious symbolism that is the substance of all
·style'. Strange forces have been liberated; we are conscious of the
·ritual, the tomb, of tragic origins, and of oracles of the dead.
   The second movement opens —

> The miracle that gave them such a death
> Transfigured to pure substance what had once
> Been bone and sinew; when such bodies join
> There is no touching here, nor touching there,
> Nor straining joy, but whole is joined to whole;
> For the intercourse of angels is a light
> Where for its moment both seem lost, consumed.

In the second stanza the liturgical or prophetical anticipation is
fulfilled: with its paradox,

> The *miracle* that gave them such a *death*

for Ribh is a critic of early Christianity: and the two lovers are
at once a Christian and a non-Christian symbol.[1] The paradox
is reinforced by the word *transfigured*, with the rhythm dwelling
on it, since it is *transfigured* to *pure substance*, and we are at once in
the web of Neo-platonism, with Plotinus, and More's 'Psychozoia',
and his speculations on reality; remembering

> her form all full
> As though with magnanimity of light,
> Yet a most gentle woman; who can tell
> Which of her forms has shown her substance right?
> Or maybe substance can be composite,
> Profound McTaggart thought so. . . .[2]

The lovers are *transfigured*: *join* in the next line (in relation to *bone*
and *sinew*) recalls the Ezekiel-image, and yet there is again the
paradoxical *join*, to set against *transfigured*, earth against spirit
'There is no touching . . .' (is it in tenderness, or half-contempt as
in Donne?): perhaps with a memory of its use before:

[1] Cleanth Brooks, in *The Hidden God* has an admirably sensitive and
just discussion of Yeats' view of Christianity.
[2] 'A Bronze Head', *C.P.*, 382.

> He fancied that I gave a soul
> Did but our bodies touch. . . .

*Straining* joy is at once the sexual image, as of Leda, and the *straining* of the mind; before the experience is clenched on the authoritative *For* of the next line

> For the intercourse of angels is a light
> Where for its moment both seem lost, consumed.

*Intercourse*, laboured and made heavy by the preceding *the* unelided, gives the theological connotations overlaying the sexual. It is a light, with all the liberation associated with light symbolism;[1] where for *its* moment (note the precision of the *its*, for the experience is not asserted as a miracle, and therefore becomes more credible, more intricately related to the lovers) both *seem lost, consumed*. Again, I think (as in 'Stream and Sun at Glendalough') *seem* is accented, for Ribh's experience is subjective: *consumed* carries the overtone of 'consummated'. The purification in the fire is too common an image to suggest a source: perhaps it is from the *Paradiso*,[2] or Blake's illustrations to it, or from Plotinus, or from Berkeley.[3]

The movement goes on: picking up the first stanza with consummate art, bringing yet more overtones, with a thickening on the heavy-stressed *atmosphere*:

> Here in the pitch-dark atmosphere above
> The trembling of the apple and the yew,

(symbols of lover and the grave now left behind, *below*, the *transfigured* lovers).

---

[1] See, for example, Miss Bodkin's analysis: *Archetypal Patterns*, p. 267; and *Paradise Lost*, VIII, 626. Compare, too, *Vita Nuova*:

> *De li occhi suoi come che'lla li muova,*
> *escono spirti d'amore infiammati. . . .*

[2] E.g., Canto V—

> If beyond earthly wont the flame of love
> Illumine me, so that I overcome thy power
> Of vision, marvel not.

[3] There is a suggestive passage in *Siris*, p. 205.

> Here on the anniversary of their death,
> The anniversary of their first embrace,

(Is this a memory of 'The Second Anniversarie'?)

> These lovers, purified by tragedy,
> Hurry into each other's arms;

The tragedy, and the triumph, are re-enacted at the tomb: *hurry*, the common word, enforces the credibility of it. The cycle, the great love-story is complete. There remains the hermit, the critic of St Patrick, the Neo-platonist, the saint: concerned with his own love-story that is one with Baile and Aillinn, or Helen, or Beatrice; the saint who may be Dante, or Yeats.

> . . . these eyes,
> By water, herb and solitary prayer
> Made aquiline, are open to that light.
> Though somewhat broken by the leaves, that light
> Lies in a circle on the grass; therein
> I turn the pages of my holy book.

The image of wisdom in age, 'this voice that ninety years have cracked', the eyes made *aquiline* (with memory of his own prayer)[1] with the eagle as the soul image for loneliness, pride, power to gaze upon the sun, a face like that of Dante,[2] all are of Yeats himself. This momentary desire for discipline is characteristic: 'I see clearly that when I rewrite *The Adoration of the Magi* the message given to the old men must be a series of seemingly arbitrary commands: A year of silence, certain rules of diet, and so on. Without the arbitrary there cannot be religion, because there cannot be the last sacrifice, that of the spirit.'[3] The verse slows instinctively, perhaps ironically, on *somewhat*; for the light by which Ribh sees is not yet complete. He is still below the tree foliage of the apple and the yew, sensual love and the grave. Perhaps *the leaves* have overtones of the Sibylline Leaves (and this would fit the prophetic context) as in *Paradiso*,

[1]          Grant me . . .
             An old man's eagle mind.

It is of interest that the Cuala Press Edition (1934) has *acquiline*, with yet another sharpened sound-image from this spelling.

[2] See, for example, the end of *Purgatorio*, xxii, for 'fasting, herb and solitary prayer'.

[3] *Autobiographies*, p. 466.

xxxiii. But the circle of light, the circle with its normal symbolism, thrown upon the grass, is now sufficient for him to turn (at least) the pages. It would be entirely consonant with Yeats' method of allusiveness to have remembered his favourite Nōh *Nishikigi*: 'The lovers, now that in an aery body they must sorrow for unconsummated love, are "tangled up as the grass patterns are tangled" . . . and in the end bride and bridegroom show themselves for a moment "from under the shadow of the love-grass".'[1] It is *his* holy book, his own philosophy.

The whole poem has this faint pre-Raphaelite tint, but with a strength and energy far beyond the capacity of that tradition. It has a curious power of radiating new significances; a balanced symbolism set out cumulatively and logically, controlled and organized to its end. The fusion of religious and human love is an age-old theme; but the richness of suggestion, the tact and restraint, marks the poem as among the six perfect achievements of Yeats. Of such work the appreciation is never easy; and it is just, here as always, to leave the final word with him:

> A poetical passage cannot be understood without a rich memory, and like the older school of painting appeals to a tradition, and that not merely when it speaks of 'Lethe's Wharf' or 'Dido on the wild sea-banks' but in rhythm, in vocabulary; for the ear must notice slight variations upon old cadences and customary words, all that high breeding of poetical style where there is nothing ostentatious, nothing crude, no breath of parvenu or journalist.[2]

Yet for all its learned and complex overtones this language is 'public', as he intended it to be. Its qualities of life and precision are given it in part by the exquisite and subtle ear, in part by the exact rhythmic correspondence with the emotion that runs underneath it. Its 'high breeding' is the product, not of preciosity or aloofness, but of the double layer of speech on which he drew, the speech of the 'noble and beggarman'; the one remembering the past and the momentum of tradition, the other accustomed to give to living words their fierce dignity and brutality.

[1] *E. & I.*, p. 234.
[2] Ibid., pp. 227–8.

# CHAPTER SEVENTEEN

# Last Poems

Neither loose imagination,
Nor the mill of the mind
Consuming its rag and bone,
Can make the truth known.
'An Acre of Grass.'

The mental world of Yeats' last poetry is like that of Renan in his old age, mischievous, volatile, passingly profound and secretly diverting in its sophistries. – AUSTIN CLARKE.[1]

... I am grateful for your letter. At my time of life a man wonders if the time has not come to cease from verse. Your letter makes me hope that I have found a little wisdom to take the place of the passion I once had.
– *Letters*, W. B. Y. to T. R. Henn (12 March 1938).

I

Critical opinion has diverged sharply both as to the merits of *Last Poems and Plays* and its place in Yeats' poetic development. Some expressed a pained surprise at the obsession with lust and rage, the brutality and violence of an elderly and sex-ridden poet, who had lost sight of his original objective, or forgotten the synthesis achieved in 'Byzantium', and whose last writings were aimless and perverse, with something of the wildness of senility. Others recognized the sense of excitement communicated in the poems, but gave no explanation of it; others, again, concentrated on the virtues of the ballad poetry, and the 'nobility' of the verses to Dorothy Wellesley. It seems desirable to attempt to view the collection in some sort of perspective: for I believe that the derogatory criticisms are based most often upon a single quatrain, accepted at its face value, and, superficially, a convenient salient for the reviewer:

[1] *The Dublin Magazine*, April–June 1939.

You think it horrible that lust and rage
Should dance attention upon my old age;
They were not such a plague when I was young;
What else have I to spur me into song?[1]

I have argued previously that 'Byzantium' should not be considered as the final synthesis; that Yeats' prose, particularly that of
*On the Boiler*,[2] should be read in relation to this period; and that
the poems of *A Full Moon in March* are closely related to *Last
Poems*. I suggest that the whole can be seen as a clearly defined
pattern, a projection of previous thought and technique; neither a
regression nor a senile perversity, but a reconsideration and readjust-
ment (in the light of contemporary events) of nearly everything
that had gone before.

It seems to me that *Last Poems* falls into four main divisions.
There are first the 'cosmic' poems, projections or restatements of
Yeats' previous thought on the great mutations of the world. These
are 'The Gyres', 'Lapis Lazuli', 'An Acre of Grass', 'The Statues',
'A Bronze Head', and 'The Circus Animals' Desertion'. They merge
in one respect into the Cuchulain group, culminating in the play
on the hero's death; mystical, death-haunted, linked to *The King
of the Great Clock Tower* in *A Full Moon in March*. They represent
the last identification of the poet with the heroic defeat of his hero,
expressing the tragic exaltation of gaiety which I find to be the
dominant theme of the whole collection. And since, through the
Cuchulain image and the Statue in the Post Office, Cuchulain is an
emblem of the Easter Rising, there is a link with the ballad poetry,
both patriotic and dramatic; and this itself is related to the first
group (particularly through the *Marching Songs*) as a final aspect of
the function and value of the Rising in the processional cycles of
history. The fourth group concerns the so-called 'lust and rage'
poems; related to the 'cosmic' poems of the first group, to the heroic
love of the second, and to the 'book of the people' in the third. This
mood finds expression in 'The Three Bushes' and the related songs,
and in 'Hound Voice'. Finally, the four groups are, as it were,
straddled or bracketed by three other central poems: 'The Municipa'
Gallery Revisited', 'The Man and the Echo', and 'Under Ben Bulbenl.

[1] 'The Spur', *C.P.*, p. 359. The first draft has 'should dance attendance'
which is a better line (Allt).
[2] In its original text.

## II

The first poem, 'The Gyres', makes a double assertion. It is another
view of the ending of a civilization, both in Ireland and in the world
at large. Yeats' view, as always from the period of *Responsibilities*
onwards, is that of Heraclitus and Plato rather than of Shelley.
The threads are picked up from 'The Second Coming' —

> Irrational streams of blood are straining earth

and from 'Coole Park and Ballylee' (remembering the pictures of the
dead to be reviewed in 'The Municipal Gallery Revisited')

> – And ancient lineaments are blotted out.

Among those 'blotted out' is Lady Gregory, who died in 1932.

> A year ago I found I had written no verse for two years: I had
> never been so long barren; I had nothing in my head, and there used
> to be more than I could write. Perhaps Coole Park, where I had
> escaped from politics, from all that Dublin talked of, when it was shut,
> shut me out from my theme; or did the subconscious drama that was
> my imaginative life end with its owner?[1]

His friends have gone; the Irish political scene has changed beyond
recognition; but the oracle, Shelley's ancient philosopher in the
shell-strewn cavern by the Mediterranean,[2] who might be Oedipus,
or Ribh the heretic Hermit-Saint, or Yeats himself – an Irish
Delphic oracle – in the 'Cleft that's christened Alt', near Sligo,
accepts the mutability of things:

> Out of cavern comes a voice,
> And all it knows is that one word 'Rejoice!'

> Conduct and work grow coarse, and coarse the soul. . . .

It was the complaint that he had made of the years of drudgery
at the Abbey, when he half-doubted that his gift had been blunted;
it is echoed from the passage on 'drudgery' in 'The Phases of the
Moon'. But now the tone has changed. The comment is 'Rejoice!'
and 'What matter?' There will be a new civilization, a new aristocracy, to take the place of the old. 'As we approach the phoenix nest

---

[1] Preface to *The King of the Great Clock Tower*. Cuala Press, 1934.
[2] See *Autobiographies*, pp. 171 *et seq.*

the old classes, with their power of co-ordinating events, evaporate, the mere multitude is everywhere with its empty photographic eyes. Yet we who have hated the age are joyous and happy. The new discipline wherever enforced or thought will recall forgotten beautiful faces. . . .'[1] The poem is shot through and through with memories of Shelley, and particularly of *Hellas*. 'Old Rocky Face' was 'Old Cavern Face' in the first draft.[2] A passage from the *Letters to 'A.E.'* is pertinent:

> Had some young Greek found Shelley's 'Ahasuerus' in that shell-strewn cavern, the sage would not have talked mathematics or even 'those strong and secret thoughts . . . which others fear and know not', but given, I think, very simple advice, not indeed fitted to any momentary crisis but fitted perhaps for the next fifty years.[3]

But there is also a passage from Spengler which serves to tie this symbolism to the world-stream of events:

> The second wave swelled up steeply in the Apocalyptic currents after 300. Here it was the Magian waking-consciousness that arose and built itself a metaphysic of Last Things, based already 'upon the prime symbol of the coming Culture, the Cavern.'[4]

The invocation may be addressed to Ahasuerus, or to the Sphinx, timeless and omnipresent, whether in the desert or on the Rock of Cashel; or heard as the 'Rocky Voice' as of the Delphic Oracle in 'The Man and the Echo', associated with the strange beast that stirs in the desert at the second coming. His civilization, and with it all civilization, is decaying.[5] Maud Gonne has lost her beauty, Lady Gregory of the 'ancient lineaments' is dead. The 'irrational streams of blood' that accompanied the rise of Christianity, recur in the Easter Rising, and perhaps again (though I do not know when this poem was composed) in the events of Europe between 1934 and 1938. 'Empedocles has thrown all things about'; the allusion may have many sources. There is evidence that he read Cary's translation

[1] *On the Boiler*, p. 25. Note the 'empty photographic eyes', as of the Roman statues.

[2] I am indebted to A. N. Jeffares for this. But I do not know what significance (if any) is to be found in the carved stone head, high in the S.E. wall of Thoor Ballylee, and facing towards Coole.

[3] *The Dublin Magazine*, July/Sept. 1939.

[4] *Decline of the West*, ii, p. 249.

[5] Consider (especially in view of what follows) Donne's 'Anniversarie': 'All other things, to their destruction draw'.

of Dante, and Shadwell's (which he preferred), and Lawrence Binyon's *Inferno*; and there is a note on the reference to Empedocles in Canto IV of Cary's *Inferno*:

> . . . [he] taught that the universe exists by reason of the discord of the elements, and that if harmony were to take the place of this discord, a state of chaos would ensue.[1]

Perhaps it is also a reference to the alternate cycles of movement.

> Empedocles is cited as saying that 'of necessity Love and Strife control things and move them part of the time, and that they are at rest during the intervening time.'[2]

Or the proper reference may be to *A Vision*:

> 'When Discord,' writes Empedocles, 'has fallen into the lowest depths of the vortex' – the extreme bound, not the centre, Burnet points out – 'Concord has reached the centre, into it do all things come together so as to be only one, not all at once but gradually from different quarters, and as they come Discord retires to the extreme boundary . . . in proportion as it runs out Concord in a soft immortal boundless stream runs in.'[3]

And so Yeats realizes and affirms his place in the cycle of events. 'Hector is dead and there's a light in Troy' – the image that recurs perpetually, whether of Maud Gonne's beauty, or Iseult's. This age is just such another, of violence and disintegration. Quiescent Being passes into active Becoming; the tragic joy is also the theme of 'Lapis Lazuli':

> Yet they, should the last scene be there,
> The great stage curtain about to drop,
> If worthy their prominent part in the play,
> Do not break up their lines to weep.[4]

The second stanza of 'The Gyres' is dispassionate. All is part of the cycle:

> What matter though numb nightmare ride on top,
> And blood and mire the sensitive body stain?
> What matter? Heave no sigh, let no tear drop,
> A greater, a more gracious time has gone;

[1] Dante, Everyman, p. 17.
[2] McNeile Dixon, *The Human Situation*, p. 407. I am indebted for the allusion to E. M. M. Milne.
[3] (B), p. 67.
[4] *C.P.*, p. 338.

> For painted forms or boxes of make-up
> In ancient tombs I sighed, but not again;
> What matter? Out of cavern comes a voice,
> And all it knows is that one word 'Rejoice!'

The 'numb nightmare' has been thought of before in relation to the Troubles: now it is world-wide. The sensitive body is stained – note the paradox – by its components, the mire and blood of the rescuing dolphin of 'Byzantium'. But there is to be no lamentation; the phrase

> A greater, a more gracious time has gone

picks up the thought of the first stanza. He has rejected Egyptian thaumaturgy, the pursuit of the dead into the labyrinth (compare 'no dark tomb-haunter once' of 'A Bronze Head'[1]). The voice out of the cavern is that of Sibyl or oracle: and the overtones of 'Rejoice!' set the mind wandering towards the Christian exhortation.

The third stanza opens with an allusion to the poet's own thought of himself in the last Phases of the Moon. The comment 'What matter?' is exactly right: in its arrogance comparable with

> And when that story's finished, what's the news?
> of 'The Choice'[2] The new gyre will begin:
> Conduct and work grow coarse, and coarse the soul,
> What matter? Those that Rocky Face holds dear,
> Lovers of horses and of women, shall,
> From marble of a broken sepulchre,
> Or dark betwixt the polecat and the owl,
> Or any rich, dark nothing disinter
> The workman, noble and saint, and all things run
> On that unfashionable gyre again.

The tradition of aristocracy, of the great virile men, will return. The tone drops, labours with the complexity of its meaning, full of its allusions; *from marble* – the enduring thing – *of a broken sepulchre* – suggests the Second Coming ('I have a series of dramatic poems – very short – of Christ coming out of the tomb')[3] or the Second Resurrection, or a city rebuilt from the masonry of tombs; all this complexity is there, and more so in the next line —

---

[1] *C.P.*, p. 382.
[2] Ibid., p. 278.
[3] Hone, *Life*, p. 402.

> Or dark betwixt the polecat and the owl,

I doubt whether it is possible to fix the meaning precisely. The polecat and the owl, are, in the first place, associated with desolate places and ruins;[1] the owl with wisdom and the supernatural, the polecat (as, in many poems, the weasel) with destruction. The resurrection or disinterment of the new age will take place *betwixt* them (the ambiguity is obvious). It will be disinterred from *any rich dark nothing*, and there is the thought of Donne again: both in 'A Nocturnal upon St Lucies Day'

> But I am by her death (which word wrongs her)
> Of the first nothing, the Elixir grown —

and in 'The Relique'. The end will be the new gyre of an hierarchy, an order, that is prophesied in 'Under Ben Bulben', flaunted in the epitaph of 'Horseman, pass by!'

The same theme is developed in 'Lapis Lazuli' – 'almost the best I have made of recent years'.[2] He is meditating over a Chinese carving, and this is one more addition to the list of poems in English literary history that have been stimulated by such an object. 'Some one had sent me a present of a great piece carved by some Chinese sculptor into the semblance of a mountain with temple, trees, paths and an ascetic or pupil about to climb the mountains. Ascetic, pupil, hard stone, eternal theme of the sensual east. The heroic cry in the midst of despair. But I am wrong, the east has its solutions always, and therefore knows nothing of tragedy. It is we, not the east, that must raise the heroic cry.' There is expressed in it the exaltation in tragedy and defeat which he had found in the Rising, and which is now to be integrated with his own life, even though he hates the age. It is the last knowledge that 'comes to turbulent men':

> They know that Hamlet and Lear are gay;
> Gaiety transfiguring all that dread.
> All men have aimed at, found and lost;
> Black out; Heaven blazing into the head:
> Tragedy wrought to its uttermost.

So in a significant passage in *On the Boiler*:

[1] Compare Leonardo da Vinci's portrait of *Lady Cecilia*; and (in Synge's *Deirdre*) . . . 'weasels and wild cats crying on a lonely wall' . . .
[2] *D.W. Letters*, p. 91.

The arts are all the bridal chambers of joy. No tragedy is legitimate unless it leads some great character to his final joy. Polonius may go out wretchedly, but I can hear the dance music in 'Absent thee from felicity awhile', or in Hamlet's speech over the dead Ophelia, and what of Cleopatra's last farewells, Lear's rage under the lightning, Oedipus sinking down at the story's end into an earth 'riven' by love? Some Frenchman has said that farce is the struggle against a ridiculous object, comedy against a movable object, tragedy against an immovable; and because the will, or energy, is greatest in tragedy, tragedy is the more noble; but I add that 'will or energy is eternal delight,' and when its limit is reached it may become a pure, aimless joy, though the man, the shade, still mourns his lost object.[1]

I suggest that this statement clarifies the whole issue. He himself may 'mourn his lost object'; he may see himself and his purpose defeated; he may suffer the decay of body and of desire. The 'pure, aimless joy' is that of the Fool, in the last of the Phases, who has all things from God. The other mask-figures support this: Timon, for passion and rage at ingratitude, Blake for his energy, Lear for his progress through madness to peace: this last image fitting perfectly with Yeats' theory of purification through exhaustion of desire, and his image of himself as the dispassionate spectator of the political chaos of 1936:

> – so we'll live,
> And pray, and sing, and tell old tales, and laugh
> At gilded butterflies, and hear poor rogues
> Talk of court news —

(compare the poem 'Politics'),

> – and we'll talk with them too,
> Who loses and who wins; who's in, who's out;
> And take upon 's the mystery of things,
> As if we were God's spies; and we'll wear out,
> In a wall'd prison, packs and sets of great ones
> That ebb and flow by the moon.

'The Statues' picks up one of the threads of *A Vision*, which recurs again in 'Under Ben Bulben'. It is the old argument (repeated in *On the Boiler*) for the traditional sculpture, Greek deriving from Egyptian and its 'measurement'; and Alexander's conquest of the East by that achievement. (I believe that this apparent obsession with

[1] Page 35

measurement is more profound than any mere numerology, and
that it derives from Blake's engraving 'The Ancient of Days' that
hung at Woburn Buildings,[1] in which God is measuring the world
with compasses of lightning thrust down through the clouds.
Compare 'Measurement began our might.'[2]) The artist's function in
depicting the perfection of physical form 'to fill the cradles right',
the guidance of sexual desire:

> But boys and girls, pale from the imagined love
> Of solitary beds, knew what they were,
> That passion could bring character enough,
> And pressed at midnight in some public place
> Live lips upon a plummet-measured face.[3]

This is perhaps the most difficult poem that Yeats wrote. Much
light is thrown on it by Stallworthy's study of the drafts,[4] which
supplements most admirably Vivienne Koch's essay in *The Tragic
Phase*. The intensely difficult 'Grimalkin' of stanza 3 has been
explained by Wilson;[5] I am not wholly convinced, but I do not
know of a better exegesis. At the end, the poem is linked to the
Easter Rising, and its mystical implications; a theme in one sense
complementary to that of 'The Gyres'. 'Measurement' will bring
about a Greek aristocratic stability as the myths converge:

> When Pearse summoned Cuchulain to his side,
> What stalked through the Post Office? What intellect,
> What calculation, number, measurement, replied?
> We Irish, born into that ancient sect
> But thrown upon this filthy modern tide
> And by its formless spawning fury wrecked,
> Climb to our proper dark, that we may trace
> The lineaments of a plummet-measured face.

There is, surely, no loss of control in this verse. The heroic arrogance of the two legendary figures, equated against each other, is

---

[1] Masefield, *Some Memoirs of W. B. Yeats*, p. 5. It is the illustration to
*Paradise Lost*, vii, 225.
[2] 'Under Ben Bulben'. But this concern with 'measurement' has many
possible sources. He would have met it everywhere in his Cabalistic, Egyptian,
Arabic and Renaissance studies.
[3] *C.P.*, p. 375.
[4] *Review of English Studies*, Vol. I, No. 3, July 1963.
[5] *Iconography*, p. 301.

linked mysteriously to the secrets of the ultimate philosophy, the perfection of form; which is in its turn the knowledge of God.

The strange 'Cuchulain Comforted'[1] is a prophetic poem on his own entrance to the Kingdom of the Dead, with memories of Dante (and this is the only poem in which Yeats employs *terza rima*) cutting across Celtic legend. The hero is welcomed by the souls in the Country of the Blessed:

> They had changed their throats and had the throats of birds

– which I believe to be connected with the stage-direction at the end of *The Death of Cuchulain* following the dance of the Morrigu:

> Then she stands motionless. There is silence and in the silence a few faint bird notes.[2]

I shall deal in the final chapter with what I believe to be the implications of the Cuchulain-image in *The Death of Cuchulain*. I do not yet understand the full meaning of the play; though I am clear that it must be read side by side with *The King of the Great Clock Tower* and with 'Cuchulain Comforted', and that it is, in some sense, a projection of the theme of the former. The play is obscure because Yeats is trying to achieve a kind of desperate compression, working by juxtaposition of incidents in the hero's life which form a pattern at once too definite and too vague to be apprehended as a unity. The symbolism is not conceived as an integral part of the structure; the binding of Cuchulain by Aoife in the folds of her veil, the perception of Aoife as a Clytemnestra-figure, the Blind Man who kills him for twelve pennies, at the order of Queen Maeve – all these are set in a strained relationship to the Easter Rising and the Statue of Cuchulain in the Post Office. It is the not uncommon failing of the poet who has thought so deeply over a given theme that he moves among its intricacies with an ease which vitiates communication in the crude theatrical form.

[1] *C.P.*, p. 395
[2] But the mystery extends to the séance room: 'We sang, and then there was silence, and in the silence from somewhere close to the ceiling the clear song of a bird.' *Explorations*, p. 365.

### III

The ballads of *Last Poems* appear at first to be in a class of their own, but are, I think, to be related closely to the other poems. There are four main themes; the glorification of the Easter Rising, and its establishment as part of the mythology, perhaps with the intention, however unconscious, of confirming in Yeats' own mind his organic part in the event. Such are 'The O'Rahilly', the Casement poems, 'Three Songs to the One Burden', and the much revised 'Three Marching Songs', of which an earlier variant is accessible in *A Full Moon in March*. They are a little strident, with whistle and concertina behind all of them, and not 'Colonel Martin' alone: the jerky excited rhythms reflect a feverish half-ecstatic mood, trying desperately to pull into the framework the characteristic relationships of his figures to the pattern of Love and War. The Steinach operation which he caused to be performed in 1934 resulted beyond doubt in a temporary recrudescence of vitality, but is insufficient of itself to account for the new excitement in the technique of 'Supernatural Songs', and the steady joyous contemplation of tragedy; which is, as I have suggested, a logical development of Yeats' thought. Nor can we attribute to it, as critics and 'the mirror of malicious eyes' have lately done, the alleged obsession with 'lust and rage'. Yeats was very much concerned with world events. 'Europe seems to be under a waning moon.' It was characteristic of him that the world disintegration should be reflected subjectively in terms of his personal experiences and theories. To Dorothy Wellesley he wrote:

> At this moment I am expressing my rage against the intellegentsia by writing about Oliver Cromwell who was the Lennin of his day – I speak through the mouth of some wandering peasant poet in Ireland.[1]

The poem is 'The Curse of Cromwell',[2] and is a lament for his decaying world:

> All neighbourly content and easy talk are gone,
> But there's no good complaining, for money's rant is on.
> He that's mounting up must on his neighbour mount,
> And we and all the Muses are things of no account.

[1] *D.W. Letters*, p. 131. The spelling is Yeats'.
[2] *C.P.*, p. 350.

School of Mantegna: Triumph of Death

*'The years like great black oxen tread the world'*

Leda and the Swan

*'A sudden blow : the great wings beating still*
*Above the staggering girl . . .'*

The Tower in Snow, 1963

*'  . . . and I seem to know*
*That everything outside us is*
*Mad as the mist and snow'*

They have schooling of their own, but I pass their schooling by,
What can they know that we know that know the time to die?
> O what of that, O what of that,
> What is there left to say?

At first the verse seems clumsy and the third and fourth lines strained, until we realize that it is written for a tune's sake: but (as so often in the ballads) the whole poem is softened and widened by the strange and shifting overtones of the refrain. It gains immeasurably by reading aloud. It is the theme of 'The Gyres' and 'The Statues', complicated by the preparation for death; and that finds an image in the poem 'In Tara's Halls'. 'The Pilgrim' is a return to the thought that the holy places of Ireland might effect a union of the two religions. It is a ballad that recalls, intensely, the world of some of Jack Yeats' paintings, the ritual of pilgrimage, and its ambivalent aspects.

The best of the other ballads is 'The O'Rahilly';[1] in which the effect depends on the tone, which varies from verse to verse, of the sea refrain (as at the changing of the watch) 'How goes the weather?' It is part questioning, part ironic, part a sort of chorus to move the action outside reality. It means in effect, *What of the Rising? What is going on in the day-to-day world of the farmer, the huntsman, or sailor?* – the background of the war; and perhaps, *What is the news of happenings in the world beyond these?* These overtones should be brought out by accent and tone of each verse[2] (all the ballads must be read aloud), the idiom being organic: for it seems to me that here, perhaps for the first time, Yeats achieves true colloquial speech:

> Sing of the O'Rahilly
> That had such little sense
> He told Pearse and Connolly
> He'd gone to great expense
>
> Keeping all the Kerry men
> Out of that crazy fight;

[1] *C.P.*, p. 354. The raw material of the poem was provided by a newspaper account of The O'Rahilly's death.

[2] The Accent of Last Poems, *E. & S., E. Assn.*, 1956. (Henn)
It is possible that there is yet another overtone; for it was the weather that wrecked Casement's landing, and that contributed to the failure of the Rising.

M

> That he might be there himself
> Had travelled half the night.
>           *How goes the weather?*

By comparison with this, the Casement poems are forced, crude, factitiously violent – as if (and it may well have been so) they were the products of Yeats' pondering on an event which was mere political hearsay, of whose truth he was himself not wholly sure, but in which it was important to believe.

'Colonel Martin'[1] is a special achievement in this technique. It is perfectly adapted to the narrative qualities of the Irish street-ballad: it allows for dramatic emphasis, for dialogue in character, even to the *tourneurs de phrase* suited to the social rank of each speaker; it has a little of the rapidity of movement, and of the artistic inconsequentiality of the true ballad. An irony that is uncommon in Yeats flickers over the poem, and, in the denouement, shows a vivid knowledge of the ballad's prototype; a tragic and cruel accentuation of the bathos of the events, which is entirely in keeping. If we examine these ballads side by side with those of *Crossways* – 'Moll Magee' and 'The Foxhunter' – there is no comparison for the vitality, the organic sense of rhythm,[2] the delicate adjustment (even in such an apparently coarse medium) to tone and character in dialogue:

> 'And did you keep no gold, Tom?
> You had three kegs,' said he.
> 'I never thought of that, Sir.'
> 'Then want before you die.'
> And want he did; for my own grand-dad
> Saw the story's end,
> And Tom make out a living
> From the seaweed on the strand.
> *The Colonel went out sailing*

#### IV

'The Three Bushes' grew out of a ballad by Dorothy Wellesley. It was continually modified and revised, and the account of its making is to be read in the *Letters*. It is another handling of the old problem, whether love be of the body, or of the soul, or of both: the whole complicated, I believe, by the dramatic fantasy-solution

---

[1] *C.P.*, p. 361.
[2] Note, e.g. the dramatic change in Stanza VII.

which the poem offered. There are the two women, the 'daylight
lady' and the chambermaid, soul and sense; the one tortured by
sexual passion, yet inhibited: showing precisely the same conflict
as the Queen in *A Full Moon in March*:

> I am in love
> And that is my shame.
> What hurts the soul
> My soul adores,
> No better than a beast
> Upon all fours.[1]

There are memories here of earlier work: the realism of woman in
her attitude to this fulfilment, the Lear–Swift reduction to unaccommodated man, recalls

> And laughed upon his breast to think
> Beast gave beast as much.

By contrast, the Chambermaid is complete knowledge, complete
objectively. Her knowledge of the body is without amazement:

> How came this ranger
> Now sunk in rest,
> Stranger with stranger,
> On my cold breast?
> What's left to sigh for,
> Strange night has come;
> God's love has hidden him
> Out of all harm,
> Pleasure has made him
> Weak as a worm.

What may, perhaps, be missed at a first reading is the rightness
of the word *ranger*; it is a common Anglo-Irish term, expressing
at once admiration for manhood and virility, and a shadow of alarm.
It is not a mere rhyme-word determined by the 'stranger' of the
third line. So, too, the simile at the end; both are in character with
the Chambermaid.

The Lady, in her second and third songs, struggles towards her
own synthesis: dramatized by Yeats, mocked at as the cocotte who
has not the courage of her love, and yet striving to justify her
solution:

----

[1] 'The Lady's First Song,' *C.P.*, p. 343. The quotations that follow are
from the same series of poems.

He shall love my soul as though
Body were not at all,
He shall love your body
Untroubled by the soul,
Love cram love's two divisions
Yet keep his substance whole.
            *The Lord have mercy upon us.*

It may not be immediately apparent that the liturgical refrain not only throws forward to the Chambermaid's final confession to the priest, but is a counterpointed gesture, as by some bystander, on the 'heresy' that the Lady propounds. In her third song she moves a step onwards towards a richly emblematic synthesis:

That I may hear if we should kiss
A contrapuntal serpent hiss,
You, should hand explore a thigh,
All the labouring heavens sigh.

*Contrapuntal* carries the long-drawn-out stress; the serpent as the emblem of the Fall, of the sex principle set against the neo-Platonism of, say, 'Hero and Leander'. (An ikon of the seventeenth century shows Eve in a posture as of crucifixion upon Adam's Tree, while the Serpent penetrates her.) Against these two are set the Lover with his single song: exquisitely modulated, picking up, in a different key, the theme of 'Beloved, may your sleep be sound'. I do not know of any short poem in which the workmanship is more perfect; with the virtue concentrated (as so often in Yeats' technique) on the single word *sighs* in the third line, with its depth and resonance:

Bird sighs for the air,
Thought for I know not where,
For the womb the seed sighs.
Now sinks the same rest
On mind, on nest,
On straining thighs.

For if our ear remembers the previous writings, there are in this the harmonies of all the Leda-imagery; the bird with its *straining* thighs; the symmetry of construction that draws *mind* and *nest* together, the sources of thought-in-action – the eggs of Love and War – the seed sighing, half-human but also remembering, I think, the passage in Hardy's *Woodlanders* where the low breathing of the newly-planted trees is heard.

So 'The Wild Old Wicked Man',[1] which bears upon the mask of
Synge's brutality and violence; with its ending in a negation of
purgatory, of the classic values of tragedy, and the modulation of
the whole by the refrain. It is the theme of 'Must we part, Von
Hügel', twisted ironically, and yet completely poised in knowledge:

> 'That some stream of lightning
> From the old man in the skies
> Can burn out that suffering
> No right-taught man denies.
> But a coarse old man am I,
> I choose the second-best,
> I forget it all awhile
> Upon a woman's breast.'
> *Daybreak and a candle-end.*

But there is one new aspect of the love-conflict; lifted, as it were,
to the plane of the Celtic hunting legends, and 'that wild Tristram',
and the whole archetypal image of the hound and the deer. It is now
all bare, stripped of the obscurities, the symbolism of the earlier
poems; simple and dignified:

> The women that I picked spoke sweet and low
> And yet gave tongue.

(He would choose them so, for Lear is the most strongly defined
of the latest masks, and Cordelia his dream.)

> 'Hound Voices' were they all.
> We picked each other from afar and knew
> What hour of terror comes to test the soul,
> And in that terror's name obeyed the call,
> And understood, what none have understood,
> Those images that waken in the blood.[2]

[1] *C.P.*, p. 356.
[2] 'Hound Voice', ibid., p. 385.

# CHAPTER EIGHTEEN

# 'Horseman, Pass By!'

MARTIN. There were horses – white horses rushing by, with white shining riders – there was a horse without a rider, and some one caught me up and put me upon him and we rode away, with the wind, like the wind —
FATHER JOHN. That is a common imagining.
*The Unicorn from the Stars.*

I

The three final dated poems of *Last Poems* contain, perhaps, Yeats' *Grand Testament*. 'Under Ben Bulben' is the most intelligible of the three. In it, the six dominant themes are picked up, their essential threads run lightly and almost casually through the fingers. There is the magic of his Sligo childhood; the preternatural that he had pursued in Bloomsbury, Dublin, Paris or on Croagh Patrick; the Rebellion, and the forgiveness of the dead; the exaltation of war, of the Swordsman who was to repudiate – though with reluctance – the Saint;[1] the great traditions of art, the origins going far back into the mystical mathematics of Babylon and Egypt, linked to history by the returning movements of the gyres; the aristocratic hierarchy of the Ireland of the future. The verse swaggers, with its rough rhythms, across the pages with its characteristic Berkleian boast:

> That we in coming days may be
> Still the indomitable Irishry

Then it sinks to a lower key, though still arrogant beneath its

[1] I have spent my life saying the same thing in many different ways. I denounced old age before I was twenty, and the Swordsman throughout repudiates the Saint – though with vacillation. (MS. note by W. B. Y. – Mrs Yeats.)

apparent restraint. He returns to the little churchyard of Drumcliff, under the shadow of the enchanted mountain:

> No marble, no conventional phrase;
> On limestone quarried near the spot
> By his command these words are cut:
> *Cast a cold eye*
> *On life, on death,*
> *Horseman, pass by!*[1]

The Epitaph is not great poetry, but neither is Swift's, which in part it echoes; there are no grounds in history for supposing that poets do this sort of thing for themselves with any great success. We should see it as the climax of a long discursive meditative poem, in strong and sometimes violent clipped verse. It is typical of many aspects of Yeats: a desire to mystify, to suggest his own peculiar rhetoric of the ghost, to satisfy his dramatic nostalgia for a tradition of place and ancestry, and to emphasize two aspects of desired masks. It is said that he decided to be buried at Drumcliff when he noted the crowd of 'A.E.''s enemies at 'A.E.''s funeral, but there were more cogent reasons than that.

The sense of the dramatic is held to the fall of the curtain, even to the rhythm of the galloping horses. Death must be seen with the cold dispassionateness of high breeding, with no sense of fear: for

> Death and life were not
> Till man made up the whole,
> Made lock, stock and barrel
> Out of his bitter soul . . .

It was, perhaps, as good a way as any, to dramatize that long-meditated experience so that it should reveal no trace of self-pity. The 'coldeye' – coldness is a favourite term for his own ideal of perfection in art – is this aristocratic dispassionateness and laughter that he spoke of; first in 'Upon a Dying Lady', of Mabel Beardsley, and then in 'Vacillation':

> And call those works extravagance of breath
> That are not suited for such men as come
> Proud, open-eyed and laughing to the tomb.[2]

---

[1] He dropped the original first line: 'Draw rein, draw breath': *v.* Stallworthy, op. cit., p. 6.

[2] 'Vacillation', III, *C.P.*, p. 283.

But the phrase, 'Horseman, pass by!' has many meanings. In Irish idiom, the word 'horseman' has certain overtones that may be missed in ordinary speech. It carries a note of respect, even of awe; the rider has something of Hebraic strength and mystery, or of the symbolic association of strength and wisdom that produced the centaurs, 'the holy centaurs of the hills'.[1] The horseman belongs to aristocracy,[2] he symbolizes possessions, breeding, strength, virility, and a certain 'wildness of sorrow', as in those figures of Jack Yeats' paintings of the horsemen at Irish funerals. There is much of this suggestion throughout Yeats' poetry. In his memories of the Ashmolean Museum he recalled above all 'certain pots with strange half-supernatural horses. . . .' His ancestry, with hard-riding country gentlemen among them, was, he believed, famous on that account: Major Robert Gregory, with all the virtues in Castiglione, was noted too:

> Soldier, scholar, horseman, he,
> As 'twere all life's epitome.[3]

There is the remembered image of Countess Markiewicz:

> When long ago I saw her ride
> Under Ben Bulben to the meet,
> The beauty of her country-side
> With all youth's lonely wildness stirred. . . .[4]

Horsemanship becomes an emblem of an aristocracy that will yet return:

> Those that Rocky Face holds dear,
> Lovers of horses and of women, shall,
> From marble of a broken sepulchre,
> Or dark betwixt the polecat and the owl,
> Or any rich, dark nothing disinter
> The workman, noble and saint, and all things run
> On that unfashionable gyre again.[5]

---

[1] There is a magic gateway in the side of Ben Bulben through which the faery host emerges.

[2] Sir Jonah Barrington gives the various categories of 'gentry': 'half-mounted', 'full-mounted', etc. (*Personal Sketches of His Own Times*).

[3] 'In Memory of Major Robert Gregory,' *C.P.*, p. 151. But Stanza VIII of this poem, which concerns the Galway foxhounds, was inserted to meet Mrs Gregory's wishes and against the poet's judgement.

[4] 'On a Political Prisoner,' *C.P.*, p. 206.

[5] 'The Gyres,' ibid., p. 337.

But the horseman, the images of the tomb, the memories of Sligo, and Ben Bulben, are foreshortened against earlier memories. In the prose tale of *Dhoya*, the Fomorian giant who is robbed of his fairy bride, he leaps upon the leader of a herd of wild horses, and on it gallops towards the North West along Ben Bulben 'down that valley where Dermot hid his Grania in a deep cavern', and finally plunges over a cliff into the western sea. The ghosts of horse and rider go on: 'Sometimes the cotters on the mountains of Donegal hear on windy nights a sudden sound of horses' hoofs, and say to each other, "There goes Dhoya". And at the same hour if any be abroad in the valley they see a huge shadow rushing along the mountain.'[1] Dhoya himself, the angry passionate man, of enormous strength, is – with Oisin – an early dream-image of Yeats, just as Cuchulain is the last; and it is not altogether fantastic to see in this legend a kind of prophetic self-justification in the plea: 'Only the changing, and moody, and angry, can love.'

The phrase is linked to the Rosicrucians and the mountain tomb of their leader. The cataract that 'smokes upon the mountain side'[2] can be no other than that which falls from Ben Bulben into Glencar; the horsemen riding from Knocknarea to Ben Bulben are those in the 'Song for the Severed Head':

> Saddle and ride, I heard a man say,
> Out of Ben Bulben and Knocknarea,
> *What says the Clock in the Great Clock Tower?*
> All those tragic characters ride
> But turn from Rosses' crawling tide,
> The meet 's upon the mountain side.
> *A slow low note and an iron bell.*[3]

To that procession of images come those that remain of the circus; Cuchulain, who had sought wisdom in battle, or in fighting the waves; Niamh, Aleel, Hanrahan; last and most sinister, a remembered character from *The Secret Rose*:

> The King that could make his people stare
> Because he had feathers instead of hair.[4]

[1] *John Sherman and Dhoya*, p. 195.
[2] 'The Mountain Tomb,' *C.P.*, p. 136.
[3] *C. Plays*, p. 641. They turn from the tide, I suppose, because the ghost is reluctant to cross water.
[4] 'The Wisdom of the King'.

There are, then, many images stored in those short lines. Death is to be confronted heroically and dramatically, for the two attitudes have become one. 'Cuchulain Comforted' is a vision-poem,[1] dictated near death, with its bird-like shrouds, and the strange overtones of Dante[2] and of Morris' 'Defence of Guenevere'. 'The Black Tower', the latest-dated poem of *Last Poems*, is also concerned with the two mountains, and it may well be that Yeats had in mind, not only the tower at Ballylee, but the round tower that stands beside Drumcliff Churchyard; and he celebrates the warrior Eoghan Bel buried near Maeve's cairn on the summit of Knocknarea:

> *There in the tomb stand the dead upright,*
> *But winds come up from the shore:*
> *They shake when the winds roar,*
> *Old bones upon the mountain shake.*[3]

But the poem itself is complex and obscure, as is the right of one written 'when the dark grows thicker'. Generally, the Black Tower, which has overtones perhaps from Browning, but which has its basic reference to Thoor Ballylee, becomes at the last the refuge and defence that once it was in the great period of his poetry. Now it helps to protect the King and his retainers, in their decrepitude, against the new generation. The conflict is political, philosophical, poetical, personal; perhaps all of these together. (One thinks of 'The New Faces'.) They come to bribe or threaten, to persuade the defenders to throw in their lot with the usurper; as the new government (which had rejected the Oath of Allegiance) had sought to induce Yeats to return to a more active part in affairs. At this point we may refer to the reference given by Wilson[4] to Plato's *Statesman*, where the ruler of the universe has withdrawn from active participation in it. Chaos has followed; the King waits till the return of the new order. This is the thought of 'The Gyres'; Arland Ussher has noted the Messianic yearnings of much Irish history.

So far so good. But W. J. Keith seems to have given depth to

---

[1] The prose draft, the result of a dream, was dictated at 3 a.m. on 7 Jan. 1939: the poem was finished on 13 Jan. (Mrs Yeats).
[2] *e.g. Inferno XV*, 20, 'come vecchio sartor fa nella cruna.'
[3] *C.P.*, p. 396.
[4] *W. B. Yeats and Tradition*, p. 224.

Yeats' poem by suggesting a possible reference to the Arthurian legend. For this he quotes from E. K. Chambers' *Arthur of Britain*:[1]

> Beneath the Castle of Sewingshields, near the Roman Wall in Northumberland, are vaults where Arthur sleeps with Guinivere and all his court and a pack of hounds. He waits until one blows the horn which lies ready on a table, and cuts a garter placed beside it with a sword of stone. Once a farmer, knitting on the ruins, followed his clew of wool which had fallen into a crevice and found the vault. He cut the garter and Arthur woke, but as he sheathed the sword, fell asleep again, with the words —

> O woe betide that evil day
> On which the witless wight was born,
> Who drew the sword – the garter cut,
> But never blew the bugle horn.

The old cook of the Tower then, as Keith suggests, might be explained by the legend of Sir Beaumains and Sir Kay: who, degraded from his knighthood, became a cook in the buttery.

We can then see the poem as another instance of multiple or laminated meanings. The new order is defied by the 'right king' and his enfeebled retainers, in the Tower of old age, which is black because of approaching death. He defies the corruption of the new order —

> Those banners come to bribe or threaten
> Or whisper that a man's a fool —

though the old order seems bankrupt and feeble. The blowing of the horn will announce a rescue, the return of strength and order – is there an echo of Roncesvalles? – but the rumours of its distant sound are false. The whole is pointed by the refrain which suggests the growing blackness of approaching death, *and* the increasing darkness just before the dawn; the Mountain Tomb, not far from the sea (Ben Bulben or Knocknarea) so that the sea-winds are the heralds of change; and the shaking of the bones (in fear, excitement, anticipation – *The Dreaming of the Bones*) which will return to life when the Ezekiel-like prophecy is fulfilled; remembering that between Knocknarea and Sligo there are a number of ancient

[1] MLN. LXXV February 1960: 'Yeats's Arthurian Black Tower'. But there was perhaps an additional strata of symbolism from the Golden Dawn and Rosicrucianism, and a strong case is made out for this by Virginia Moore in *The Unicorn*, pp. 439 ff.

burial-mounds. And if, as I believe possible, he remembered Ricketts' 'Don Juan and the Statue', that strange, terrifying picture of the horseman with outstretched right arm and sunken corpse-face, there would be in the words a further symbol of Juan's lonely power on which he had meditated, and which had served to embody his contempt for 'those that hated *The Playboy of the Western World*'. It is a kind of evocation of the heroes that meet him, the dramatic assertion of his kinship with the supernatural. Perhaps in the thought of the traveller there is something of the finality of Swift's own epitaph;[1] Swift, who was 'always just round the corner', and by whose side, in St Patrick's, Yeats was to be offered a final burial:

> Imitate him if you dare,
> World-besotted traveller; he
> Served human liberty.

II

'Under Ben Bulben' and the Epitaph are thus not only a testament and a gesture, but a rapid and violent tightening of the threads of past thought. The reader must accept them as such; and speculate a little on the conventional phrases that succeeding generations of critics may cut upon the stone. There have been already Celebrations and Detractions in plenty; but among them is apparent an uncertainty of judgement that arises from a reluctance to dissociate the poetic from the practical personality, and a failure to perceive the relationship between the 'magic' and the work. Of the Detractions, there appear to be four that are now in public speech: obscurity, insincerity, fascism, and escapism; Greek endings with the little passing bell. It is right to consider them.

The first charge commonly levelled against Yeats is that of obscurity, in the earlier phases because he used an imaginative mythology, in the later because his verse is too compressed, elliptical, obscure. I have suggested that neither charge holds good provided that the work is taken not in isolation, or in pieces selected for an anthology,[2] but as a whole; because new images become through

---

[1] *v.* Wade, *Letters*, p. 525. It is perhaps worth noting that the Latin is poor, as it might be that of a stonemason.

[2] 'Now I have a very great objection to making a selection from my own poems' (Wade, *Letters*, p. 416).

usage as little strange as the old, and because it is part of his greatness to discard continually all that is not living in his world of images. The poetry is never easy; it does demand this knowledge of what has gone before and what comes after; it requires a knowledge, at least in outline, of his life and background, and some sympathy with his beliefs. These demands are common to much poetry: and that poetry which demands less from its reader is, at best, of a nature utterly different from the complex laminated structure that Yeats' work reveals. And in common with all poetry, the greater the knowledge the more full and wise is the ultimate response.

It has been held that Yeats' later poetry is too analytical, too much of the mind. I have suggested that, in so far as the love-poetry is concerned, this analytical approach is, in the middle period, deliberate and at the last flares up, as it were (as all great love-poetry must surely do) into its own peculiar mysticism. It is part of his achievement that he fought against those innovations that seemed to him to deny the great tradition:

> In their pursuit of meaning, Day Lewis, MacNeice, Auden, Laura Riding have thrown off too much, as I think, the old metaphors, the sensuous tradition of the poets:
>
> > High on some mountain shelf
> > Huddle the pitiless abstractions bald about the necks,
>
> but have found, perhaps the more easily for that sacrifice, a neighbourhood where some new Upanishad, some half-asiatic masterpiece, may start up amid our averted eyes.[1]

This purpose seems to me consistently and successfully pursued. Yet it is much more than sensuous poetry in the accepted sense: its sheer muscular quality of movement has drawn familiar things into strange new patterns of thought on the edge of thought. And yet it escapes the dreaminess of 'A.E.'; its pity and horror intensified (as in the great tradition), by the injection of metaphysical normality:

> What is this flesh I purchased with my pains,
> This fallen star my milk sustains,
> This love that makes my heart's blood stop

[1] Preface to *Upanishads*, p. 10.

Or strikes a sudden chill into my bones
And bids my hair stand up?[1]

Yeats was led to the belief in the permanent significance of symbols
by dream, and vision, and the evidence, reinforced over and over
again, of a constant and cumulative historical approach to the
supra-sensuous. His views are given concisely in the celebrated essay
'Magic'. The laws laid down by Porphyry for the preparations of
the Pythian prophetess at Delphi were strangely close to those that
experience had proved necessary for the medium in a séance.[2] The
daimons of Plutarch that controlled the ecstatic powers of prophecy
had their counterparts in psychic research. And yet – he quotes
Spenser – 'And yet do not believe too much.' For, in the last resort,
all things magical might be themselves symbols or forms in the
depths of the mind. This is why there is always uncertainty, and
uncertainty that is, ultimately, of philosophy rather than of magic;
and therefore he turns to Berkeley – 'Though he could not describe
mystery – his age had no fitting language – his suave glittering
sentences suggest it; we feel perhaps for the first time that eternity
is always at our heels or hidden from our eyes by the thickness of a
door.'[3]

That is why he turns to philosophy; and I suggest again that the
thought process is supremely logical. He had drawn from Vico
the thought that all true philosophy begins in myth: but his own
poetry beginning with myth and testing the validity of myth by the
experiences of love and hatred and war, brought him inevitably
to the point where he had to seek in philosophy the justification
by thought alone of what he had already written without knowing
its intellectual justification. No one can follow the course of his
arguments with Sturge Moore, the account of his excited discovery
of Spengler's and Toynbee's justifications of his theory of history,
without a growing admiration for the integrity and energy with
which he pursued his aim. It is a curious and suggestive reversal of
the normal advice to the developing poet: get learning, get philosophy.

[1] 'The Mother of God', *C.P.*, p. 281. The poem owes, I think, something
to Rossetti's *Ave*.
[2] See G. Dempsey, *The Delphic Oracle*, p. 56.
[3] Preface to Hone and Rossi's *Berkeley*, p. xxi.

III

The first great detraction is obscurity; the second insincerity. I have tried to show that a mind essentially dramatic, believing wholly in the theory of progression by the union of opposites, is above and outside the blank and level of that term. If the mind of man were indeed so complex, if all the varied experiences and aspects of personality, linked to and drawing on the ancestral memory could produce proven and tested images of the past, no single mask could suffice, as Hardy's did, to suggest that complexity. Those who are prepared to accept the stained and skeined variety of the poetry will realize that no less complexity of personality could underlie it. Nor is it insincere in any normal sense. It is dramatic, involving the projection and interfusion of imaged aspects of personality in accordance with a specific psychological theory. I say 'imaged aspects', for this poetry has never the confiding quality by which we are aware of a warm humanity. That is not part of the design. It is to be 'cold'. At the same time, he tries to eliminate from it what he calls 'abstractions'; and the result is this strange distant impersonality that is yet unmistakably his own. It seems to me that his method was at once more honest and more suited to the complexity of mire and blood than that of poets who, professing a single-mindedness, show in their work so many evidences of the heterogeneous.

With this go the lesser detractions of snobbery, affectation, misjudgement of men's and women's work. Some of them are justified

> . . . but you, gods, will give us
> Some faults to make us men.

But it is, I think, worth while to point out that many whom he knew pay tribute to his courtesy, his almost unfailing psychological judgements of men encountered casually, but judged according to some secret method of his own: to the courteous genius of his talk.[1] But above all there was his kindness to all those who were shy, or young, or who needed help; his arrogance was reserved for the pretentious or insincere.

[1] I follow L. A. G. Strong's noble tribute: supported by my own lesser knowledge and my talk with his many friends.

IV

The third detraction will concern his politics. I do not excuse the brief association with General O'Duffy's Blue-shirts, except to suggest that he was not alone in believing, at that moment of history, that the discipline of fascist theory might impose order upon a disintegrating world: though indeed nothing could be farther from Yeats' mind than its violent and suppressive practice. It is unlikely that one who had been a target of Dublin malice for so long would escape further embroideries upon his indiscretion: it is typical that his established preference for wearing blue shirts, many years before fascism was heard of, should now be a support to a lie. But all his reading of history, all his knowledge of Elizabethan drama, of Dante, of mythology, and of Ireland's past, brought him to believe in two cardinal principles. First, an old gyre was approaching its end; if order were to be imposed at all, the new age seemed likely to be authoritarian. No one could read and accept Spengler without coming to that conclusion; Spengler's philosophy has been called 'Fascism for the non-Fascist'. Historically, the pendulum seemed to be swinging that way. 'As all realization is through opposites, men coming to believe the subjective opposite of what they do and think, we may be about to accept the most implacable authority the world has known.'[1]

The new Ireland, fighting through rebellion to sovereignty, must be, as the price of its existence, a military state. 'Desire some just war. . . .' If there was to be fighting, a hierarchy was necessary; men could be led only by aristocracy, the nation unified by its great men. 'No art can conquer the people alone – the people are conquered by an ideal of life upheld by authority. As this ideal is rediscovered, the arts, music and poetry, painting and literature, will draw closer together.'[2] And again, 'An idea of the State which is not a preparation for those three convictions,[3] a State founded on economics alone, would be a prison house. A State must be made

---

[1] *Irish Statesman* (Hone Papers).

[2] *Autobiographies*, p. 491.

[3] 'I would found literature on the three things which Kant thought we must postulate to make life liveable – Freedom, God, Immortality' (*Explorations*, p. 332).

like a Chartres Cathedral for the glory of God and the soul. It exists for the sake of the virtues and must pay their price.'[1]

Secondly, he had seen a civilization pass, and a new set of law-givers, without tradition of service, come to power. The Ireland of 1930 and after gave him little hope, except for the Shelleyan prophecy in 'The Gyres'.[2] But the anarchy and corruption that he had seen, or fancied that he saw in 'this filthy modern tide' might serve at least to produce great poetry, as it had for Dante. His experience in the Senate had not given him pleasure. Somehow, a new aristocracy would be built up: perhaps by some unification of Protestant and Catholic faith centred once again on the holy places of Ireland: perhaps by some common insistence, such as Balzac had preached and the Catholic Church had always preached, on the sanctity of the family as the essential unit of the State. He was impatient of the manner in which education was developing; and some wiser governance was necessary there. But this is not fascism; it is as old as Homer, or Castiglione, and the riots at the Abbey, the scandal of the 'blind bitter town', had confirmed it:

> What cared Duke Ercole, that bid
> His mummers to the market-place,
> What th' onion-sellers thought or did
> So that his Plautus set the pace
> For the Italian comedies?[3]

## V

The fourth and last detraction will be, I think, that Yeats' poetry is out of touch with the world about him; that though he has wisdom, he has no unifying moral subject; that he has no philosophy of life, but in its place a mythology which is personal, obscure, inconsistent and remote; that he is indeed the last of the Romantics for whom there is no place now. These charges are more difficult to answer, for they concern not only Yeats but all the values of poetry. I do not think that his cyclic theory of history leads to determinism in the life of the individual; since each man and woman is perpetually at war with the false aspects of personality, and the end of that

[1] *Explorations*, p. 335.
[2] *C.P.*, p. 337. I do not find this poem convincing.
[3] 'To a Wealthy Man . . .' ibid., p. 119.

N

struggle is the achievement of a unity of being. If it is true that a poet's significance is measured by his ability to image the contemporary dissipation and despair, or to achieve the intricate analysis of individual minds, then Yeats will be condemned: for his concern is not with these. His thought, or 'philosophy', in so far as any poet's thought can be isolated or precipitated from his poetry by the chemistry of criticism, seems to be in the main a reassertion of the great traditional values; Dante's love and war and the return of the dead, the serious things approached rhetorically and yet dispassionately, in his progress towards a synthesis. I believe that progress to be evidenced sufficiently in the development of his poetry and prose, and by his increasingly complex portrayal of a world which, however personal in its aspect as a microcosm, is yet continuously expanded and linked to the processional images of time, and therefore to what is deeply rooted in our own consciousness.

For it is perhaps true that a poet of this type has, when all is said, this essential task: to propound a system of time in which past and present are seen as a pattern, whose fundamentals and their intricate harmonics are related to yet undetermined patterns in the future, and to those that in our minds lie on the edge of consciousness. He has no 'philosophy' because he can no more mirror certainty than any of the great poets or artists of the past whose statement or speculation is implicit as positive values in their work. Hamlet, that recurrent symbol, is a type, not of morbid psychology but of the energy and brilliance and the joy in defeat of Renaissance man. What is purely destructive can be perceived and imaged almost in its completeness, and achieve a certain response precisely for that reason; what is constructive or positive, whether we perceive life as a tragedy or not, is perceived and imaged with inexactitude because of the spiritual mystery that must be shown. It is the task of such a poet as this to lead us with him through speculations. As points of departure for those speculations I do not think that Homeric or Celtic legend, Job and Dante and Blake, Spengler and Toynbee, are more or less phantastic in themselves than anthropology or ritual or experiments with time or perception. What is necessary is the establishment of a poetic usage that can be related to what is traditionally a part of the reader's background and culture, so that sympathy can be initiated and maintained.

Whether readers of the future will overcome the last barrier that exists between Yeats and his readers, his own certainty that love and war and death are fundamentally a mystery, I cannot judge. The word most commonly and most loosely used in the criticism of Yeats' work is 'magical'. It is used to denote his psychic experience, the music of his verse, the incantation of a half-understood mythology, and the complexity of perfectly controlled technique.

It is best to let Yeats speak, with the language of Job to which he returns continually: 'I must not talk to myself about "the truth" nor call myself "teacher" nor another "pupil" – these things are abstract – but see myself set in a drama where I struggle to exalt and overcome concrete realities perceived not with mind only but as with the roots of my hair.'[1] What does matter is that the poetry deals, at its greatest, with so much that is on the edge of thought and emotion; and we cannot know it until we are prepared at least to listen to that strange tide running beneath the surface, as I have heard the stream of the Shannon run out in a clear day, through the calm of its estuary, flinging up great eddies and whirlpools from below the keel of my boat.

VI

It is idle to speculate what might have come out of Yeats' poetry if he had lived to encounter the excitement of prophecy fulfilled in the events of 1939; or seen, as the result of the new gyre winding its threads from the ruins of the old, the beginnings of a new authoritarian rule in the world, or of resettlement of Ireland by a new aristocracy. I believe that in his own vision of himself he was passing from the phase of the Saint to that of the Fool:

> I shall find the dark grow luminous, the void fruitful when I understand I have nothing, that the ringers in the tower have appointed for the hymen of the soul a passing bell.[2]

*Per Amica Silentia Lunae* was published in 1918. It contains, as

[1] *Explorations*, pp. 301–2.

[2] *Mythologies*, p. 332. F. A. C. Wilson, has drawn my attention to *Die versunkene Glocke* by Hauptmann: the main point is the relevance of the play to *The Only Jealousy of Emer*, but there is also the bell-symbolism, as well as that of shell, moon, statue. *Southern Review* (Adelaide I).

many critics have pointed out, the essence of Yeats' thought, set out in the exquisitely cadenced prose that owed so much to Sir Thomas Browne. I find in this passage the most exact forecast of his latest poetry. The dark, 'the pitch-dark night', of Ribh grows luminous. The Tower that had served so greatly as a symbol, that had foreshortened history and linked Plato, and the Cromwellian men-at-arms and *Il Penseroso*, and Shelley, becomes the Black Tower of *Last Poems* whose garrison is old and broken, but remains 'on guard, oath bound'. And it is the Great Clock Tower, for time runs on and hermit and king have converged:

> A storm-beaten old watchtower,
> A blind hermit rings the hour.

It looks on Knocknarea and Ben Bulben, and its bell is tolling now

> *A slow low note and an iron bell.*

For it is the hymen of the soul, and the words are deliberate and traditional for that consummation; imagined through much thought on the nature and purpose of sexual joy,

> For the intercourse of angels is a light
> Where for its moment both seem lost, consumed.

Then the 'lust and rage' of which so many stupid and vulgar things have been written, falls into place. The fierce light of that holy intercourse made study in the sacred book a reality, remembering Donne:

> Loves mysteries in soules doe grow,
> But yet the body is his booke.[1]

'Does not all art come when a nature, that never ceases to judge itself, exhausts personal emotion in action or desire so completely that something impersonal, something that has nothing to do with action or desire, suddenly starts into its place, something which is as unforeseen, as completely organized, even as unique, as the images that pass before the mind between sleeping and waking?'[2] Even remorse for the crime committed, can serve the ultimate knowledge:

[1] 'The Extasie.'
[2] *Autobiographies*, p. 332.

The knowledge of reality is always in some measure a secret knowledge. It is a kind of death.[1]

I am not concerned here with the question of Yeats' relationship to Christianity.[2] That his poetry is in one sense profoundly religious I am certain: but there was in his heart a kind of fighting which could never let him achieve submission or acceptance. 'I am always, in all that I do, driven to a moment which is the realization of myself as unique and free, or to a moment which is the surrender to God of all that I am. . . . Again and again with remorse, a sense of defeat, I have failed when I would write of God, written coldly and conventionally.'[3] It is not inconsistent that he could accept miracles, and yet deny 'what seems most welcome in the tomb', or that he should create Ribh as the last mask, and make him a critic of early Christianity. For Christianity was but one movement of the gyres, one aspect of truth, profoundly significant and moving, but not the final knowledge. There was, too, this innate perversity, this desire for solitude, the rejection of dogma: remembering perhaps his device in the Cabalistic Society: *Demon est deus inversus*. Christian love might be insufficient, for there was no great humility in Yeats. And if no love were there, a native perversity would shape a Donne-like paradox, setting hatred in its place. 'Instead of the Saint's humility he had come to see the image of the mind in a kind of frozen passion, the virginity of the intellect.' So the critic of early Christianity, of St Patrick, had studied hatred:

> Then my delivered soul herself shall learn
> A darker knowledge and in hatred turn
> From every thought of God mankind has had.
> Thought is a garment and the soul's a bride
> That cannot in that trash and tinsel hide:
> Hatred of God may bring the soul to God.

Yet the paradoxical nature of the man remains. He could admire most passionately Toyohiko Kagawa and his 'heroic life', his 'subtlety of moral understanding', and be at pains to quote with approval the Christian doctrines of atonement and forgiveness. But however much he might approve them, Christianity was but

[1] *Autobiographies*, p. 482.
[2] See Austin Warren's 'Religio Poetae' (*Southern Review*, Winter 1941, Vol. vii, No. 3).
[3] *Explorations*, p. 305.

one movement or series of movements,[1] in the historical pattern
of the gyres; and behind the 'System' there was the solitary and
perverse mind that found it more dramatic to try the lots in Virgil
than in the Gospels, to study hatred rather than the love that they
enjoined. Out of individuality there was to come an energy resem-
bling that of Blake:

> But today the man who finds belief in God, in the soul, in immortality,
> growing and clarifying, is blasphemous and paradoxical. He must
> above all things free his energies from all prepossessions not imposed
> by those beliefs themselves. The Fascist, the Bolshevist, seeks to turn
> the idea of the State into free power and both have reached (though
> the idea of the State as it is in the mind of the Bolshevist is dry and lean)
> some shadow of that intense energy which shall come to those of whom
> I speak.
> When I speak of the three convictions and of the idea of the State
> I do not mean any metaphysical or economic theory. That belief which
> I call free power is free because we cannot distinguish between the
> things believed in and the belief; it is something forced upon us bit by
> bit; as it liberates our energies we sink in on truth.[2]

### VII

There is some justice in Yeats' description of himself as of the
last Romantics. His poetry is both traditional and intensely personal.
Its rhythms are strongly accented, and in them there is implicit the
half-chant of older poetry, and an intonation which, when he read
his verse, seemed to give it a peculiar life of its own.[3] Those rhythms,
and his idioms, are refreshed continually from common speech,
from the book of the people, from the vulgar and tavern music of the
street ballad; from Synge's brutality and violence and melancholy;
from the strong and delicate cadences of the great Elizabethans. The
poetry is built about a core of symbols, linked by history, or dream,
or woman, or event, the 'images that waken in the blood', and which
are the instruments of his thought. The symbols shape themselves

---

[1] As we should expect from his theosophical background.
[2] *Explorations*, p. 334–5.
[3] 'He stressed the rhythm till it almost became a chant; he went with
speed, marking every beat and dwelling on his vowels' (Masefield, op. cit.,
p. 13). This, too, was his method of composition: chanting lines or half-
lines aloud, wide gestures of the hands, till the words had obeyed his call.

into patterns within a framework determined by the poet-philosopher's view of time. And time involves the catastrophic interpretation of history, the great mutations of the world perceived in a dramatic foreshortening; for it is, perhaps, necessary that the romantic poet should be possessed by this sense of catastrophe or of regeneration to give urgency to his statement. Enrichment of the images springs from his own sense of his position in history. Reality crowded thickly about him; and it was living and vital because it was determined by the pressure of the past, implicit in the rhythms of history perceived and justified, from 1916 onwards, by the present. Visions were built on images, and the images, so far as his study of history, archaeology, and philosophy might give him certainty, were asserting their validity at every turn of political events. The funeral gleam of Troy, the burning roof and tower that marked the destruction of a great family; or the drunken soldiery of Byzantium or Clare-Galway, were images that caught fire backwards from the past into the present. Maud Gonne might be Laura, or Beatrice, or Helen, or Emer, but all drew a common life from the Great Memory. The poet as Renaissance man, painter, or politician, soldier or scholar or saint, justified his multiplicity by calling strong ghosts to stand by his bed. It did not matter that the statue of Cuchulain in the Post Office was a bad one; the epic of heroism and love and defeat drew its vitality from the identification with public and private history.

But in this poetry there is more than traditional romanticism. He had taken much of what was pertinent, his manner of thinking of love and death, but not of God, from the metaphysical poets. The passionate-dispassionate, the sinewy precision of words, the laminated metaphors, the redemption from the cynical or sordid by pride and steadfastness, are part of what he found and made his own. He found them and used them, not only because he refused to sacrifice his integrity as a dedicated poet, but because his instinct to understand remained alive to the end.

It is a final paradox that these qualities of balance and integrity should be related to a personality characteristically 'Romantic', in the best and worst senses. A poet who, by Chance or Choice, assumes the traditional myriad-mindedness, must play the parts that those roles demand; and he must study them, or he will fail to speak with conviction. Therefore he must posture, speak bravely, find that which is the prerogative of men of action, think himself into the heroes of mythology. Renaissance man, all that Hamlet and Lear stood for, might find its last emblem with Cuchulain's stand in the Post Office; as Robert Gregory's death as a fighter-pilot in Italy recalled the shade of Achilles:

> Though battle-joy may be so dear
> A memory, even to the dead. . . .

The end was to be gaiety, as Hamlet and Lear were gay, knowing John Synge's reality and joy, the bitter gaiety of defeat as the gyres ran on.

But there was no self-pity for the past, no blindness as to the present. Yeats was intensely aware of contemporary thought. His poetry is the outcome of a philosophy which, though he could think towards it only through the medium of the symbol, was yet unified, all detractions reckoned up, by a high and consistent purpose. That purpose is to be perceived in relation to Ireland; being, as Yeats saw it, at once the microcosm and the mirror of the world. Out of Ireland, whatever the hatred, whatever the momentary bitterness or perversity of the 'fanatic heart', would come the new and ordered society:

> Preserve that which is living and help the two Irelands, Gaelic Ireland and Anglo-Ireland, so to unite that neither shall shed its pride. Study the great problems of the world, as they have been lived in our scenery, the re-birth of European spirituality in the mind of Berkeley, the restoration of European order in the mind of Burke. Every nation is the whole world in a mirror and our mirror has twice been very bright and clear. Do not be afraid to boast so long as the boast lays burdens on the boaster. Study the educational system of Italy, the creation of the philosopher Gentile, where even religion is studied not in the abstract but in the minds and lives of Italian saints and thinkers; it becomes at once part of Italian history.
>
> As for the rest we wait till the world changes and its reflection changes in our mirror and an hieratical society returns, power descending from the few to the many, from the subtle to the gross, not because some man's policy has decreed it but because what is so overwhelming cannot be restrained. A new beginning, a new turn of the wheel.[1]

---

[1] *Explorations*, p. 337.

# Select Bibliography

| | |
|---|---|
| Adams, Hazard | *Blake and Yeats; the Contrary Vision*; New York, 1955. |
| Adams, Henry | 'History as Phase'. Essay in *The Degradation of the Democratic Dogma*. Introduction by Brooks Adams; New York. |
| Allingham, William | *Poems.* |
| Allt, G. P. D., and Alspach, R. K. | *The Variorum Edition of the Poems of W. B. Yeats*; New York, 1957. |
| Armstrong, E. A. | *The Folklore of Birds*; London, 1958. |
| Béguin | *L'Ame Romantique et Lé Rêve*; Paris, 1946. |
| Bennett, Richard | *The Black and Tans*; London, 1959. |
| Berkeley, George | *Collected Works.* Edited by G. Sampson; London, 1897–8. |
| Bjersby, Birgit | *The Cuchulain Legend in the Works of W. B. Yeats*; Upsala, 1951. |
| Blackmur, R. D. | *The Lion and the Honeycomb*; London, 1956. |
| Blake, William | *Works.* Edited by Ellis and Yeats, 3 vols. Illustrations to *Dante, Blair, Virgil, Job*, etc. |
| Bodkin, M. | *Archetypal Patterns in Poetry*; London, 1934. |
| | *Studies of Type Images . . .*; London, 1951. |
| Bowra, C. M. | *The Heritage of Symbolism*; London, 1947. |
| Brooks, Cleanth | *The Hidden God*; New Haven and London, 1963. |
| Byron, Robert, and Talbot Rice, David | *The Birth of Western Painting . . .*; London 1930. |
| Calvert, S. | *Memoir of Edward Calvert*; London, 1893. |
| Church, R. | *Eight for Immortality*; London, 1941. |
| Corkery, Daniel | *Synge and Anglo-Irish Literature*; Cork. |

Cornford, F. M.          *Plato's Cosmology*: the *Timaeus* of Plato;
                          London, 1937.
Coxhead, Elizabeth       *Lady Gregory, A Literary Portrait*; Lon-
                          don, 1961.
Damon, Samuel Foster     *William Blake; his Philosophy and Symbols*;
                          London, 1924.
Dante                    *Divine Comedy* and *Vita Nuova*.
Dalton, O. M.            *Byzantine Art and Archaeology*; Oxford,
                          1911.
d'Alviella, Count        *The Migration of Symbols*; London, 1894.
  Goblet
Dillon, Myles            *The Cycles of the King's of Ireland*; London,
                          1946.
Donoghue, Denis          *The Integrity of Yeats*; Cork, 1964.
  (Ed.)
Donoghue and Mul-        *An Honoured Guest: Critical Essays on
  ryne (Eds.)             W. B. Yeats*; London, 1964.
Eglinton, John           *Anglo-Irish Essays*; Dublin and London,
                          1917.
Eisler, R.               *The Royal Art of Astrology*; London, 1946.
Eliot, T. S.             *Poetry and Drama*; London, 1951.
Ellis-Fermor, U. M.      *The Irish Dramatic Movement*; London,
                          1957 (2nd Edn).
Ellmann, Richard         *Yeats: the Man and the Masks*; London,
                          1948.
                         *The Identity of Yeats*; London, 1954.
Empson, W.               *Seven Types of Ambiguity* (2nd Edn);
                          London, 1947.
                         *Some Versions of Pastoral*; London, 1935.
*Encyclopaedia of Religion and Ethics.*
Engelberg, E.            *The Vast Design*; Toronto, 1964.
Farrer, Austin           *A Rebirth of Images*; Westminster, 1949.
Fenollosa, E. F.         *Certain Nōh Plays of Japan*; Cuala Press,
                          1916.
Flower, Robin            *The Irish Tradition*; Oxford, 1947.
Frye, G. Northrop        *The Anatomy of Criticism*; Princeton, 1957.
Gibbon, W. Monk          *The Masterpiece and the Man: Yeats as I
                          Knew Him*; London, 1959.

| | |
|---|---|
| Gogarty, Oliver St John | *W. B. Yeats: A Memoir*; Dublin, 1963. |
| Gore-Booth, Eva | *Poems*; London, 1898. |
| Gregory, Augusta, Lady | *Journals*, 1916–30. |
| | *Cuchulain of Muirthemne*; London, 1902. |
| | *Visions and Beliefs in the West of Ireland* (2 vols.); London, 1920. |
| | *Hugh Lane's Life and Achievement*; London, 1921. |
| Grose, S. W. | *Greek Coins in the Fitzwilliam Museum*; Cambridge, 1923. |
| Guest, Lady Charlotte | *The Mabinogion* (transl.); Everyman, 1906. |
| Gwynn, Stephen | *Scattering Branches*; London, 1940. |
| Hamsa Shri Bhagwan | *The Holy Mountain*; London, 1934. |
| Hannay, J. O. | *The Wisdom of the Desert*; London, 1904. |
| Hatzfeld, H. | *Literature Through Art*; Oxford, 1952. |
| Heard, Gerald | *The Ascent of Humanity*; London, 1929. |
| Heath-Stubbs, J. | *The Darkling Plain*; London, 1950. |
| Herbert, S. | *The Unconscious Mind*; London, 1923. |
| Hermas, Shepherd of | (Ed. J. B. Lightfoot and J. R. Harmer), *The Apostolic Fathers*, 1891. |
| Hoare, D. M. | *The Works of Morris and Yeats in Relation to Early Saga Literature*; Cambridge, 1937. |
| Hone, J. M. | *W. B. Yeats: 1865–1939*; London, 1942. (Second Edition 1962). |
| Hone, J. M., and Rossi, M. M. | *Bishop Berkeley, His Life, Writings and Philosophy*, with an Introduction by W. B. Yeats. |
| Horton, W. T. | *A Book of Images*. Drawn by W. T. Horton and introduced by W. B. Yeats; London, 1898. |
| Hough, Graham | *The Last Romantics*; London, 1959. |
| Howarth, H. | *The Irish Writers, 1880–1940*; London, 1948. |
| Huxley, T. H. | *Hume, with helps to the study of Berkeley.* |
| Hyde, D. | *Love Songs of Connacht*; Dublin, 1893. |

Hyde, D.                    *The Religious Songs of Connacht*; London,
                            1906.
Images of a Poet           University of Reading Exhibition Cata-
                            logue, Manchester, 1961.
Inge, W. R.                *Studies of English Mystics*; London, 1905.
Jeffares, A. Norman        *W. B. Yeats: Man and Poet*; London, 1949.
Jeffares and Cross         *Excited Reverie: Critical Essays on W. B.*
    (Eds.)                  *Yeats*; London, 1965.
Johnson, Lionel            *Collected Poems.*
Jonson, Ben                *Works.*
*Julian, Works of the Emperor.* Translated by W. C. Wright (Loeb
    Classical Library); London, 1913.
Kenner, H.                 *Gnomon: Essays on Contemporary Litera-*
                            *ture*; New York, 1958.
Kermode, Frank             *Romantic Image*; London, 1957.
Kirby, Sheelah             *The Yeats Country*; Dublin, 1962.
Kilgannon, T.              *History of Sligo*; Dublin, 1898.
Kleinstück, Johannes       W. B. Yeats *oder der Dichter in der*
                            *Moderner Welt;* Hamburg, 1963.
Koch, Vivienne             *W. B. Yeats, The Tragic Phase*; London,
                            1951.
Leavis, F. R.              *New Bearings in English Poetry*; London,
                            1932 (New Edn. 1950).
*LETTERS*                   W.B.Y. to Katharine Tynan, ed. R. Mc-
                            Hugh; Dublin, 1953.
                            On Poetry from W.B.Y. to Dorothy
                            Wellesley; Oxford, 1940.
                            W.B.Y. and T. Sturge Moore; London,
                            1953.
                            J. B. Yeats . . . to his Son, W.B.Y. and
                            others. Ed. Joseph Hone; London, 1944.
                            Letters of W.B.Y. ed. Wade; London,
                            1954.
Lévi, Eliphas              *Transcendental Magic.* Edited by A. F.
    (A. L. Constant)        Waite; London, 1896.
Lister, Raymond            *Edward Calvert*; London, 1962.
MacBride, Madame           *A Servant of the Queen*; London, 1938.
    (Maud Gonne)

| | |
|---|---|
| MacNeice, L. | *The Poetry of W. B. Yeats*; London, 1941. |
| Martensen, H. L. | *Jacob Boehme: His Life and Teaching*; London, 1885. |
| Mathers, S. L. MacGregor | *The Kabbalah Unveiled*; London, 1887. |
| Mead, G. R. S. | *Thrice Greatest Hermes*; London, 1906. |
| Melchiori, Giorgio | *The Whole Mystery of Art*; London, 1960. |
| Menon, V. K. Naravanna | *The Development of William Butler Yeats*. Preface by Sir Herbert J. C. Grierson. 2nd Revised Edition, 1960. |
| Mercier, Vivian | *The Irish Comic Tradition*; Oxford, 1962. |
| Mitchel, John | *Jail Journal*; Dublin, 1913. |
| Moore, George | *Works*. |
| Moore, T. Sturge | *Poems*. |
| Moore, Virginia | *The Unicorns*; New York, 1954. |
| More, Henry | *Philosophical Poems*, ed. Geoffrey Bullough; Manchester, 1937. |
| Murray, A. S. | *History of Greek Sculpture*; London, 1890. |
| Murray, M. A. | *Egyptian Sculpture*; London, 1930. |
| Myers, F. W. H. | *Human Personality and its Survival after Death*; London, 1903. |
| Nietzsche | *The Birth of Tragedy*: trans. W. Haussman; London, 1909. |
| O'Grady, Standish | *History of Ireland*; Dublin, 1881. |
| O'Malley, Ernie | *On Another Man's Wounds*; Dublin, 1936. |
| Oshima, Shotaro | *Modern Irish Literature*; Tokyo, 1962. |
| Oura, Yukio | *W. B. Yeats, Poet of The Lonely Tower*; Tokyo, 1962. |
| Palladius | *The Lausiac History of Palladius*. By W. K. L. Clarke; London, 1918. |
| Palmer, Samuel | *Catalogue of Etchings*, 1937. |
| Parkinson, T. | *W. B. Yeats, Self-Critic*; California, 1951. *W. B. Yeats, The Later Poetry*; California, 1964. |
| Pater, Walter | *Notebooks, Appreciations, The Renaissance.* |
| Pearce, D. R. (Ed.) | *The Senate Speeches of W. B. Yeats*; London, 1961. |

| | |
|---|---|
| *Permanence of Yeats, The* | Selected Criticism, Edited by James Hall and Martin Steinmann; New York, 1950. |
| Plato | *Timaeus*, etc. |
| Plotinus | *Enneads*. Trans. by Stephen Mackenna; London, 1917. Revised Edn. 1956. *Select Works*. Edited by G. R. S. Mead; London, 1895. |
| Pound, Ezra | *'No', or Accomplishment*; New York, 1917. *The Translations*; London, 1951. *Certain Nōh Plays of Japan*. Introduced by W.B.Y.; Cuala, 1916 |
| Propertius | *Elegies*. Trans. by S. G. Tremenheere; London, 1899. |
| Regardie, Israel | *The History of the Golden Dawn* (4 vols.); Chicago, 1936. |
| Rhys, Sir John | *Lectures on Origin and Growth of Religion as Illustrated by Celtic Heathendom*; London, 1888. |
| Ricketts, Charles | *Self Portrait*. Letters and Journals. *Sixty-Five Illustrations*. Introduction by T. Sturge Moore; London, 1933. |
| Robinson, Lennox | *Curtain Up*; London, 1942. |
| Rossetti, Dante Gabriel | *Collected Works*. |
| Rudd, M. | *Divided Image*; London, 1953. |
| Russell, George ('A.E.') | *The Candle of Vision*; London, 1918. *Imaginations and Reveries*; Dublin, 1925. *Song and Its Fountains*; London, 1932. |
| Seymour, St John, D. | *Anglo-Irish Literature, 1200–1582*; Cambridge; 1929. |
| Saul, George Brandon | *Prolegomena to the Study of Yeats' Poems*; Philadelphia, 1957 *Prolegomena to the Study of Yeats' Plays*; Philadelphia, 1958. |
| Shaw, Bernard and Yeats, W. B. | *Letters to Florence Farr*. Edited by Clifford Bax. |
| Shree Pandit Swami and Yeats, W. B. | *The Ten Principal Upanishads*; London, 1937. |

| | |
|---|---|
| Sinnett, A. P. | *Esoteric Buddhism* (3rd Edn.); London, 1884. |
| Sparling, H. Halliday | *Irish Minstrelsy*; London, 1888. |
| Spender, S. | *The Destructive Element*; London, 1935. |
| Spengler, Oswald | *The Decline of the West*; London, 1926. |
| Stallworthy, J. M. | *Between the Lines*; Oxford, 1963. |
| Stauffer, D. A. | *The Golden Nightingale*; New York, 1949. |
| Stewart, J. I. M. | *Eight Modern Writers*; Oxford, 1963. |
| Stock, A. G. | *W. B. Yeats, His Poetry and Thought*; Cambridge, 1961. |
| Strong, Eugenie (Mrs A.) | *Apotheosis and The After Life*; London, 1915. |
| Strong, L. A. G. | *The Sacred River*; London, 1949. |
| | *Green Memory*; London, 1961. |
| Strzygowski, Josef | *Origin of Christian Church Art.* Trans. by O. M. Dalton and H. J. Braunholz; Oxford, 1923. |
| Symons, A. | *The Symbolist Movement in Literature*; London, 1899. |
| | *Collected Works*; London, 1924. |
| Taylor, Thomas | *A Dissertation*; Amsterdam, 1790. |
| | *Iamblichus: Life of Pythagoras*; London (1926 Edn.). |
| Tillyard, E. M. W. | *Poetry: Direct and Oblique*; London, 1934 (Revised Edn, London, 1945). |
| Todhunter, J. | *Helena in Troas*; London, 1886. |
| Tuve, Rosemond | *Elizabethan and Metaphysical Imagery*; Chicago, 1947. |
| Tynan (Hinkson), Katharine | *Twenty-Five Years: Reminiscences*; London, 1913. |
| | *Irish Love Songs*; London, 1892. |
| Unterecker, John | *A Reader's Guide to W. B. Yeats*; London, 1959. |
| Ure, Peter | *Towards a Mythology: Studies in the Poetry of W. B. Yeats*; London, 1958. |
| | *Yeats the Playwright*; London, 1963. |
| Ussher, Arland | *The Mind and Face of Ireland*; London, 1944. |
| | *Three Great Irishmen*; London, 1952. |

Ussher, Arland — *The Twilight of the Ideas*; Dublin, 1948.

Vendler, H. H. — *A Vision and the Later Plays*; Harvard and Oxford, 1963.

Venturi, Lionello — *Modern Painters*; New York and London, 1957.

Villiers de l'Isle-Adam, Count — *Axël*. Translated by H. P. R. Finsbury, Preface by Yeats; London, 1952.

Von Hügel, Baron — *The Mystical Element in Religion*; London, 1908.

Waddell, Helen — *The Desert Fathers*; London, 1936.

Wade, A. — *A Bibliography of the Writings of W. B. Yeats*; London, 1931.

*The Letters of W. B. Yeats*; London, 1954.

Waite, A. E. — *The Real History of the Rosicrucians*; London, 1887.

Waley, A. — *Introduction to the study of Chinese painting*; London, 1923.

Wellesley, Dorothy — *Selections from the Poems of*: Introduction by W. B. Yeats; London, 1936.

Wells, H. G. — *The Outline of History*.

Welsford, E. — *The Fool . . .*; London, 1935.

Whalley, George — *Poetic Process*; London, 1953.

Wilde, Lady — *Ancient Legends, Mystic Charms and Superstitions of Ireland, &c.* 2 vols. London, 1887.

Wind, Edgar — *Pagan Mysteries in the Renaissance*; London, 1958.

*Art and Anarchy*; London, 1963

Wilson, Edmund — *Axel's Castle*; New York, 1931.

*The Wound and the Bow*; London, 1941.

Wilson, F. A. C. C. — *W. B. Yeats and Tradition*; London, 1958.

*Yeats' Iconography*; London, 1960.

Witcutt, W. P. — *Blake, A Psychological Study*; London, 1946.

Wood-Martin, W. G. — *Traces of the Elder Faiths of Ireland*; London, 1892.

Yeats, Jack B. — *Sligo*; Glasgow, 1930.

*Life in the West of Ireland*; Dublin, 1912.

# Index

# University Paperbacks

## A COMPLETE LIST OF TITLES

Titles marked thus: * are to be published during 1965

### ARCHAEOLOGY AND ANTHROPOLOGY

UP   94  Antiquities of the Irish Countryside, *Seán P. O'Ríordáin*
UP    1  Archaeology and Society, *Grahame Clark*
*UP 118  Archaeology in the Holy Land, *Kathleen Kenyon*
UP   58  Habitat, Economy and Society, *C. Daryll Forde*

### ART AND ARCHITECTURE

UP   33  The Architecture of Humanism, *Geoffrey Scott*
UP 101  The Classical Language of Architecture, *John Summerson*

### BIOGRAPHY

*UP 102  An Autobiography, *Edwin Muir*
*UP 130  Elizabeth the Great, *Elizabeth Jenkins*
UP   50  The Great Mathematicians, *H. W. Turnbull*
UP   90  Horace Walpole, *R. W. Ketton-Cremer*
*UP 100  Mozart: The Man and His Works, *W. J. Turner*
UP    9  Plato: The Man and His Work, *A. E. Taylor*
UP   76  Thackeray the Novelist, *Geoffrey Tillotson*
UP   13  William the Silent, *C. V. Wedgewood*

### ECONOMICS

*UP 134  Beyond the Welfare State, *Gunnar Myrdal*
UP   21  An Economic History of the British Isles, *Arthur Birnie*
UP   52  An Economic History of Europe, *Arthur Birnie*
UP   66  Economic Theory and Underdeveloped Regions, *Gunnar Myrdal*
UP 104  Economics, *H. Speight*
UP   58  Habitat, Economy and Society (See under Archaeology and Anthropology)

## LAW

## LITERATURE

## SCIENCE